CONTENTS

ALSO BY NAOMI NOVIK

His Majesty's Dragon
Throne of Jade
Black Powder War
Empire of Ivory
Victory of Eagles
Tongues of Serpents

ALSO BY YISHAN LI

Cutie B
500 Manga Creatures
Shojo Art Studio
Shounen Art Studio
The Clique

WILL SUPER VILLAINS BE ON THE FINAL?

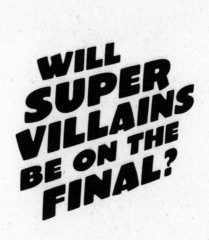

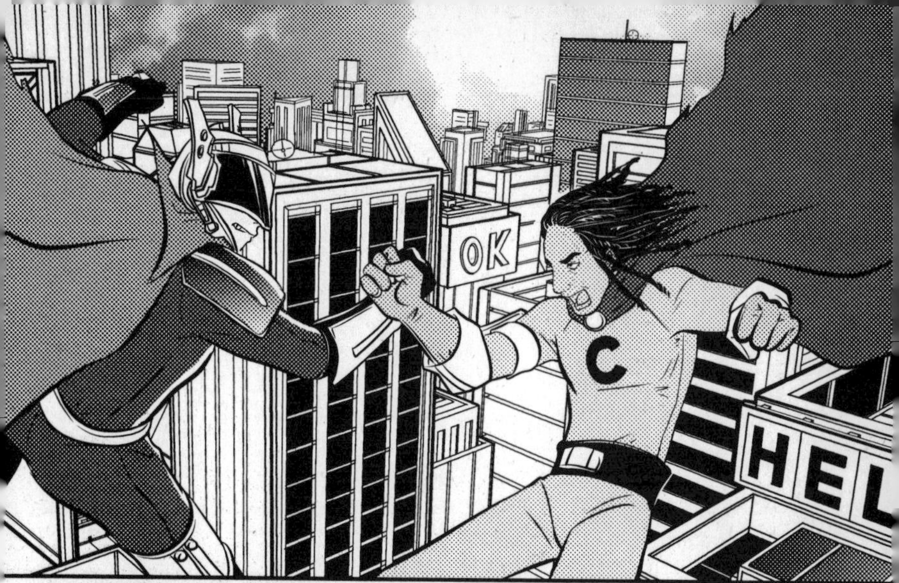
OK
C
HEL

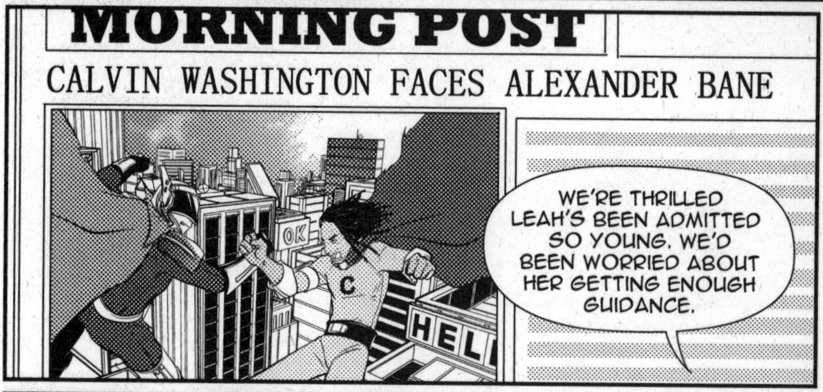
MORNING POST
CALVIN WASHINGTON FACES ALEXANDER BANE
OK
C
HEL
WE'RE THRILLED LEAH'S BEEN ADMITTED SO YOUNG. WE'D BEEN WORRIED ABOUT HER GETTING ENOUGH GUIDANCE.

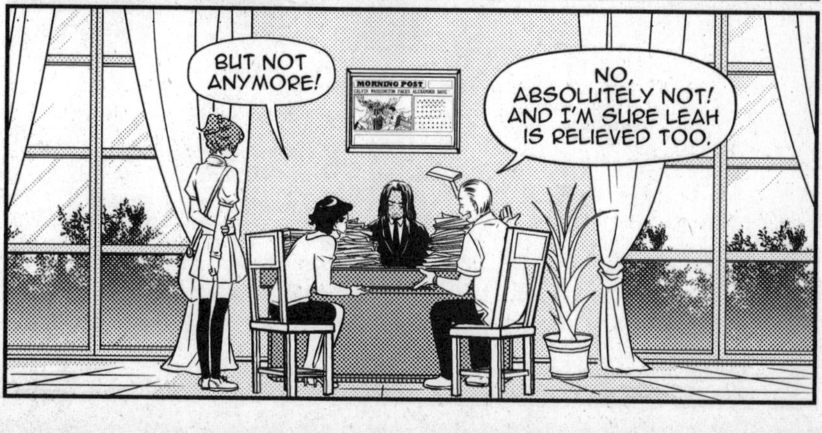
BUT NOT ANYMORE!
MORNING POST
CALVIN WASHINGTON FACES ALEXANDER BANE
NO, ABSOLUTELY NOT! AND I'M SURE LEAH IS RELIEVED TOO.

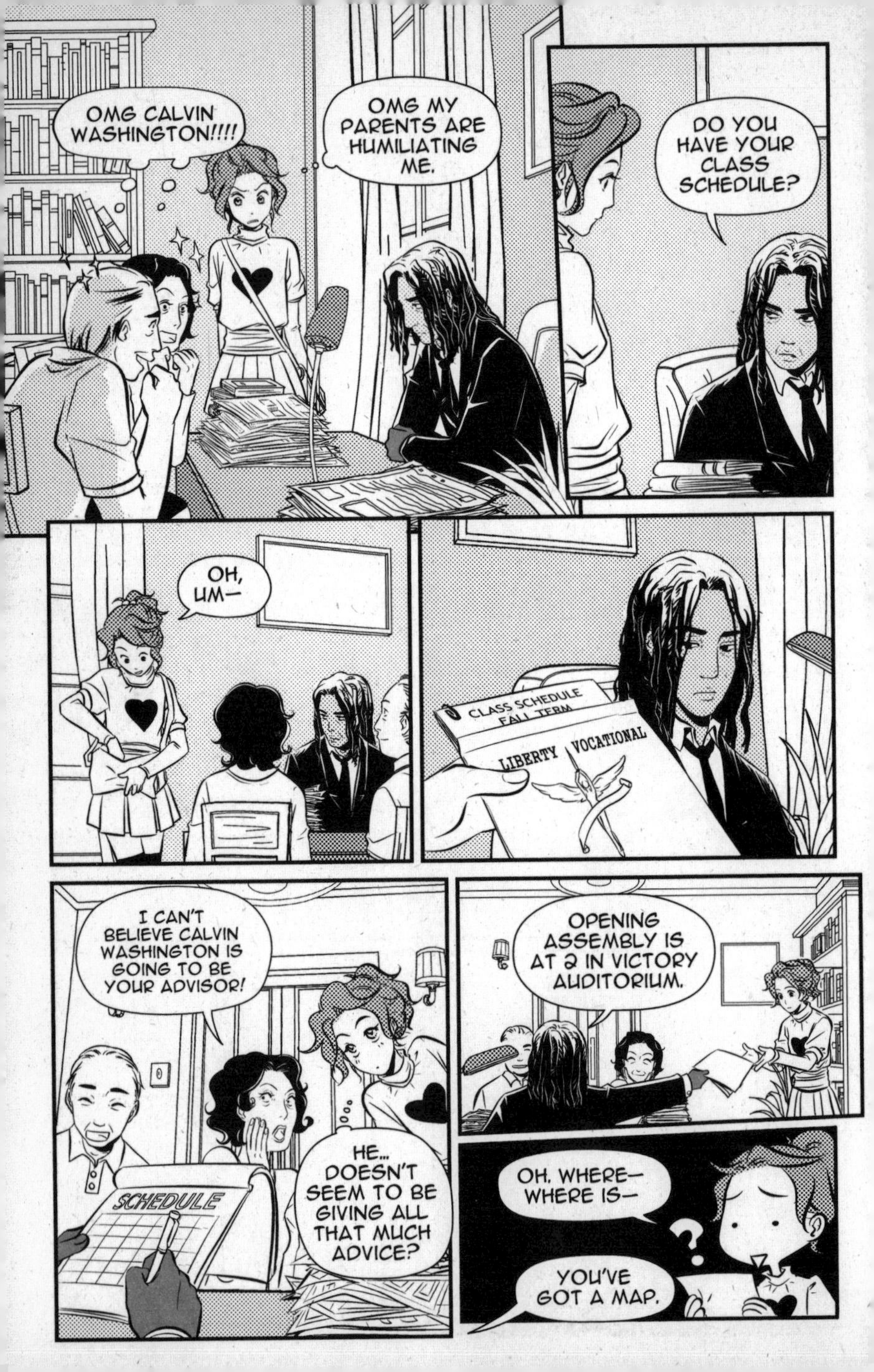
OMG CALVIN WASHINGTON!!!!
OMG MY PARENTS ARE HUMILIATING ME.
DO YOU HAVE YOUR CLASS SCHEDULE?
OH, UM—
CLASS SCHEDULE FALL TERM
LIBERTY VOCATIONAL
I CAN'T BELIEVE CALVIN WASHINGTON IS GOING TO BE YOUR ADVISOR!
SCHEDULE
HE... DOESN'T SEEM TO BE GIVING ALL THAT MUCH ADVICE?
OPENING ASSEMBLY IS AT 2 IN VICTORY AUDITORIUM.
OH. WHERE— WHERE IS—
YOU'VE GOT A MAP.

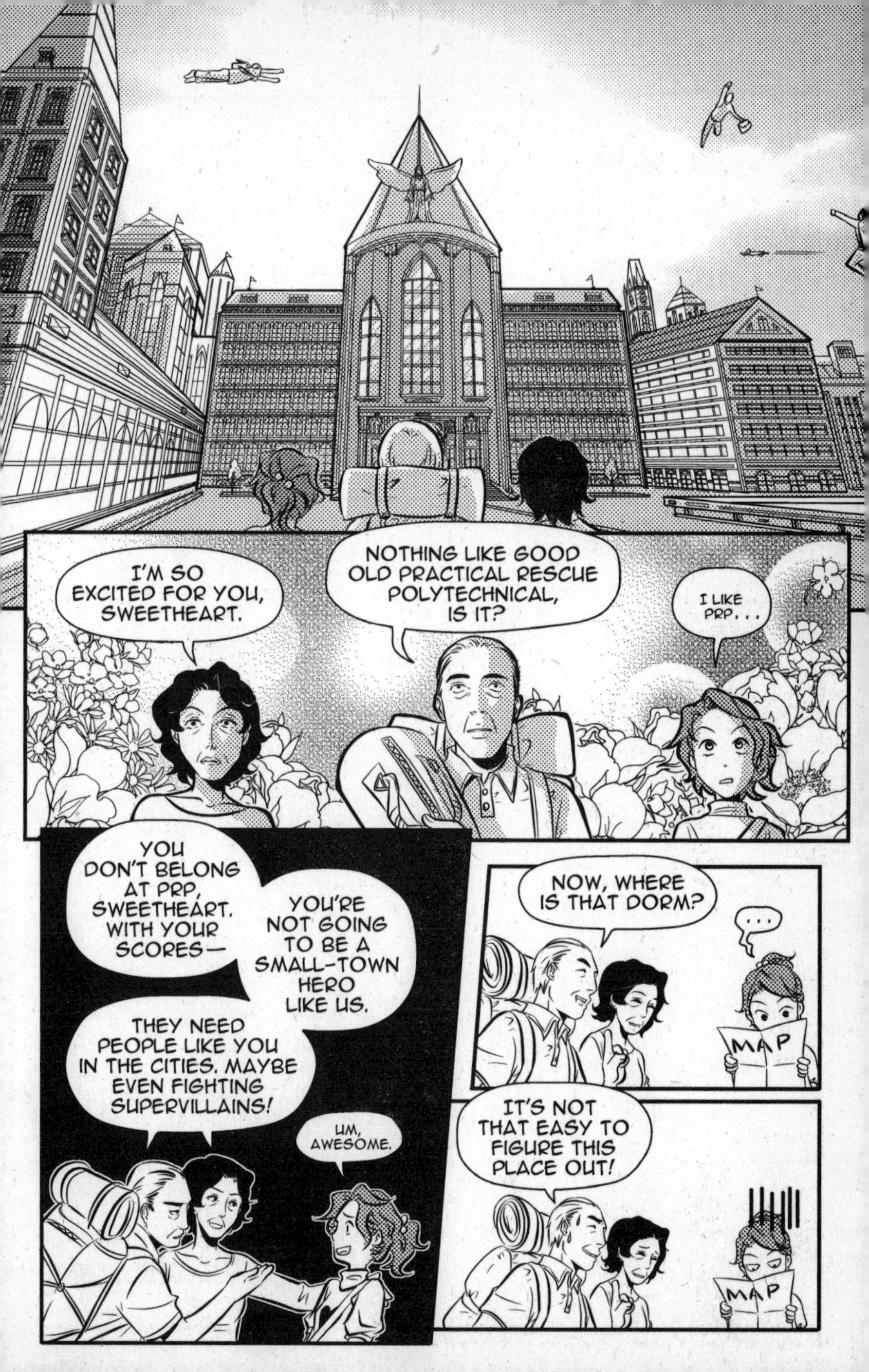
I'M SO EXCITED FOR YOU, SWEETHEART.
NOTHING LIKE GOOD OLD PRACTICAL RESCUE POLYTECHNICAL, IS IT?
I LIKE PRP...
YOU DON'T BELONG AT PRP, SWEETHEART. WITH YOUR SCORES—
YOU'RE NOT GOING TO BE A SMALL-TOWN HERO LIKE US.
THEY NEED PEOPLE LIKE YOU IN THE CITIES. MAYBE EVEN FIGHTING SUPERVILLAINS!
UM, AWESOME.
NOW, WHERE IS THAT DORM?
...
MAP
IT'S NOT THAT EASY TO FIGURE THIS PLACE OUT!
MAP

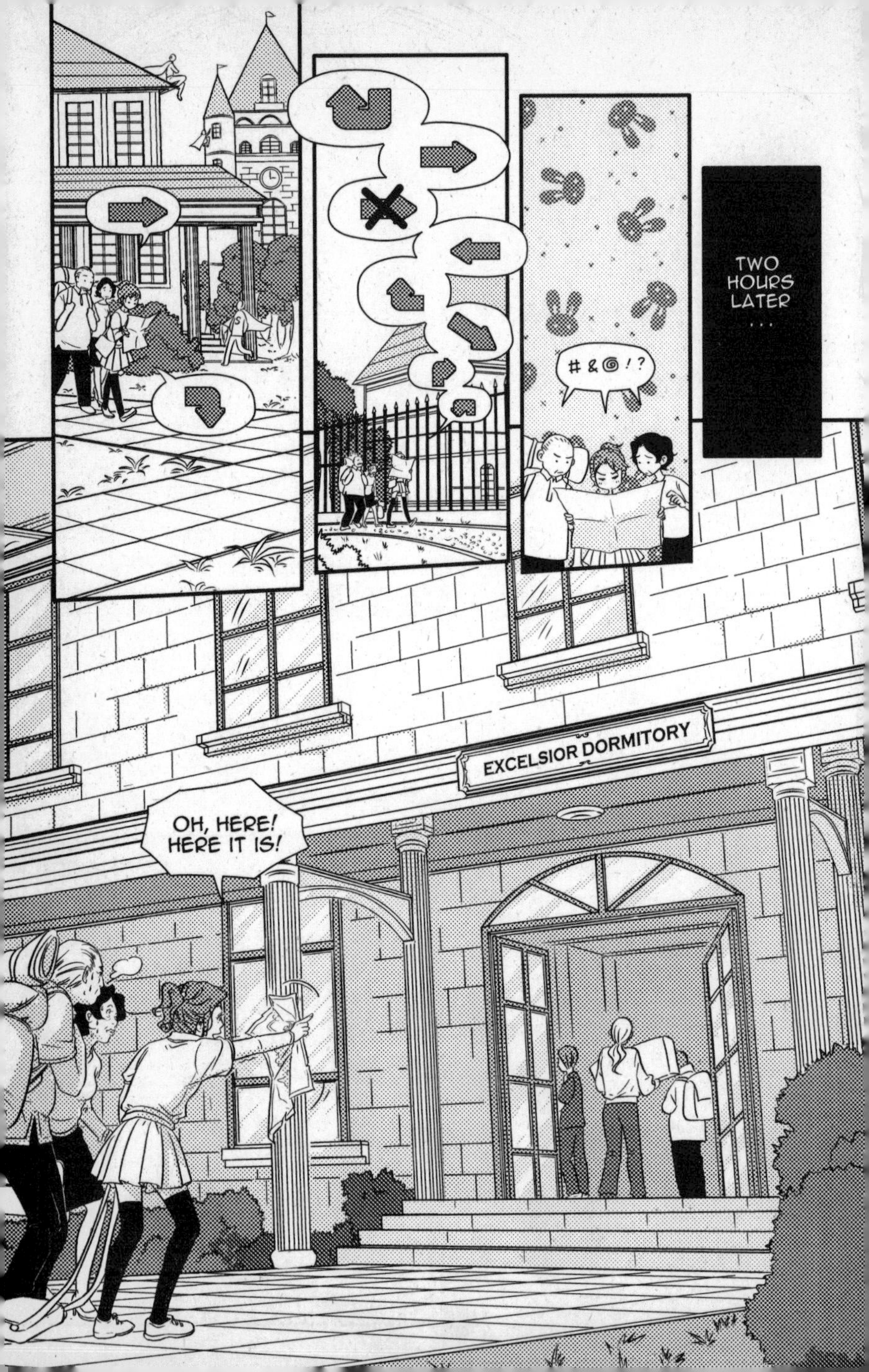
#&@!?
TWO HOURS LATER . . .
EXCELSIOR DORMITORY
OH, HERE! HERE IT IS!

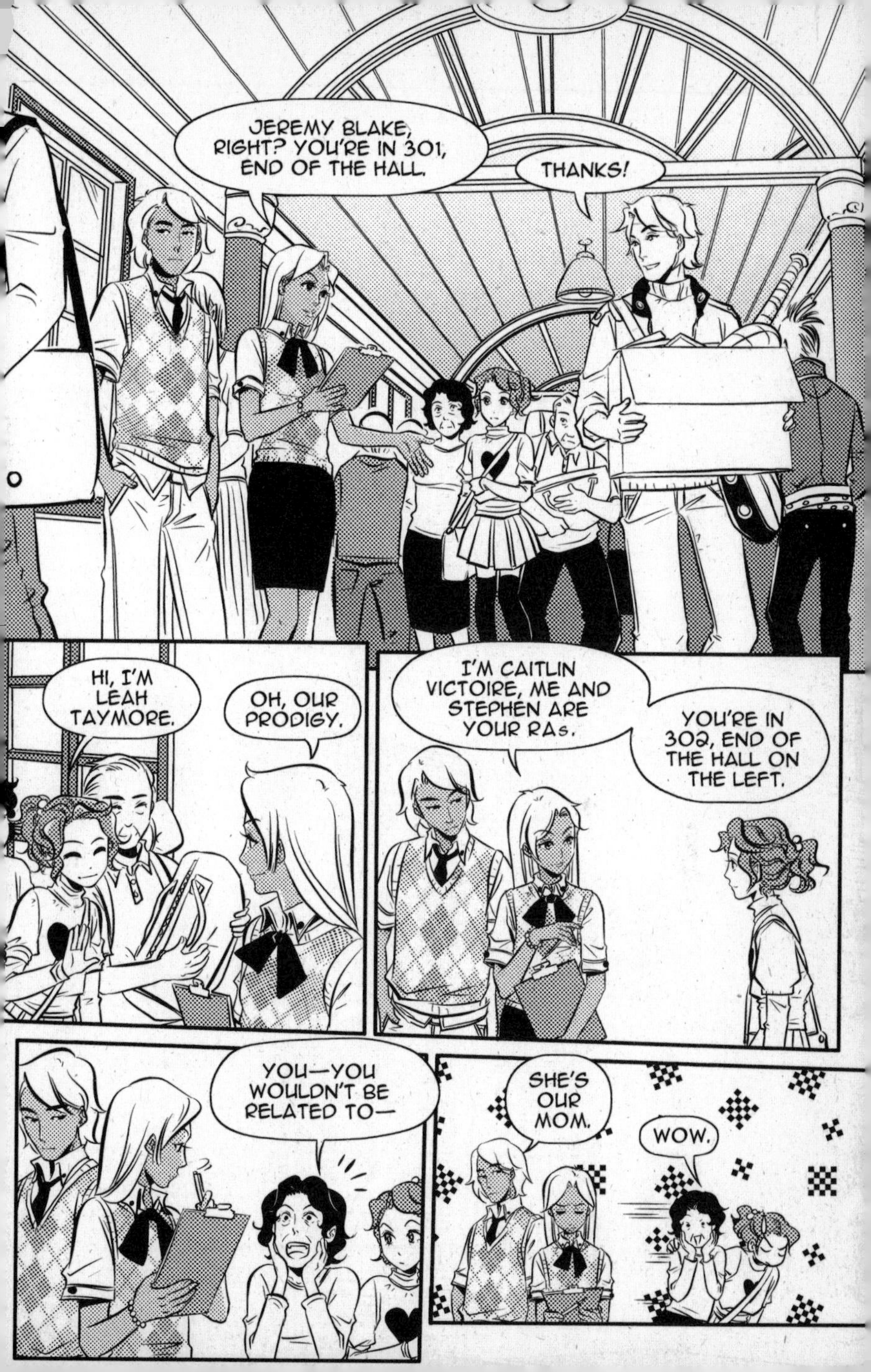

JEREMY BLAKE, RIGHT? YOU'RE IN 301, END OF THE HALL.
THANKS!
HI, I'M LEAH TAYMORE.
OH, OUR PRODIGY.
I'M CAITLIN VICTOIRE, ME AND STEPHEN ARE YOUR RAs.
YOU'RE IN 302, END OF THE HALL ON THE LEFT.
YOU—YOU WOULDN'T BE RELATED TO—
SHE'S OUR MOM.
WOW.

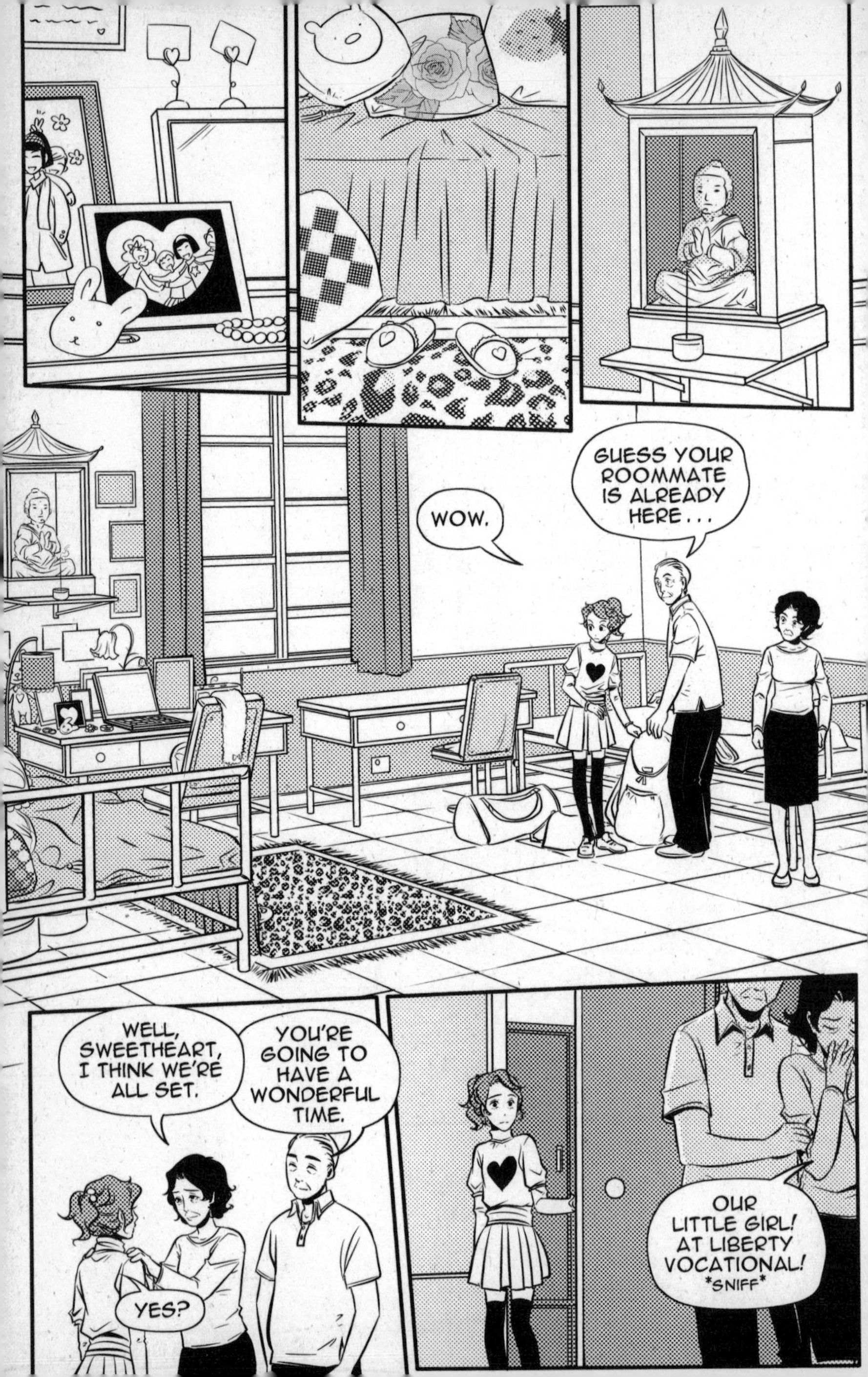
WOW.
GUESS YOUR ROOMMATE IS ALREADY HERE...
WELL, SWEETHEART, I THINK WE'RE ALL SET.
YOU'RE GOING TO HAVE A WONDERFUL TIME.
YES?
OUR LITTLE GIRL! AT LIBERTY VOCATIONAL! *SNIFF*

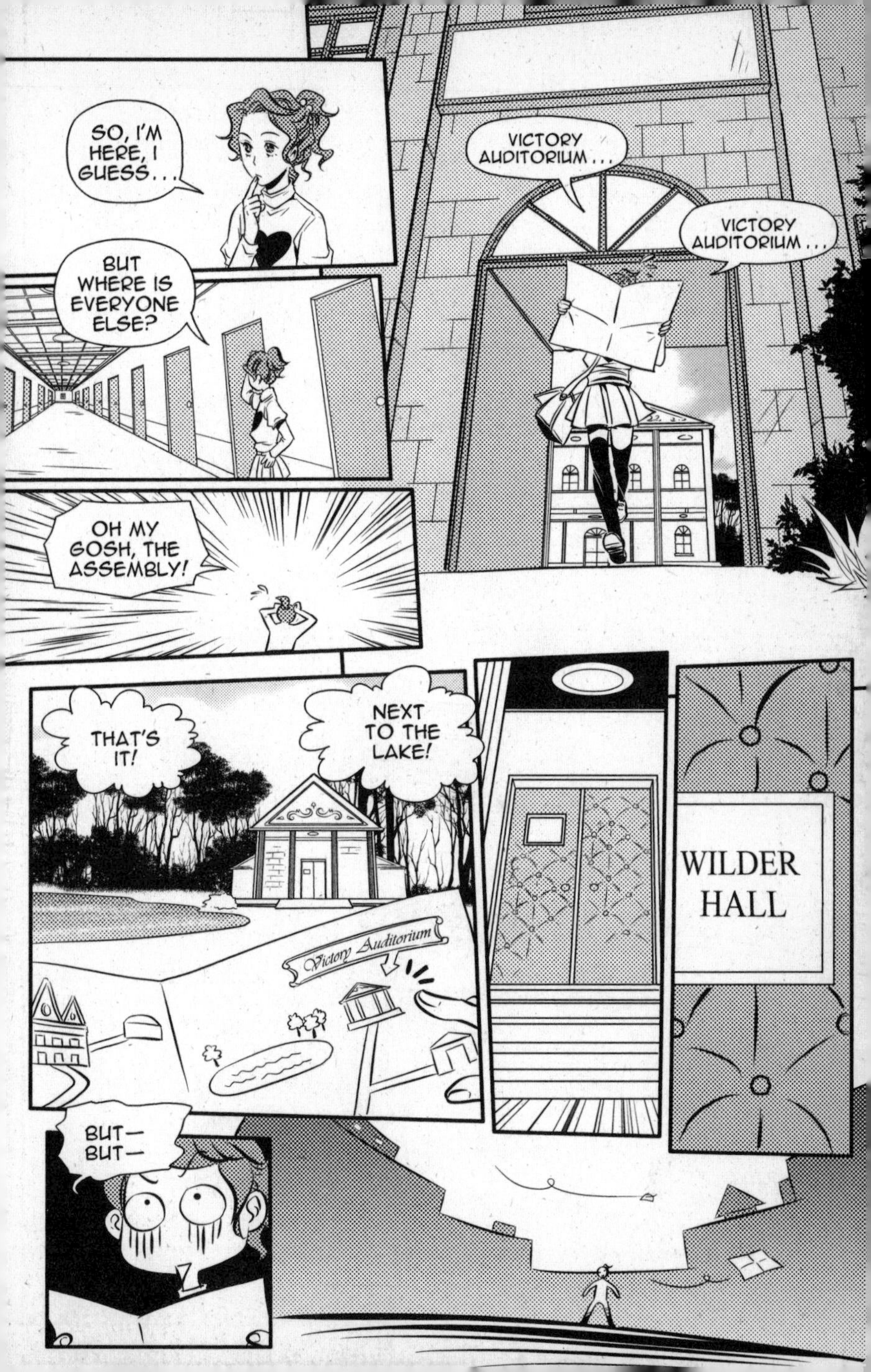
SO, I'M HERE, I GUESS...
BUT WHERE IS EVERYONE ELSE?
OH MY GOSH, THE ASSEMBLY!
VICTORY AUDITORIUM...
VICTORY AUDITORIUM...
THAT'S IT!
NEXT TO THE LAKE!
Victory Auditorium
WILDER HALL
BUT— BUT—

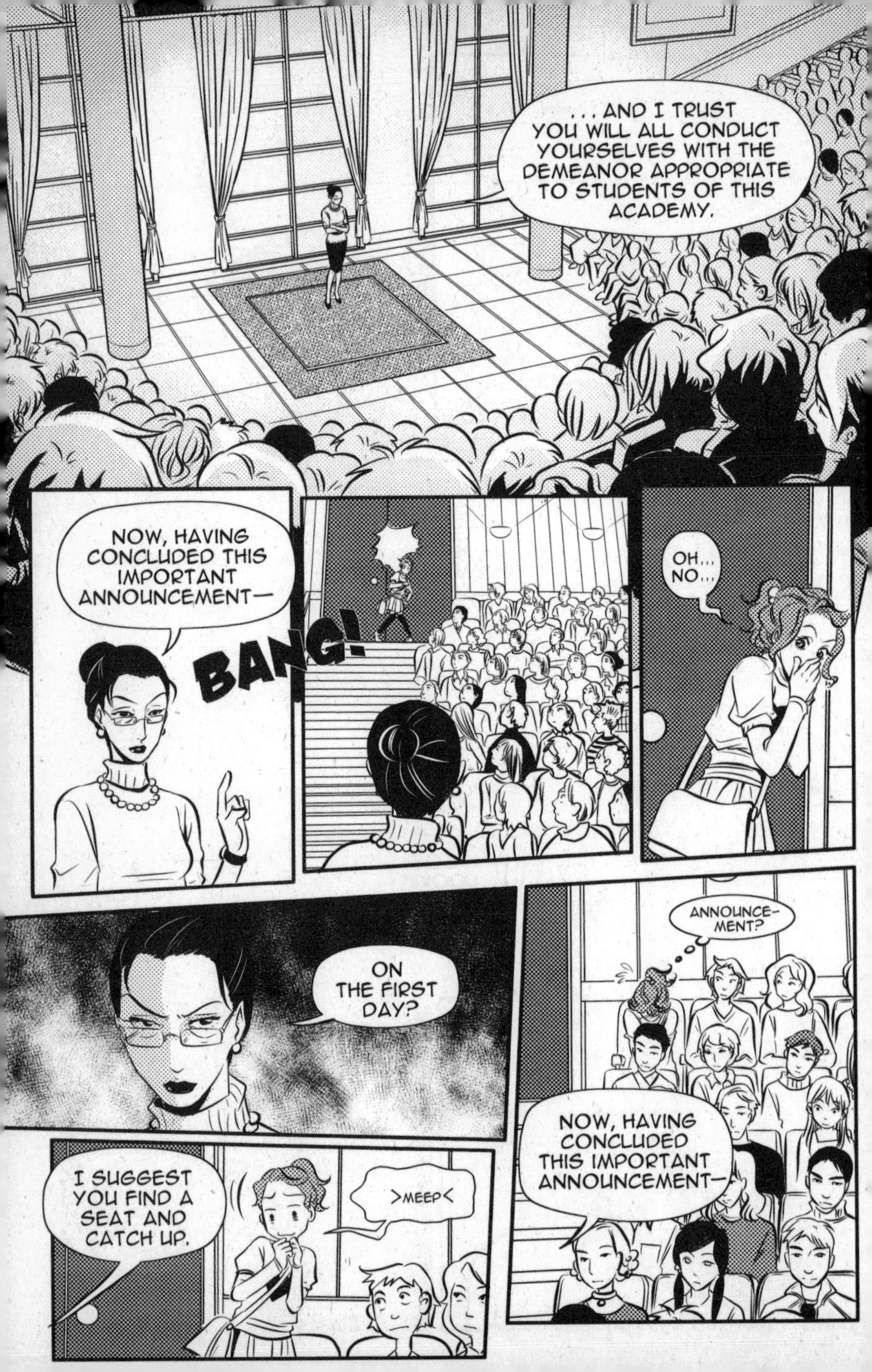
. . . AND I TRUST YOU WILL ALL CONDUCT YOURSELVES WITH THE DEMEANOR APPROPRIATE TO STUDENTS OF THIS ACADEMY.
NOW, HAVING CONCLUDED THIS IMPORTANT ANNOUNCEMENT—
BANG!
OH... NO...
ON THE FIRST DAY?
I SUGGEST YOU FIND A SEAT AND CATCH UP.
>MEEP<
ANNOUNCE-MENT?
NOW, HAVING CONCLUDED THIS IMPORTANT ANNOUNCEMENT—

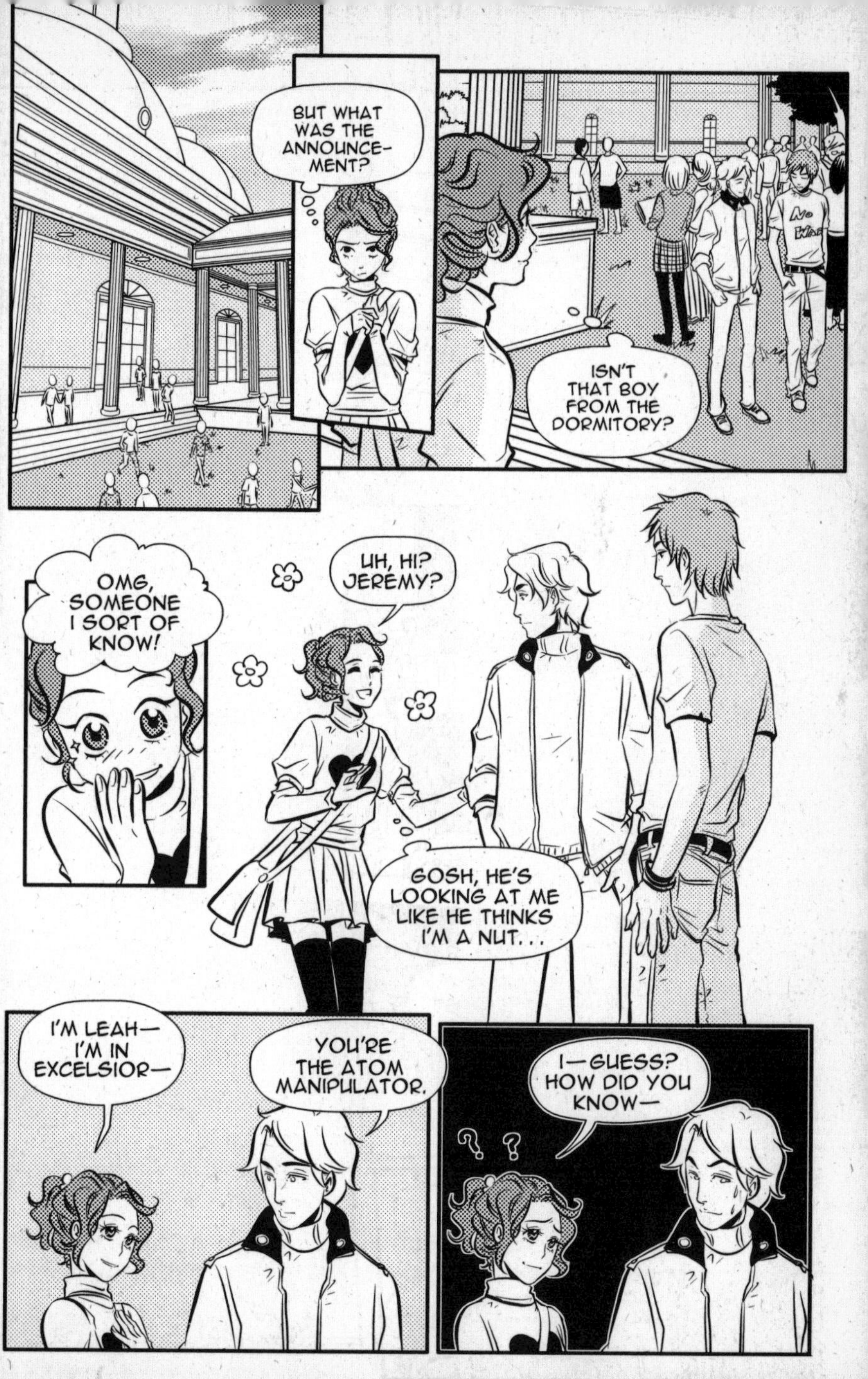

BUT WHAT WAS THE ANNOUNCE-MENT?
ISN'T THAT BOY FROM THE DORMITORY?
OMG, SOMEONE I SORT OF KNOW!
UH, HI? JEREMY?
GOSH, HE'S LOOKING AT ME LIKE HE THINKS I'M A NUT...
I'M LEAH— I'M IN EXCELSIOR—
YOU'RE THE ATOM MANIPULATOR.
I—GUESS? HOW DID YOU KNOW—
? ?

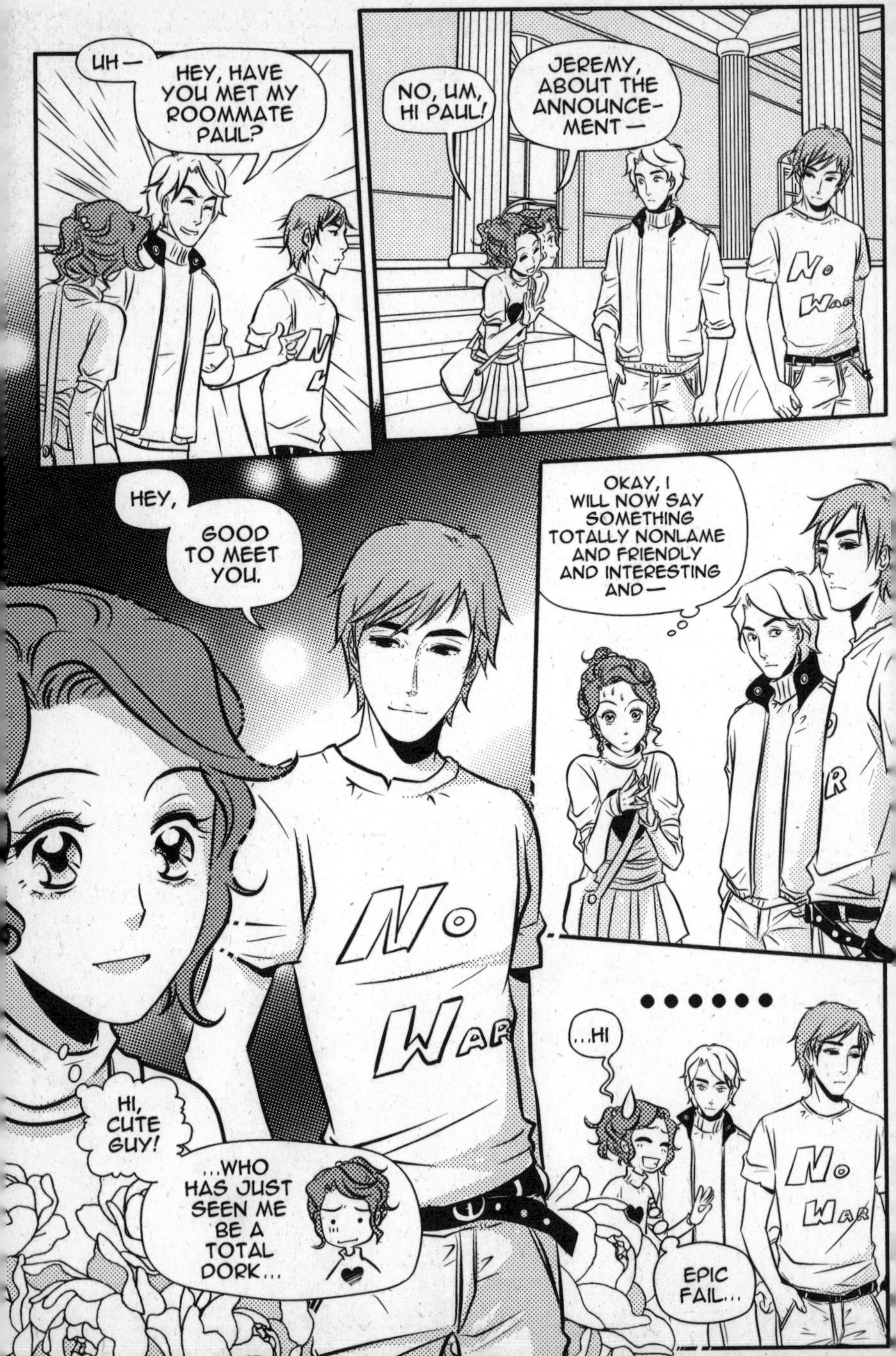
UH—
HEY, HAVE YOU MET MY ROOMMATE PAUL?
NO, UM, HI PAUL!
JEREMY, ABOUT THE ANNOUNCE-MENT—
HEY,
GOOD TO MEET YOU.
HI, CUTE GUY!
...WHO HAS JUST SEEN ME BE A TOTAL DORK...
OKAY, I WILL NOW SAY SOMETHING TOTALLY NONLAME AND FRIENDLY AND INTERESTING AND—
NO
WAR
......
...HI
EPIC FAIL...

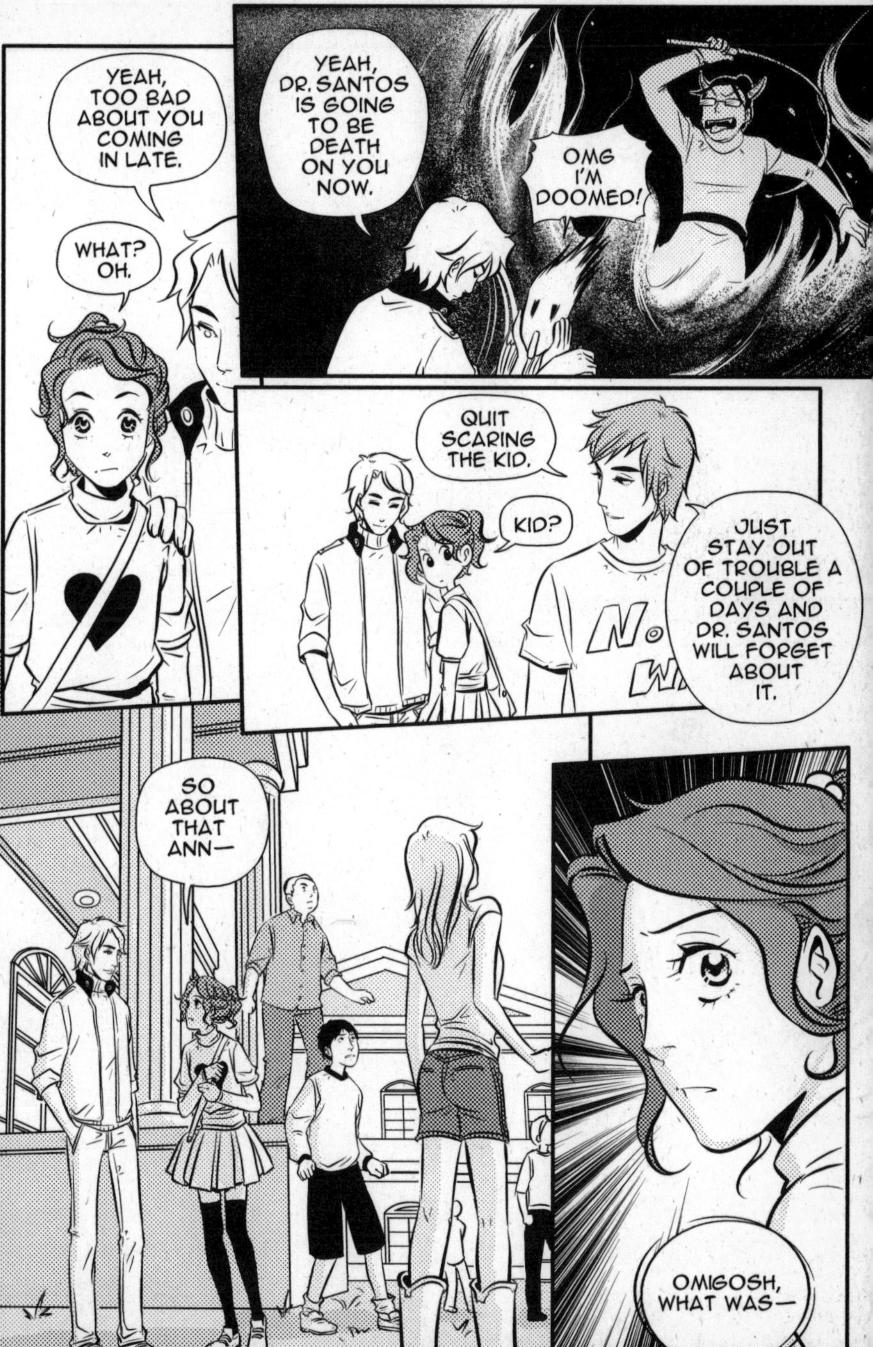
YEAH, TOO BAD ABOUT YOU COMING IN LATE.
WHAT? OH.
YEAH, DR. SANTOS IS GOING TO BE DEATH ON YOU NOW.
OMG I'M DOOMED!
QUIT SCARING THE KID.
KID?
JUST STAY OUT OF TROUBLE A COUPLE OF DAYS AND DR. SANTOS WILL FORGET ABOUT IT.
SO ABOUT THAT ANN—
OMIGOSH, WHAT WAS—

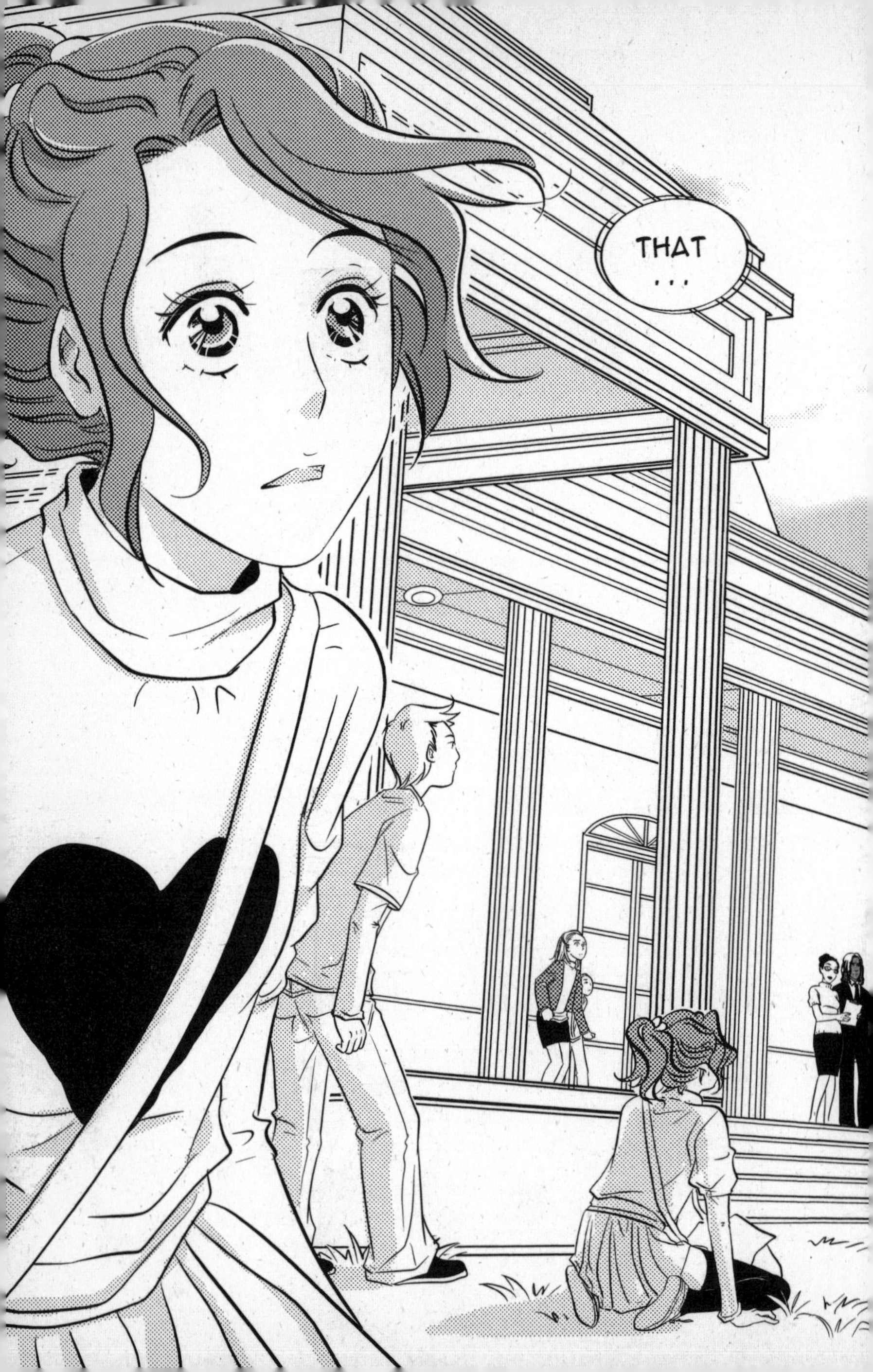
THAT . . .

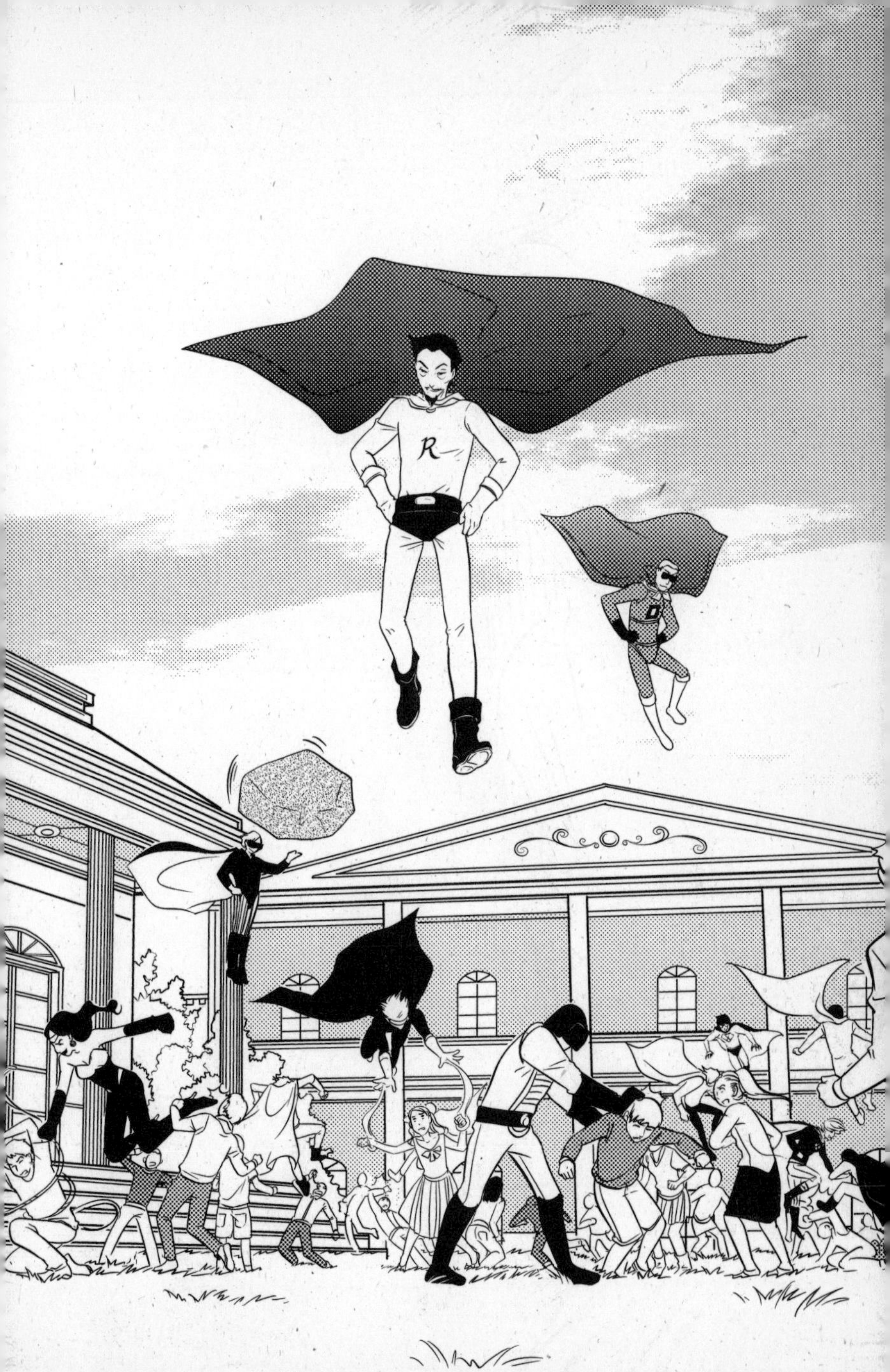

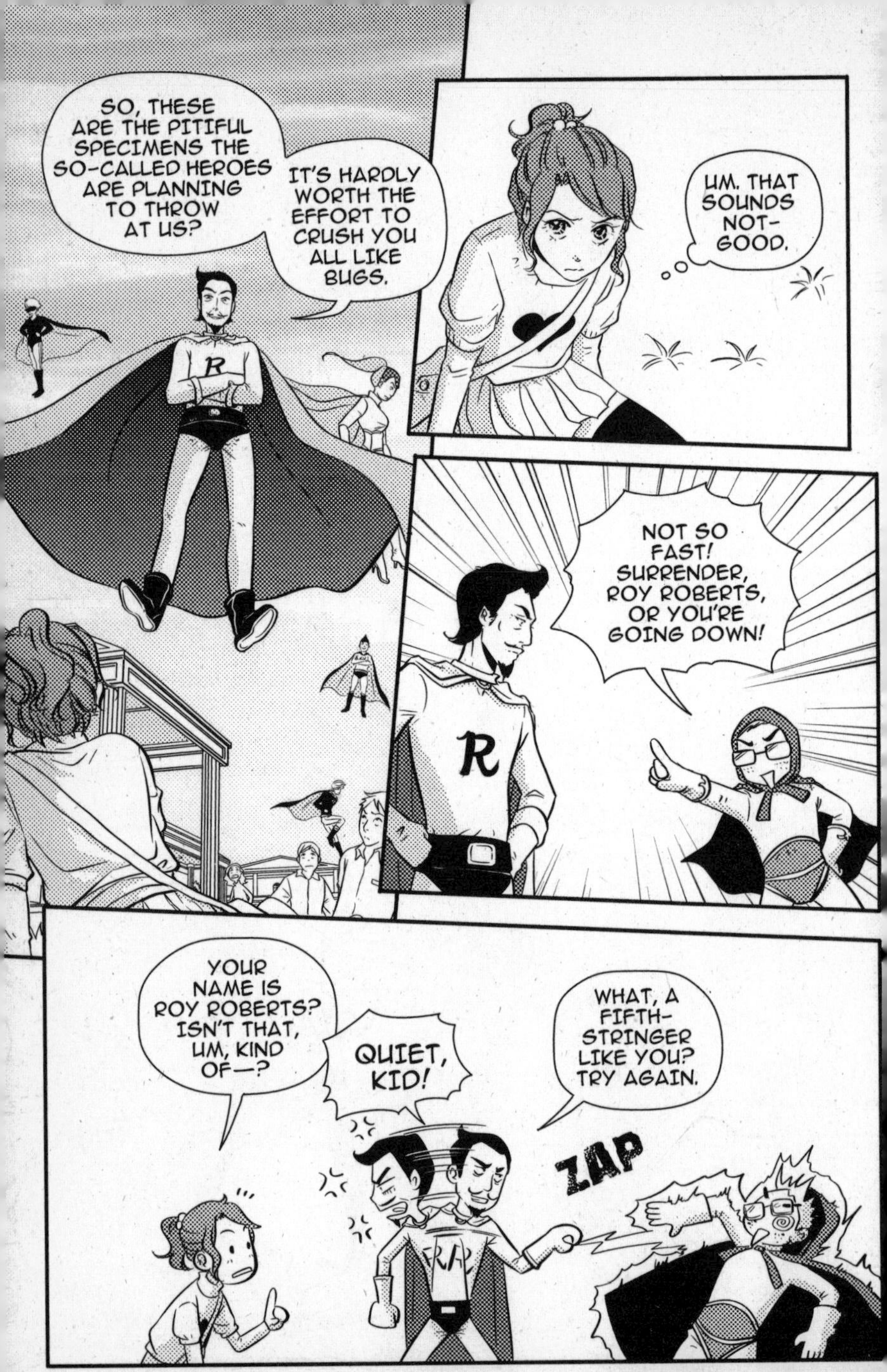

SO, THESE ARE THE PITIFUL SPECIMENS THE SO-CALLED HEROES ARE PLANNING TO THROW AT US?
IT'S HARDLY WORTH THE EFFORT TO CRUSH YOU ALL LIKE BUGS.
R
UM. THAT SOUNDS NOT-GOOD.
NOT SO FAST! SURRENDER, ROY ROBERTS, OR YOU'RE GOING DOWN!
R
YOUR NAME IS ROY ROBERTS? ISN'T THAT, UM, KIND OF—?
QUIET, KID!
WHAT, A FIFTH-STRINGER LIKE YOU? TRY AGAIN.
ZAP

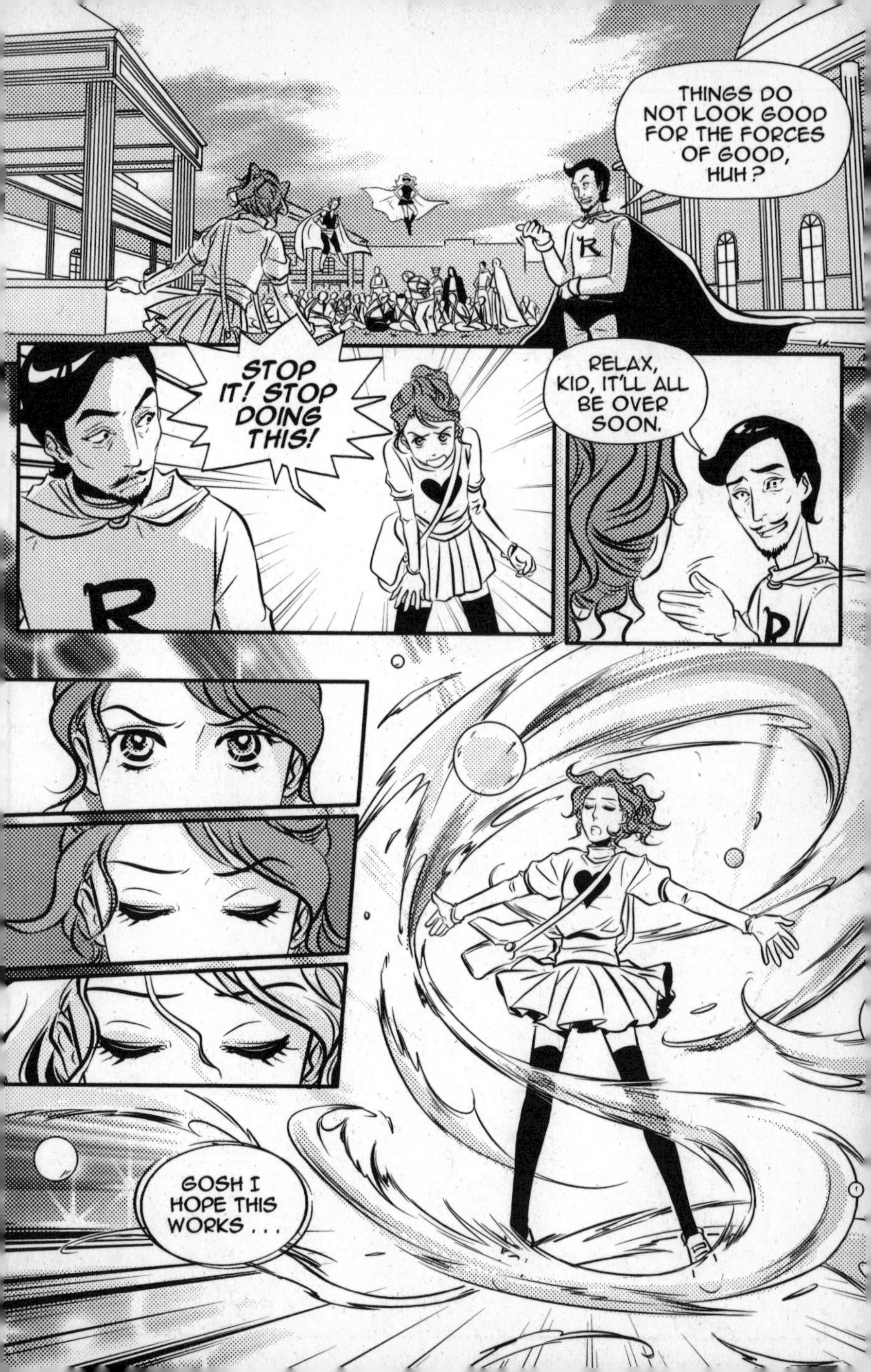
THINGS DO NOT LOOK GOOD FOR THE FORCES OF GOOD, HUH?
STOP IT! STOP DOING THIS!
RELAX, KID, IT'LL ALL BE OVER SOON.
GOSH I HOPE THIS WORKS . . .

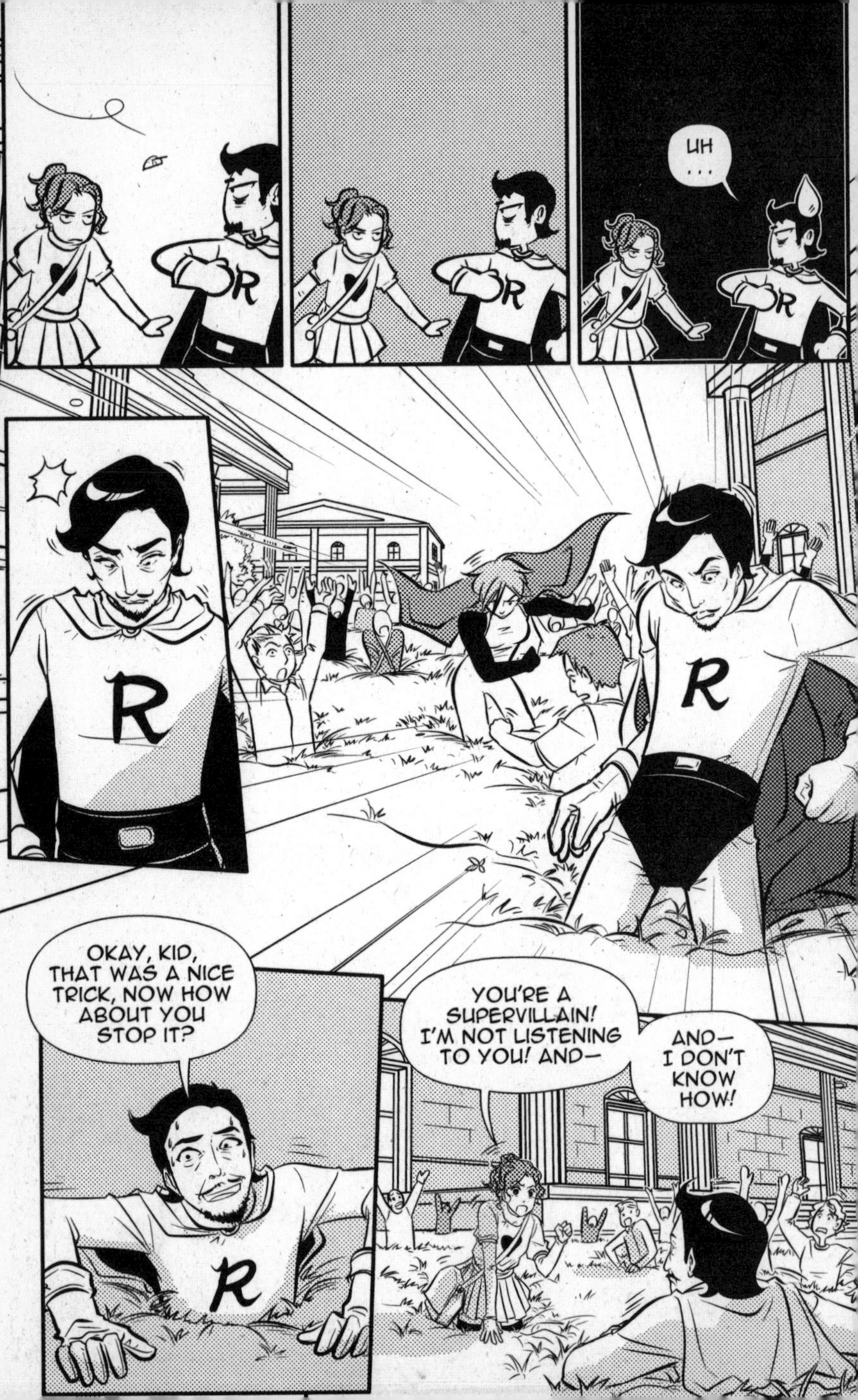
UH . . .
OKAY, KID, THAT WAS A NICE TRICK, NOW HOW ABOUT YOU STOP IT?
YOU'RE A SUPERVILLAIN! I'M NOT LISTENING TO YOU! AND—
AND— I DON'T KNOW HOW!

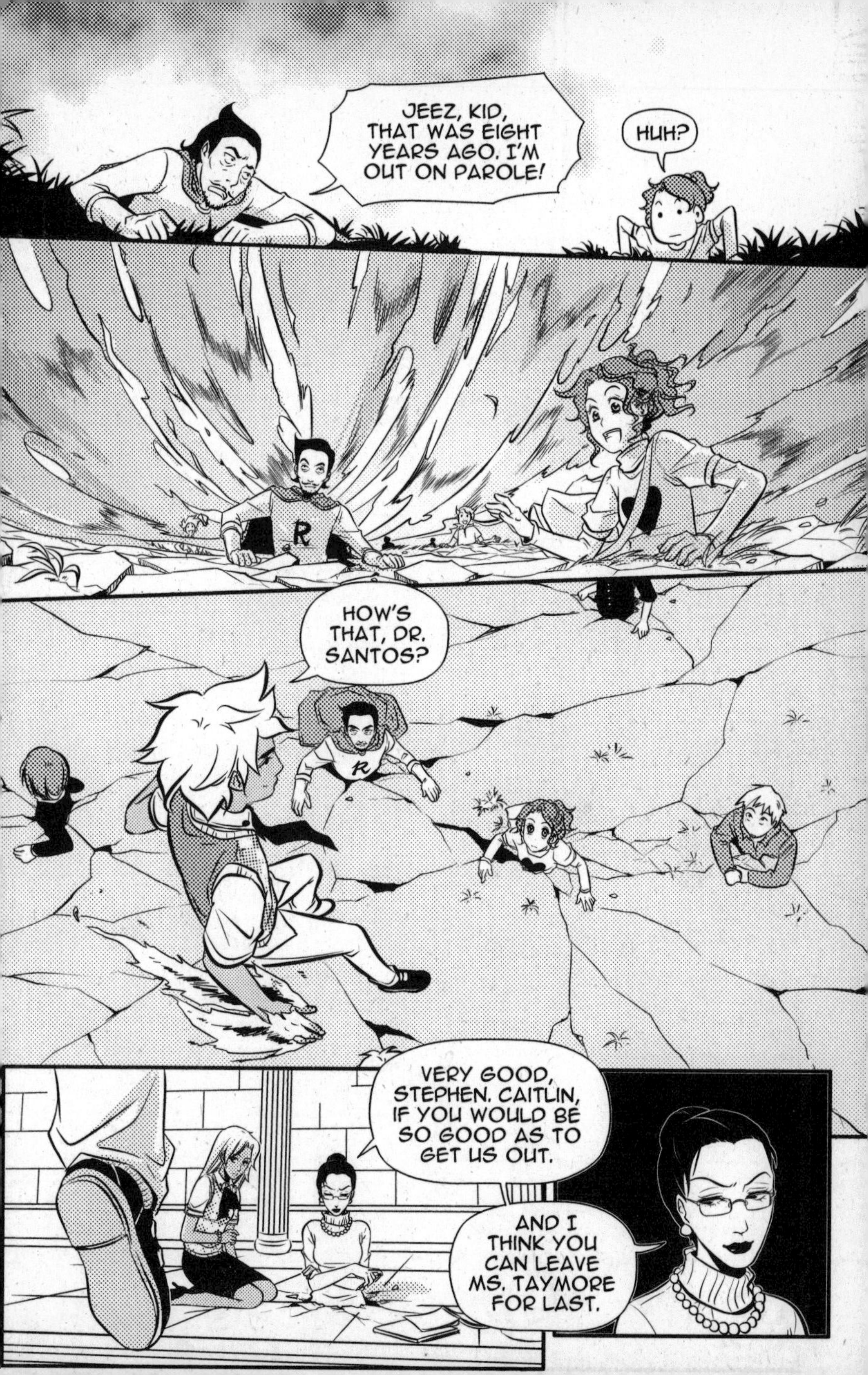
JEEZ, KID, THAT WAS EIGHT YEARS AGO. I'M OUT ON PAROLE!
HUH?
HOW'S THAT, DR. SANTOS?
VERY GOOD, STEPHEN. CAITLIN, IF YOU WOULD BE SO GOOD AS TO GET US OUT.
AND I THINK YOU CAN LEAVE MS. TAYMORE FOR LAST.

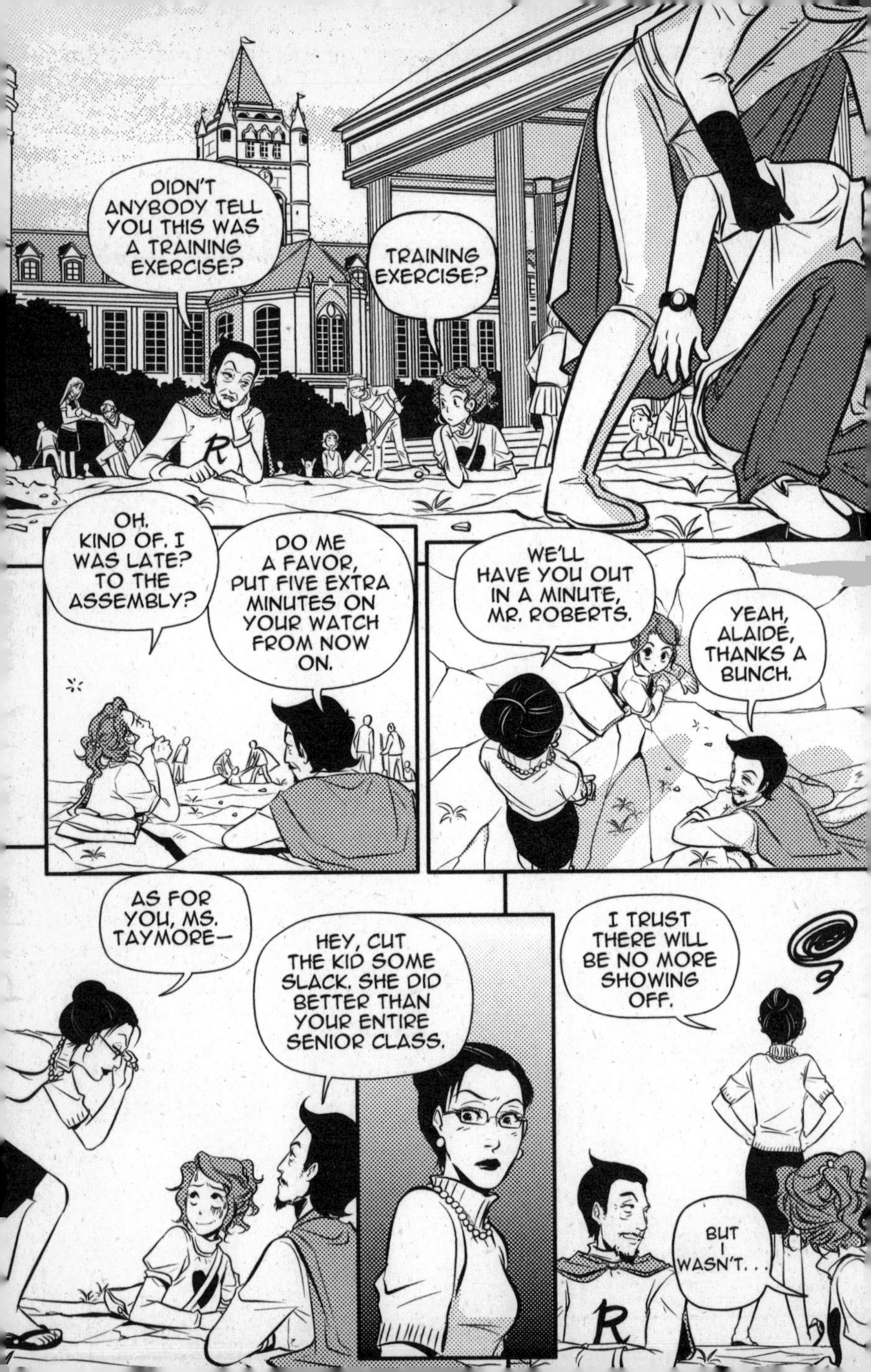
DIDN'T ANYBODY TELL YOU THIS WAS A TRAINING EXERCISE?
TRAINING EXERCISE?
OH. KIND OF. I WAS LATE? TO THE ASSEMBLY?
DO ME A FAVOR, PUT FIVE EXTRA MINUTES ON YOUR WATCH FROM NOW ON.
WE'LL HAVE YOU OUT IN A MINUTE, MR. ROBERTS.
YEAH, ALAIDE, THANKS A BUNCH.
AS FOR YOU, MS. TAYMORE—
HEY, CUT THE KID SOME SLACK. SHE DID BETTER THAN YOUR ENTIRE SENIOR CLASS.
I TRUST THERE WILL BE NO MORE SHOWING OFF.
BUT I WASN'T. . .

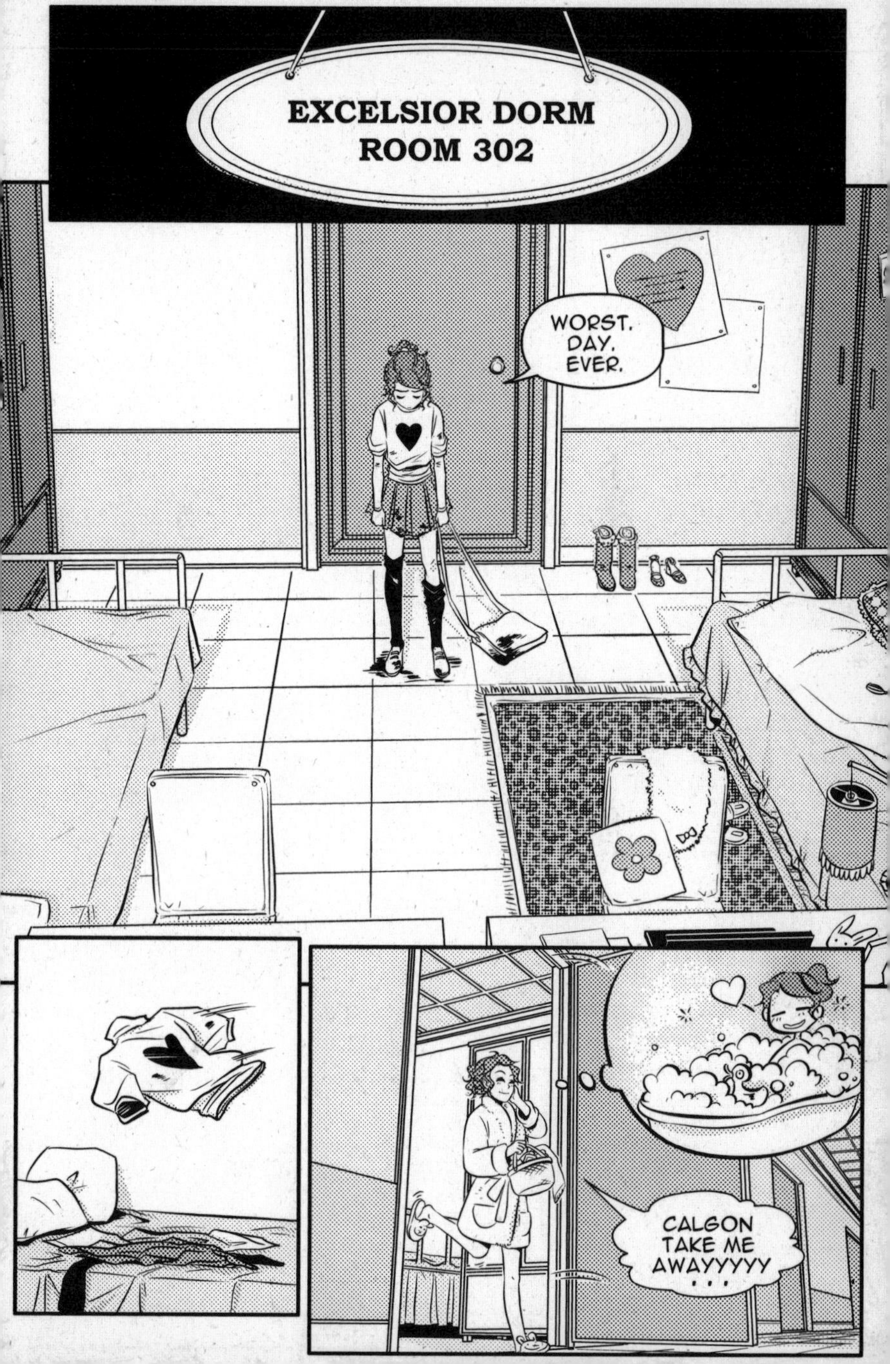
EXCELSIOR DORM
ROOM 302
WORST. DAY. EVER.
CALGON TAKE ME AWAYYYYY . . .

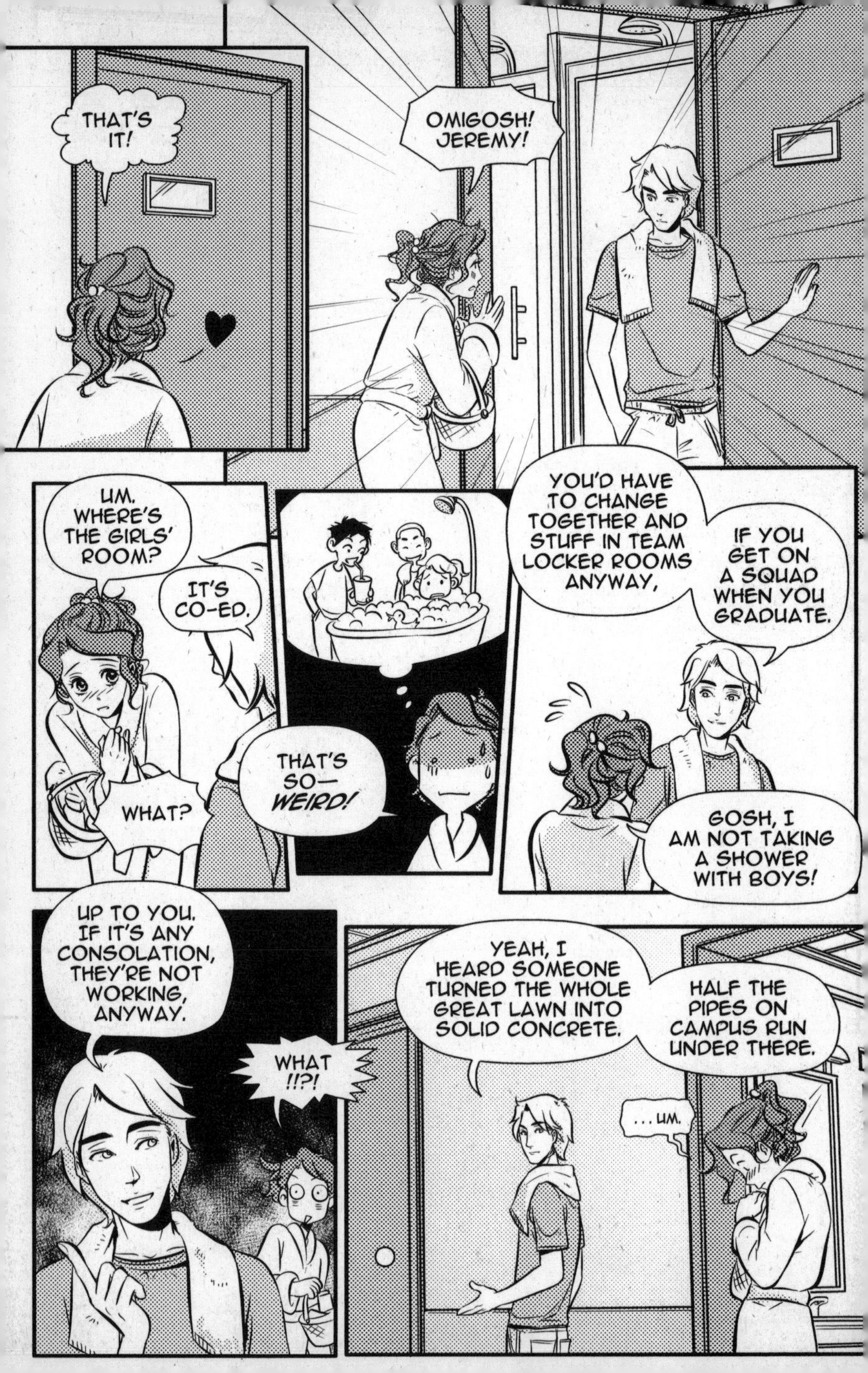
THAT'S IT!
OMIGOSH! JEREMY!
UM. WHERE'S THE GIRLS' ROOM?
IT'S CO-ED.
WHAT?
THAT'S SO— WEIRD!
YOU'D HAVE TO CHANGE TOGETHER AND STUFF IN TEAM LOCKER ROOMS ANYWAY,
IF YOU GET ON A SQUAD WHEN YOU GRADUATE.
GOSH, I AM NOT TAKING A SHOWER WITH BOYS!
UP TO YOU. IF IT'S ANY CONSOLATION, THEY'RE NOT WORKING, ANYWAY.
WHAT !!?!
YEAH, I HEARD SOMEONE TURNED THE WHOLE GREAT LAWN INTO SOLID CONCRETE.
HALF THE PIPES ON CAMPUS RUN UNDER THERE.
...UM.

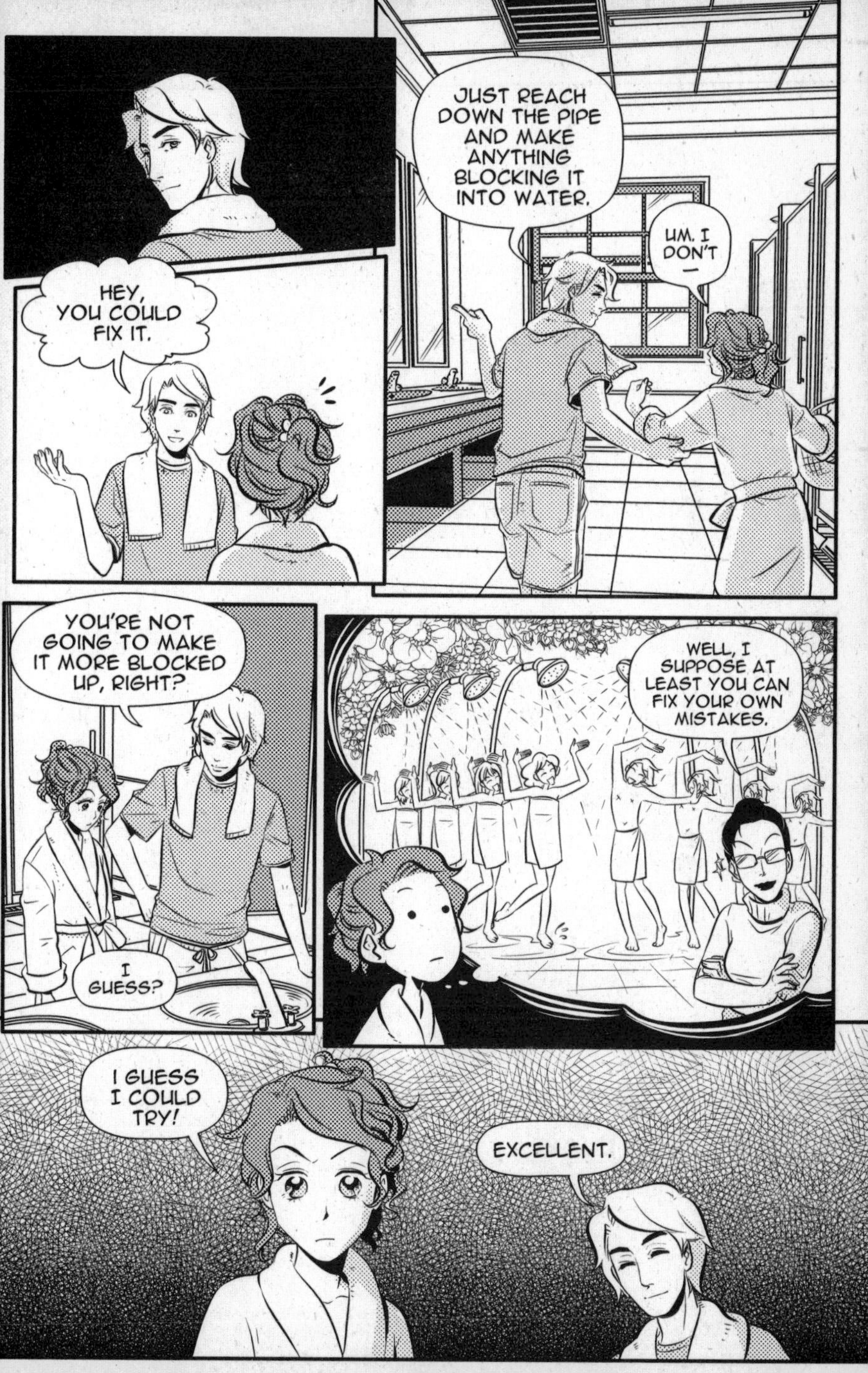
HEY, YOU COULD FIX IT.
JUST REACH DOWN THE PIPE AND MAKE ANYTHING BLOCKING IT INTO WATER.
UM. I DON'T—
YOU'RE NOT GOING TO MAKE IT MORE BLOCKED UP, RIGHT?
I GUESS?
WELL, I SUPPOSE AT LEAST YOU CAN FIX YOUR OWN MISTAKES.
I GUESS I COULD TRY!
EXCELLENT.

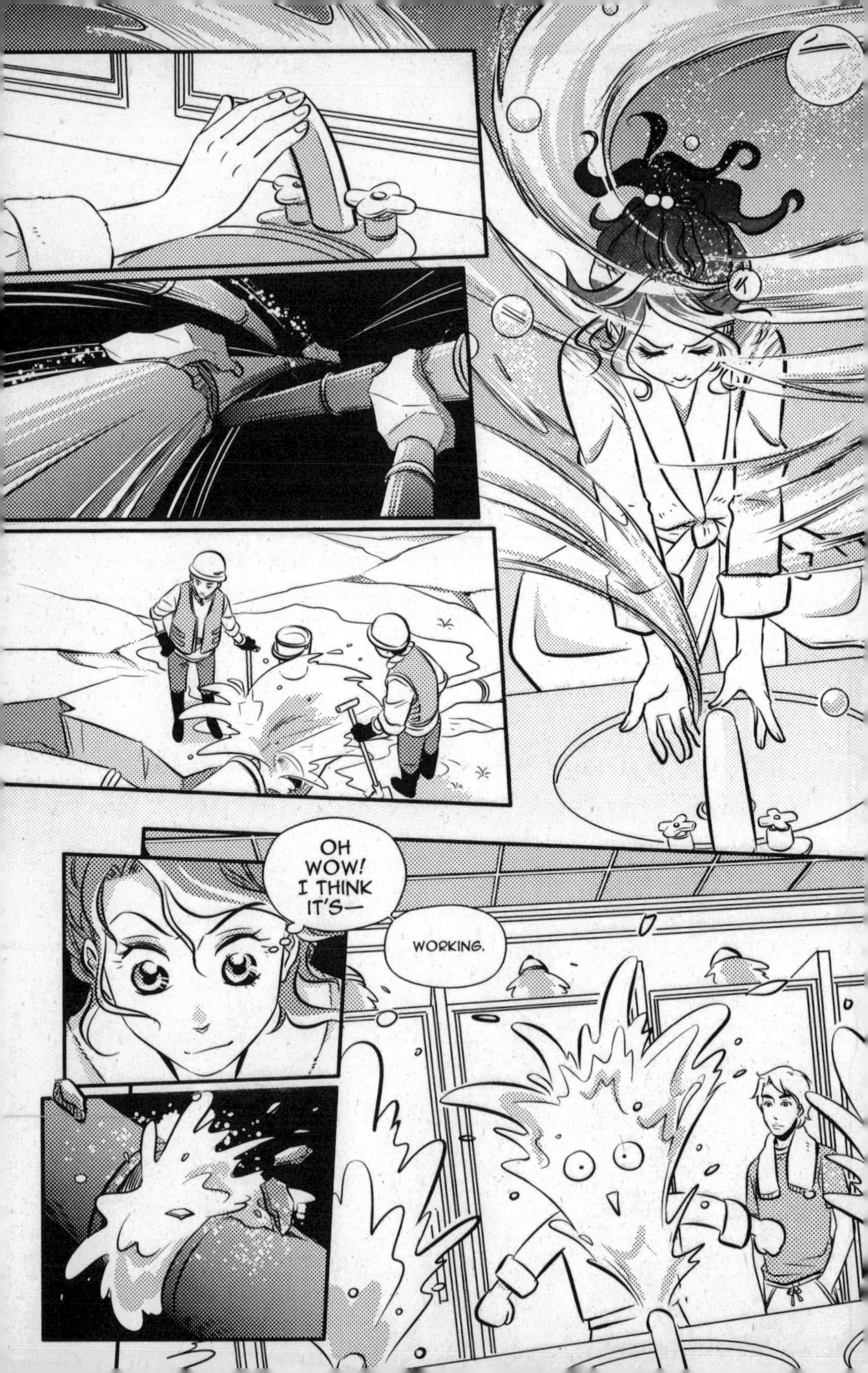
OH WOW! I THINK IT'S—
WORKING.

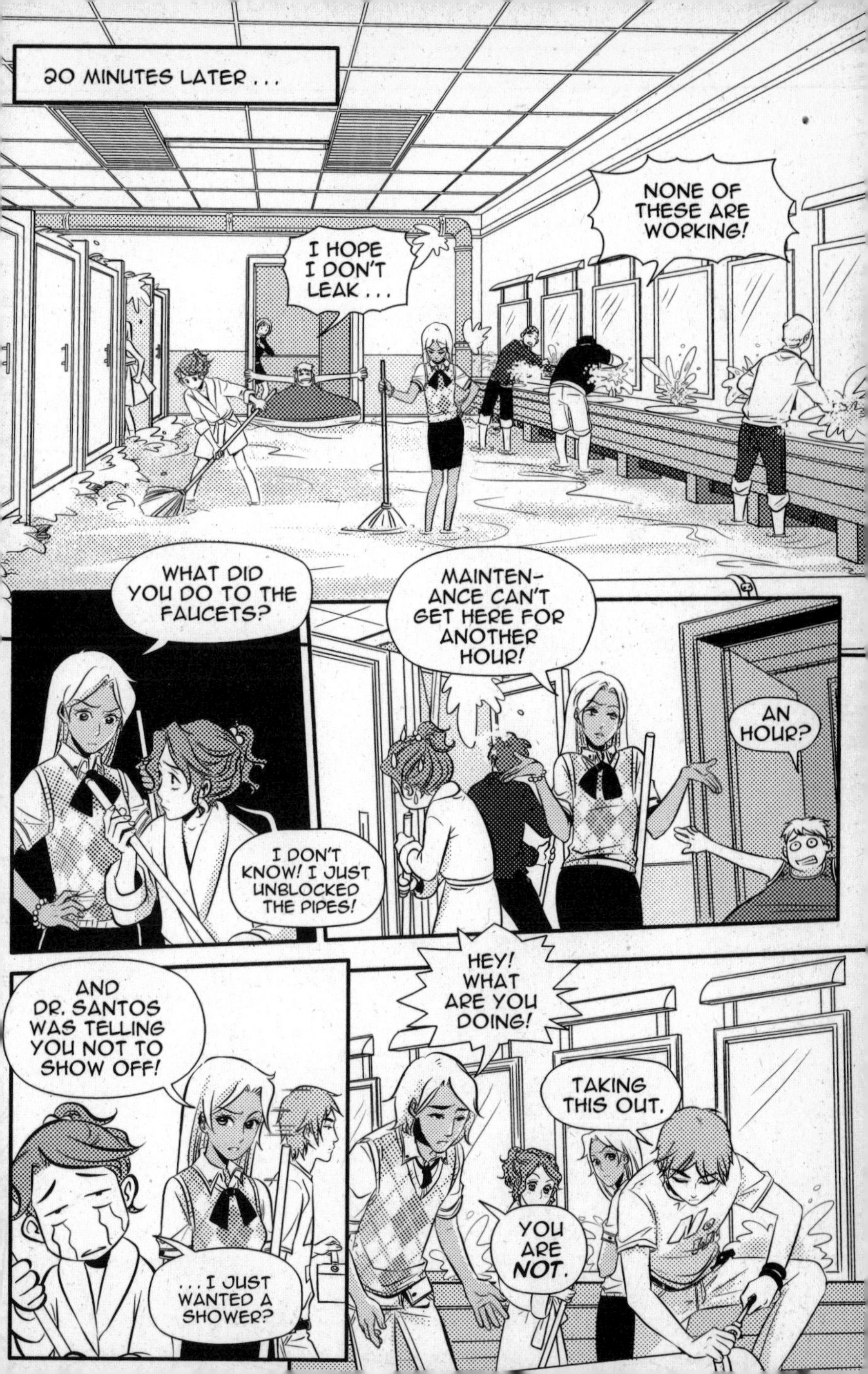
20 MINUTES LATER . . .
I HOPE I DON'T LEAK . . .
NONE OF THESE ARE WORKING!
WHAT DID YOU DO TO THE FAUCETS?
I DON'T KNOW! I JUST UNBLOCKED THE PIPES!
MAINTEN-ANCE CAN'T GET HERE FOR ANOTHER HOUR!
AN HOUR?
AND DR. SANTOS WAS TELLING YOU NOT TO SHOW OFF!
. . . I JUST WANTED A SHOWER?
HEY! WHAT ARE YOU DOING!
TAKING THIS OUT.
YOU ARE NOT.

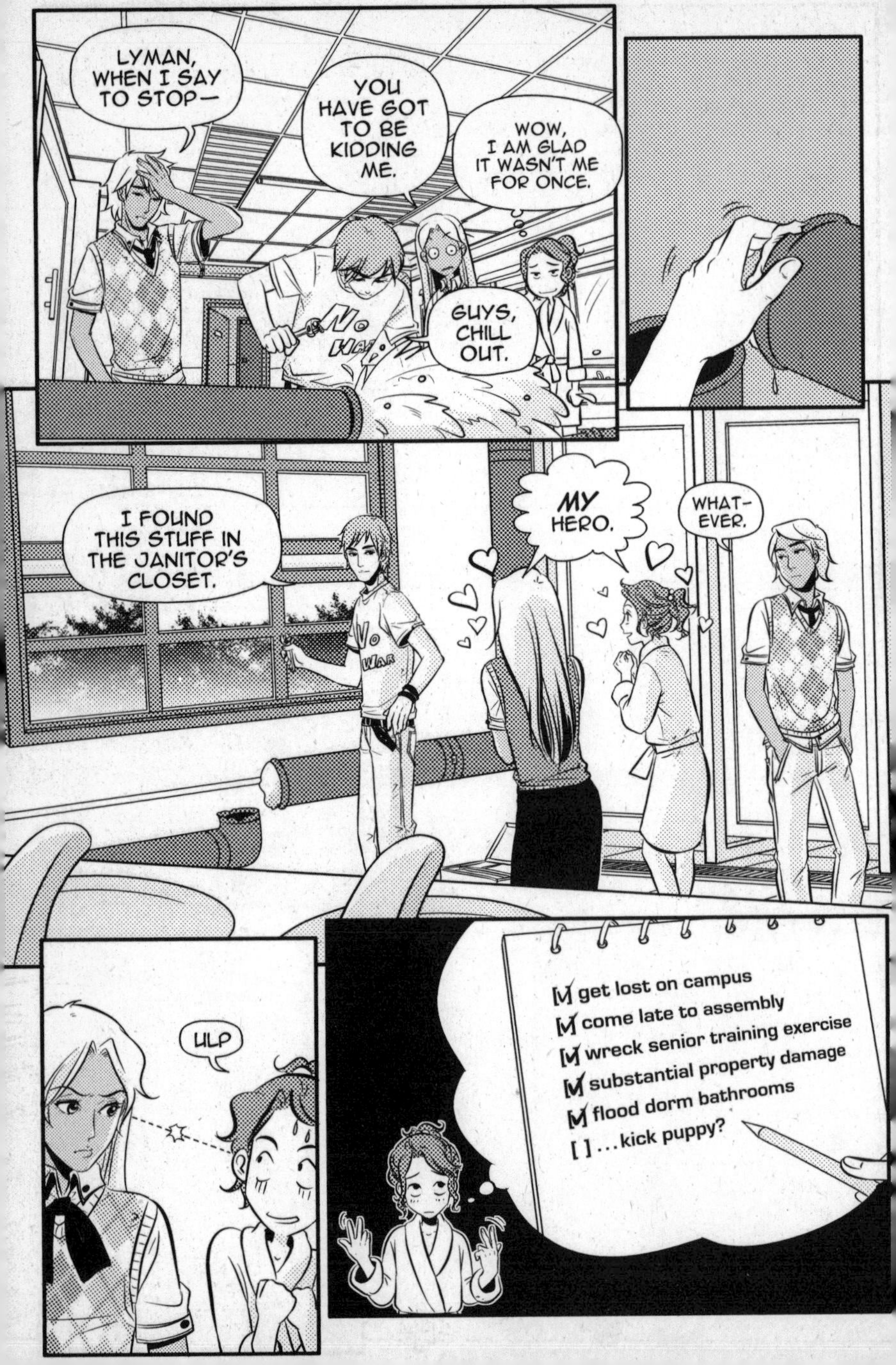
LYMAN, WHEN I SAY TO STOP—
YOU HAVE GOT TO BE KIDDING ME.
WOW, I AM GLAD IT WASN'T ME FOR ONCE.
GUYS, CHILL OUT.
I FOUND THIS STUFF IN THE JANITOR'S CLOSET.
MY HERO.
WHAT-EVER.
ULP
[✓] get lost on campus
[✓] come late to assembly
[✓] wreck senior training exercise
[✓] substantial property damage
[✓] flood dorm bathrooms
[ ] . . . kick puppy?

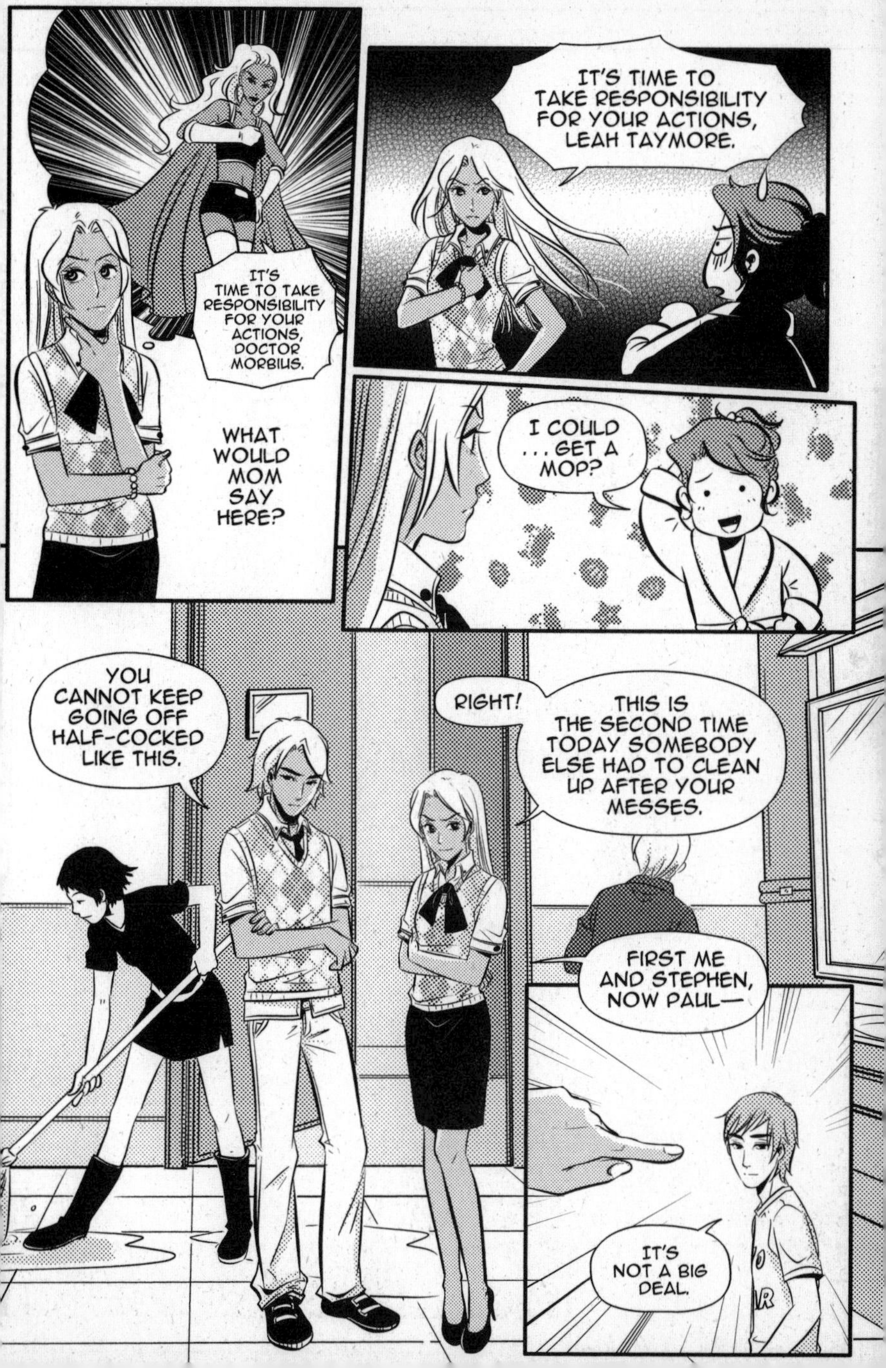
IT'S TIME TO TAKE RESPONSIBILITY FOR YOUR ACTIONS, DOCTOR MORBIUS.
WHAT WOULD MOM SAY HERE?
IT'S TIME TO TAKE RESPONSIBILITY FOR YOUR ACTIONS, LEAH TAYMORE.
I COULD . . . GET A MOP?
YOU CANNOT KEEP GOING OFF HALF-COCKED LIKE THIS.
RIGHT!
THIS IS THE SECOND TIME TODAY SOMEBODY ELSE HAD TO CLEAN UP AFTER YOUR MESSES.
FIRST ME AND STEPHEN, NOW PAUL—
IT'S NOT A BIG DEAL.

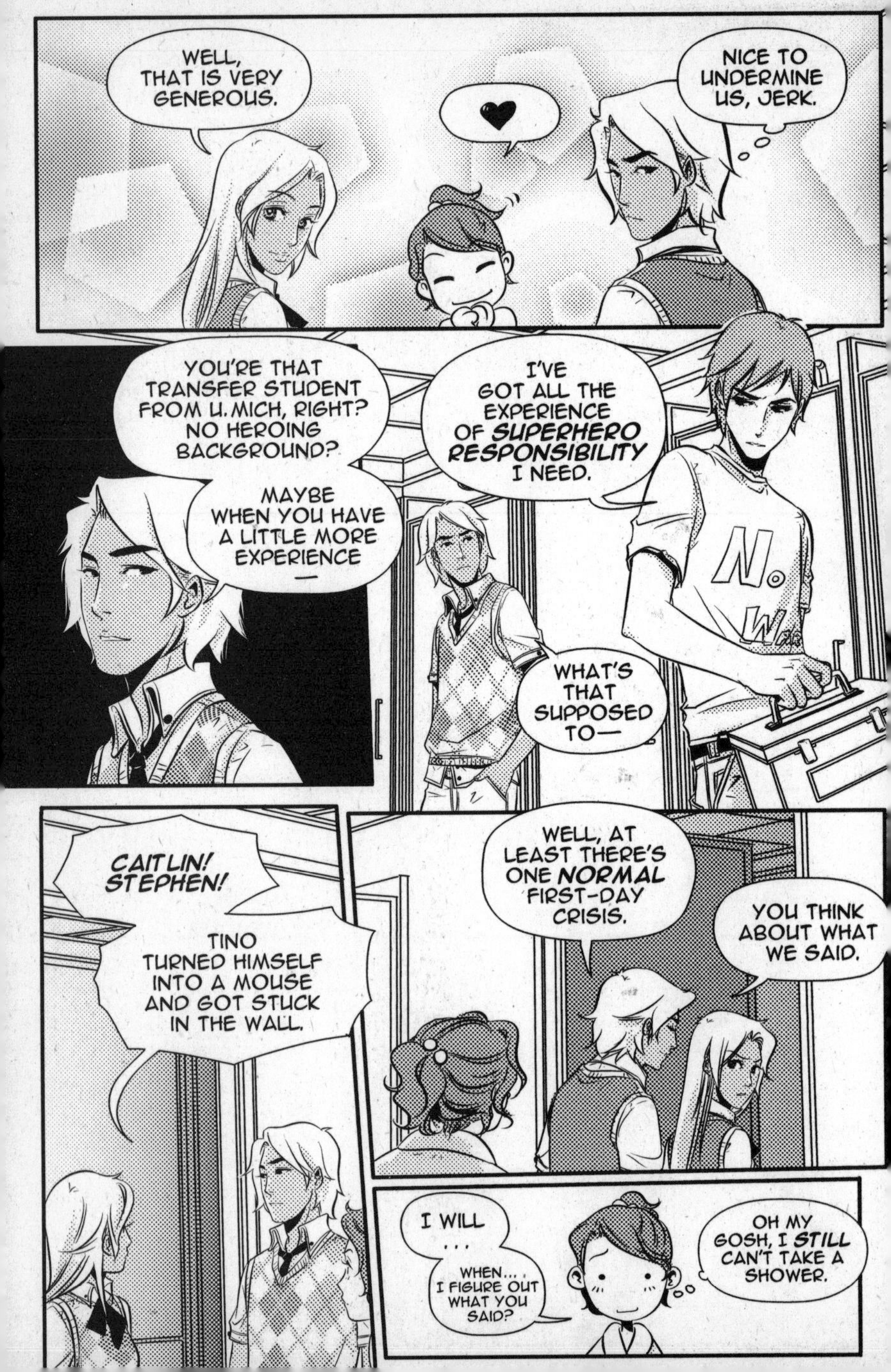
WELL, THAT IS VERY GENEROUS.
♥
NICE TO UNDERMINE US, JERK.
YOU'RE THAT TRANSFER STUDENT FROM U. MICH, RIGHT? NO HEROING BACKGROUND?
MAYBE WHEN YOU HAVE A LITTLE MORE EXPERIENCE —
I'VE GOT ALL THE EXPERIENCE OF *SUPERHERO RESPONSIBILITY* I NEED.
WHAT'S THAT SUPPOSED TO—
CAITLIN! STEPHEN!
TINO TURNED HIMSELF INTO A MOUSE AND GOT STUCK IN THE WALL.
WELL, AT LEAST THERE'S ONE *NORMAL* FIRST-DAY CRISIS.
YOU THINK ABOUT WHAT WE SAID.
I WILL . . .
WHEN... I FIGURE OUT WHAT YOU SAID?
OH MY GOSH, I *STILL* CAN'T TAKE A SHOWER.

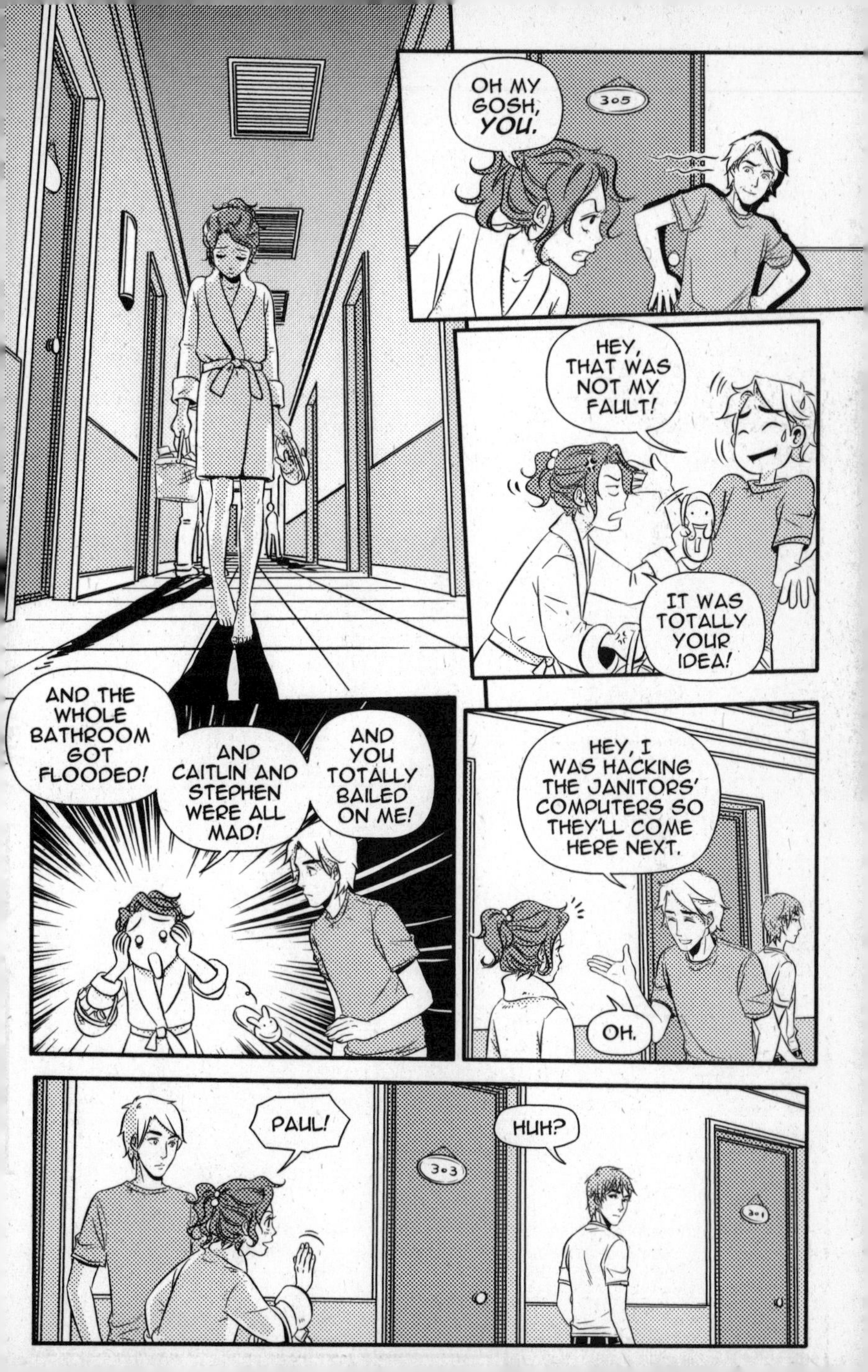
OH MY GOSH, *YOU.*
305
HEY, THAT WAS NOT MY FAULT!
IT WAS TOTALLY YOUR IDEA!
AND THE WHOLE BATHROOM GOT FLOODED!
AND CAITLIN AND STEPHEN WERE ALL MAD!
AND YOU TOTALLY BAILED ON ME!
HEY, I WAS HACKING THE JANITORS' COMPUTERS SO THEY'LL COME HERE NEXT.
OH.
PAUL!
HUH?
303
301

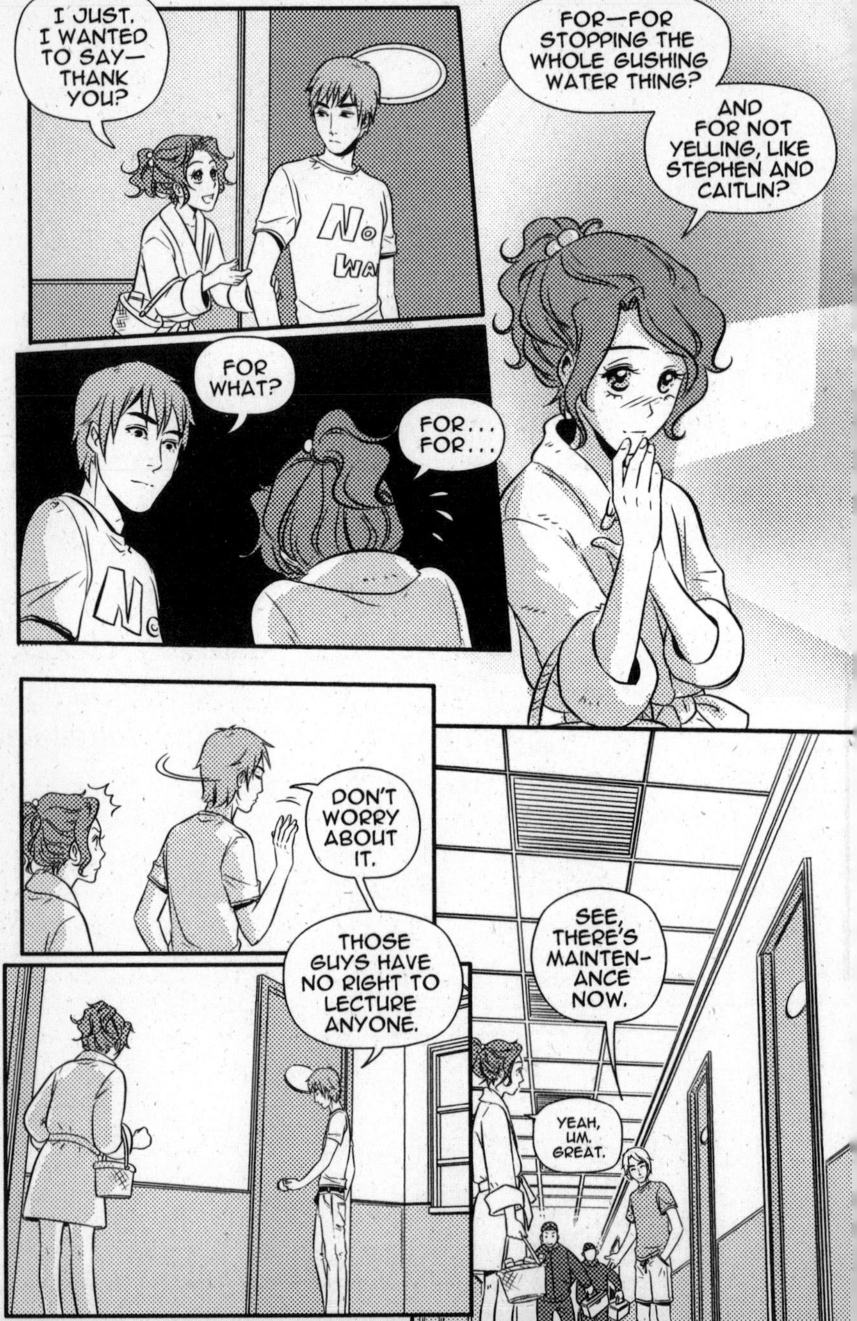
I JUST. I WANTED TO SAY— THANK YOU?
FOR WHAT?
FOR... FOR...
FOR—FOR STOPPING THE WHOLE GUSHING WATER THING?
AND FOR NOT YELLING, LIKE STEPHEN AND CAITLIN?
DON'T WORRY ABOUT IT.
THOSE GUYS HAVE NO RIGHT TO LECTURE ANYONE.
SEE, THERE'S MAINTEN-ANCE NOW.
YEAH, UM. GREAT.

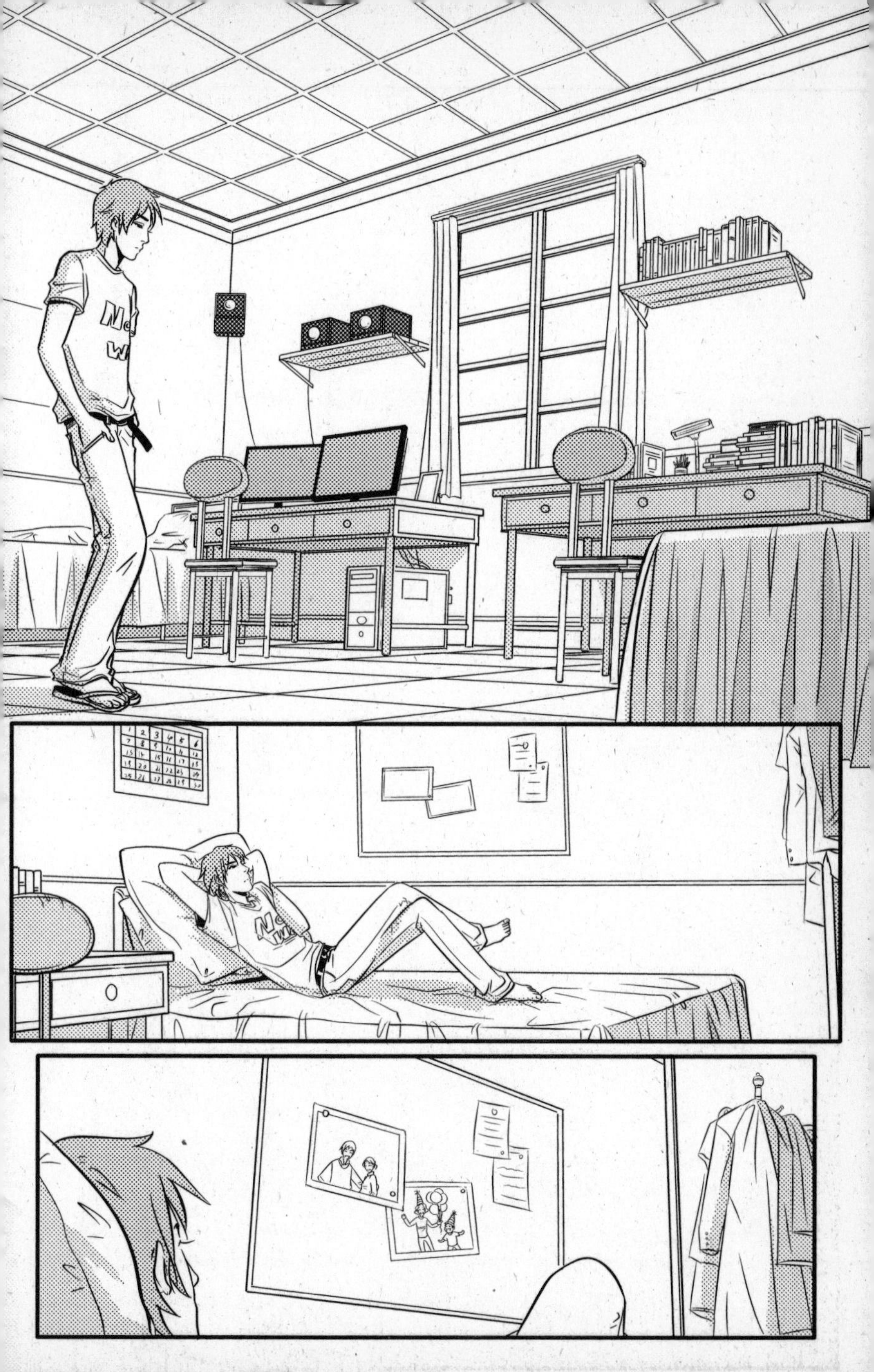

LIBERTY VOCATIONAL

Felicia Groves
Dean of Transfer Students
Admissions Office
Liberty Vocational Academy
May 14, 2012

Dear Paul Lyman,

Pursuant to a formal nomination from Detective Mina Reclerc of the Ann Arbor police, we have reviewed your records and wish to offer you a place in the class of 2016.

Please inform us by August 1 if you intend to join the class.

Regards,

Felicia Groves

Sorry, kid, I know you said you weren't interested, so I faked your address and applied for you.

You might not have as much as Calvin Washington under the hood, but you used what you had that day, and you saved ten people's lives.

We need people like you on the superhero squads. Too many of these high-octane costumes think about racking up their supervillain counts more than about taking care of people.

— Mina Reclerc

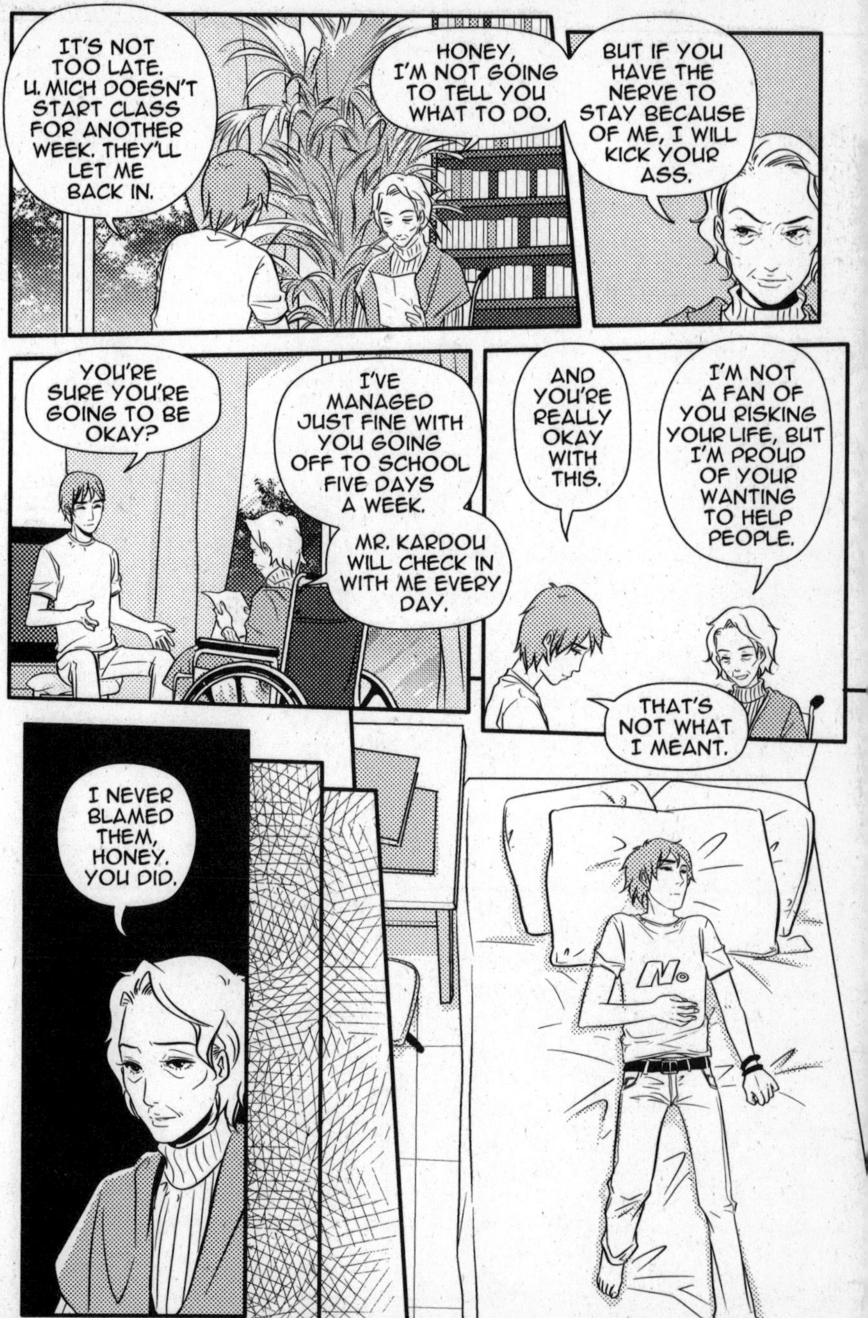
IT'S NOT TOO LATE. U. MICH DOESN'T START CLASS FOR ANOTHER WEEK. THEY'LL LET ME BACK IN.
HONEY, I'M NOT GOING TO TELL YOU WHAT TO DO.
BUT IF YOU HAVE THE NERVE TO STAY BECAUSE OF ME, I WILL KICK YOUR ASS.
YOU'RE SURE YOU'RE GOING TO BE OKAY?
I'VE MANAGED JUST FINE WITH YOU GOING OFF TO SCHOOL FIVE DAYS A WEEK.
MR. KARDOU WILL CHECK IN WITH ME EVERY DAY.
AND YOU'RE REALLY OKAY WITH THIS.
I'M NOT A FAN OF YOU RISKING YOUR LIFE, BUT I'M PROUD OF YOUR WANTING TO HELP PEOPLE.
THAT'S NOT WHAT I MEANT.
I NEVER BLAMED THEM, HONEY. YOU DID.
N

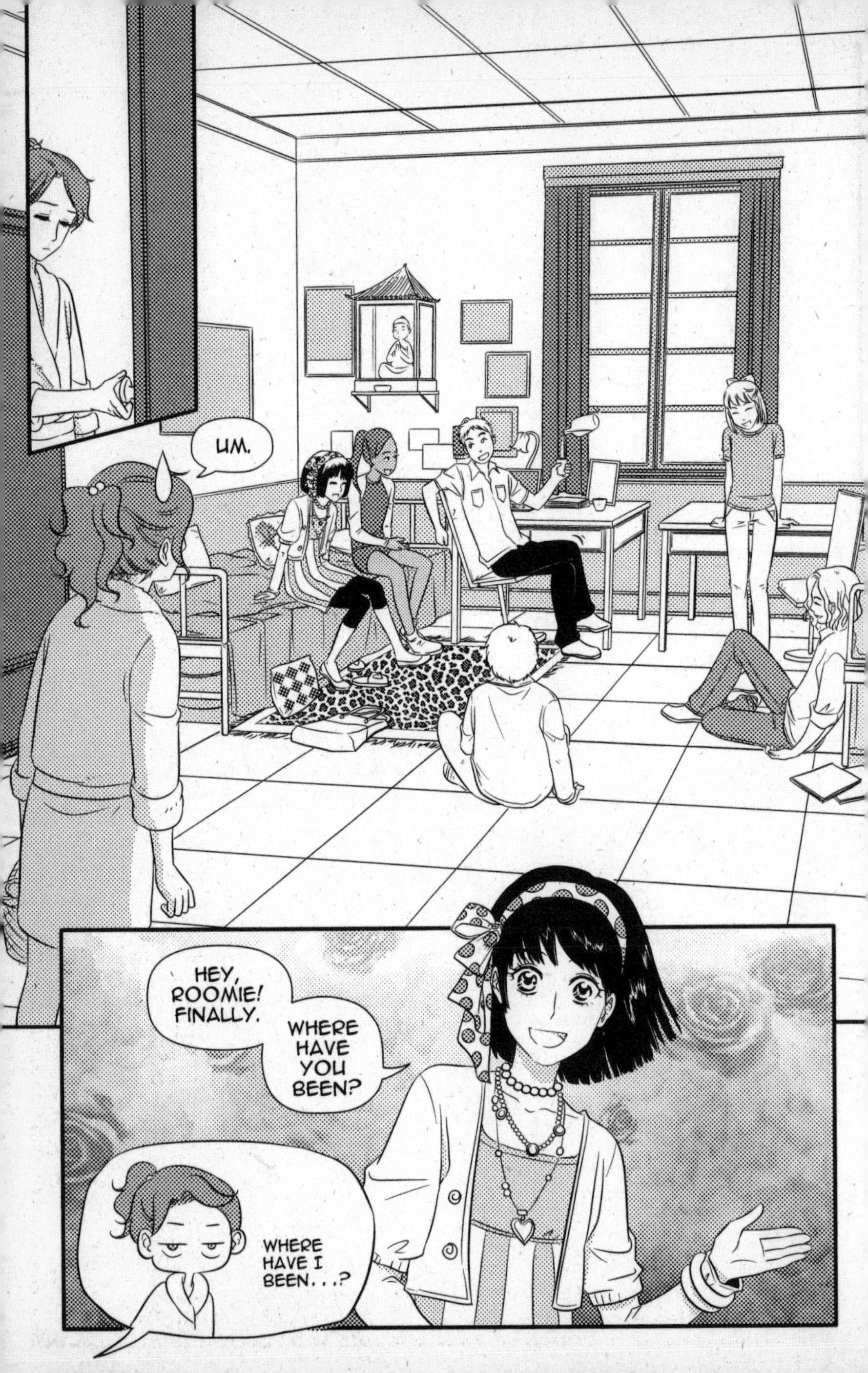
UM.
HEY, ROOMIE! FINALLY.
WHERE HAVE YOU BEEN?
WHERE HAVE I BEEN...?

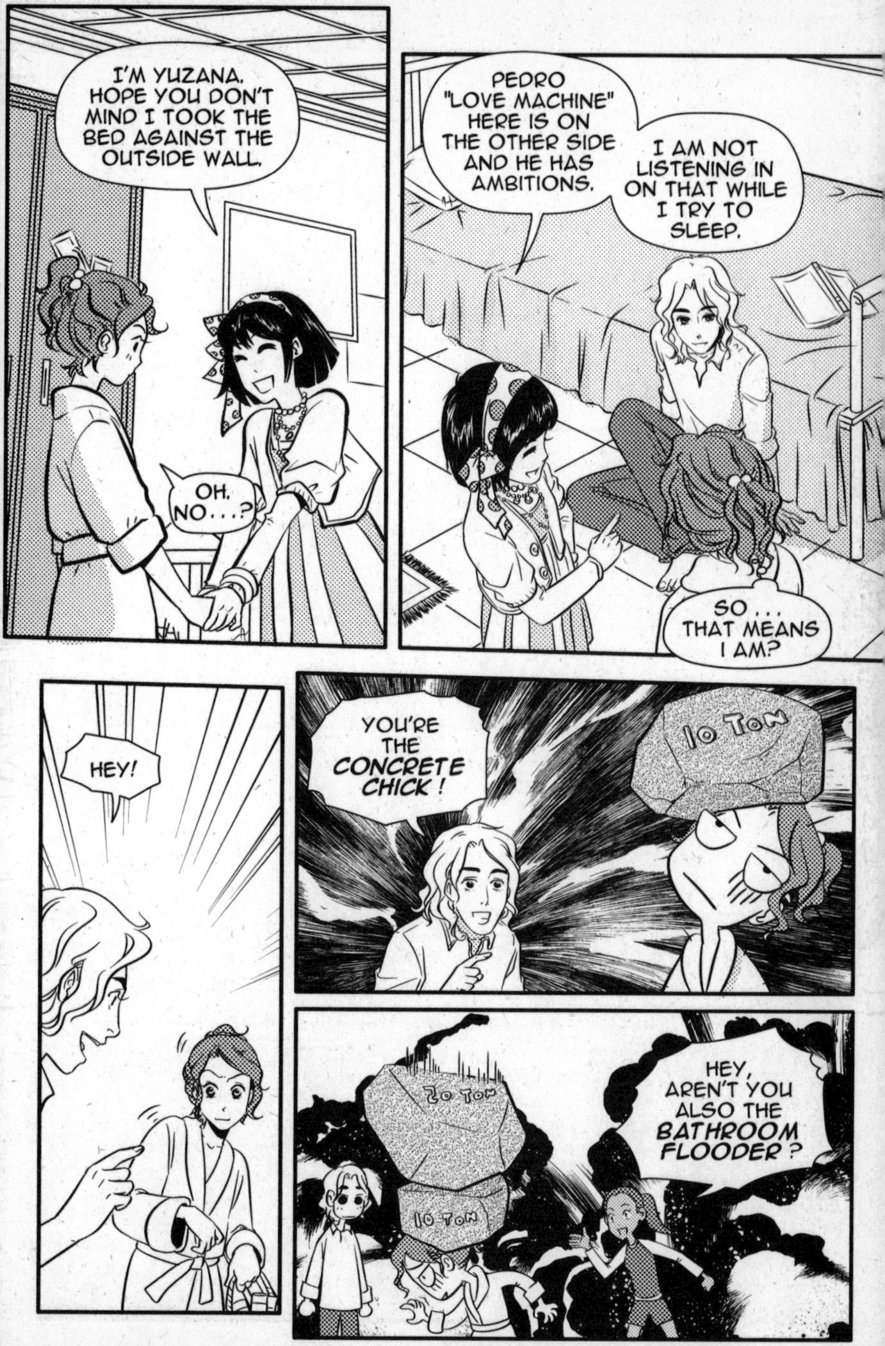
I'M YUZANA. HOPE YOU DON'T MIND I TOOK THE BED AGAINST THE OUTSIDE WALL.
OH. NO...?
PEDRO "LOVE MACHINE" HERE IS ON THE OTHER SIDE AND HE HAS AMBITIONS.
I AM NOT LISTENING IN ON THAT WHILE I TRY TO SLEEP.
SO... THAT MEANS I AM?
HEY!
YOU'RE THE CONCRETE CHICK!
10 TON
HEY, AREN'T YOU ALSO THE BATHROOM FLOODER?
20 TON
10 TON

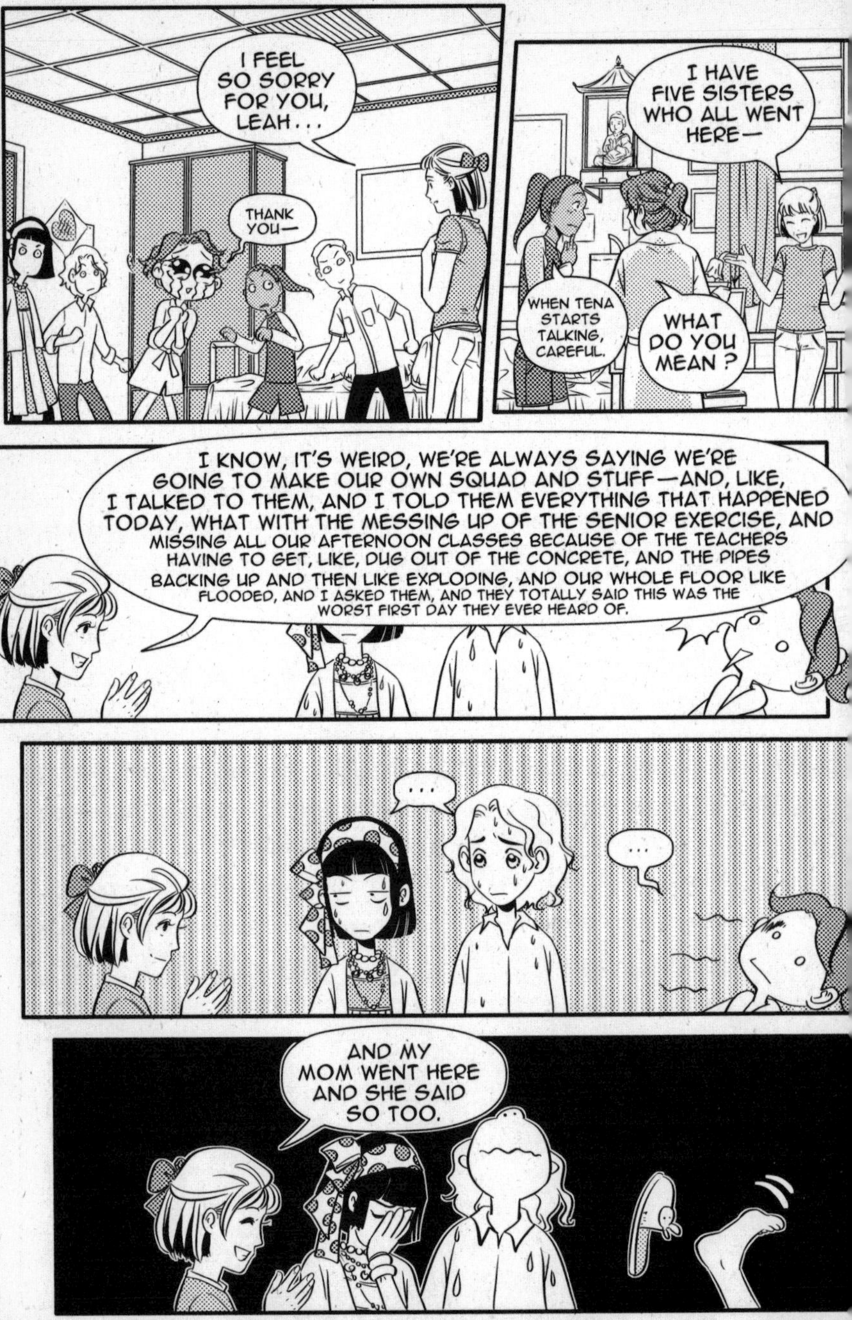
I FEEL SO SORRY FOR YOU, LEAH...
THANK YOU—
I HAVE FIVE SISTERS WHO ALL WENT HERE—
WHEN TENA STARTS TALKING, CAREFUL.
WHAT DO YOU MEAN?
I KNOW, IT'S WEIRD, WE'RE ALWAYS SAYING WE'RE GOING TO MAKE OUR OWN SQUAD AND STUFF—AND, LIKE, I TALKED TO THEM, AND I TOLD THEM EVERYTHING THAT HAPPENED TODAY, WHAT WITH THE MESSING UP OF THE SENIOR EXERCISE, AND MISSING ALL OUR AFTERNOON CLASSES BECAUSE OF THE TEACHERS HAVING TO GET, LIKE, DUG OUT OF THE CONCRETE, AND THE PIPES BACKING UP AND THEN LIKE EXPLODING, AND OUR WHOLE FLOOR LIKE FLOODED, AND I ASKED THEM, AND THEY TOTALLY SAID THIS WAS THE WORST FIRST DAY THEY EVER HEARD OF.
...
...
AND MY MOM WENT HERE AND SHE SAID SO TOO.

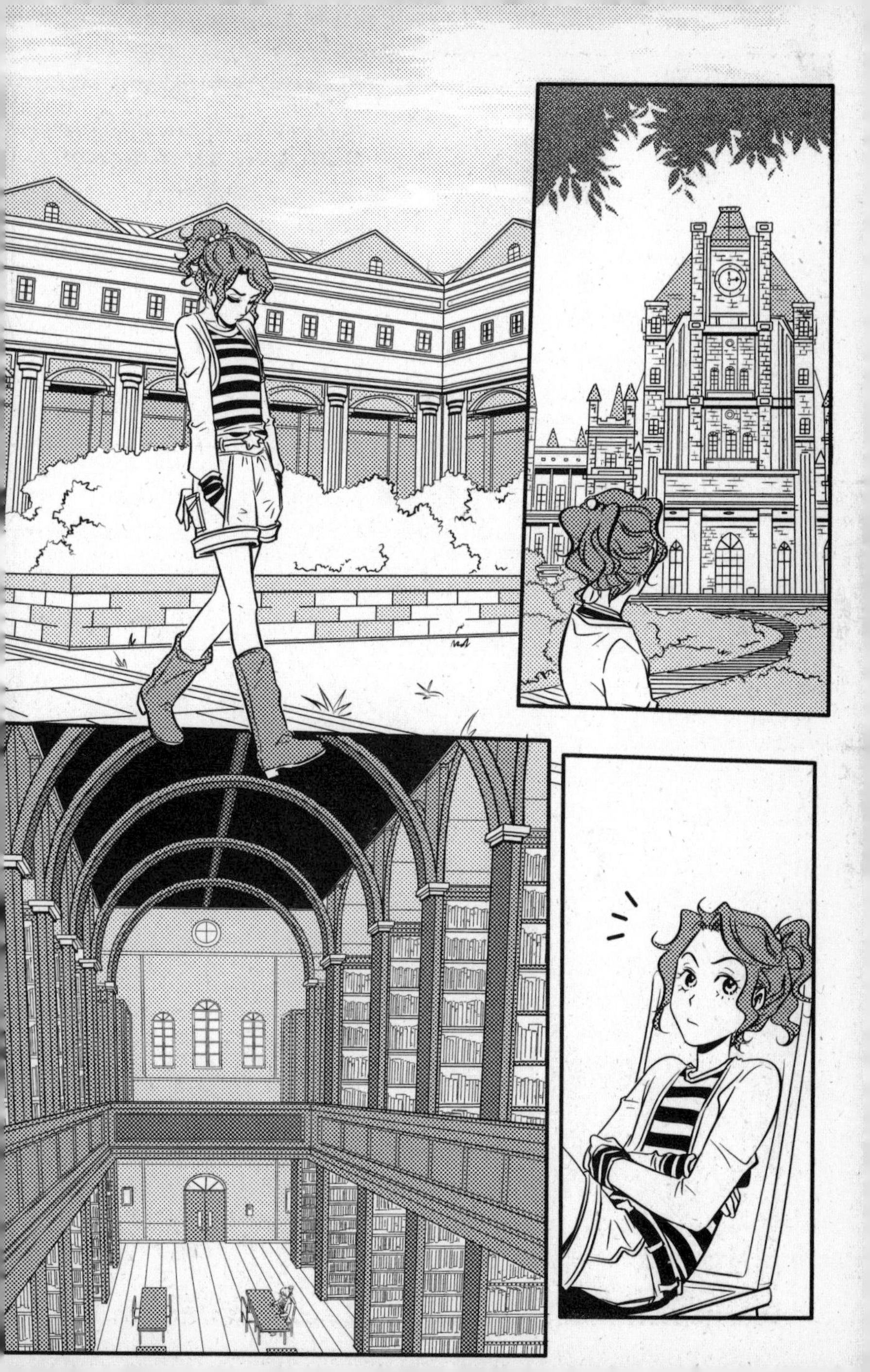

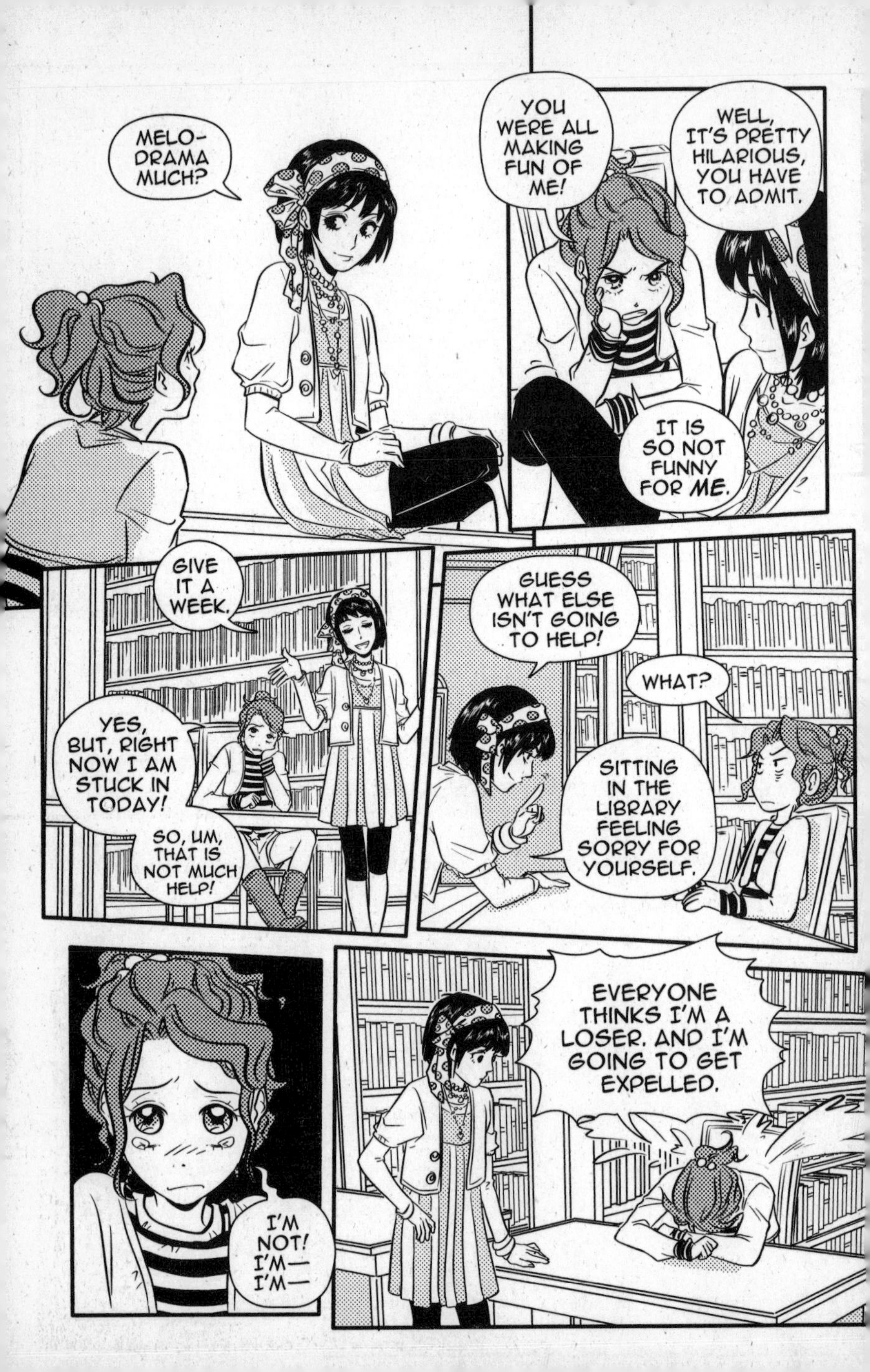
MELO-DRAMA MUCH?
YOU WERE ALL MAKING FUN OF ME!
WELL, IT'S PRETTY HILARIOUS, YOU HAVE TO ADMIT.
IT IS SO NOT FUNNY FOR *ME*.
GIVE IT A WEEK.
YES, BUT, RIGHT NOW I AM STUCK IN TODAY!
SO, UM, THAT IS NOT MUCH HELP!
GUESS WHAT ELSE ISN'T GOING TO HELP!
WHAT?
SITTING IN THE LIBRARY FEELING SORRY FOR YOURSELF.
I'M NOT! I'M— I'M—
EVERYONE THINKS I'M A LOSER. AND I'M GOING TO GET EXPELLED.

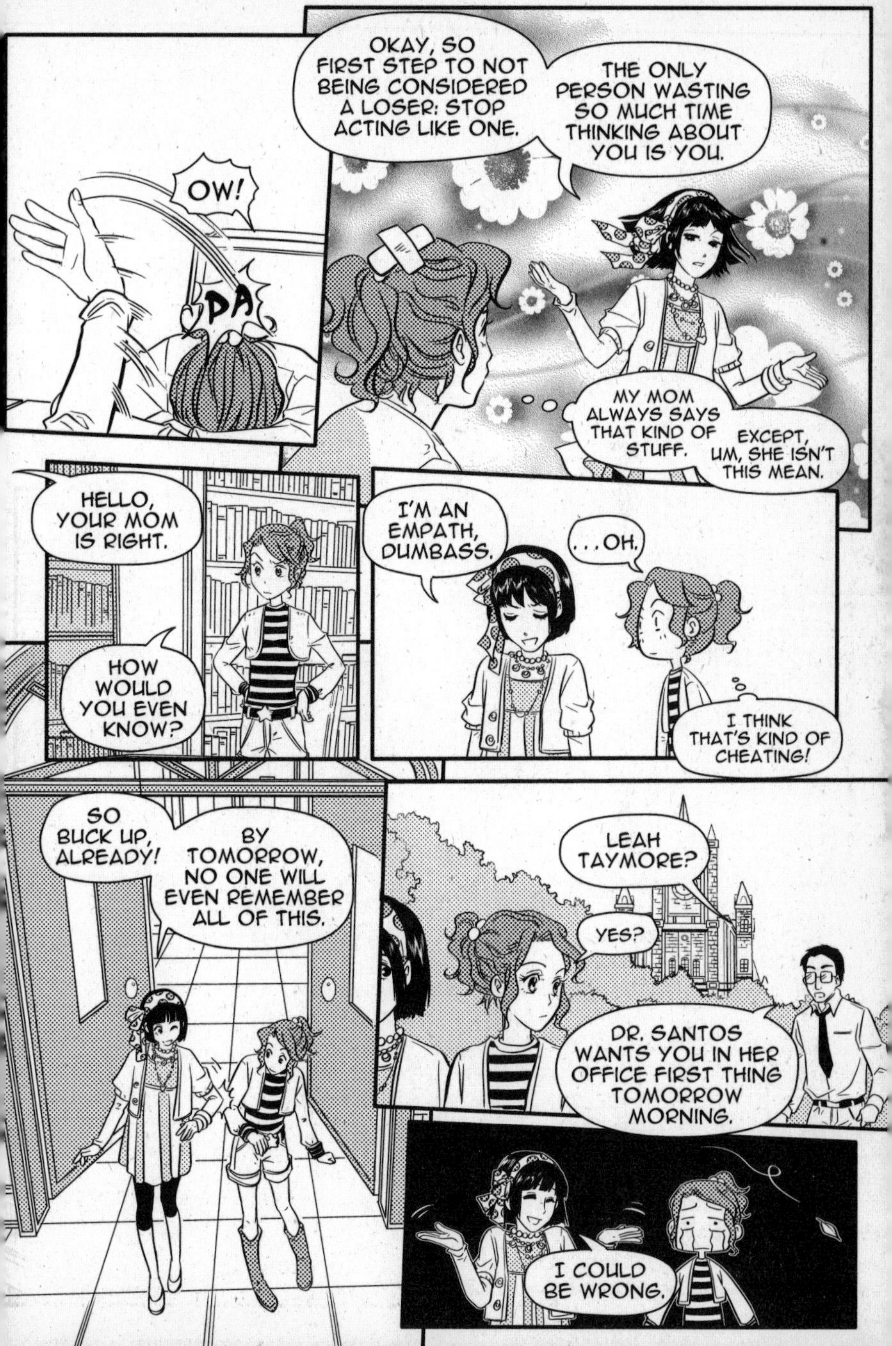
OW!
DA
OKAY, SO FIRST STEP TO NOT BEING CONSIDERED A LOSER: STOP ACTING LIKE ONE.
THE ONLY PERSON WASTING SO MUCH TIME THINKING ABOUT YOU IS YOU.
MY MOM ALWAYS SAYS THAT KIND OF STUFF.
EXCEPT, UM, SHE ISN'T THIS MEAN.
HELLO, YOUR MOM IS RIGHT.
HOW WOULD YOU EVEN KNOW?
I'M AN EMPATH, DUMBASS.
...OH.
I THINK THAT'S KIND OF CHEATING!
SO BUCK UP, ALREADY!
BY TOMORROW, NO ONE WILL EVEN REMEMBER ALL OF THIS.
LEAH TAYMORE?
YES?
DR. SANTOS WANTS YOU IN HER OFFICE FIRST THING TOMORROW MORNING.
I COULD BE WRONG.

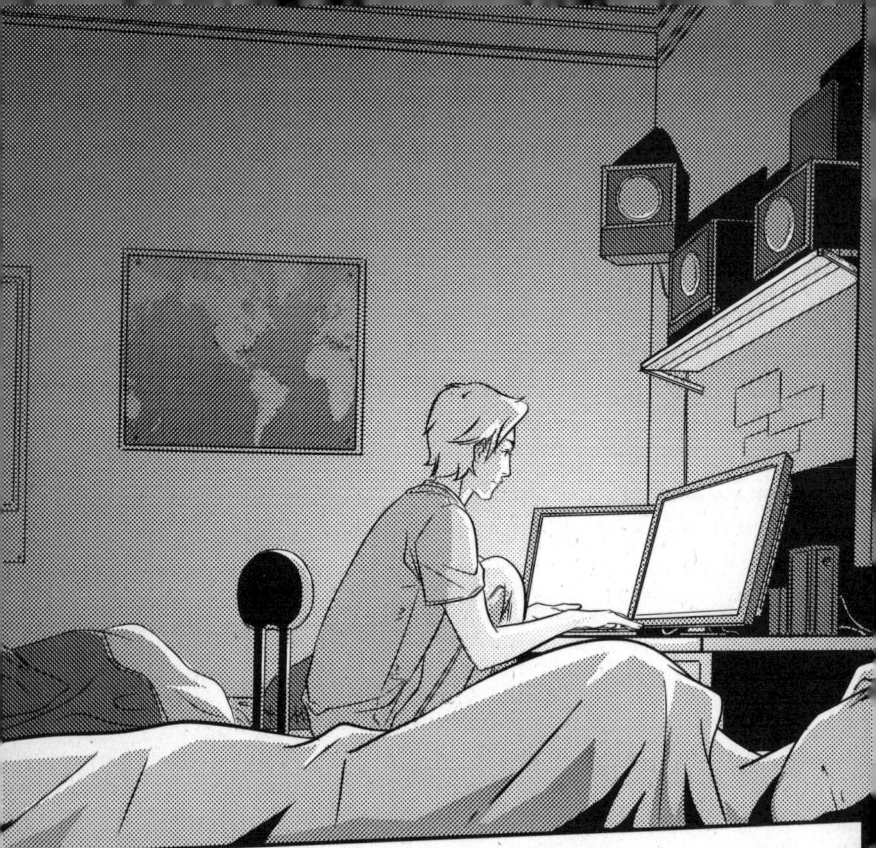

JEREMEISTER: Yeah, first day was great.
JEREMEISTER: My roommate is cool. Doesn't mind the setup.
JEREMEISTER: He's pretty excellent at Halo.
ALEXANDRB: Well, there's a high encomium.
JEREMEISTER: Daaaad.
ALEXANDRB: Oh, I'm sorry, am I being lame again? Out of touch with the kids these days?
JEREMEISTER: *eyeroll*
JEREMEISTER: There are some pretty hot girls on my hall. Hey, you didn't tell me Caitlin Victoire was smoking.
ALEXANDRB: I can't imagine how I omitted that vital piece of information.
ALEXANDRB: Dare I ask, did you have any actual classes today?
JEREMEISTER: Not a one.
ALEXANDRB: What happened?

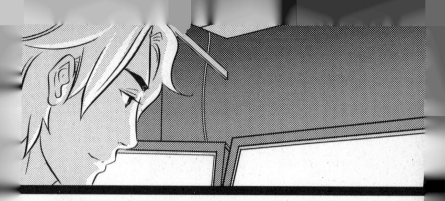

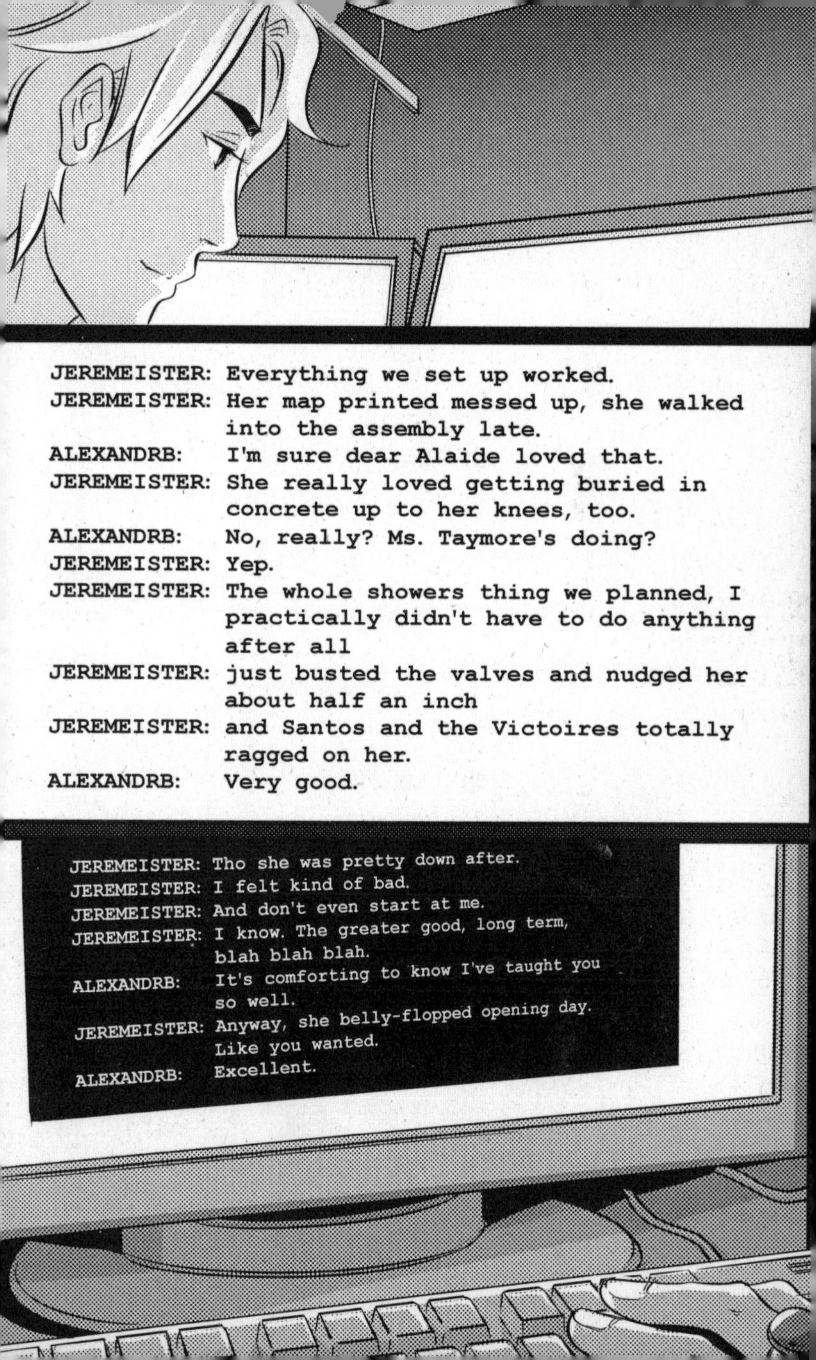

JEREMEISTER: Everything we set up worked.
JEREMEISTER: Her map printed messed up, she walked into the assembly late.
ALEXANDRB: I'm sure dear Alaide loved that.
JEREMEISTER: She really loved getting buried in concrete up to her knees, too.
ALEXANDRB: No, really? Ms. Taymore's doing?
JEREMEISTER: Yep.
JEREMEISTER: The whole showers thing we planned, I practically didn't have to do anything after all
JEREMEISTER: just busted the valves and nudged her about half an inch
JEREMEISTER: and Santos and the Victoires totally ragged on her.
ALEXANDRB: Very good.

JEREMEISTER: Tho she was pretty down after.
JEREMEISTER: I felt kind of bad.
JEREMEISTER: And don't even start at me.
JEREMEISTER: I know. The greater good, long term, blah blah blah.
ALEXANDRB: It's comforting to know I've taught you so well.
JEREMEISTER: Anyway, she belly-flopped opening day. Like you wanted.
ALEXANDRB: Excellent.

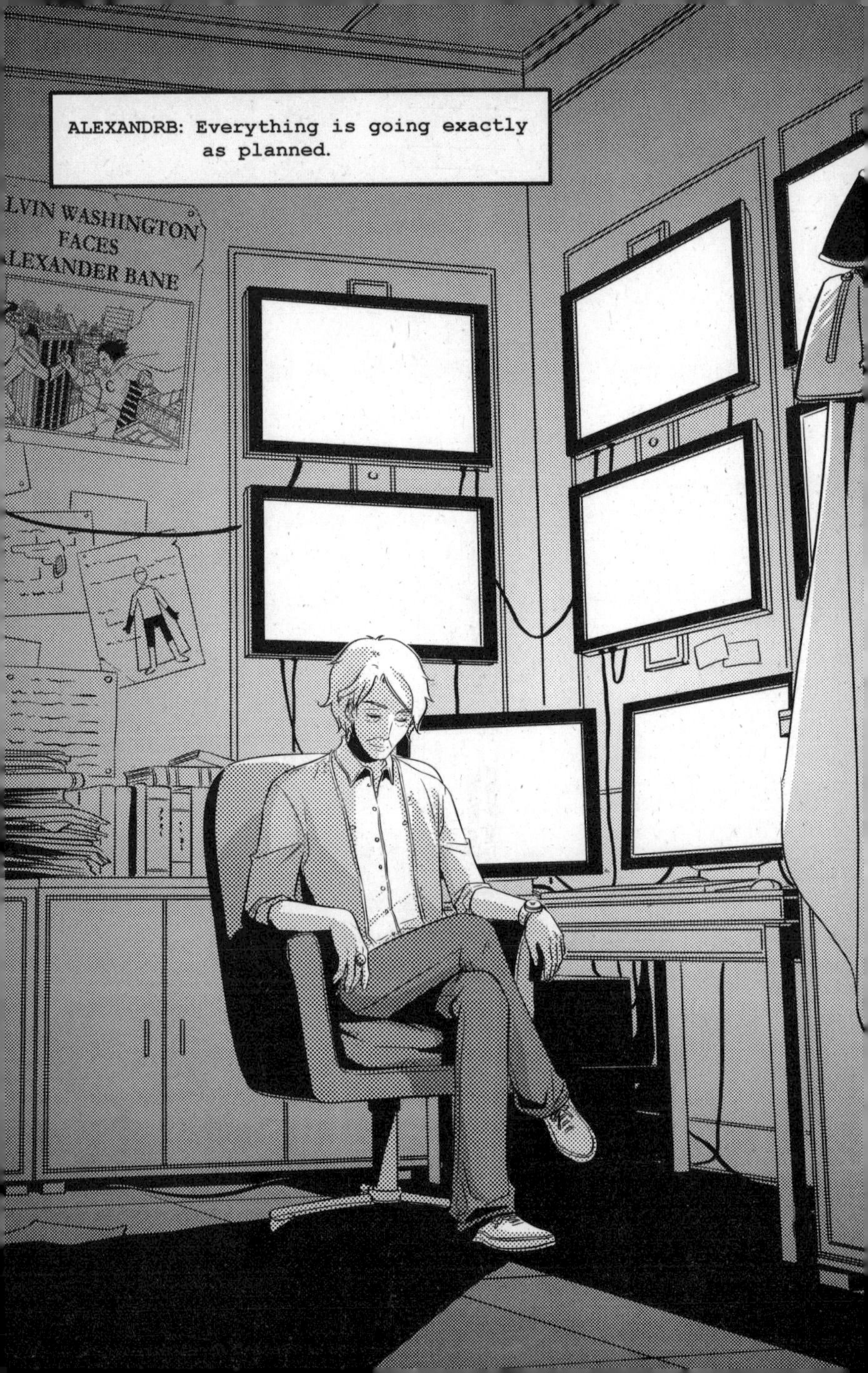
ALEXANDRB: Everything is going exactly as planned.
LVIN WASHINGTON FACES LEXANDER BANE

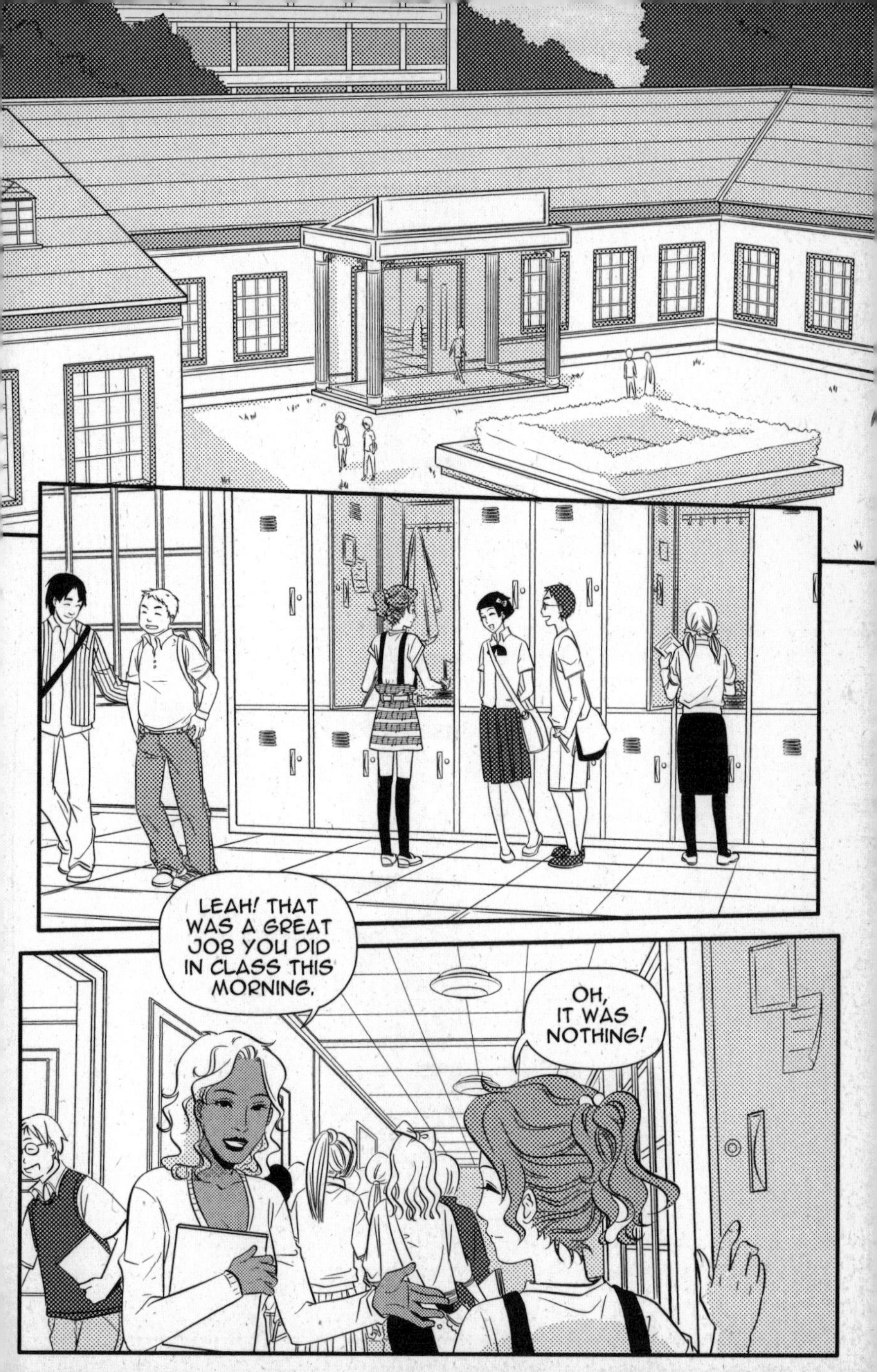
LEAH! THAT WAS A GREAT JOB YOU DID IN CLASS THIS MORNING.
OH, IT WAS NOTHING!

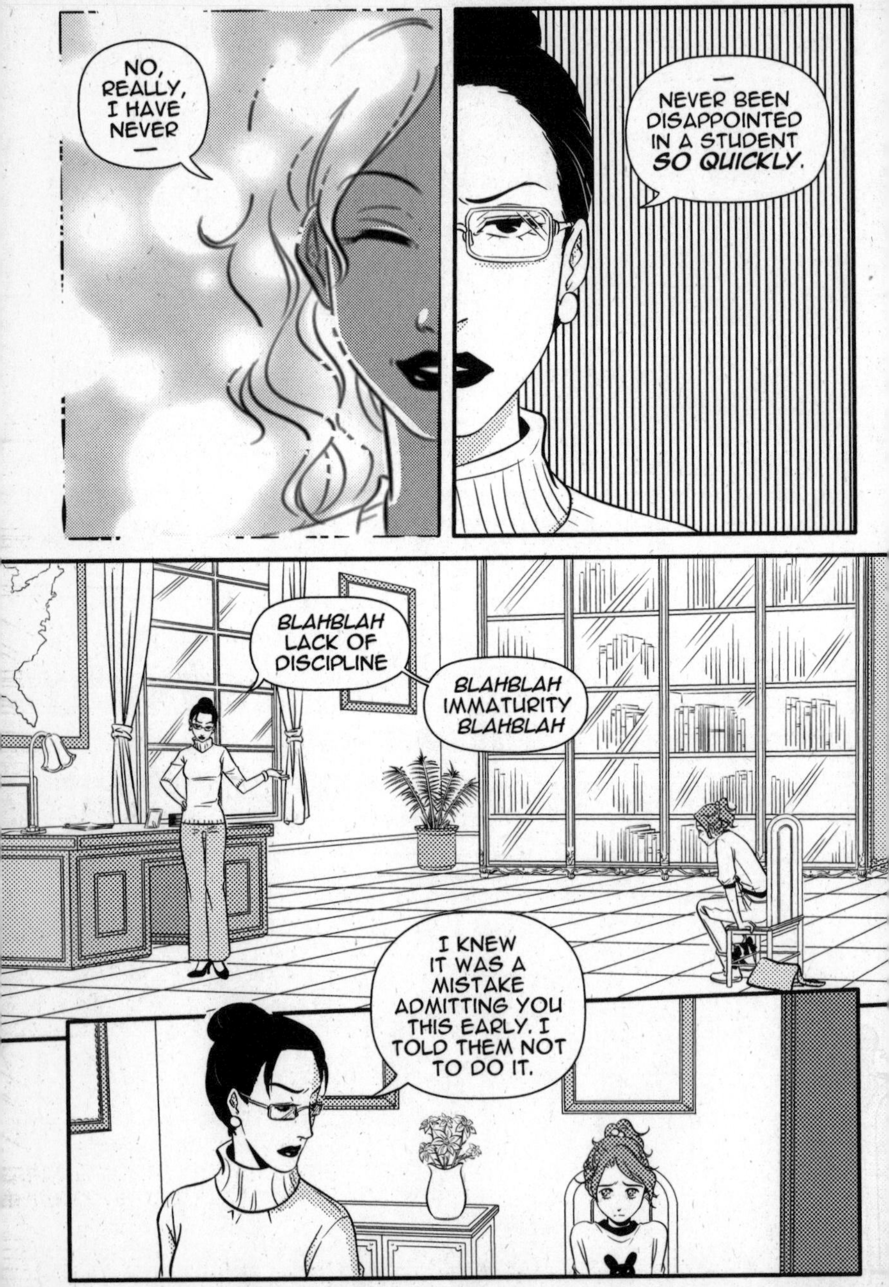
NO, REALLY, I HAVE NEVER —
— NEVER BEEN DISAPPOINTED IN A STUDENT SO QUICKLY.
BLAHBLAH LACK OF DISCIPLINE
BLAHBLAH IMMATURITY BLAHBLAH
I KNEW IT WAS A MISTAKE ADMITTING YOU THIS EARLY. I TOLD THEM NOT TO DO IT.

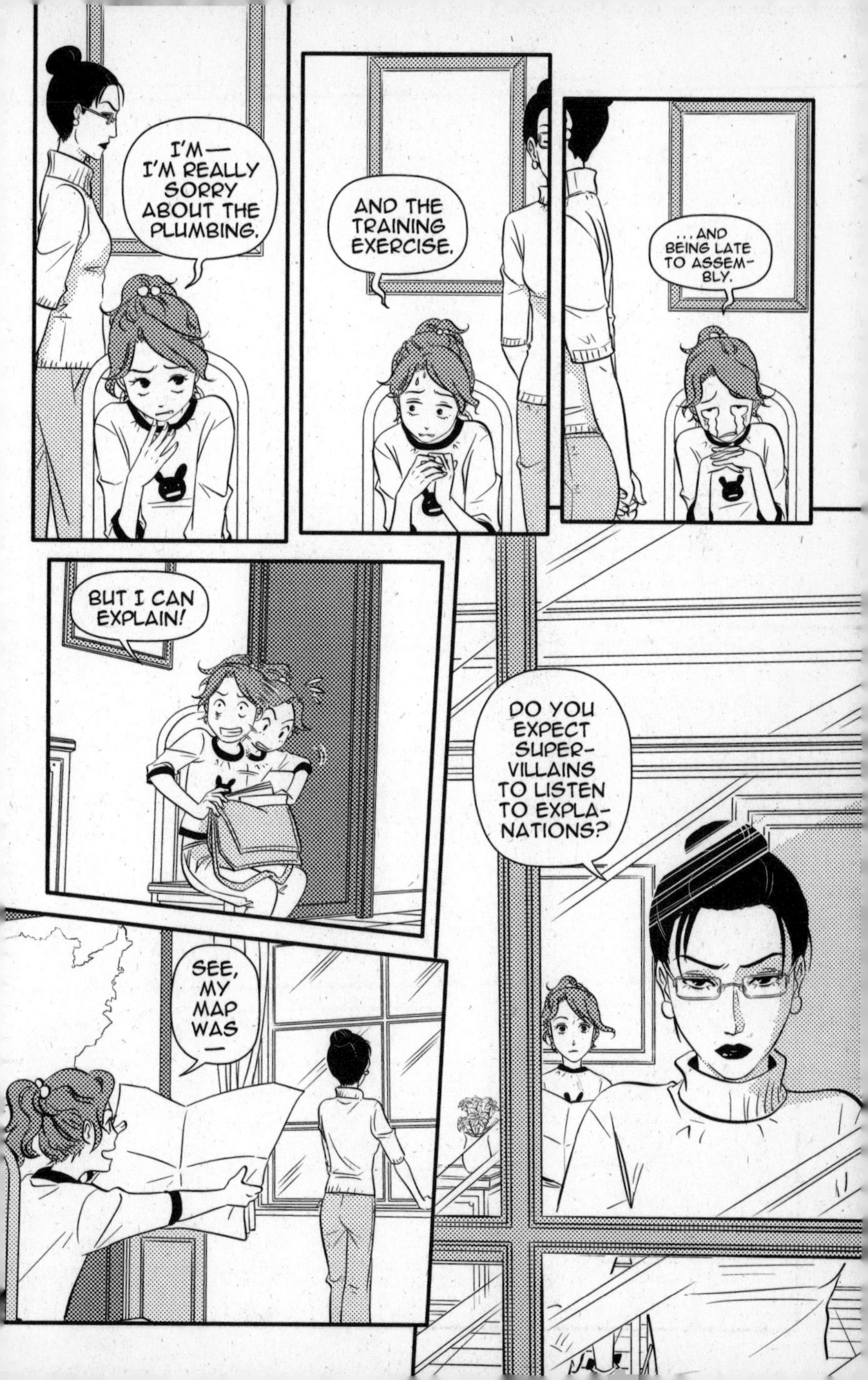
I'M— I'M REALLY SORRY ABOUT THE PLUMBING.
AND THE TRAINING EXERCISE.
...AND BEING LATE TO ASSEM-BLY.
BUT I CAN EXPLAIN!
DO YOU EXPECT SUPER-VILLAINS TO LISTEN TO EXPLA-NATIONS?
SEE, MY MAP WAS —

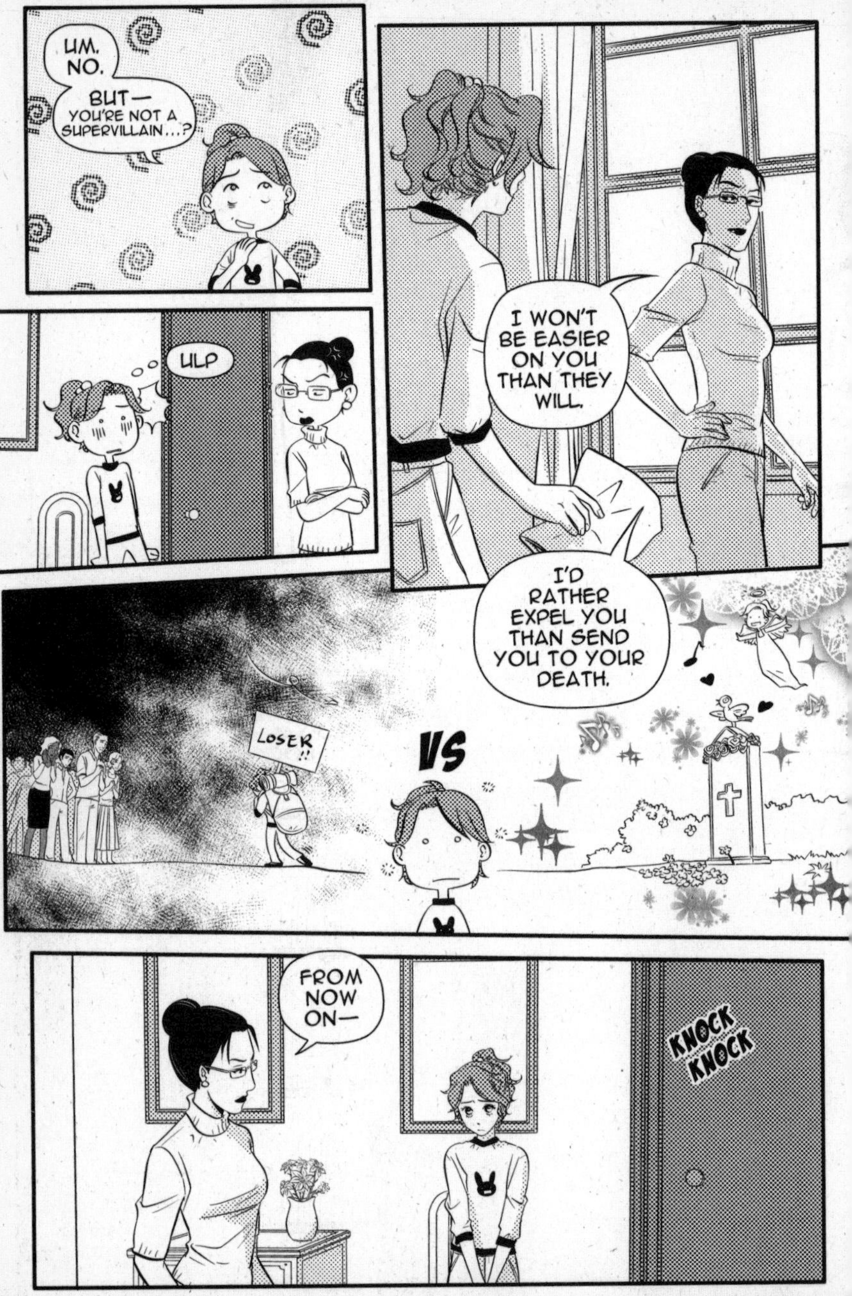
UM. NO.
BUT— YOU'RE NOT A SUPERVILLAIN...?
ULP
I WON'T BE EASIER ON YOU THAN THEY WILL.
I'D RATHER EXPEL YOU THAN SEND YOU TO YOUR DEATH.
LOSER !!
VS
FROM NOW ON—
KNOCK KNOCK

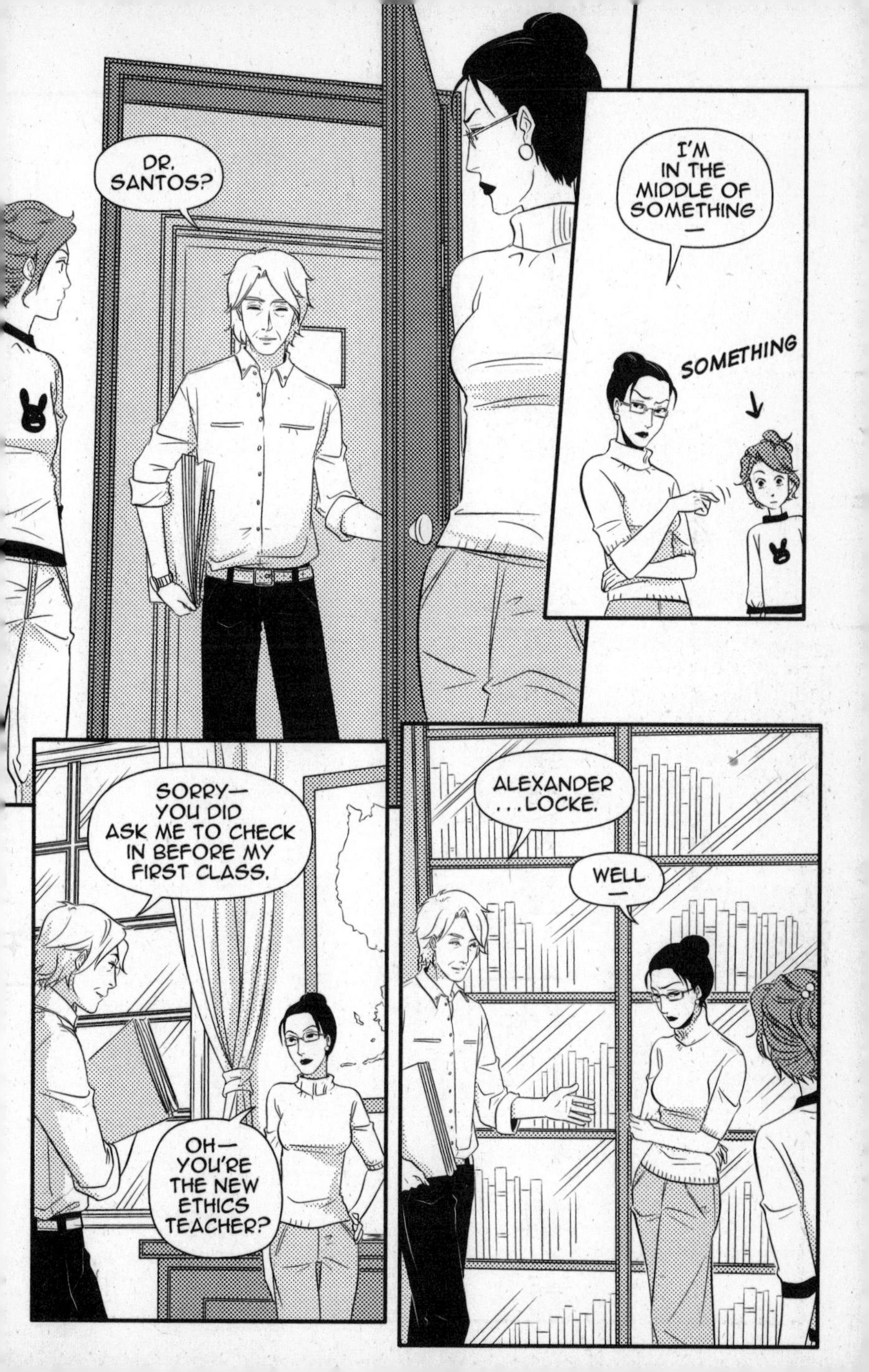
DR. SANTOS?
I'M IN THE MIDDLE OF SOMETHING —
SOMETHING
SORRY— YOU DID ASK ME TO CHECK IN BEFORE MY FIRST CLASS.
OH— YOU'RE THE NEW ETHICS TEACHER?
ALEXANDER . . . LOCKE.
WELL —

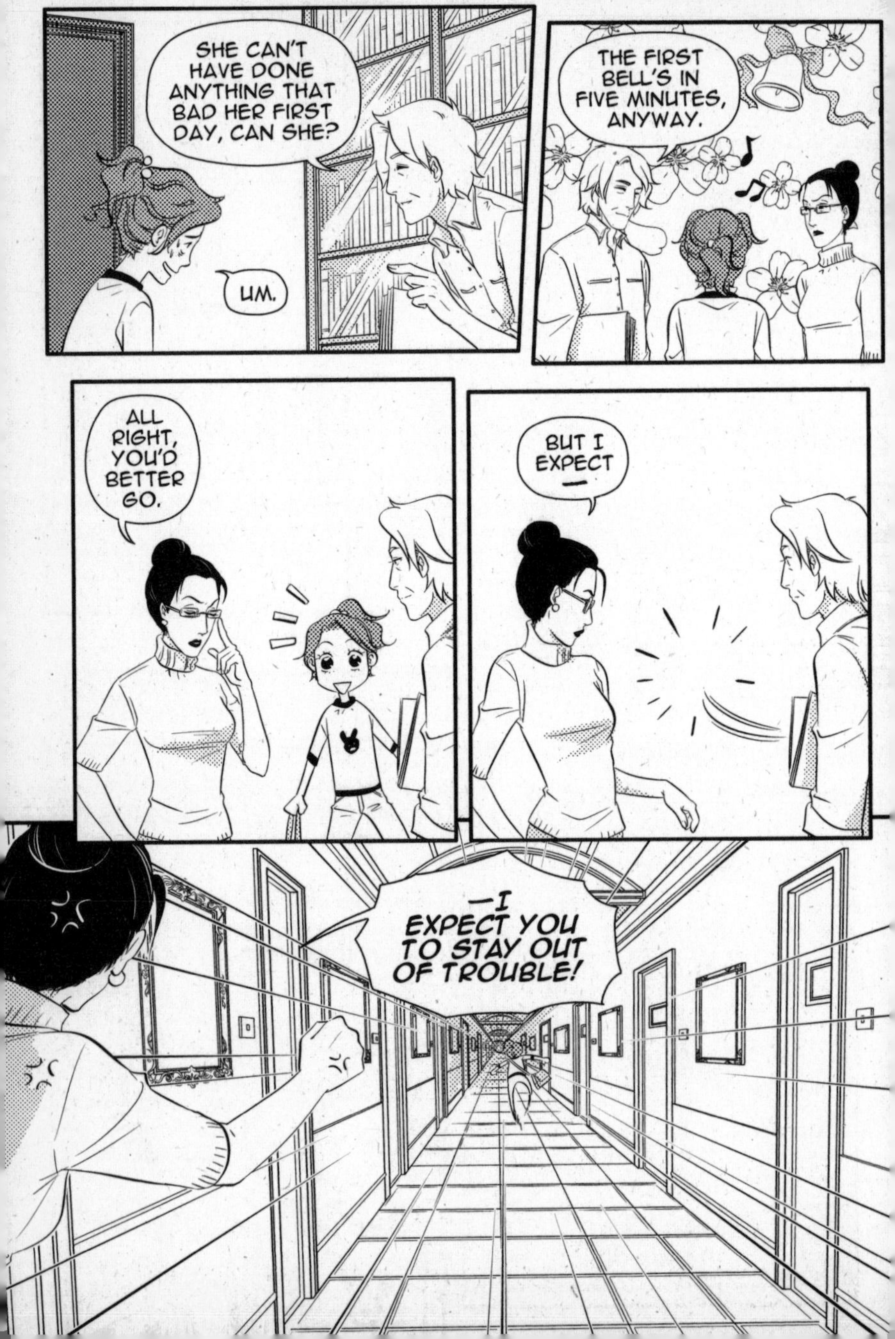
SHE CAN'T HAVE DONE ANYTHING THAT BAD HER FIRST DAY, CAN SHE?
UM.
THE FIRST BELL'S IN FIVE MINUTES, ANYWAY.
ALL RIGHT, YOU'D BETTER GO.
BUT I EXPECT —
—I EXPECT YOU TO STAY OUT OF TROUBLE!

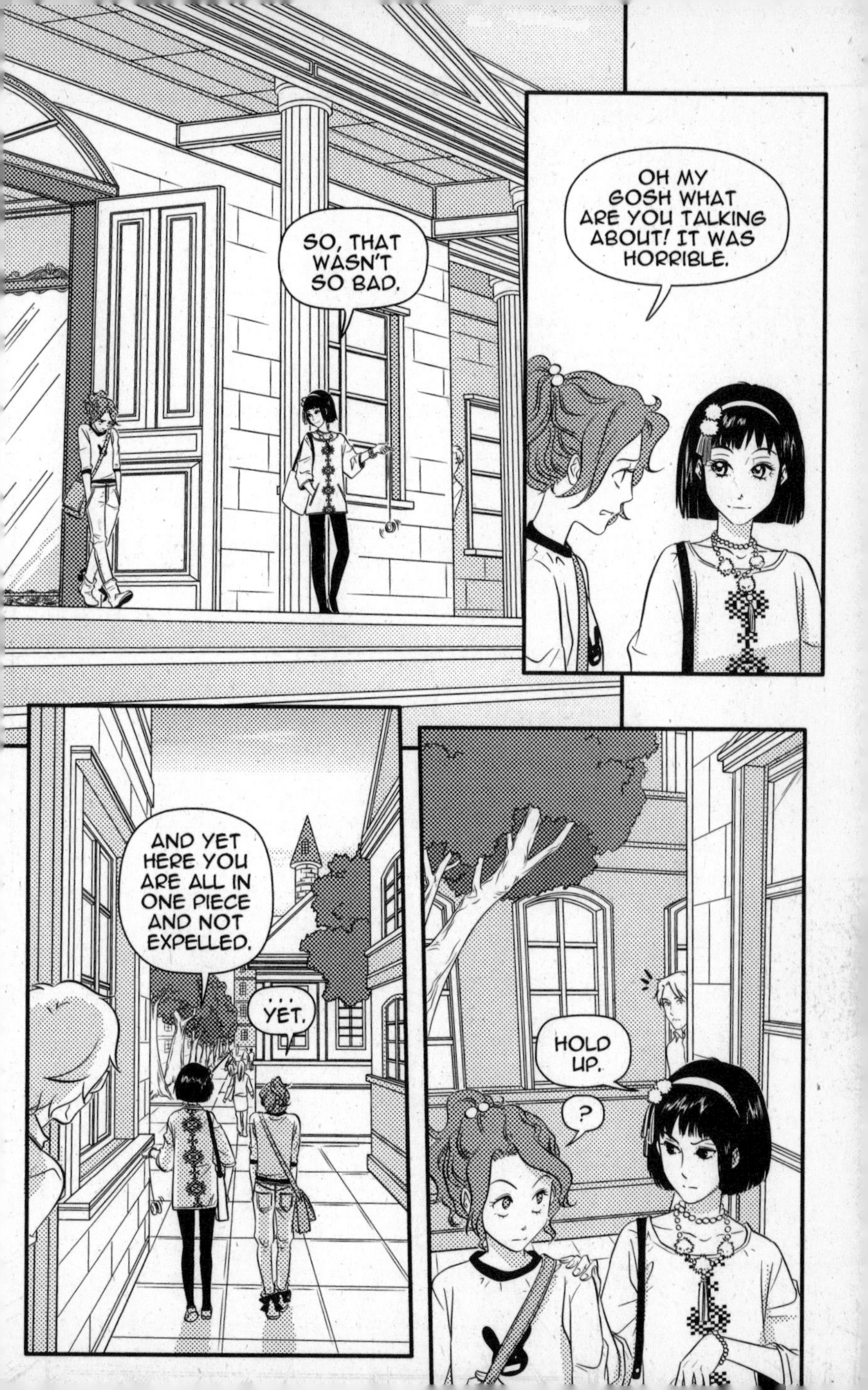
SO, THAT WASN'T SO BAD.
OH MY GOSH WHAT ARE YOU TALKING ABOUT! IT WAS HORRIBLE.
AND YET HERE YOU ARE ALL IN ONE PIECE AND NOT EXPELLED.
... YET.
HOLD UP.
?

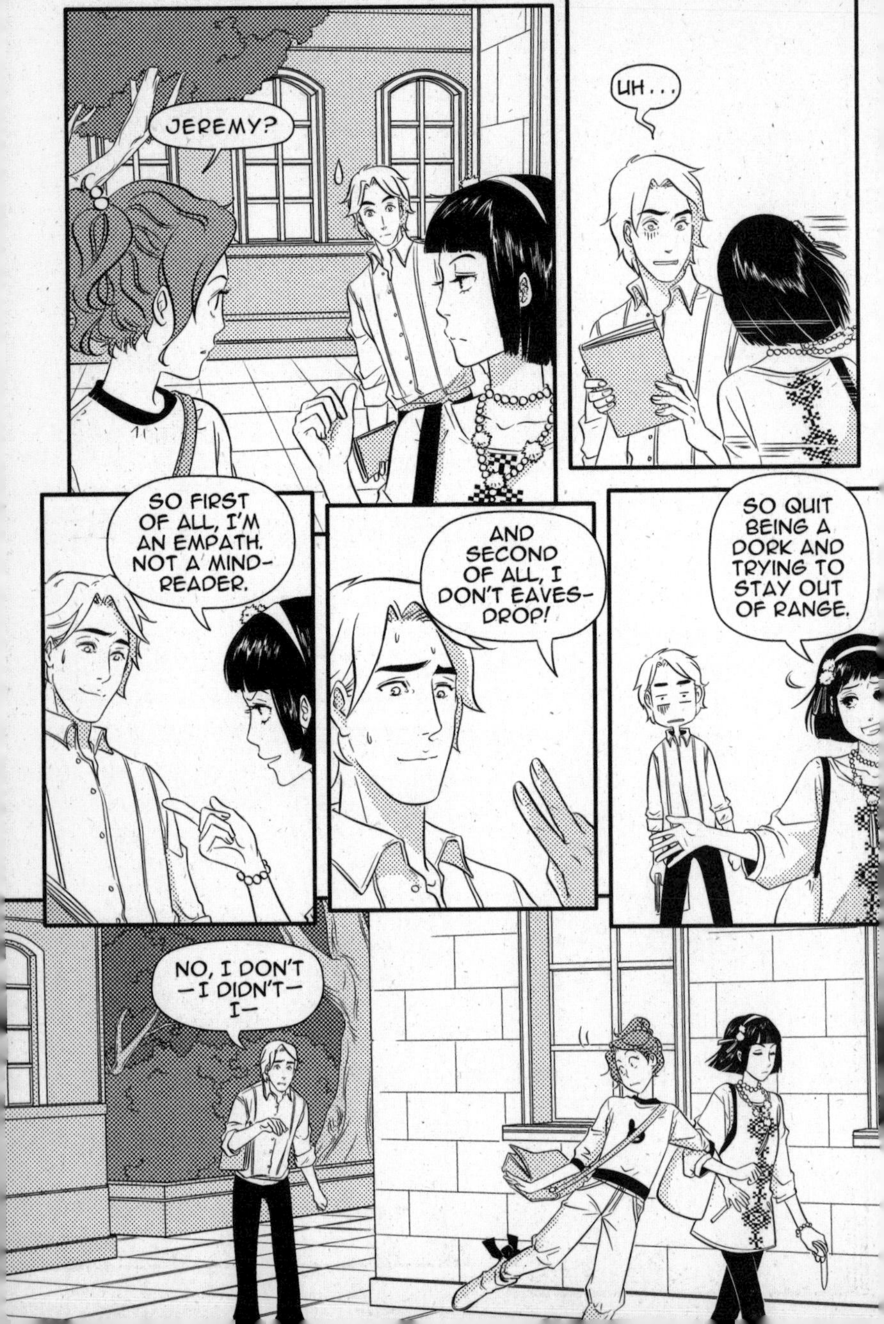
JEREMY?
UH...
SO FIRST OF ALL, I'M AN EMPATH. NOT A MIND-READER.
AND SECOND OF ALL, I DON'T EAVES-DROP!
SO QUIT BEING A DORK AND TRYING TO STAY OUT OF RANGE.
NO, I DON'T —I DIDN'T— I—

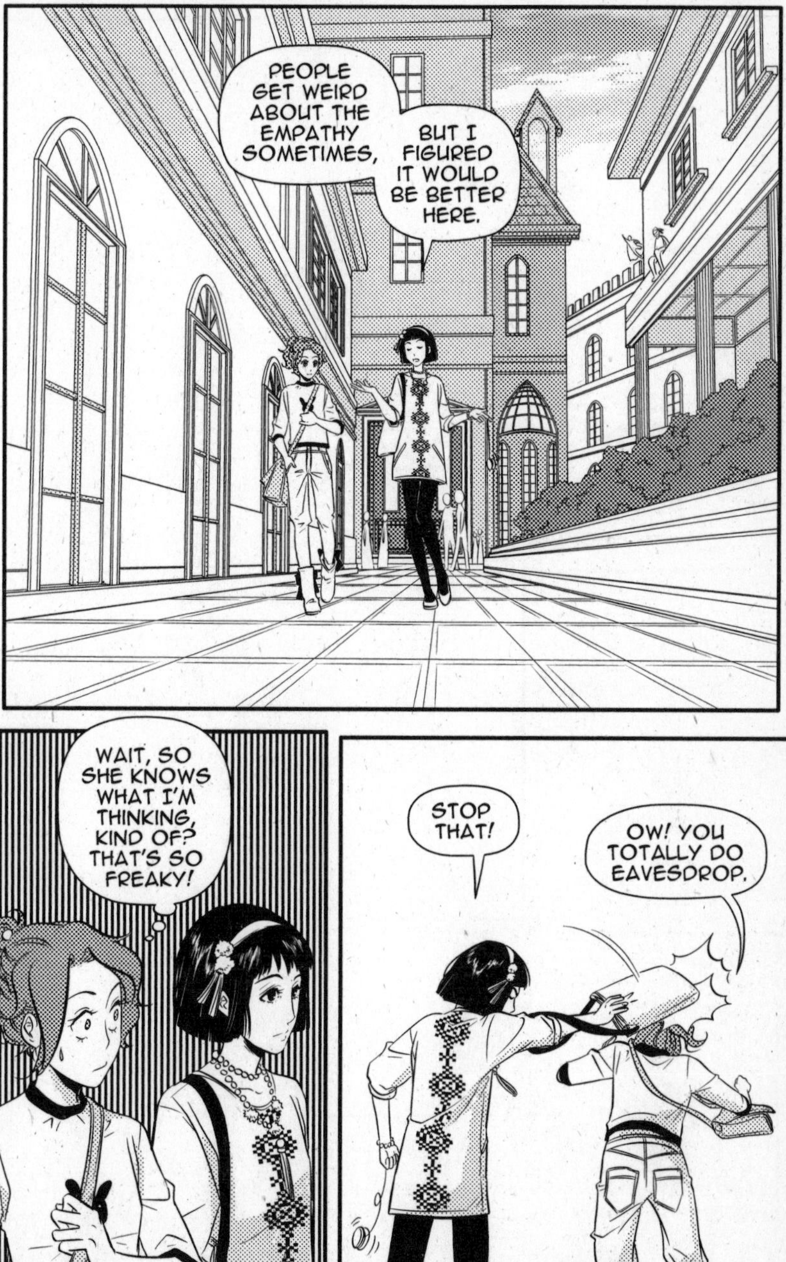
PEOPLE GET WEIRD ABOUT THE EMPATHY SOMETIMES,
BUT I FIGURED IT WOULD BE BETTER HERE.
WAIT, SO SHE KNOWS WHAT I'M THINKING, KIND OF? THAT'S SO FREAKY!
STOP THAT!
OW! YOU TOTALLY DO EAVESDROP.

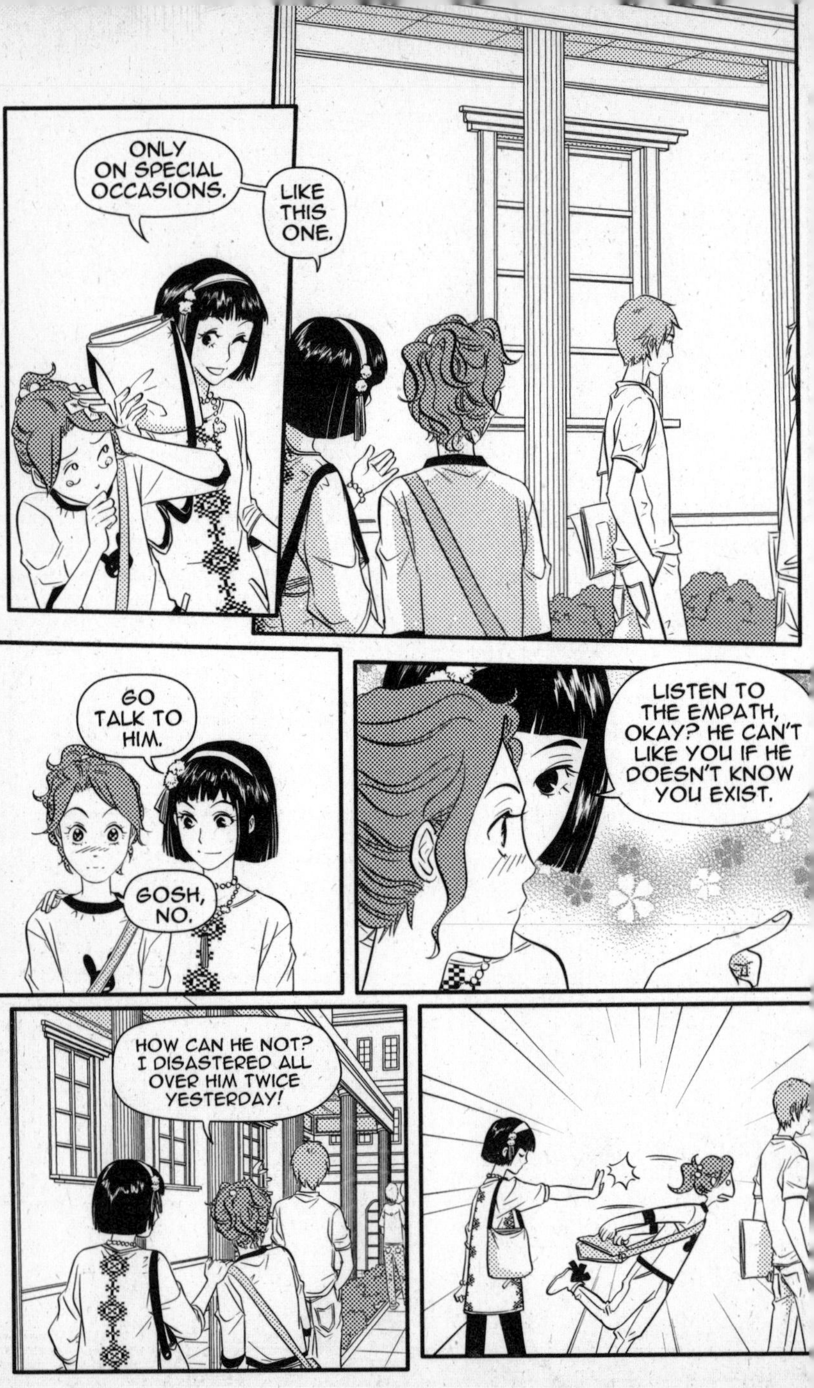
ONLY ON SPECIAL OCCASIONS.
LIKE THIS ONE.
GO TALK TO HIM.
GOSH, NO.
LISTEN TO THE EMPATH, OKAY? HE CAN'T LIKE YOU IF HE DOESN'T KNOW YOU EXIST.
HOW CAN HE NOT? I DISASTERED ALL OVER HIM TWICE YESTERDAY!

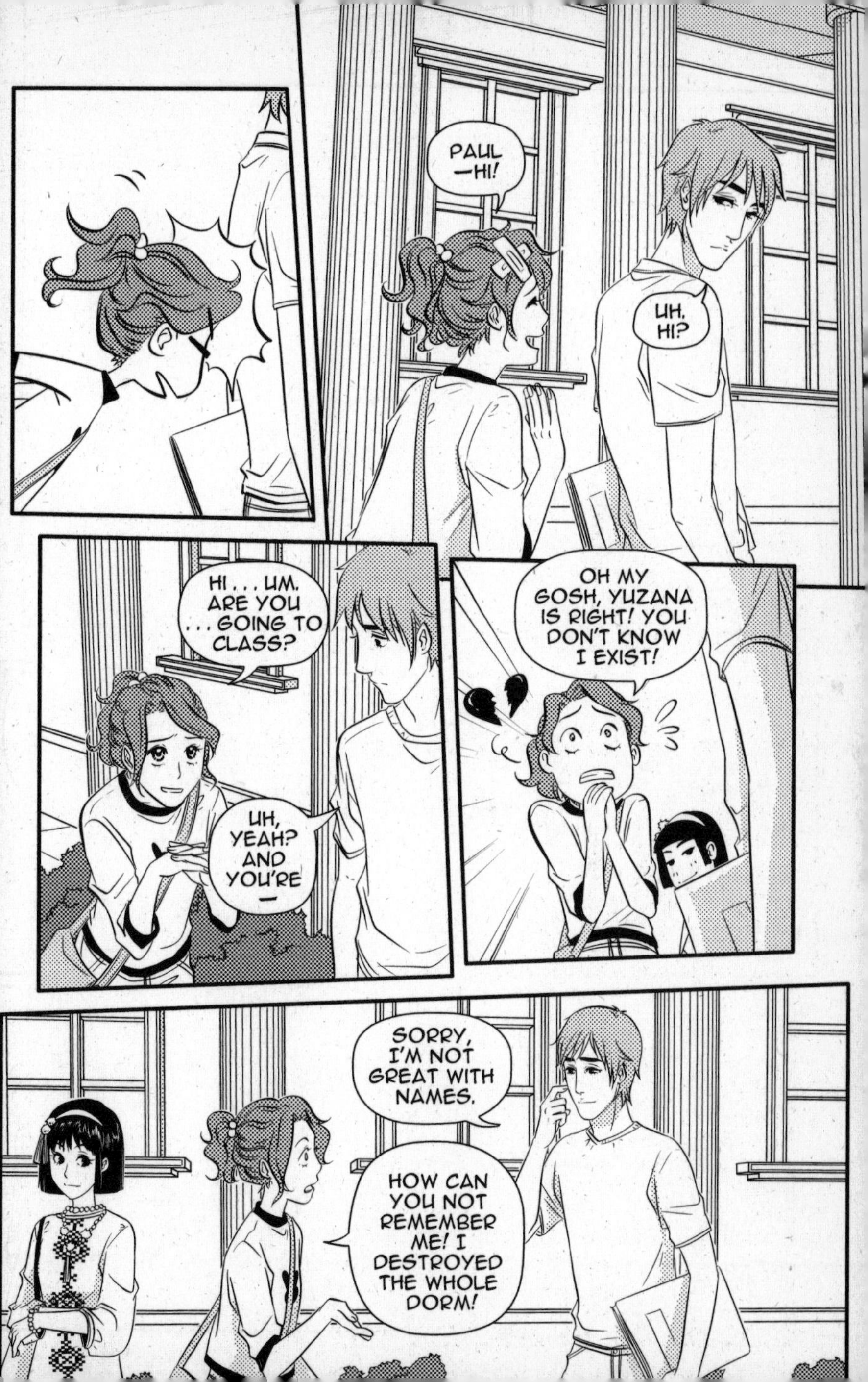
PAUL—HI!
UH, HI?
HI . . . UM. ARE YOU . . . GOING TO CLASS?
UH, YEAH? AND YOU'RE—
OH MY GOSH, YUZANA IS RIGHT! YOU DON'T KNOW I EXIST!
SORRY, I'M NOT GREAT WITH NAMES.
HOW CAN YOU NOT REMEMBER ME! I DESTROYED THE WHOLE DORM!

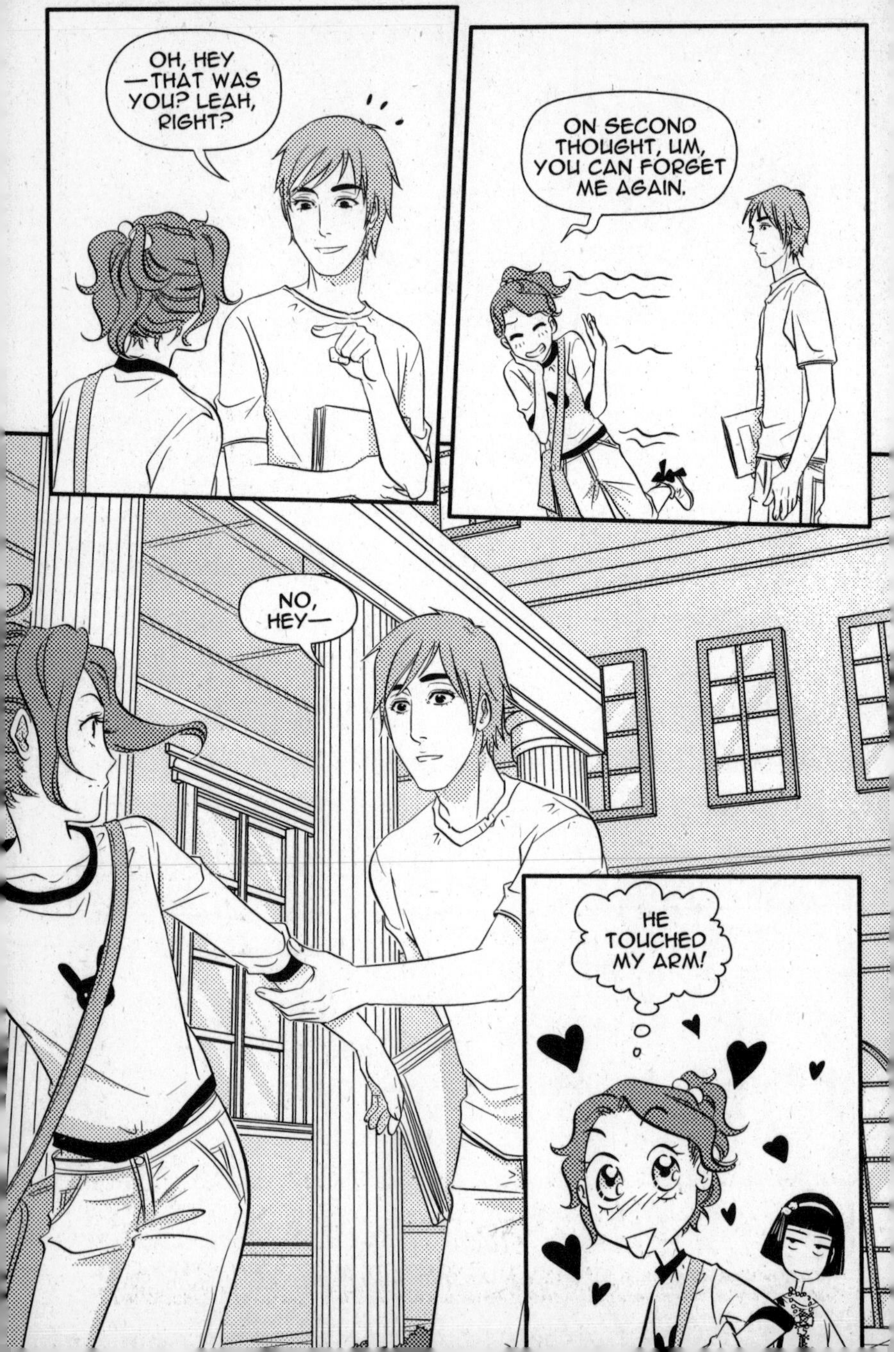
OH, HEY —THAT WAS YOU? LEAH, RIGHT?
ON SECOND THOUGHT, UM, YOU CAN FORGET ME AGAIN.
NO, HEY—
HE TOUCHED MY ARM!

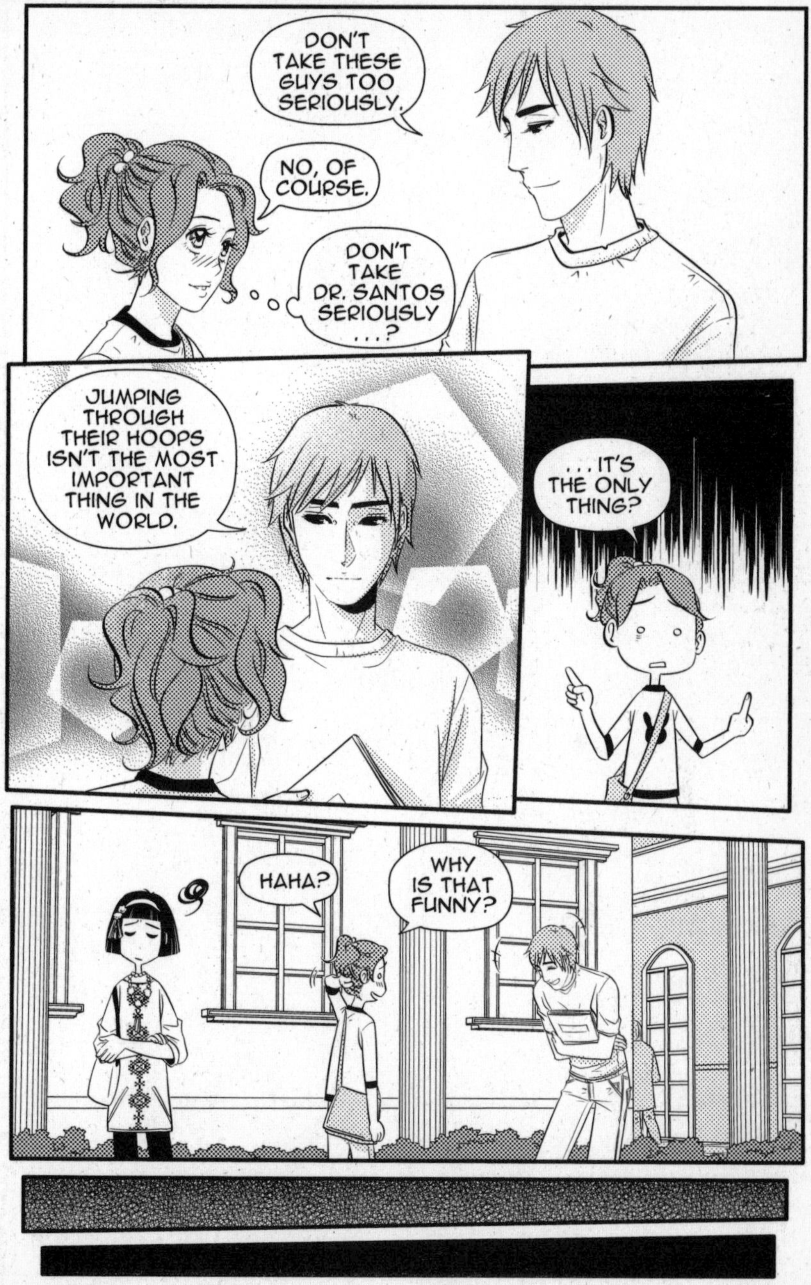
DON'T TAKE THESE GUYS TOO SERIOUSLY.
NO, OF COURSE.
DON'T TAKE DR. SANTOS SERIOUSLY . . . ?
JUMPING THROUGH THEIR HOOPS ISN'T THE MOST IMPORTANT THING IN THE WORLD.
. . . IT'S THE ONLY THING?
HAHA?
WHY IS THAT FUNNY?

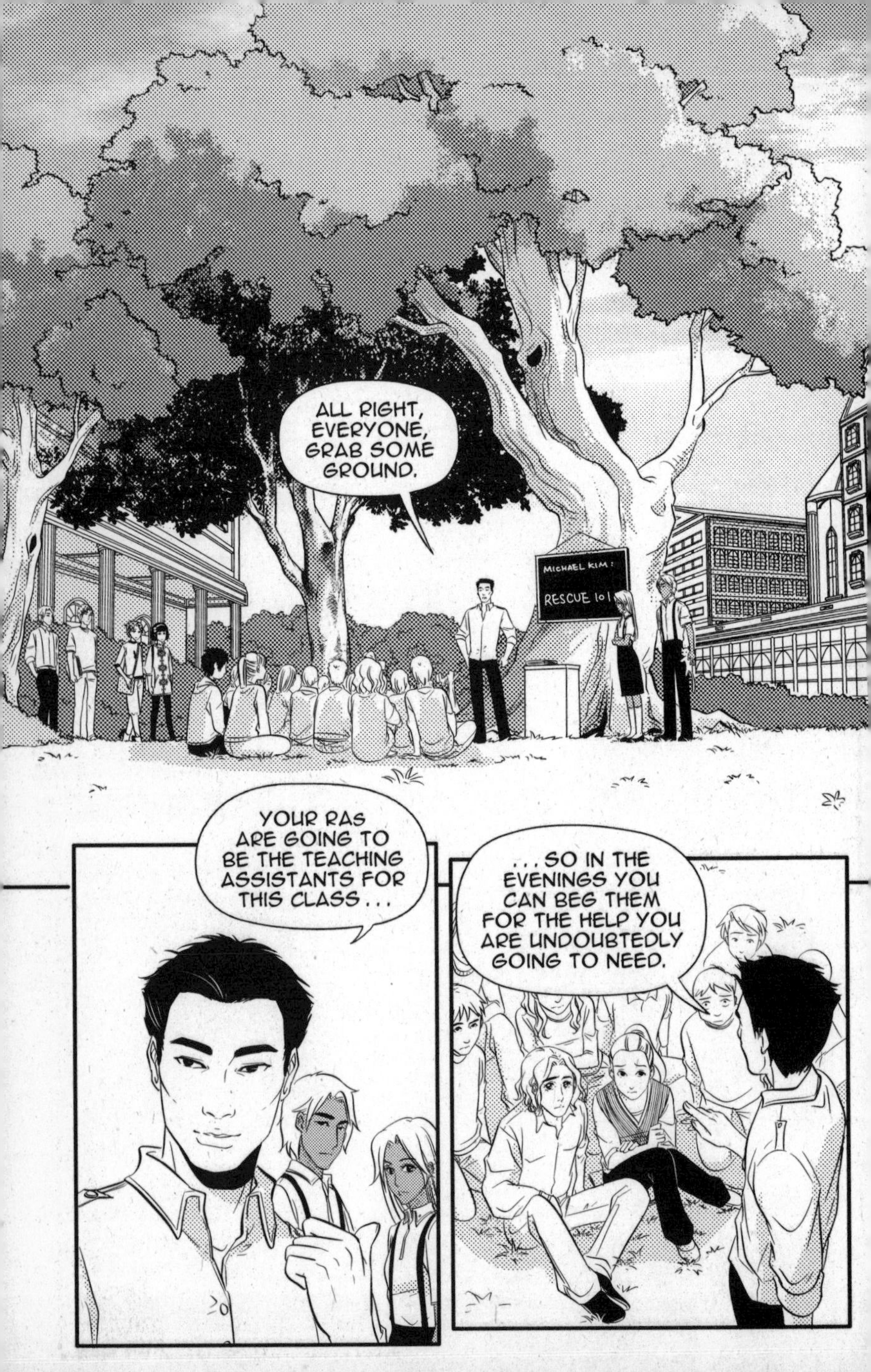
ALL RIGHT, EVERYONE, GRAB SOME GROUND.
MICHAEL KIM: RESCUE 101
YOUR RAS ARE GOING TO BE THE TEACHING ASSISTANTS FOR THIS CLASS . . .
. . . SO IN THE EVENINGS YOU CAN BEG THEM FOR THE HELP YOU ARE UNDOUBTEDLY GOING TO NEED.

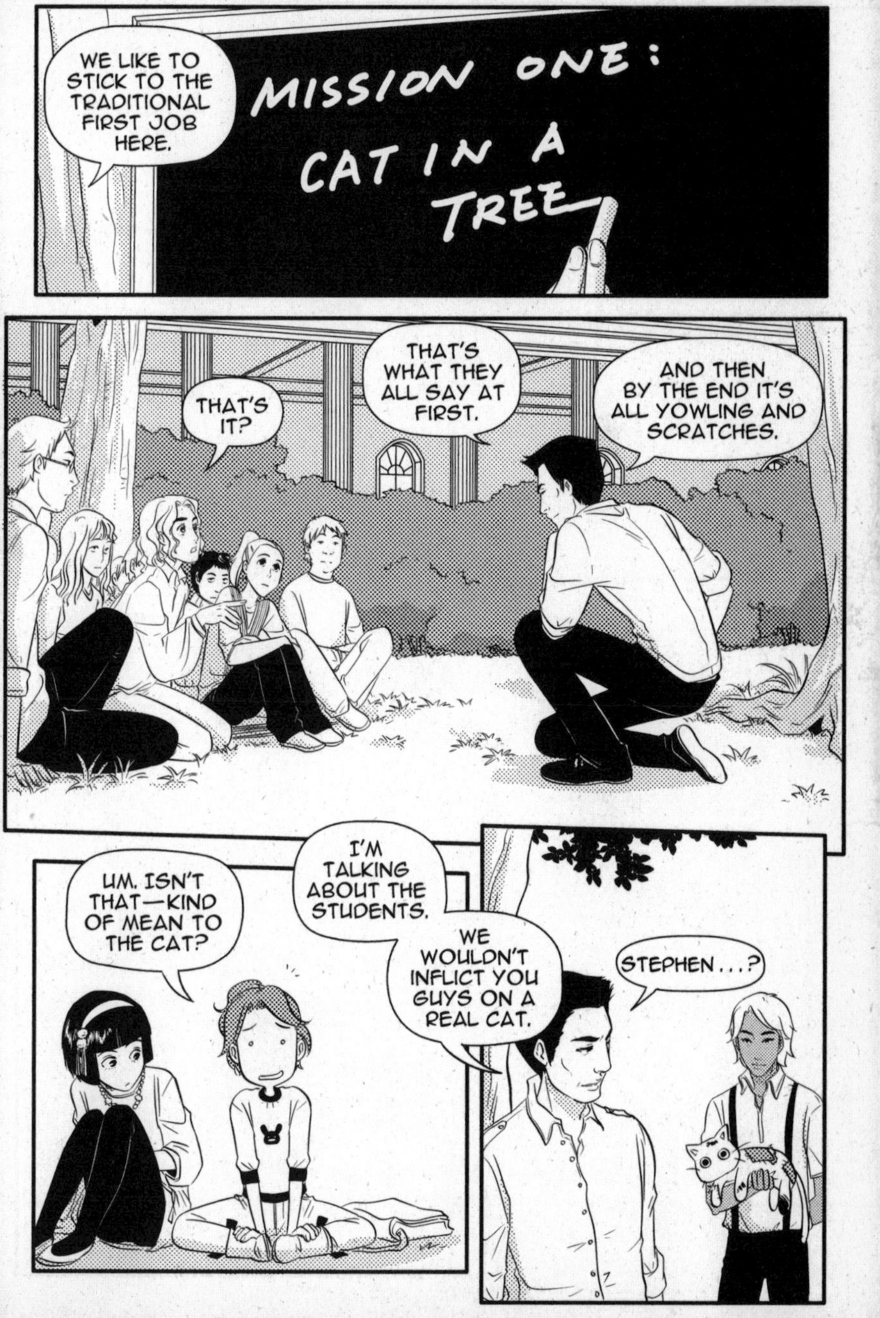
WE LIKE TO STICK TO THE TRADITIONAL FIRST JOB HERE.
MISSION ONE: CAT IN A TREE
THAT'S IT?
THAT'S WHAT THEY ALL SAY AT FIRST.
AND THEN BY THE END IT'S ALL YOWLING AND SCRATCHES.
UM. ISN'T THAT—KIND OF MEAN TO THE CAT?
I'M TALKING ABOUT THE STUDENTS.
WE WOULDN'T INFLICT YOU GUYS ON A REAL CAT.
STEPHEN . . . ?

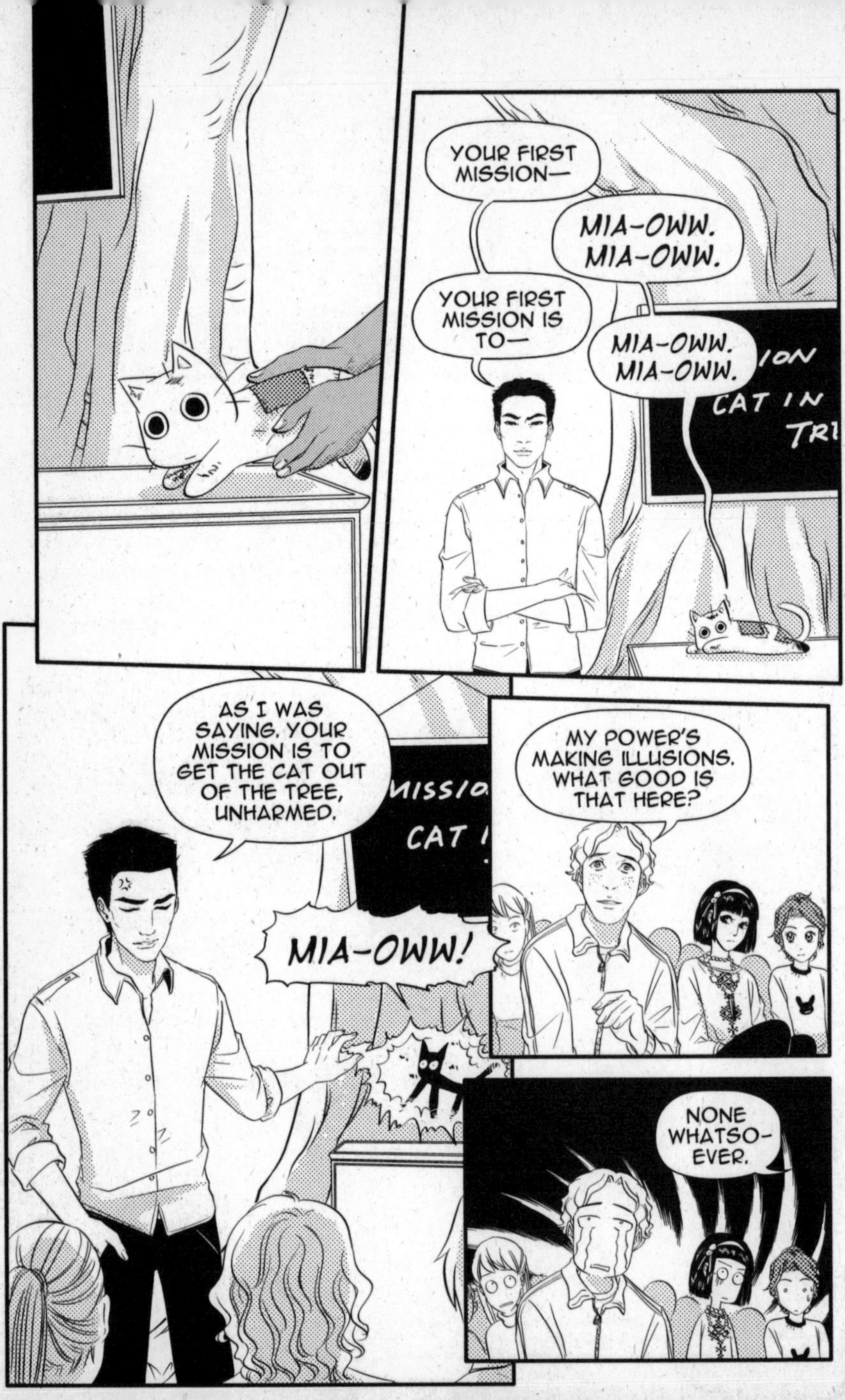
YOUR FIRST MISSION—
MIA-OWW. MIA-OWW.
YOUR FIRST MISSION IS TO—
MIA-OWW. MIA-OWW.
AS I WAS SAYING. YOUR MISSION IS TO GET THE CAT OUT OF THE TREE, UNHARMED.
MIA-OWW!
MY POWER'S MAKING ILLUSIONS. WHAT GOOD IS THAT HERE?
NONE WHATSO-EVER.

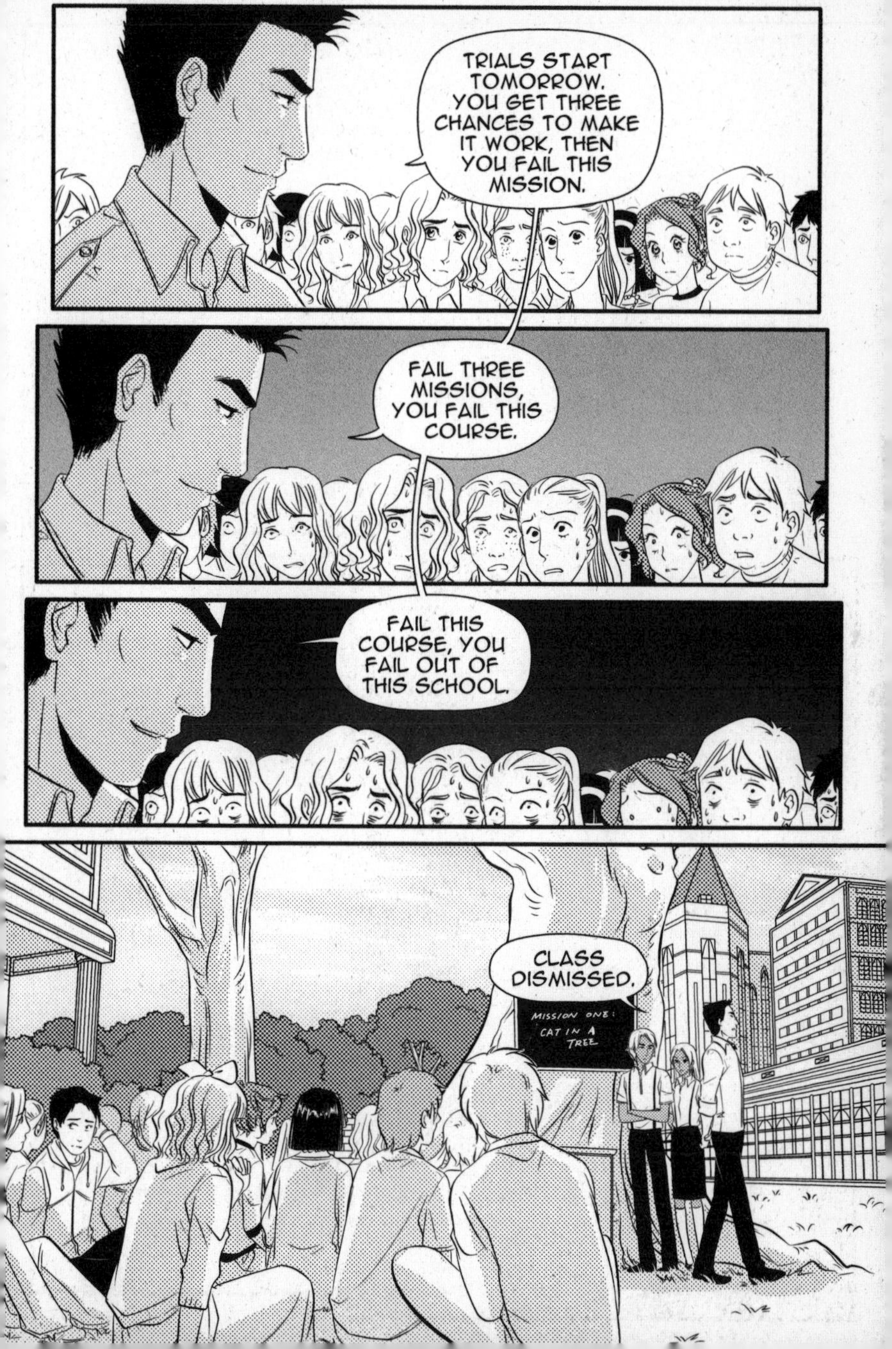
TRIALS START TOMORROW. YOU GET THREE CHANCES TO MAKE IT WORK, THEN YOU FAIL THIS MISSION.
FAIL THREE MISSIONS, YOU FAIL THIS COURSE.
FAIL THIS COURSE, YOU FAIL OUT OF THIS SCHOOL.
CLASS DISMISSED.
MISSION ONE: CAT IN A TREE

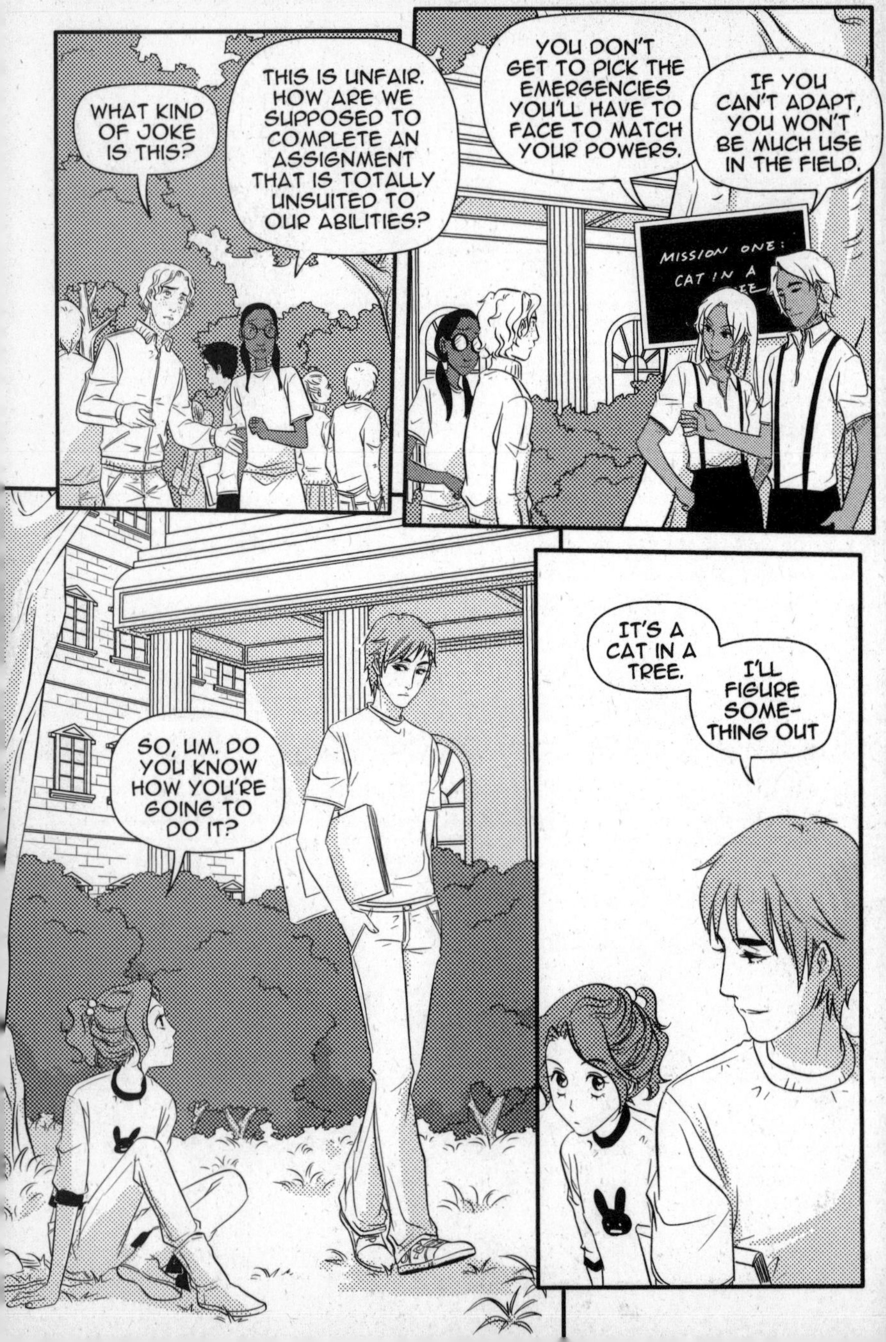
WHAT KIND OF JOKE IS THIS?
THIS IS UNFAIR. HOW ARE WE SUPPOSED TO COMPLETE AN ASSIGNMENT THAT IS TOTALLY UNSUITED TO OUR ABILITIES?
YOU DON'T GET TO PICK THE EMERGENCIES YOU'LL HAVE TO FACE TO MATCH YOUR POWERS.
IF YOU CAN'T ADAPT, YOU WON'T BE MUCH USE IN THE FIELD.
MISSION ONE:
CAT IN A
SO, UM. DO YOU KNOW HOW YOU'RE GOING TO DO IT?
IT'S A CAT IN A TREE.
I'LL FIGURE SOME-THING OUT

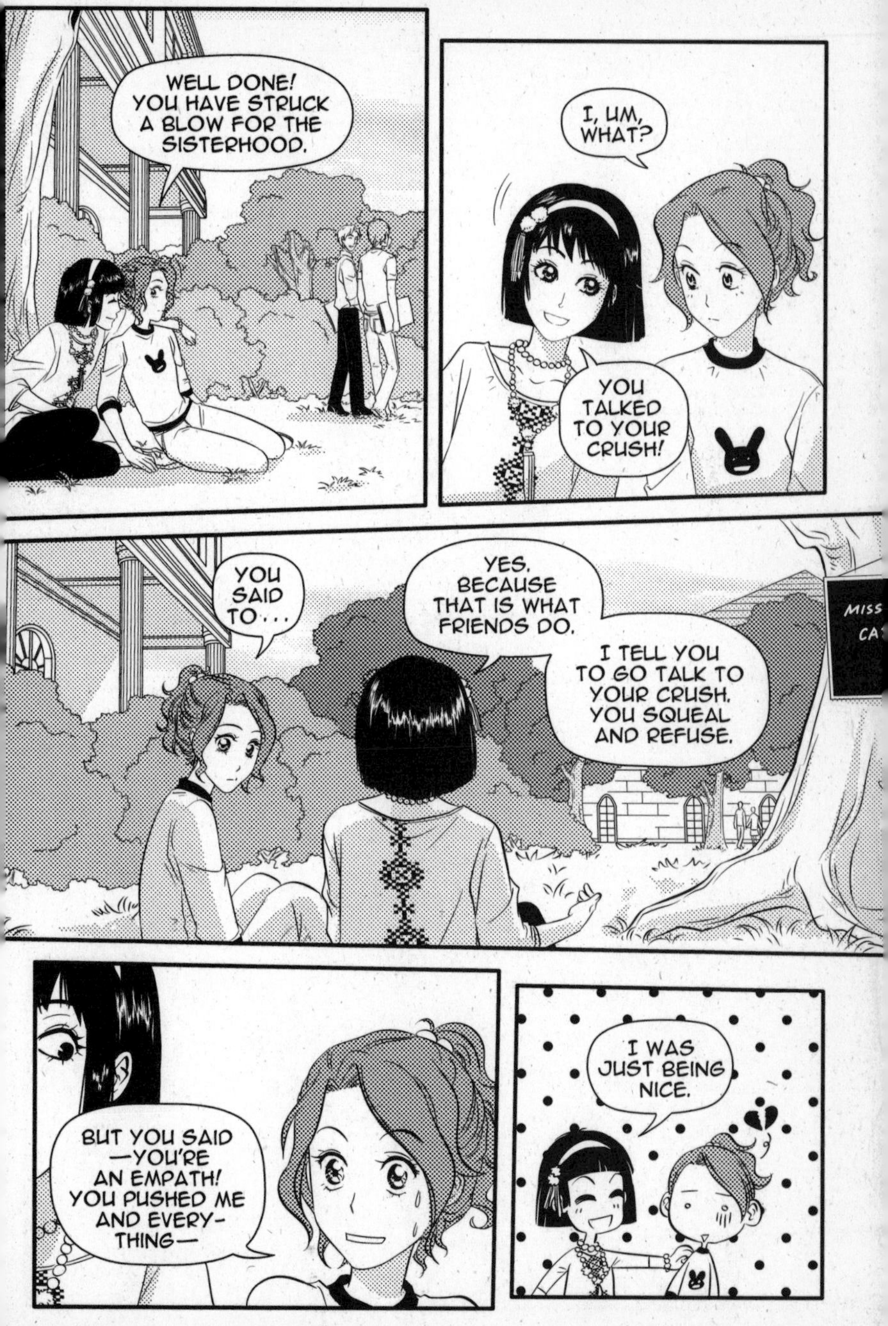
WELL DONE! YOU HAVE STRUCK A BLOW FOR THE SISTERHOOD.
I, UM, WHAT?
YOU TALKED TO YOUR CRUSH!
YOU SAID TO . . .
YES. BECAUSE THAT IS WHAT FRIENDS DO.
I TELL YOU TO GO TALK TO YOUR CRUSH. YOU SQUEAL AND REFUSE.
BUT YOU SAID —YOU'RE AN EMPATH! YOU PUSHED ME AND EVERY-THING—
I WAS JUST BEING NICE.

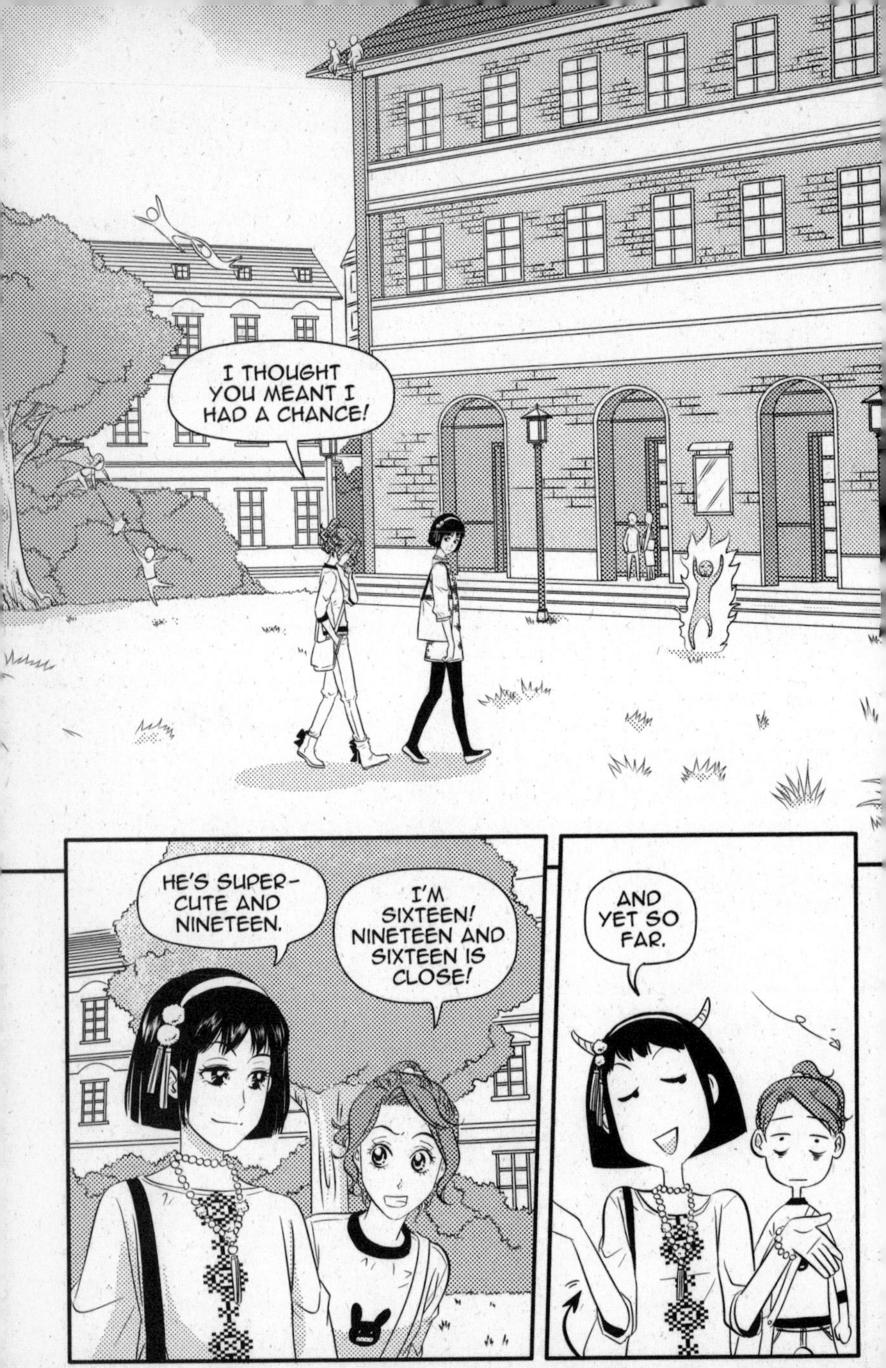
I THOUGHT YOU MEANT I HAD A CHANCE!
HE'S SUPER-CUTE AND NINETEEN.
I'M SIXTEEN! NINETEEN AND SIXTEEN IS CLOSE!
AND YET SO FAR.

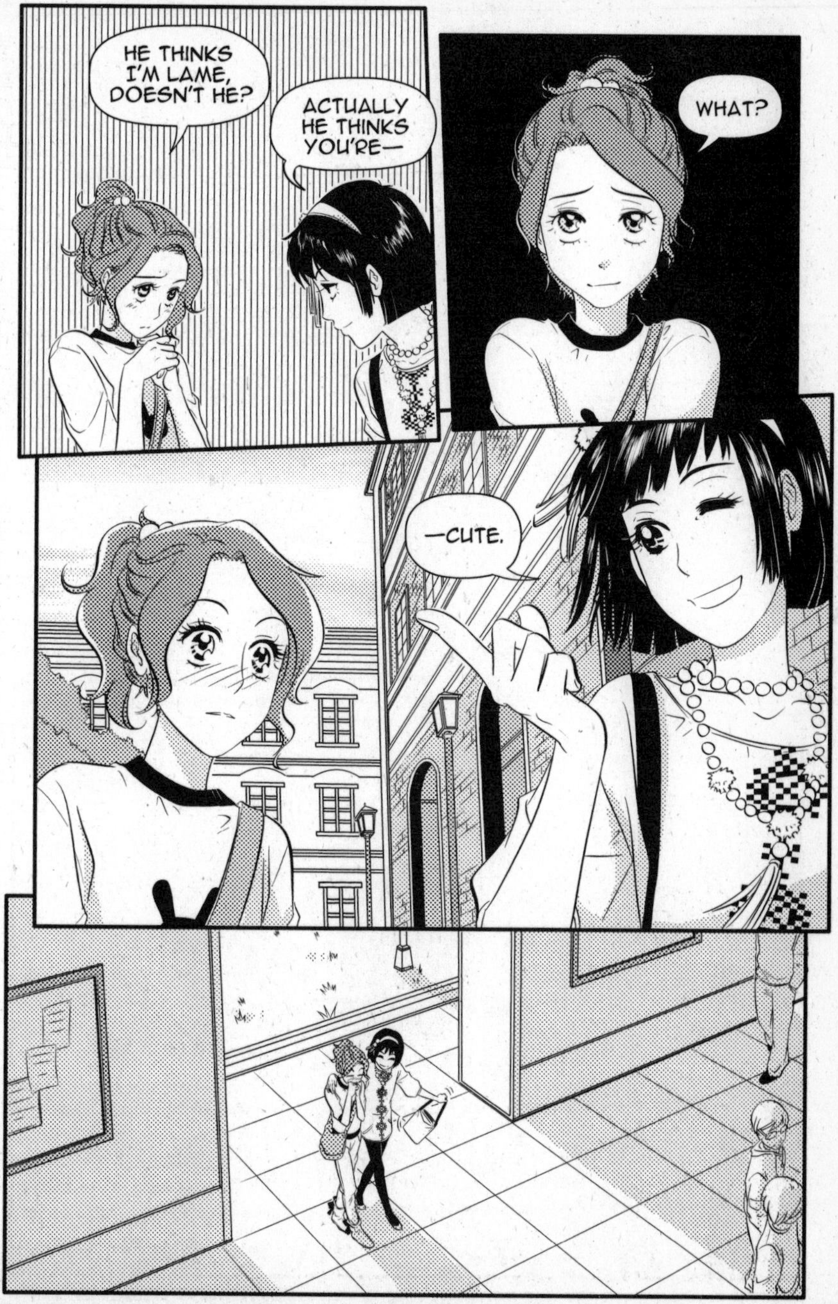
HE THINKS I'M LAME, DOESN'T HE?
ACTUALLY HE THINKS YOU'RE—
WHAT?
—CUTE.

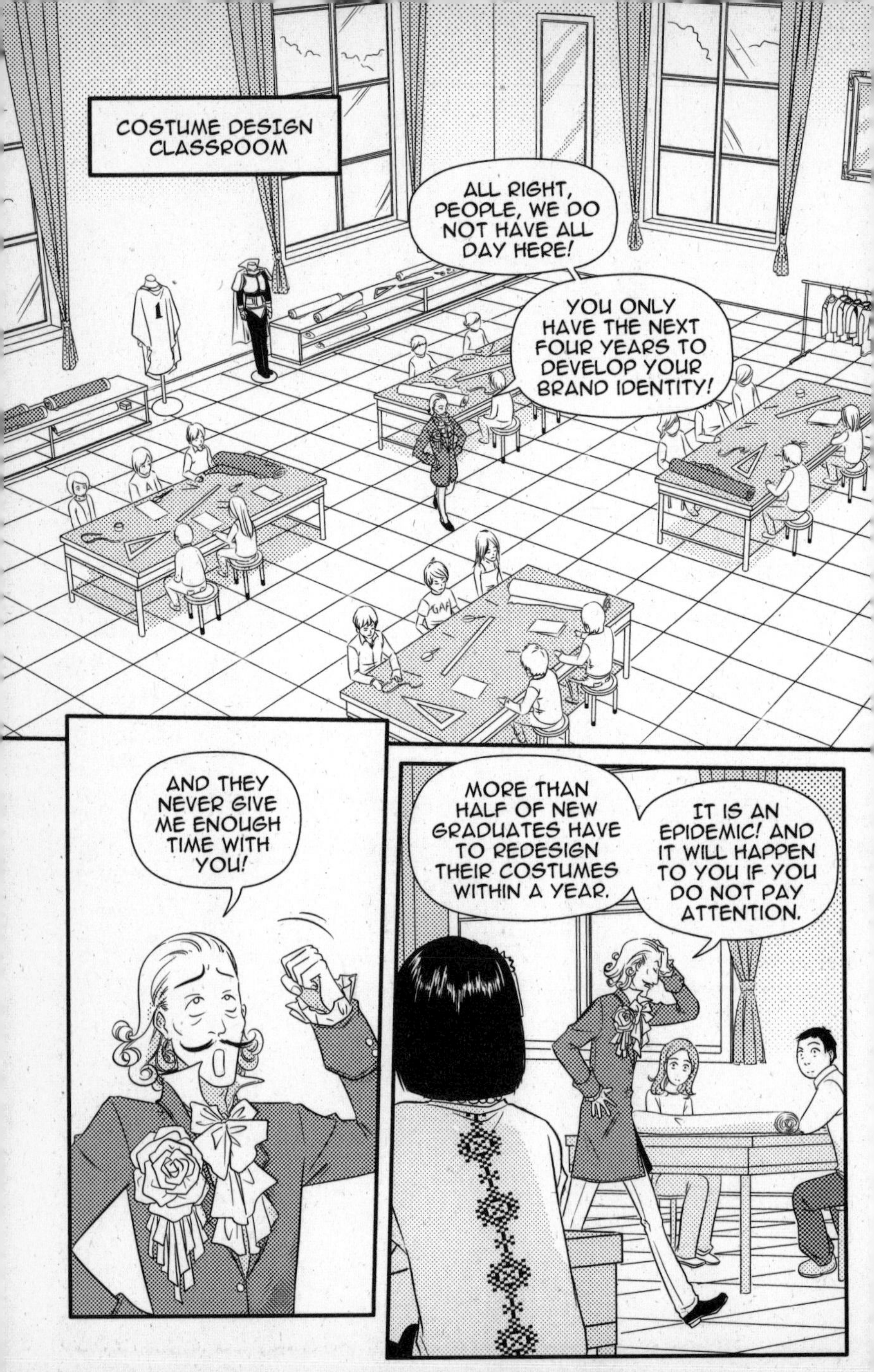
COSTUME DESIGN CLASSROOM
ALL RIGHT, PEOPLE, WE DO NOT HAVE ALL DAY HERE!
YOU ONLY HAVE THE NEXT FOUR YEARS TO DEVELOP YOUR BRAND IDENTITY!
AND THEY NEVER GIVE ME ENOUGH TIME WITH YOU!
MORE THAN HALF OF NEW GRADUATES HAVE TO REDESIGN THEIR COSTUMES WITHIN A YEAR.
IT IS AN EPIDEMIC! AND IT WILL HAPPEN TO YOU IF YOU DO NOT PAY ATTENTION.

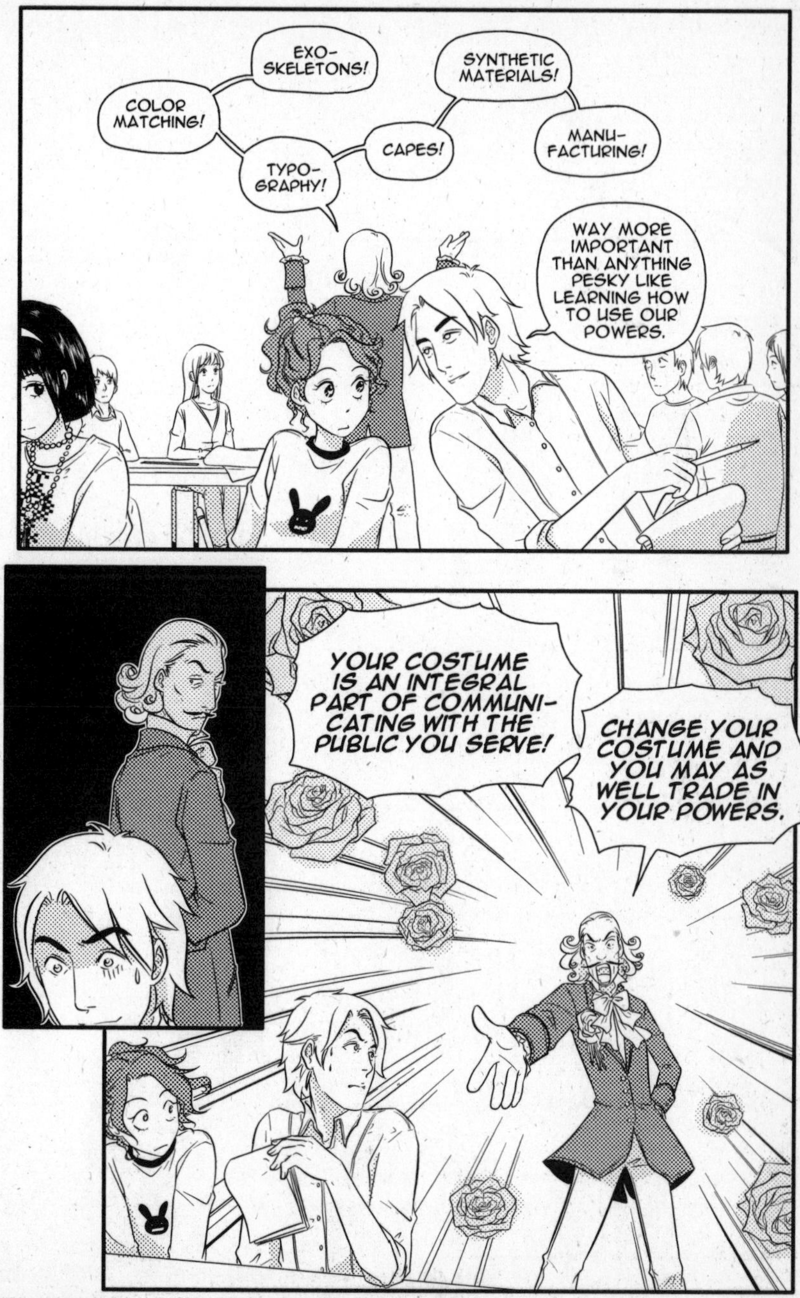
EXO-SKELETONS!
SYNTHETIC MATERIALS!
COLOR MATCHING!
MANU-FACTURING!
CAPES!
TYPO-GRAPHY!
WAY MORE IMPORTANT THAN ANYTHING PESKY LIKE LEARNING HOW TO USE OUR POWERS.
YOUR COSTUME IS AN INTEGRAL PART OF COMMUNI-CATING WITH THE PUBLIC YOU SERVE!
CHANGE YOUR COSTUME AND YOU MAY AS WELL TRADE IN YOUR POWERS.

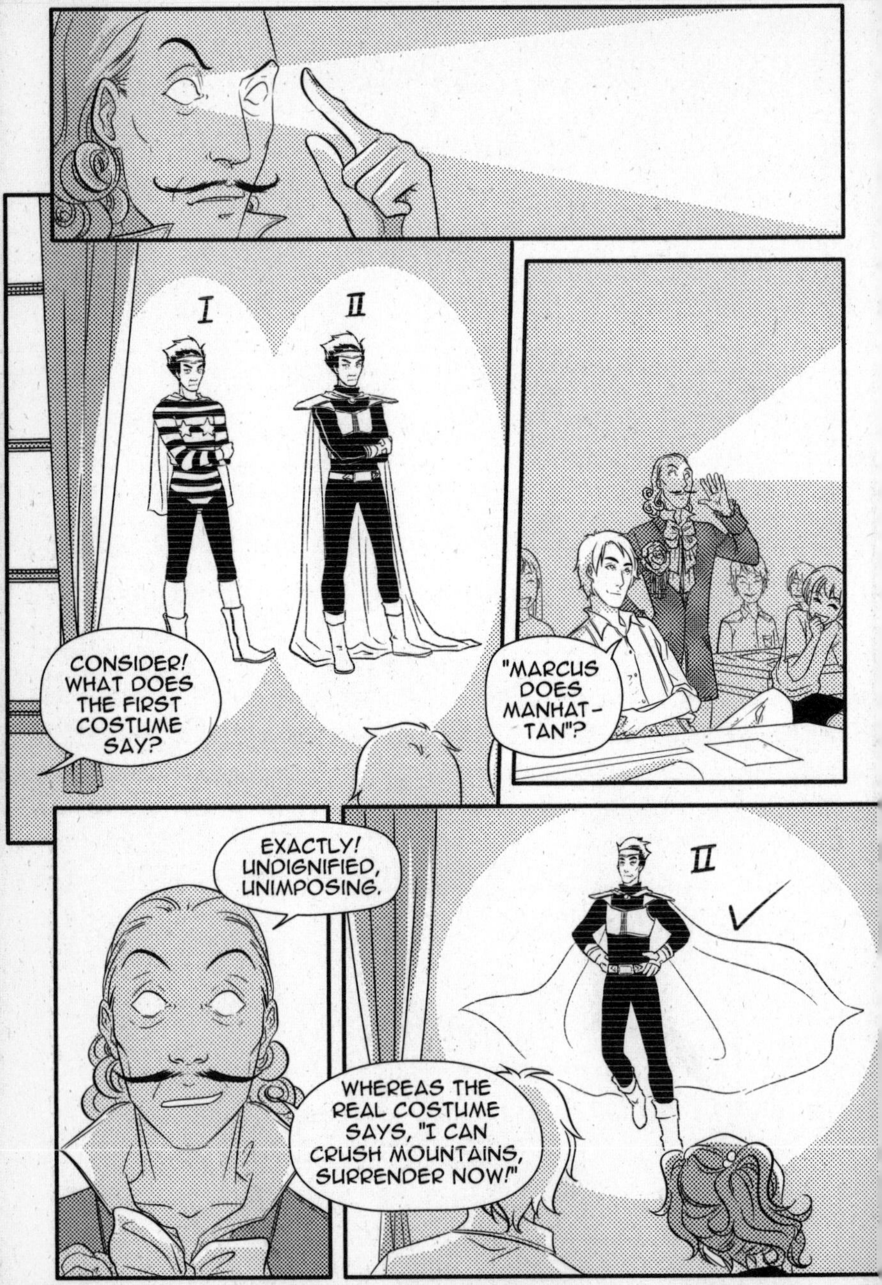
I
II
CONSIDER! WHAT DOES THE FIRST COSTUME SAY?
"MARCUS DOES MANHAT-TAN"?
EXACTLY! UNDIGNIFIED, UNIMPOSING.
II
WHEREAS THE REAL COSTUME SAYS, "I CAN CRUSH MOUNTAINS, SURRENDER NOW!"

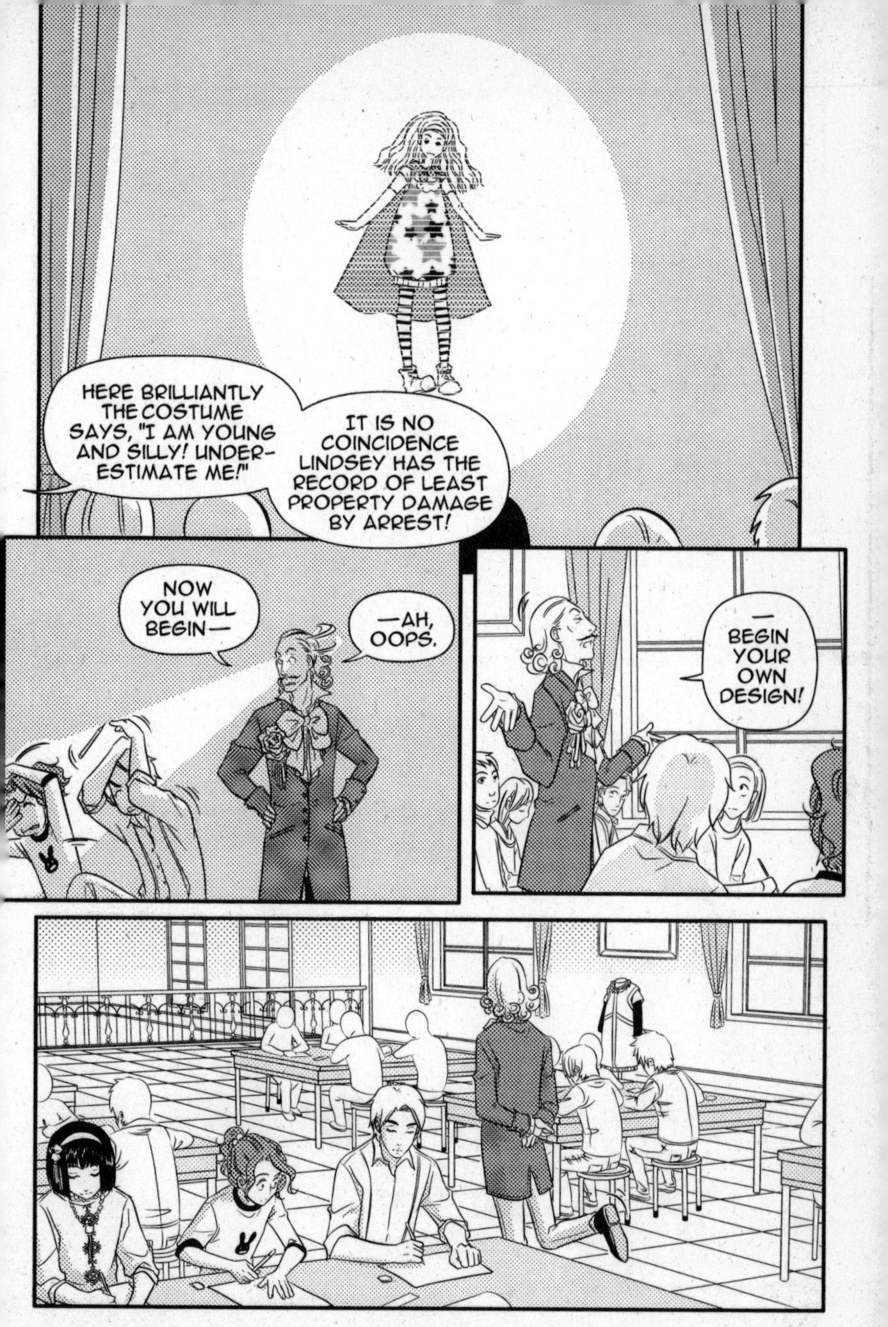
HERE BRILLIANTLY THE COSTUME SAYS, "I AM YOUNG AND SILLY! UNDER-ESTIMATE ME!"
IT IS NO COINCIDENCE LINDSEY HAS THE RECORD OF LEAST PROPERTY DAMAGE BY ARREST!
NOW YOU WILL BEGIN—
—AH, OOPS.
—BEGIN YOUR OWN DESIGN!

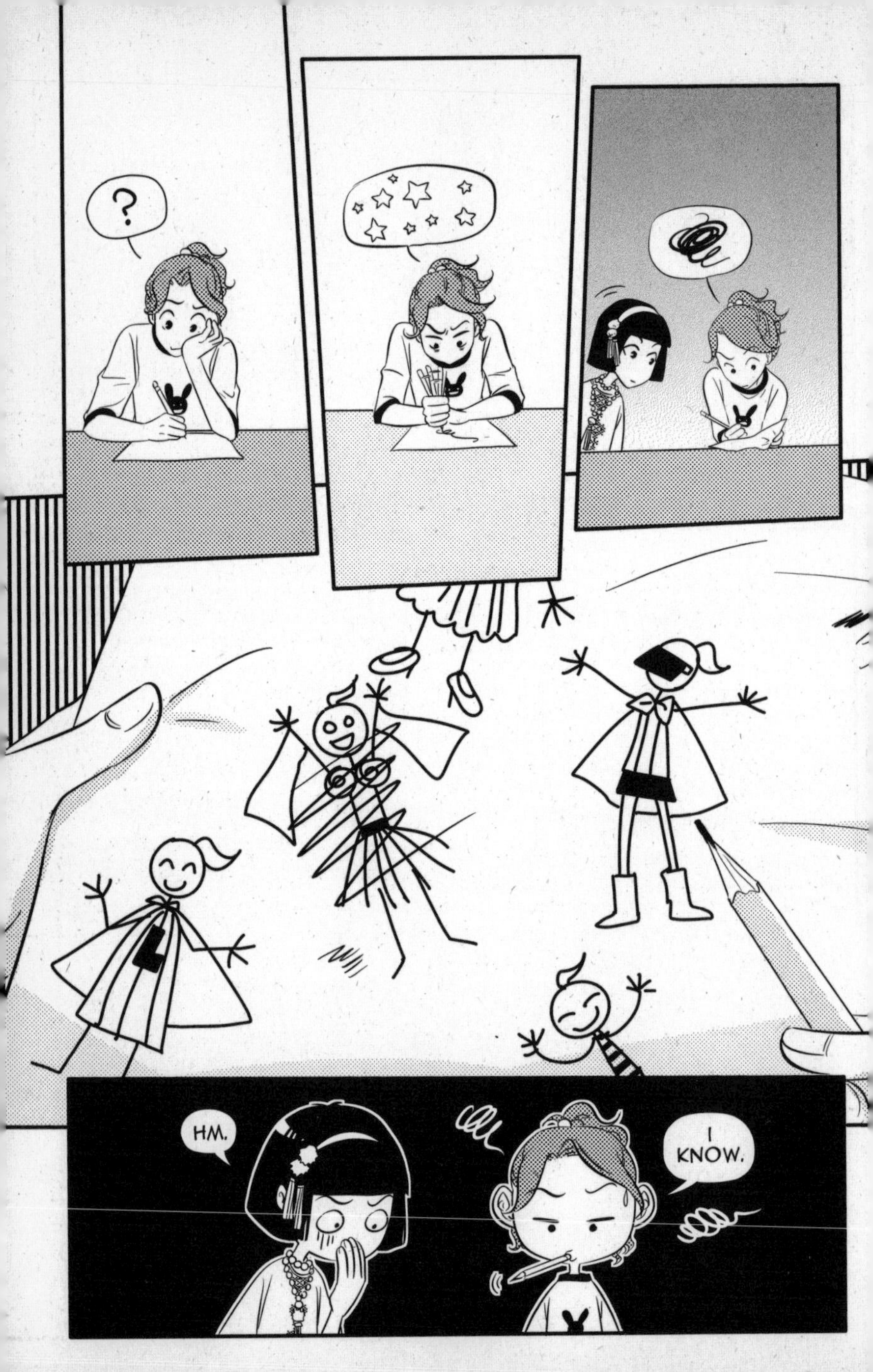
?
HM.
I KNOW.

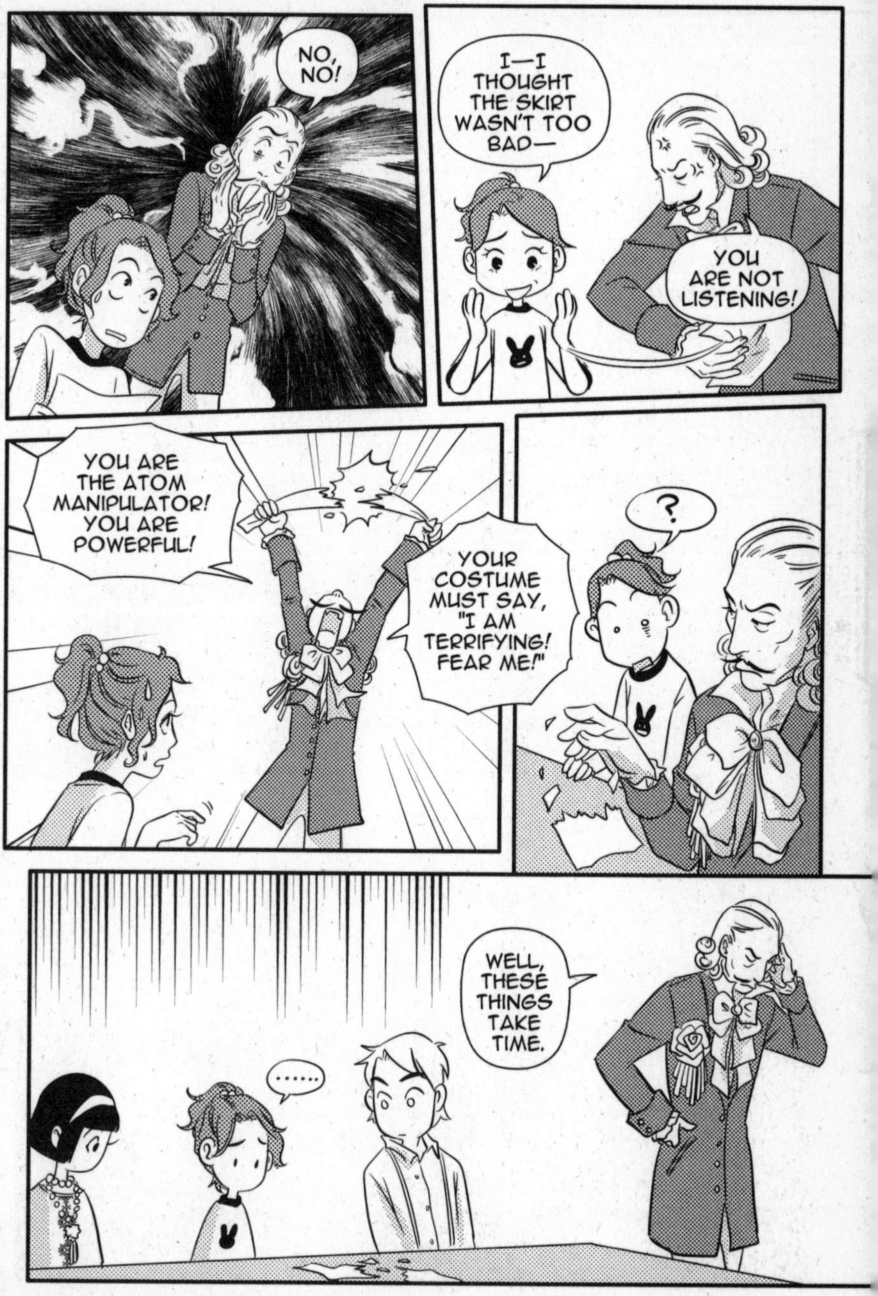
NO, NO!
I—I THOUGHT THE SKIRT WASN'T TOO BAD—
YOU ARE NOT LISTENING!
YOU ARE THE ATOM MANIPULATOR! YOU ARE POWERFUL!
YOUR COSTUME MUST SAY, "I AM TERRIFYING! FEAR ME!"
?
WELL, THESE THINGS TAKE TIME.
......

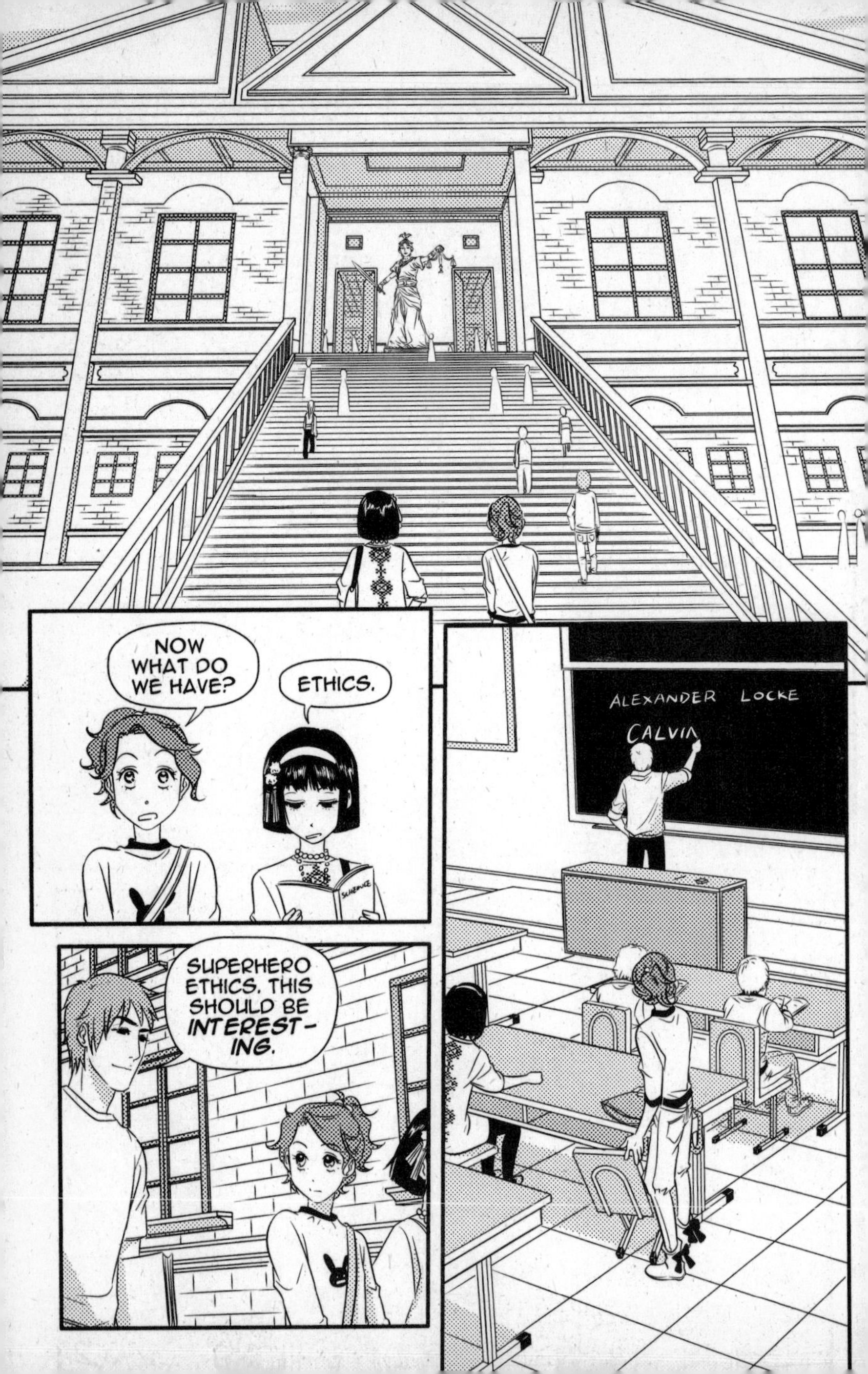
NOW WHAT DO WE HAVE?
ETHICS.
SUPERHERO ETHICS. THIS SHOULD BE **INTEREST-ING.**
ALEXANDER LOCKE
CALVIN

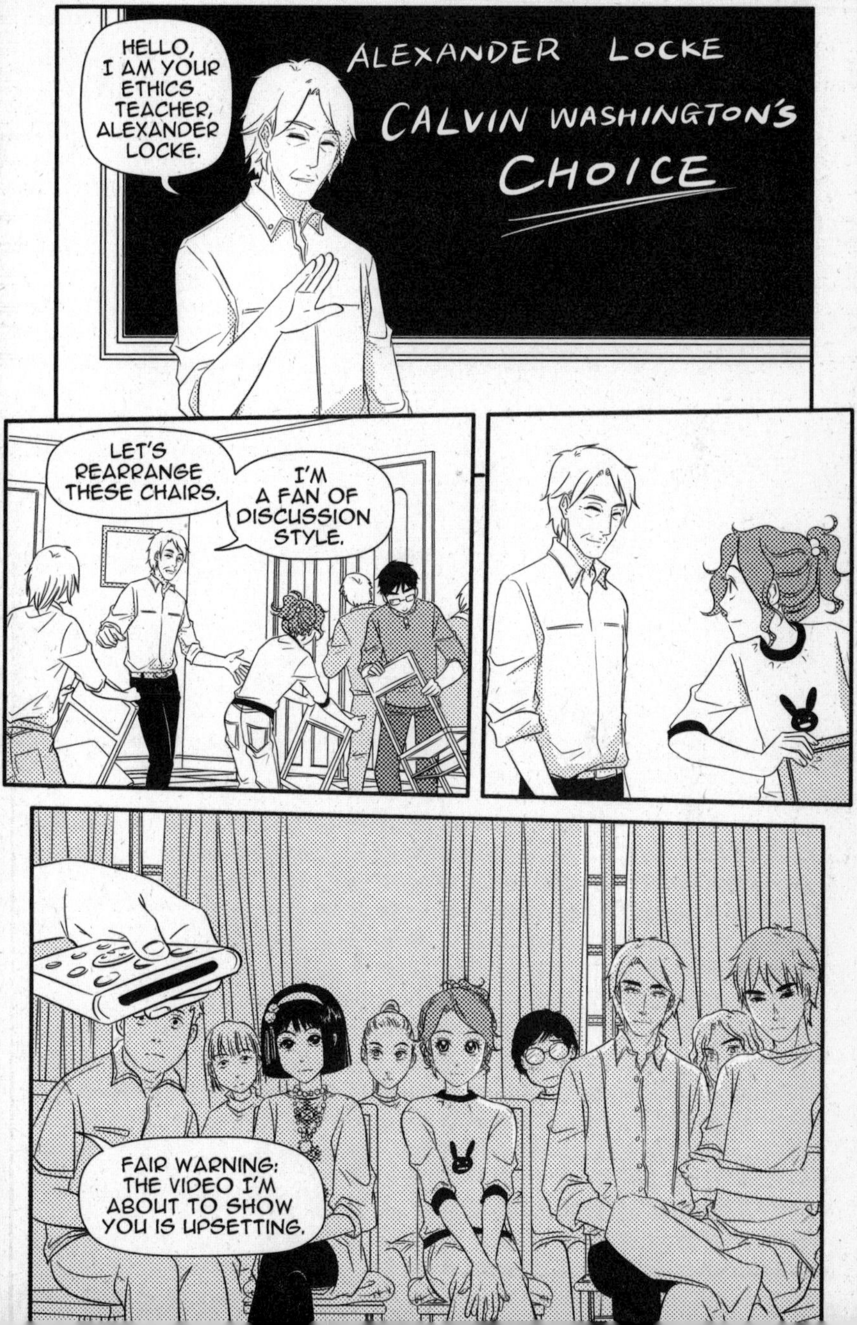
HELLO, I AM YOUR ETHICS TEACHER, ALEXANDER LOCKE.
ALEXANDER LOCKE
CALVIN WASHINGTON'S CHOICE
LET'S REARRANGE THESE CHAIRS.
I'M A FAN OF DISCUSSION STYLE.
FAIR WARNING: THE VIDEO I'M ABOUT TO SHOW YOU IS UPSETTING.

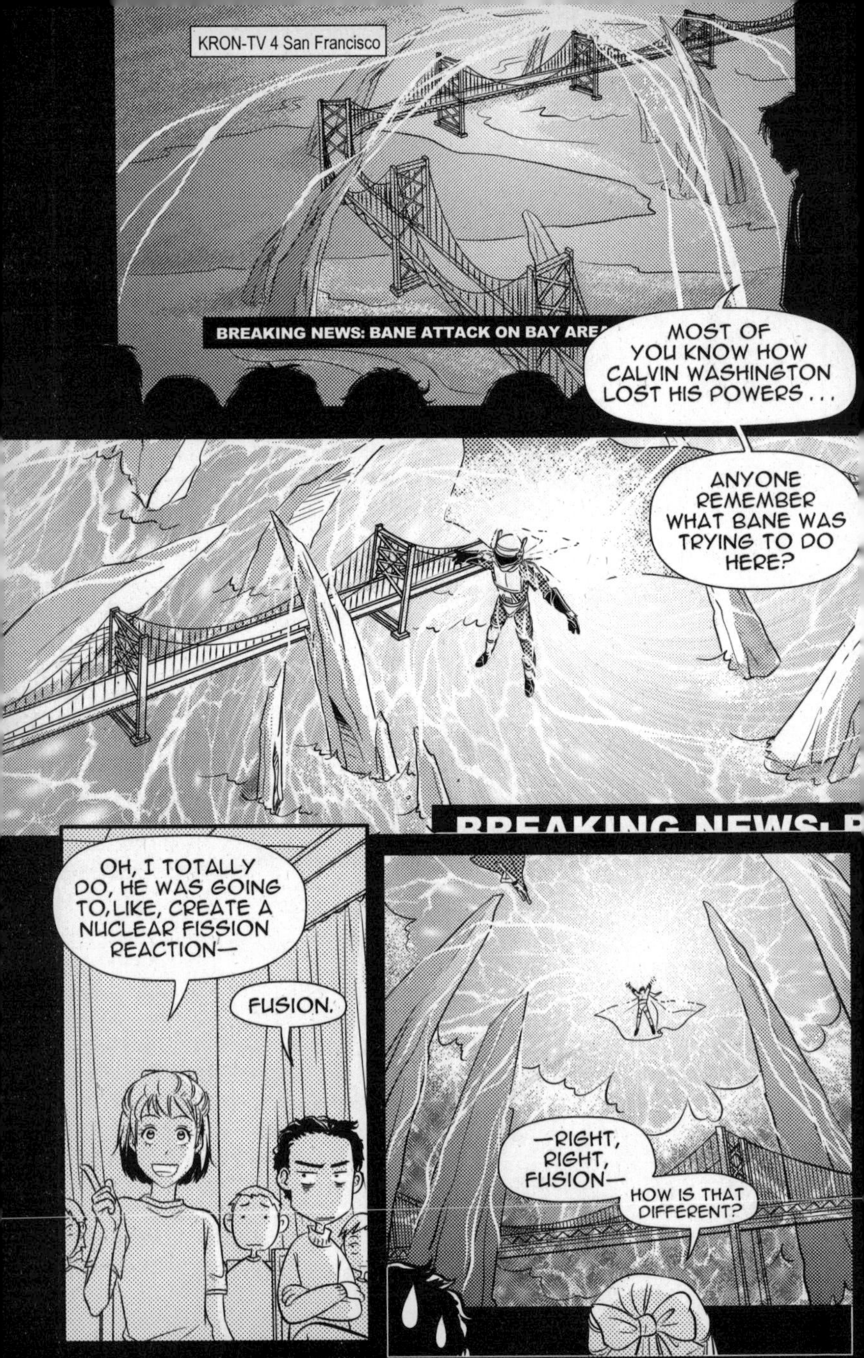

KRON-TV 4 San Francisco
BREAKING NEWS: BANE ATTACK ON BAY ARE
MOST OF YOU KNOW HOW CALVIN WASHINGTON LOST HIS POWERS . . .
ANYONE REMEMBER WHAT BANE WAS TRYING TO DO HERE?
OH, I TOTALLY DO, HE WAS GOING TO, LIKE, CREATE A NUCLEAR FISSION REACTION—
FUSION.
—RIGHT, RIGHT, FUSION—
HOW IS THAT DIFFERENT?

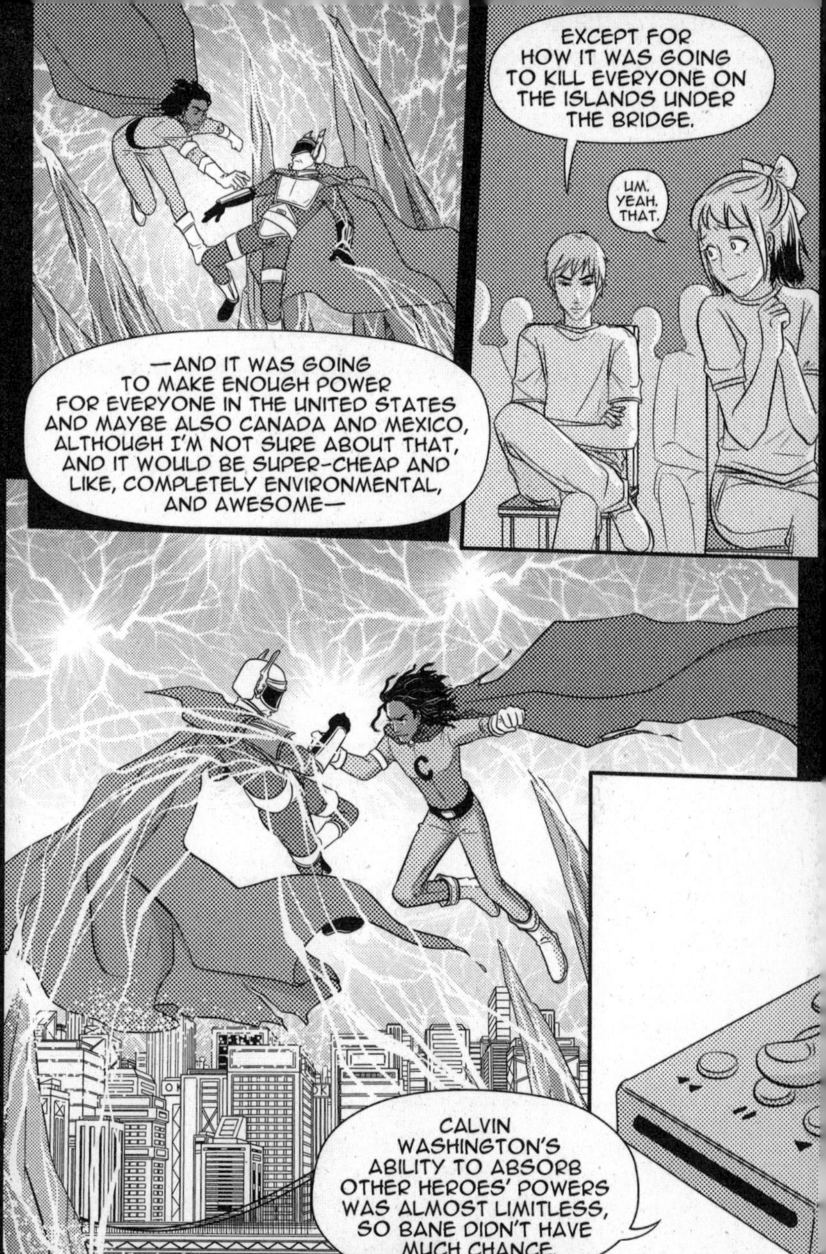
—AND IT WAS GOING TO MAKE ENOUGH POWER FOR EVERYONE IN THE UNITED STATES AND MAYBE ALSO CANADA AND MEXICO, ALTHOUGH I'M NOT SURE ABOUT THAT, AND IT WOULD BE SUPER-CHEAP AND LIKE, COMPLETELY ENVIRONMENTAL, AND AWESOME—
EXCEPT FOR HOW IT WAS GOING TO KILL EVERYONE ON THE ISLANDS UNDER THE BRIDGE.
UM. YEAH. THAT.
CALVIN WASHINGTON'S ABILITY TO ABSORB OTHER HEROES' POWERS WAS ALMOST LIMITLESS, SO BANE DIDN'T HAVE MUCH CHANCE.

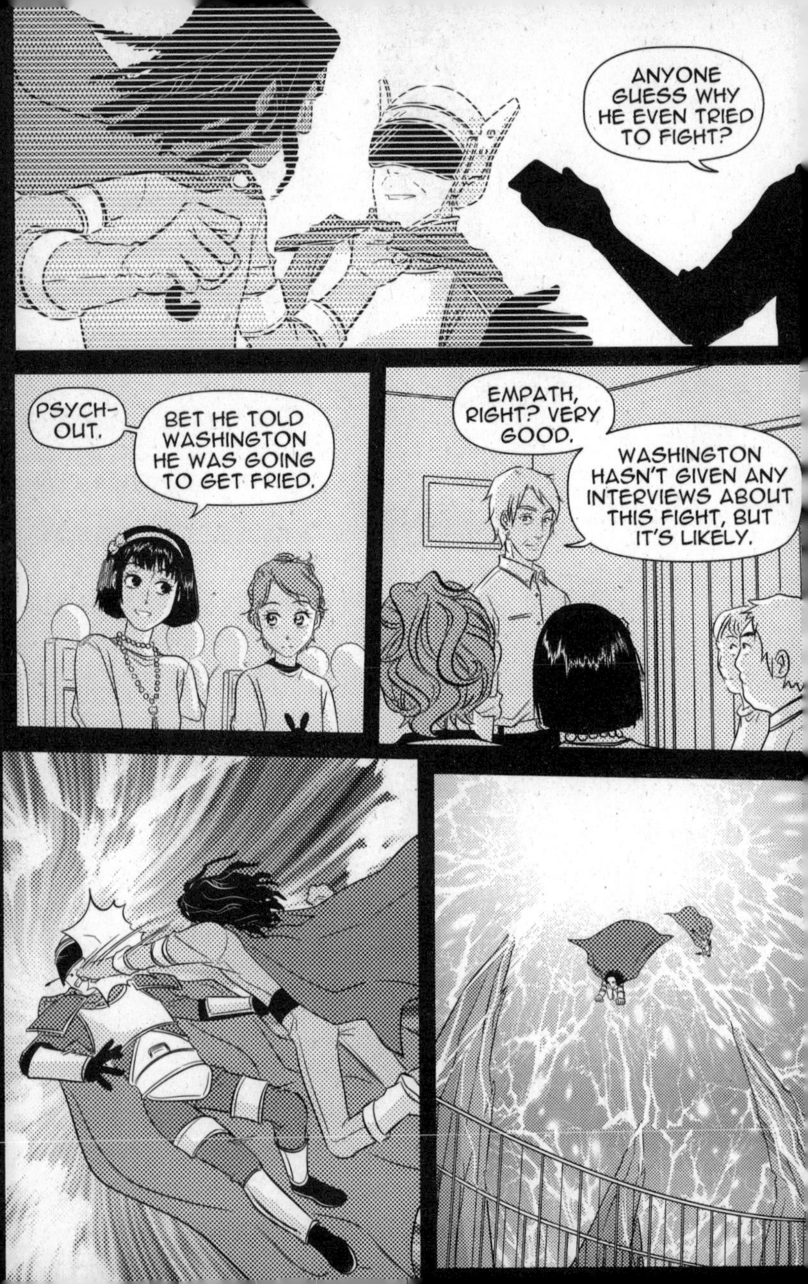
ANYONE GUESS WHY HE EVEN TRIED TO FIGHT?
PSYCH-OUT.
BET HE TOLD WASHINGTON HE WAS GOING TO GET FRIED.
EMPATH, RIGHT? VERY GOOD.
WASHINGTON HASN'T GIVEN ANY INTERVIEWS ABOUT THIS FIGHT, BUT IT'S LIKELY.

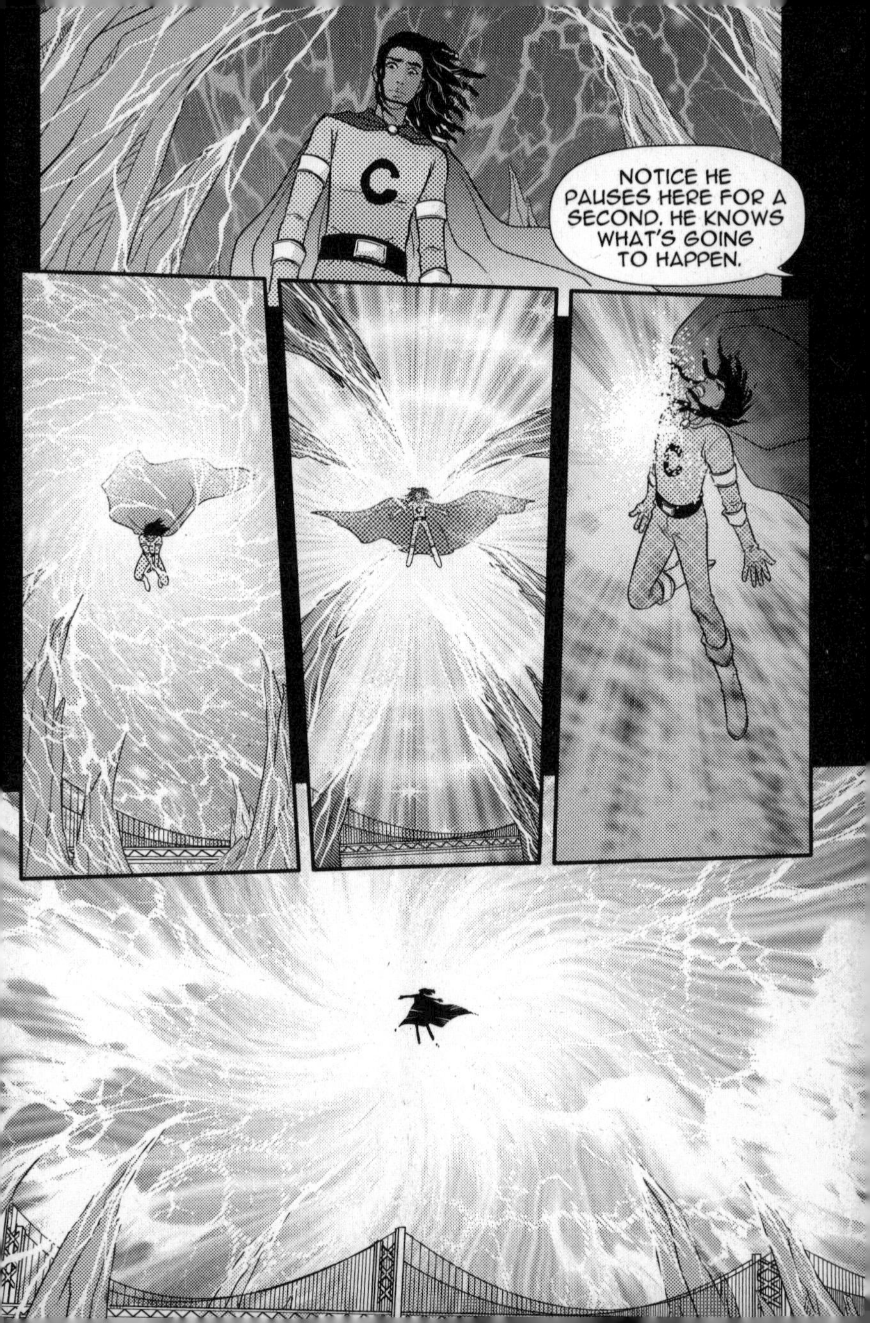
NOTICE HE PAUSES HERE FOR A SECOND. HE KNOWS WHAT'S GOING TO HAPPEN.

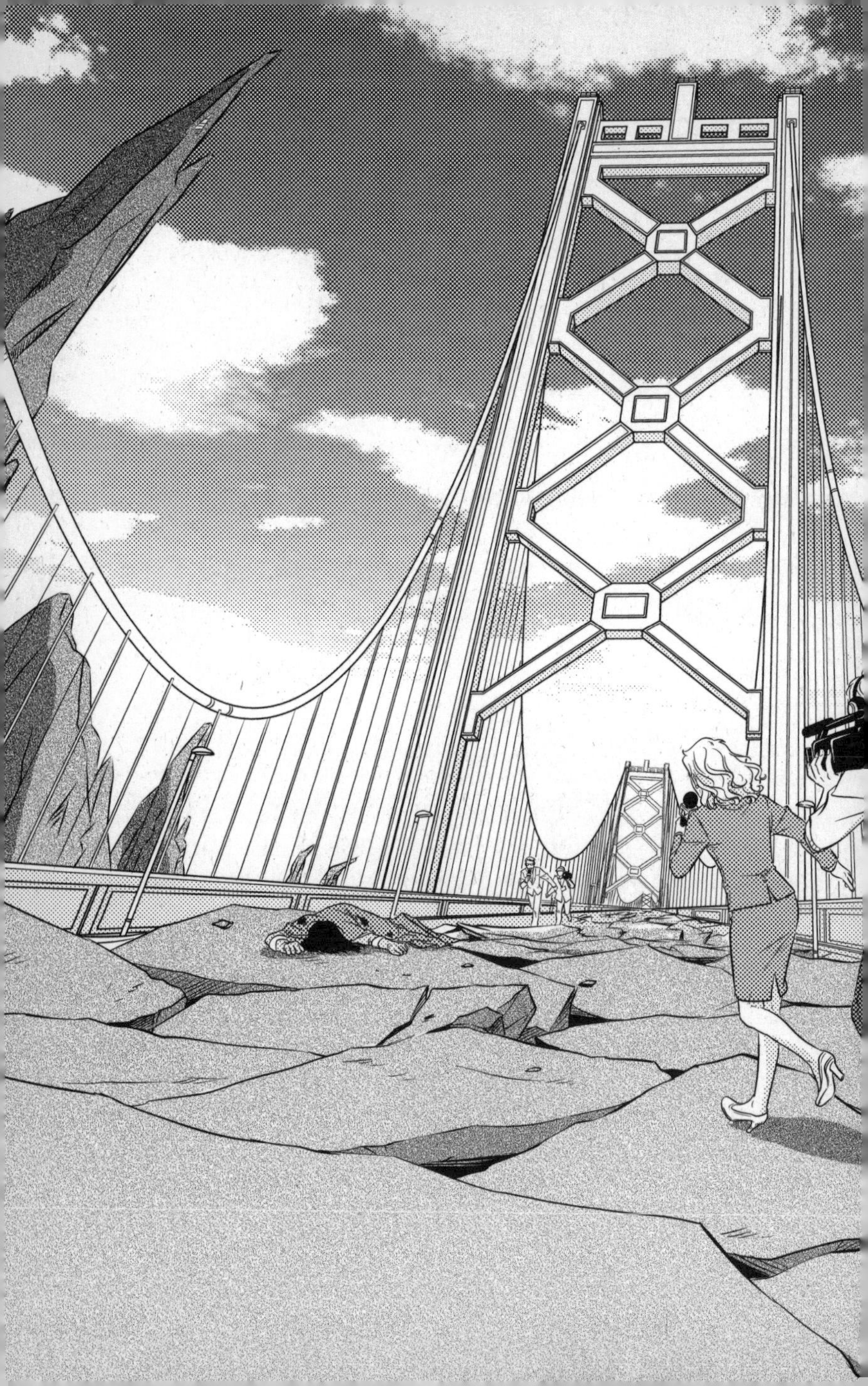

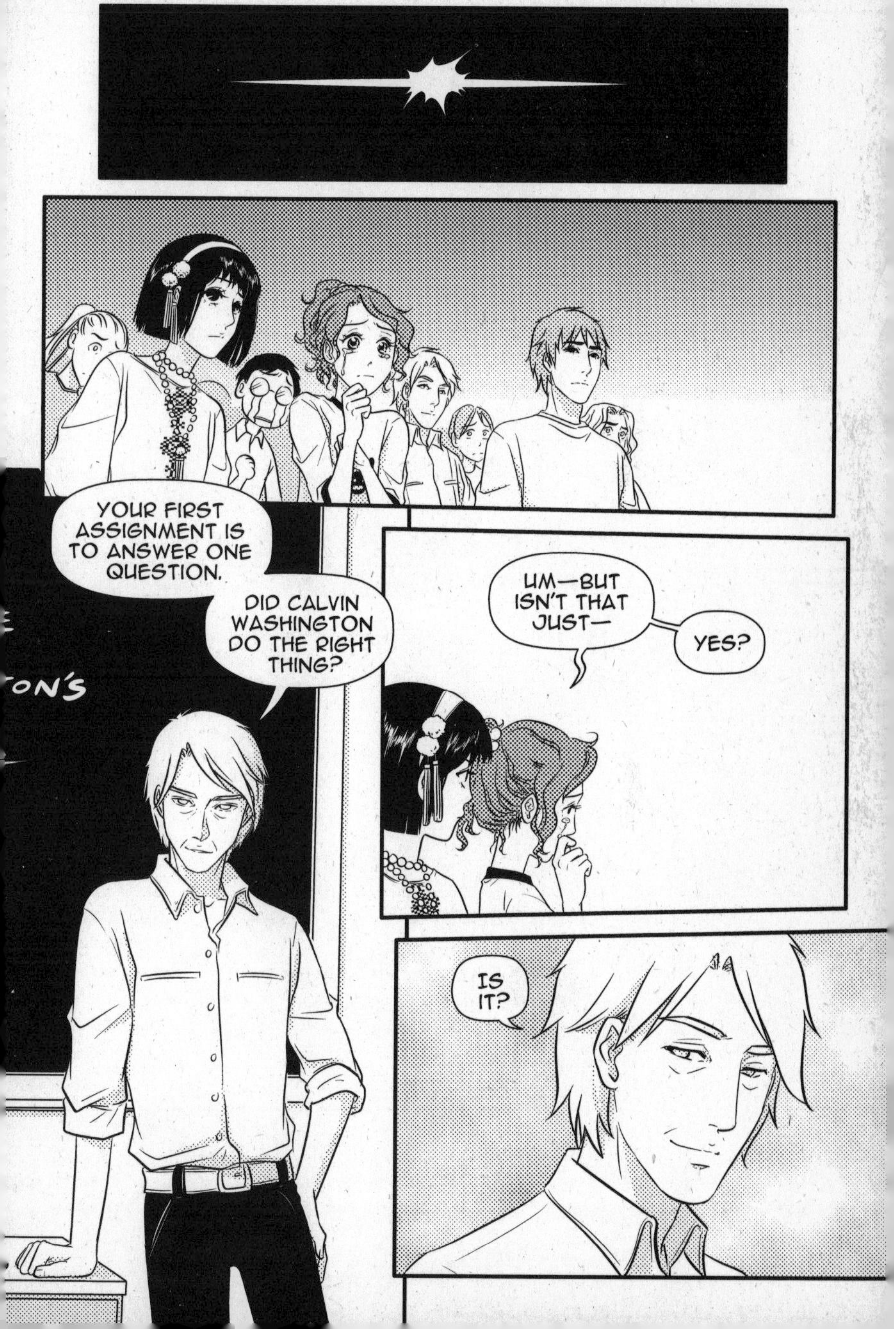
YOUR FIRST ASSIGNMENT IS TO ANSWER ONE QUESTION.
DID CALVIN WASHINGTON DO THE RIGHT THING?
UM—BUT ISN'T THAT JUST—
YES?
IS IT?

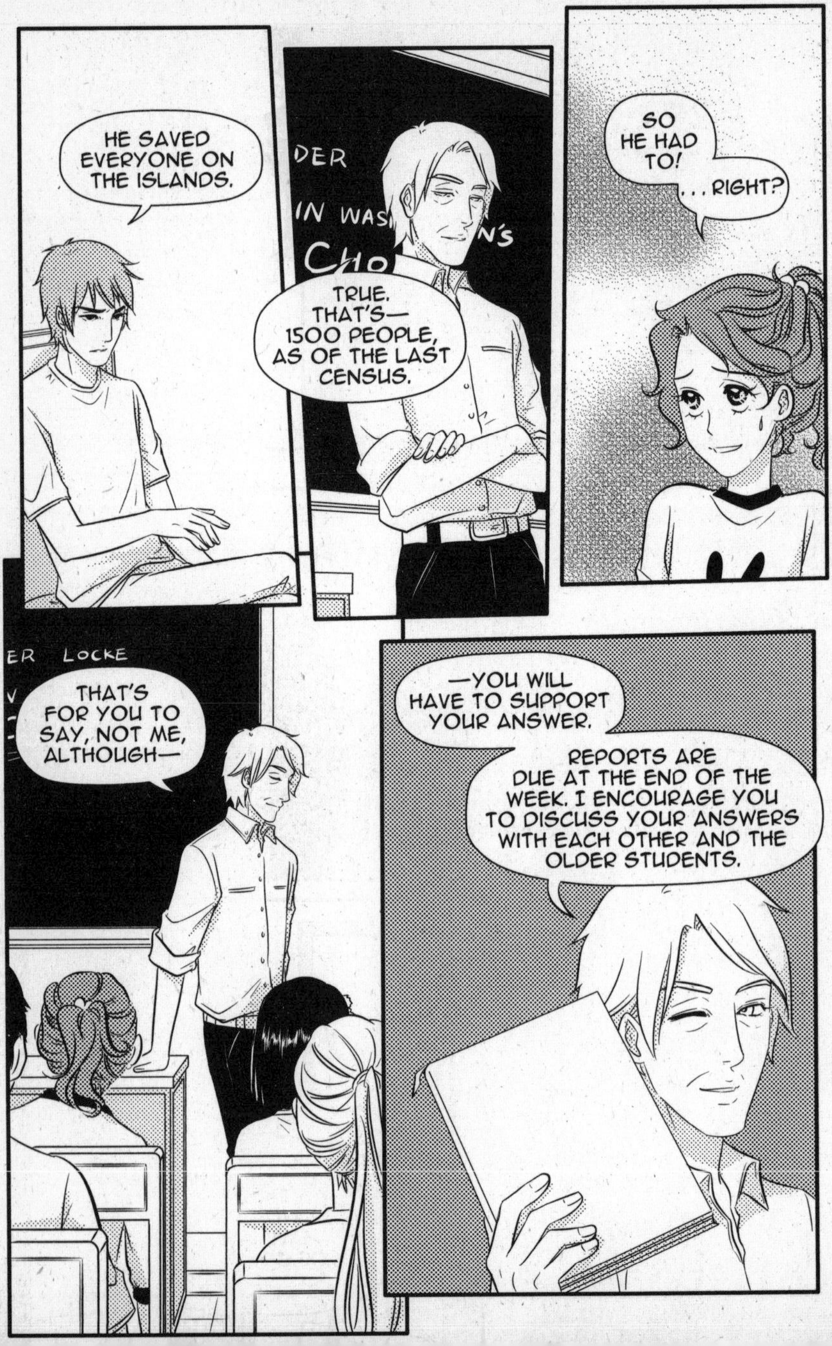

HE SAVED EVERYONE ON THE ISLANDS.
DER
IN WAS
N'S
CHO
TRUE. THAT'S— 1500 PEOPLE, AS OF THE LAST CENSUS.
SO HE HAD TO!
. . . RIGHT?
ER LOCKE
THAT'S FOR YOU TO SAY, NOT ME, ALTHOUGH—
—YOU WILL HAVE TO SUPPORT YOUR ANSWER.
REPORTS ARE DUE AT THE END OF THE WEEK. I ENCOURAGE YOU TO DISCUSS YOUR ANSWERS WITH EACH OTHER AND THE OLDER STUDENTS.

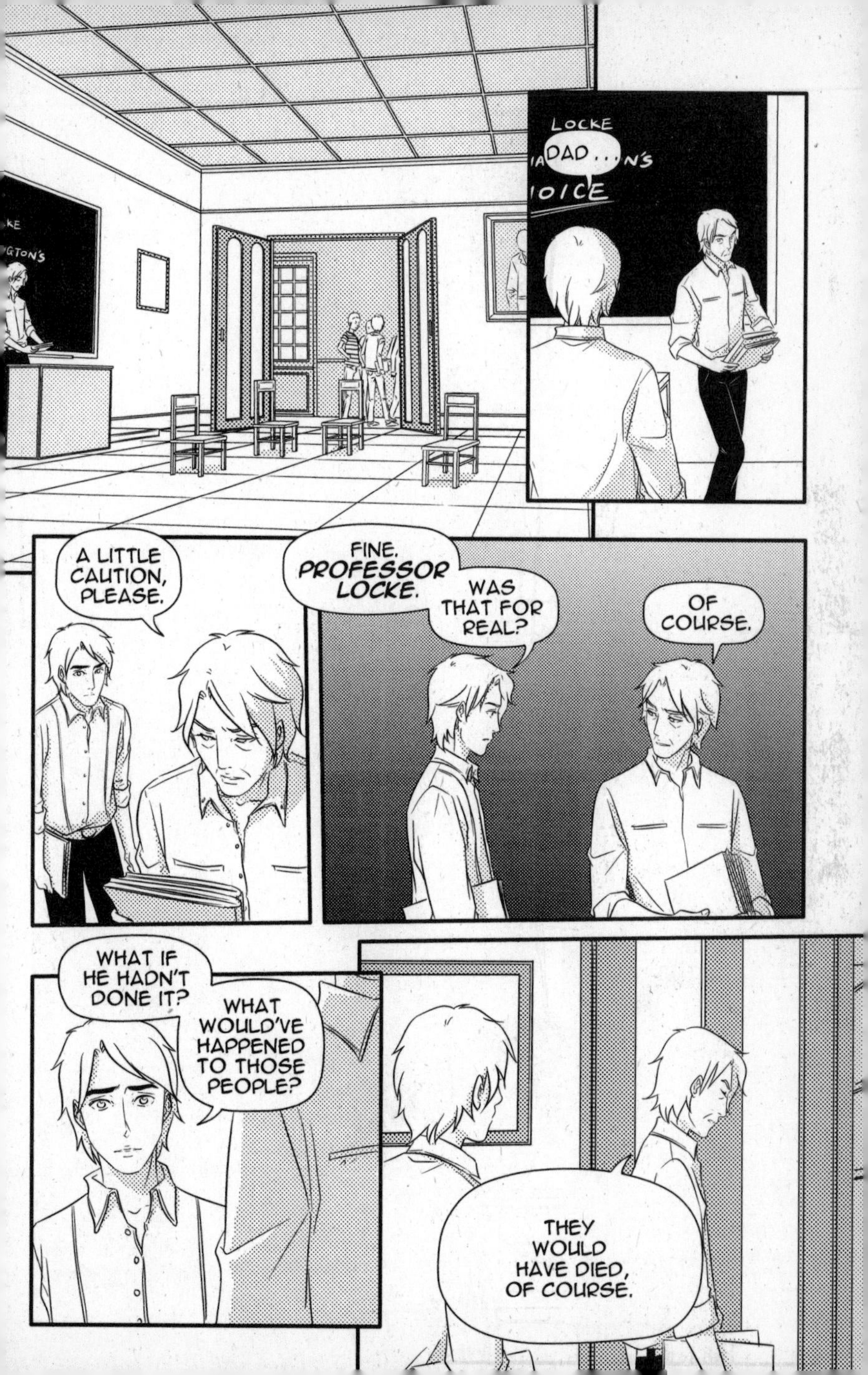
LOCKE
DAD . . .
N'S
OICE
A LITTLE CAUTION, PLEASE.
FINE. PROFESSOR LOCKE.
WAS THAT FOR REAL?
OF COURSE.
WHAT IF HE HADN'T DONE IT?
WHAT WOULD'VE HAPPENED TO THOSE PEOPLE?
THEY WOULD HAVE DIED, OF COURSE.

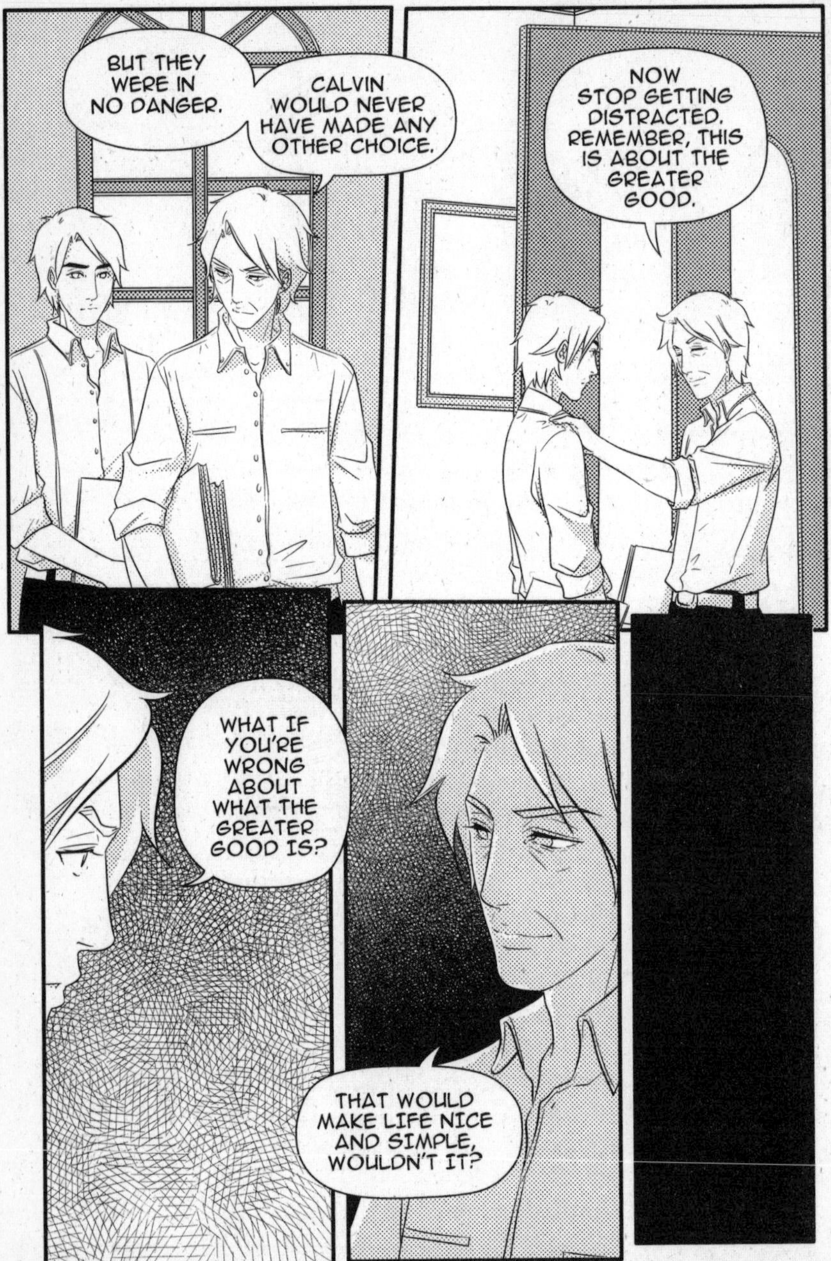
BUT THEY WERE IN NO DANGER.
CALVIN WOULD NEVER HAVE MADE ANY OTHER CHOICE.
NOW STOP GETTING DISTRACTED. REMEMBER, THIS IS ABOUT THE GREATER GOOD.
WHAT IF YOU'RE WRONG ABOUT WHAT THE GREATER GOOD IS?
THAT WOULD MAKE LIFE NICE AND SIMPLE, WOULDN'T IT?

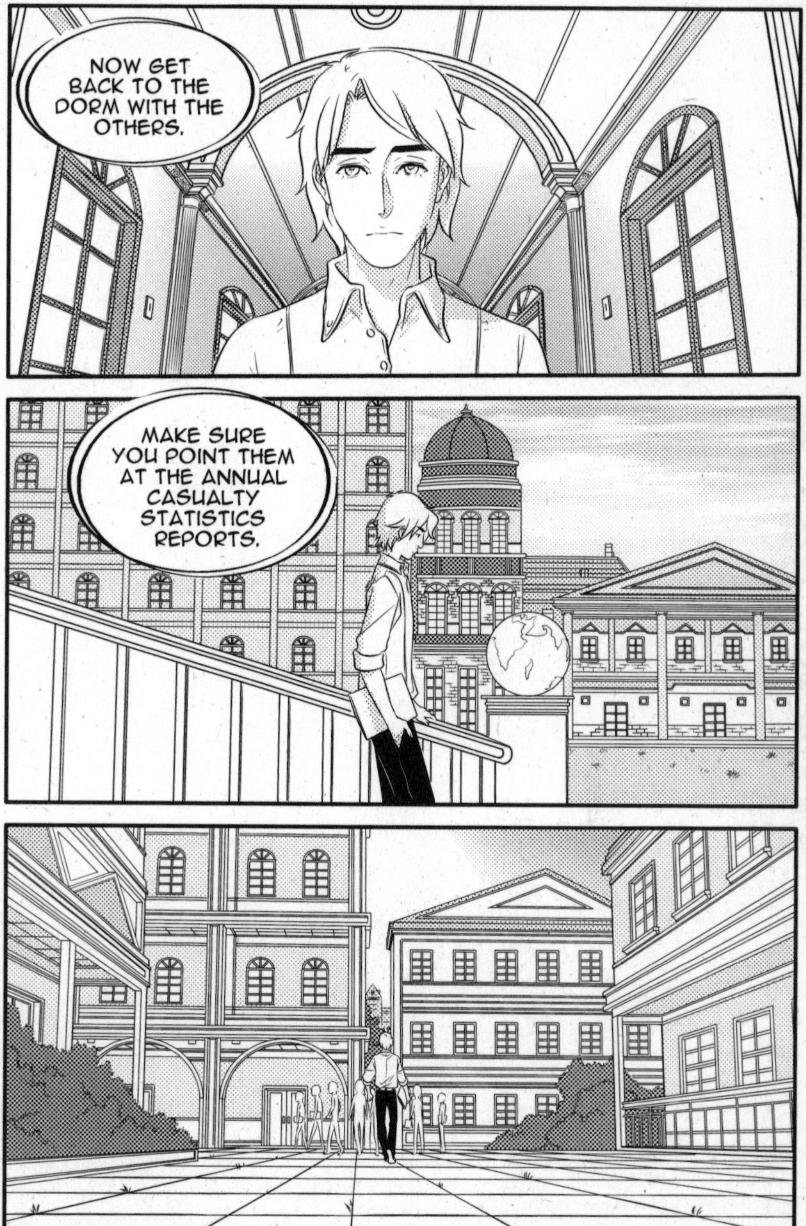
NOW GET BACK TO THE DORM WITH THE OTHERS.
MAKE SURE YOU POINT THEM AT THE ANNUAL CASUALTY STATISTICS REPORTS.

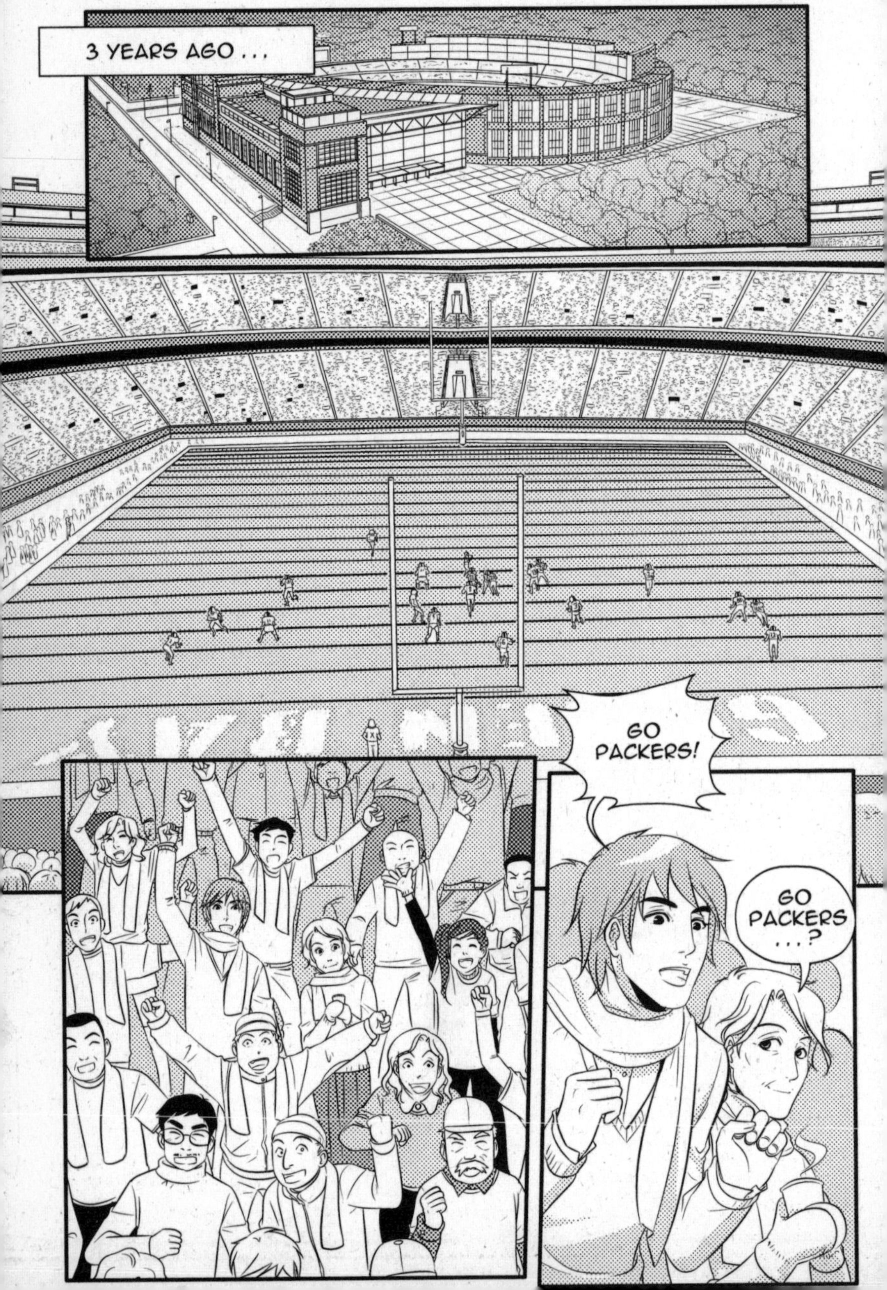
3 YEARS AGO . . .
GO PACKERS!
GO PACKERS . . . ?

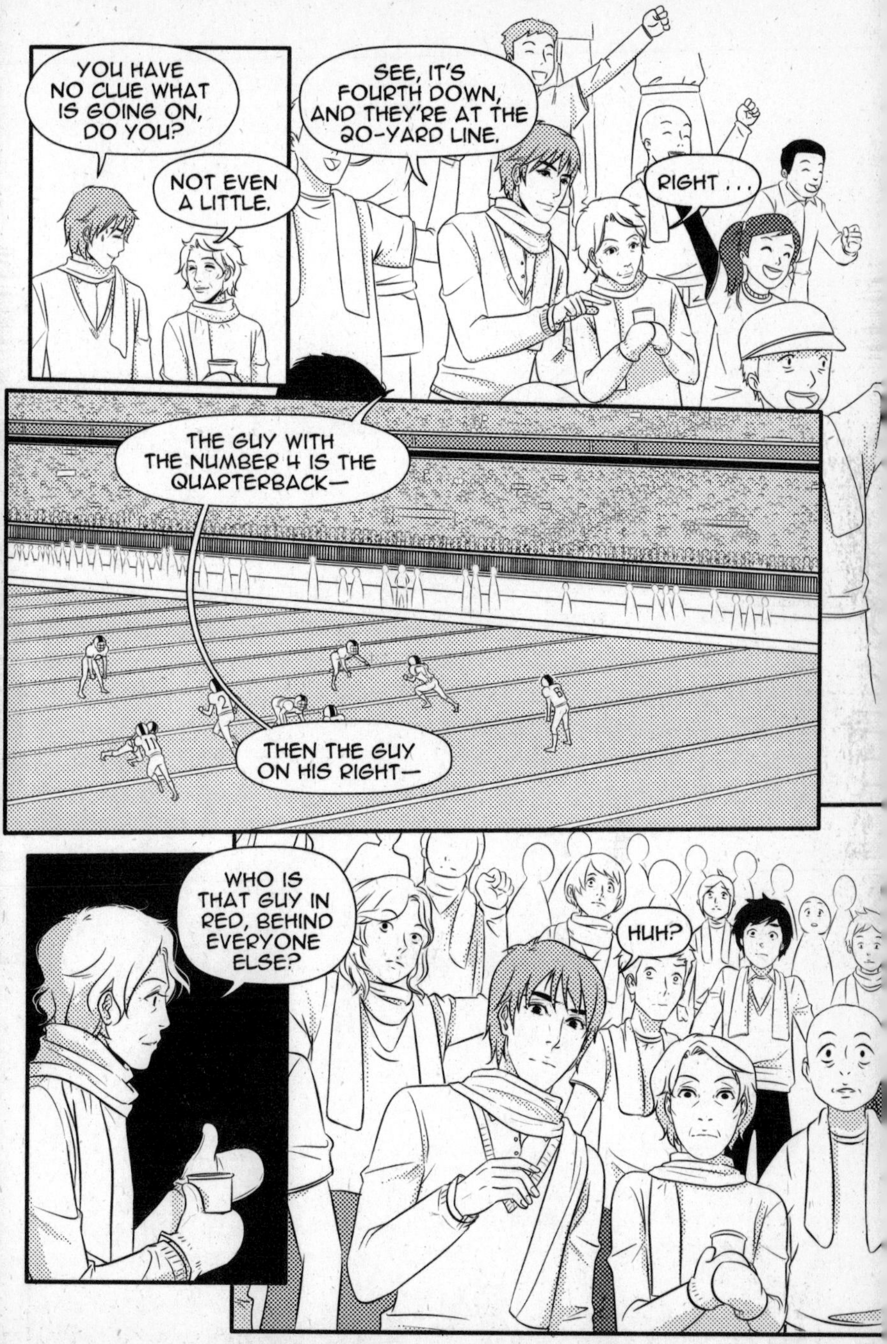
YOU HAVE NO CLUE WHAT IS GOING ON, DO YOU?
NOT EVEN A LITTLE.
SEE, IT'S FOURTH DOWN, AND THEY'RE AT THE 20-YARD LINE.
RIGHT . . .
THE GUY WITH THE NUMBER 4 IS THE QUARTERBACK—
THEN THE GUY ON HIS RIGHT—
WHO IS THAT GUY IN RED, BEHIND EVERYONE ELSE?
HUH?

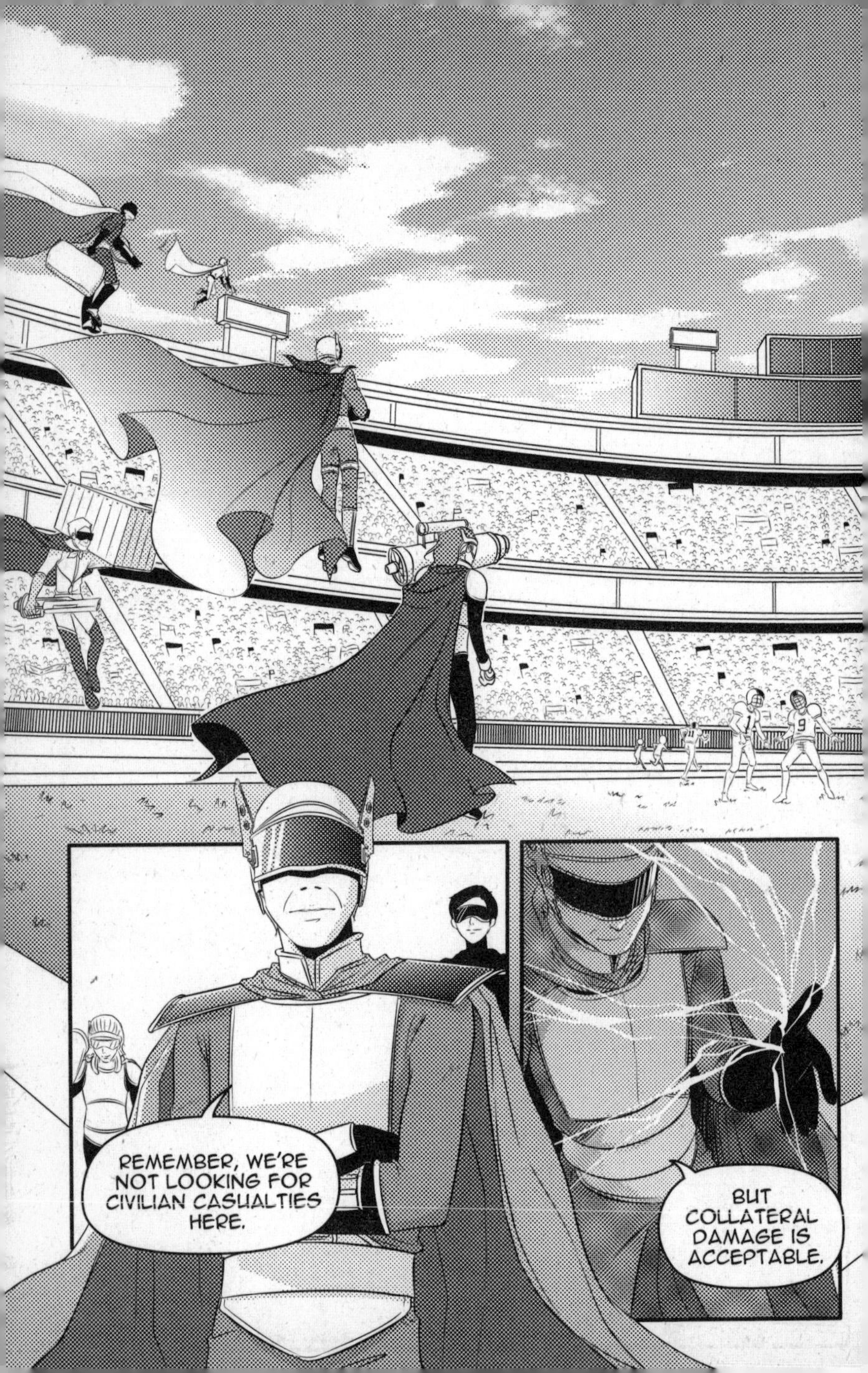
REMEMBER, WE'RE NOT LOOKING FOR CIVILIAN CASUALTIES HERE.
BUT COLLATERAL DAMAGE IS ACCEPTABLE.

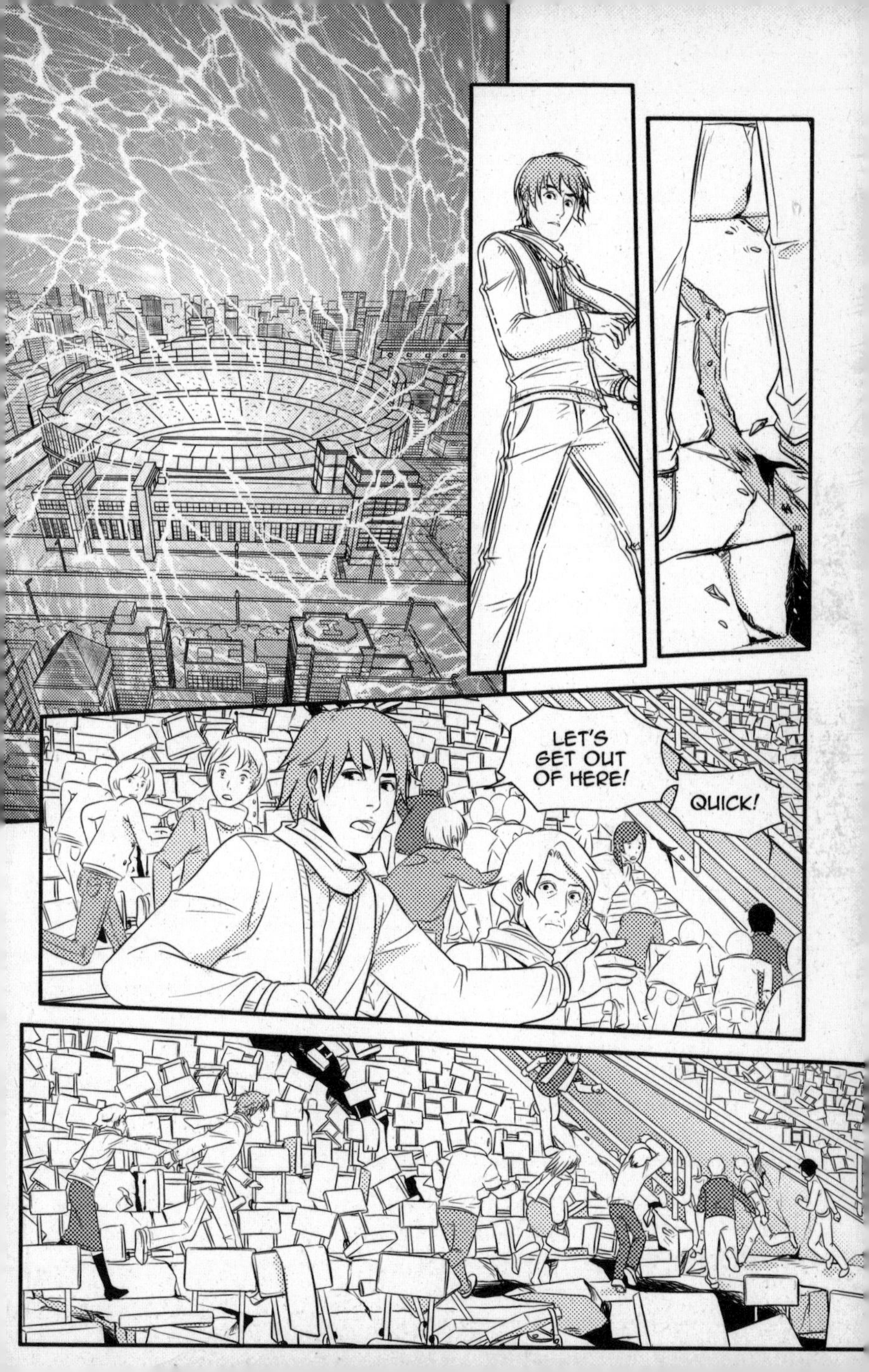
LET'S GET OUT OF HERE!
QUICK!

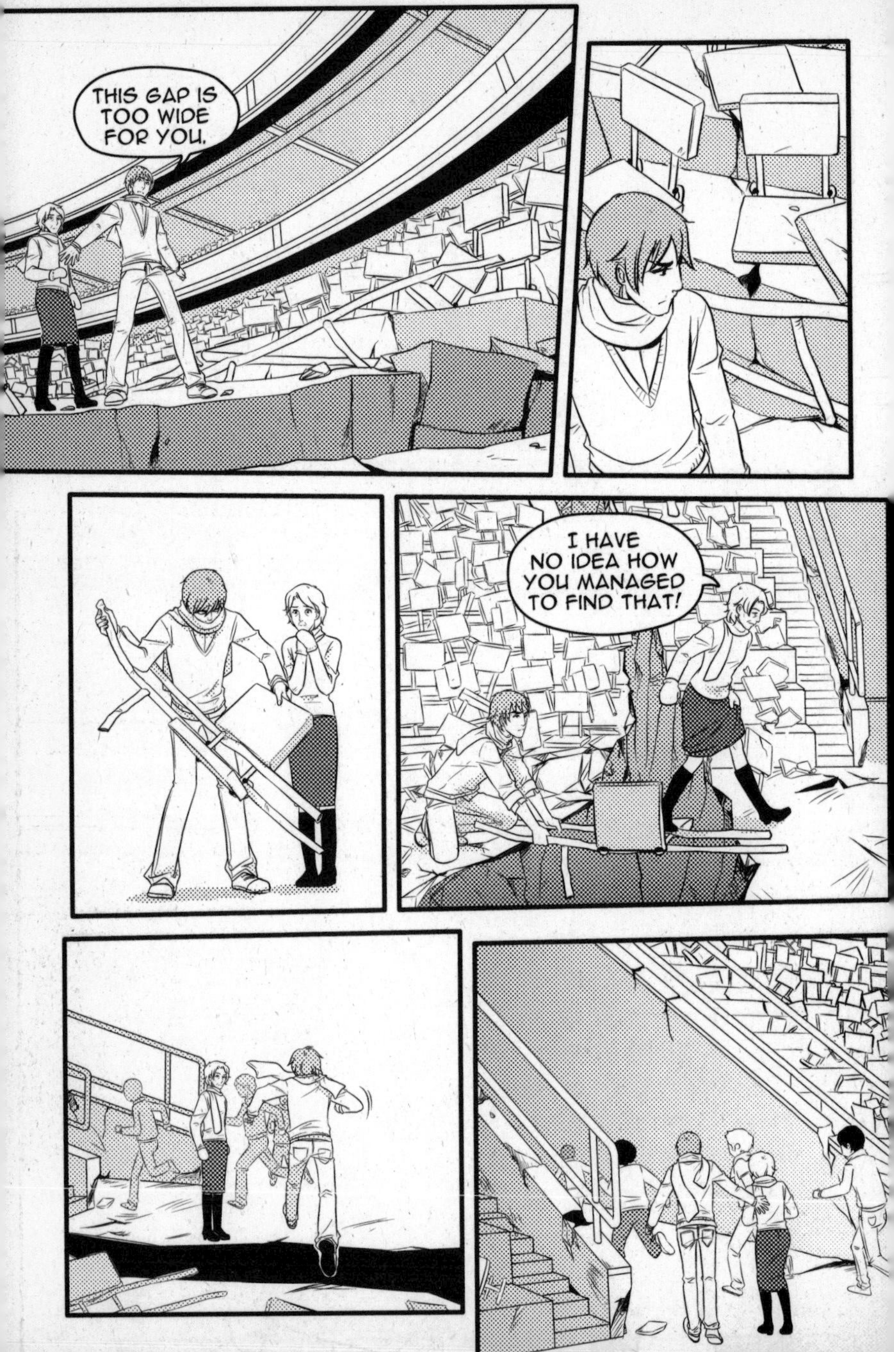
THIS GAP IS TOO WIDE FOR YOU.
I HAVE NO IDEA HOW YOU MANAGED TO FIND THAT!

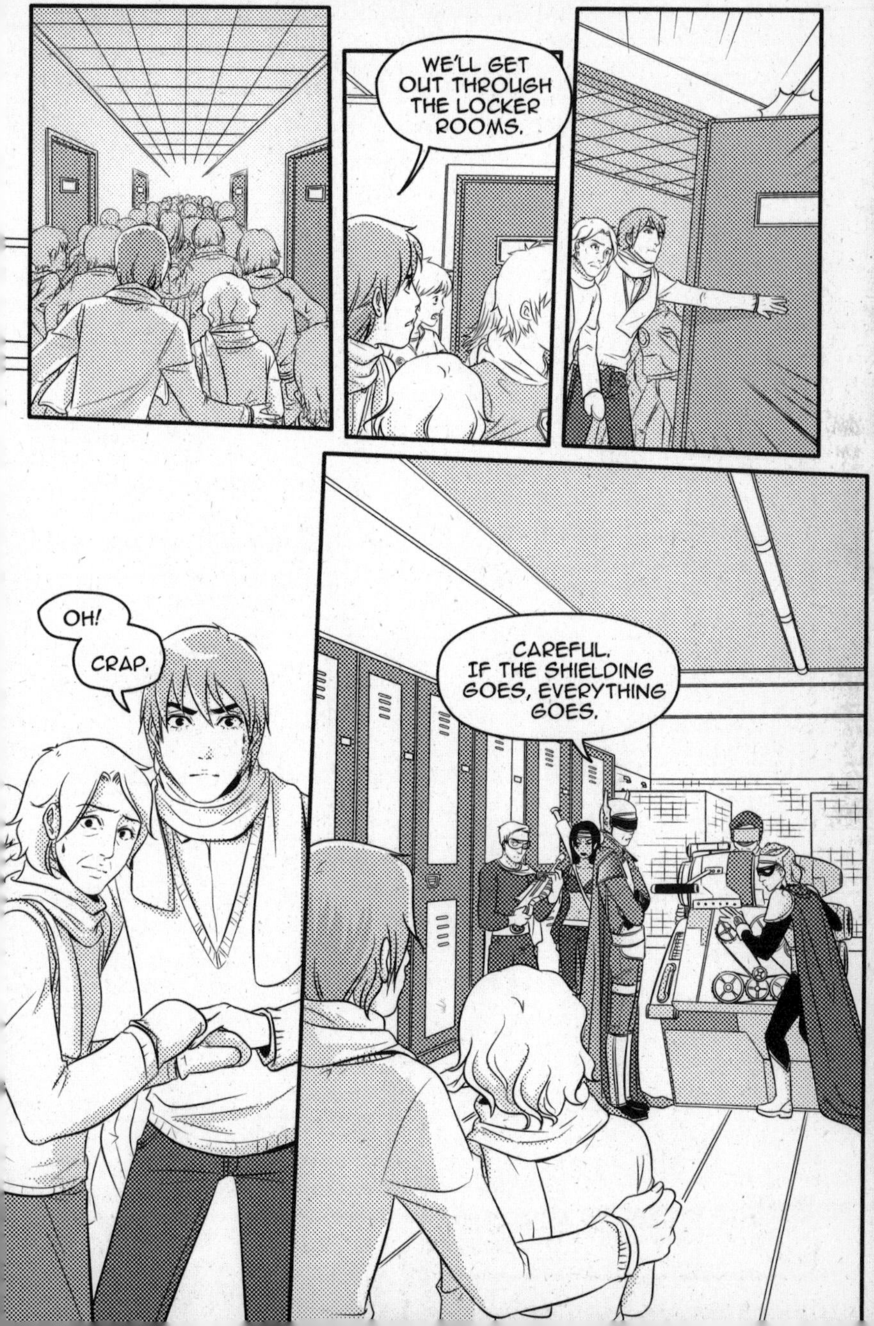
WE'LL GET OUT THROUGH THE LOCKER ROOMS.
OH!
CRAP.
CAREFUL. IF THE SHIELDING GOES, EVERYTHING GOES.

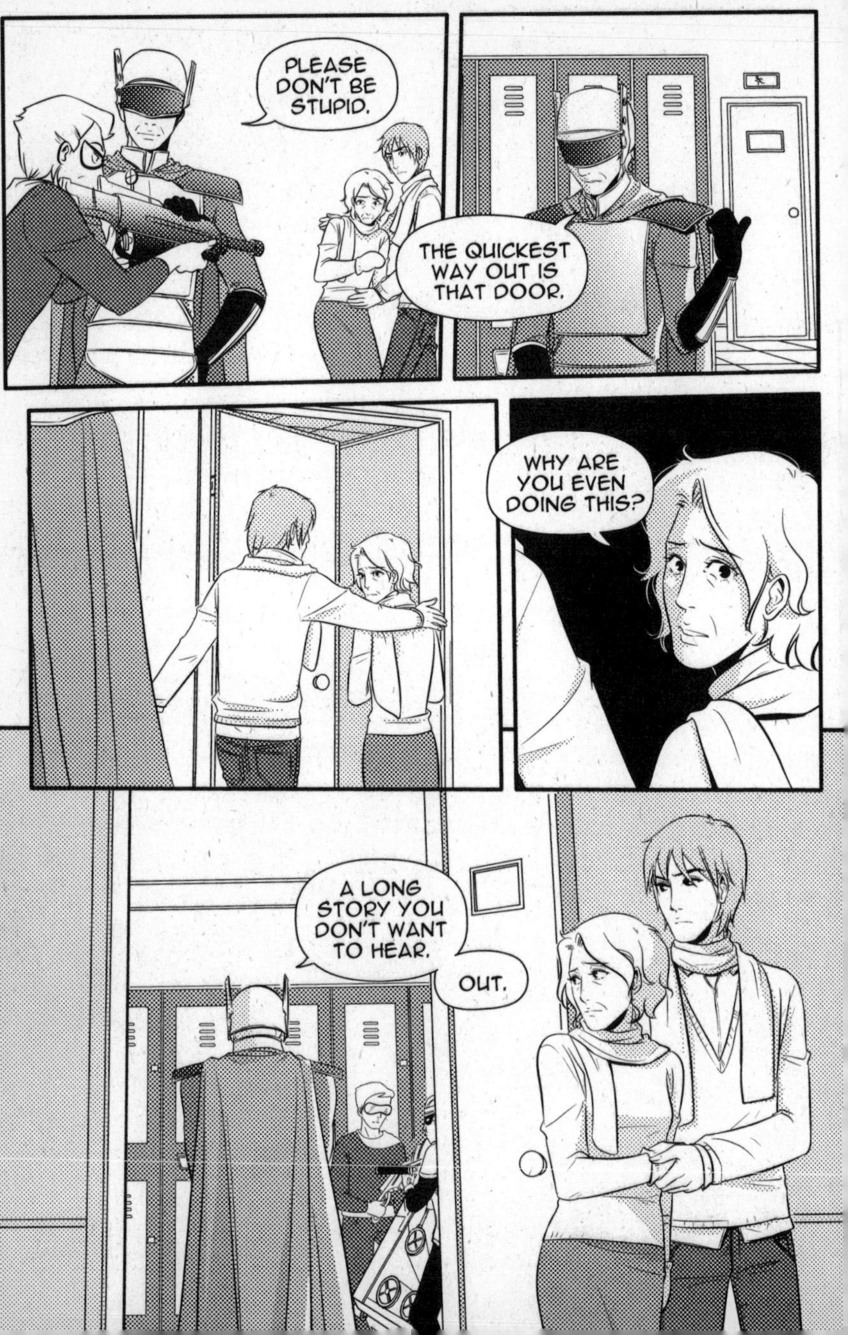
PLEASE DON'T BE STUPID.
THE QUICKEST WAY OUT IS THAT DOOR.
WHY ARE YOU EVEN DOING THIS?
A LONG STORY YOU DON'T WANT TO HEAR.
OUT.

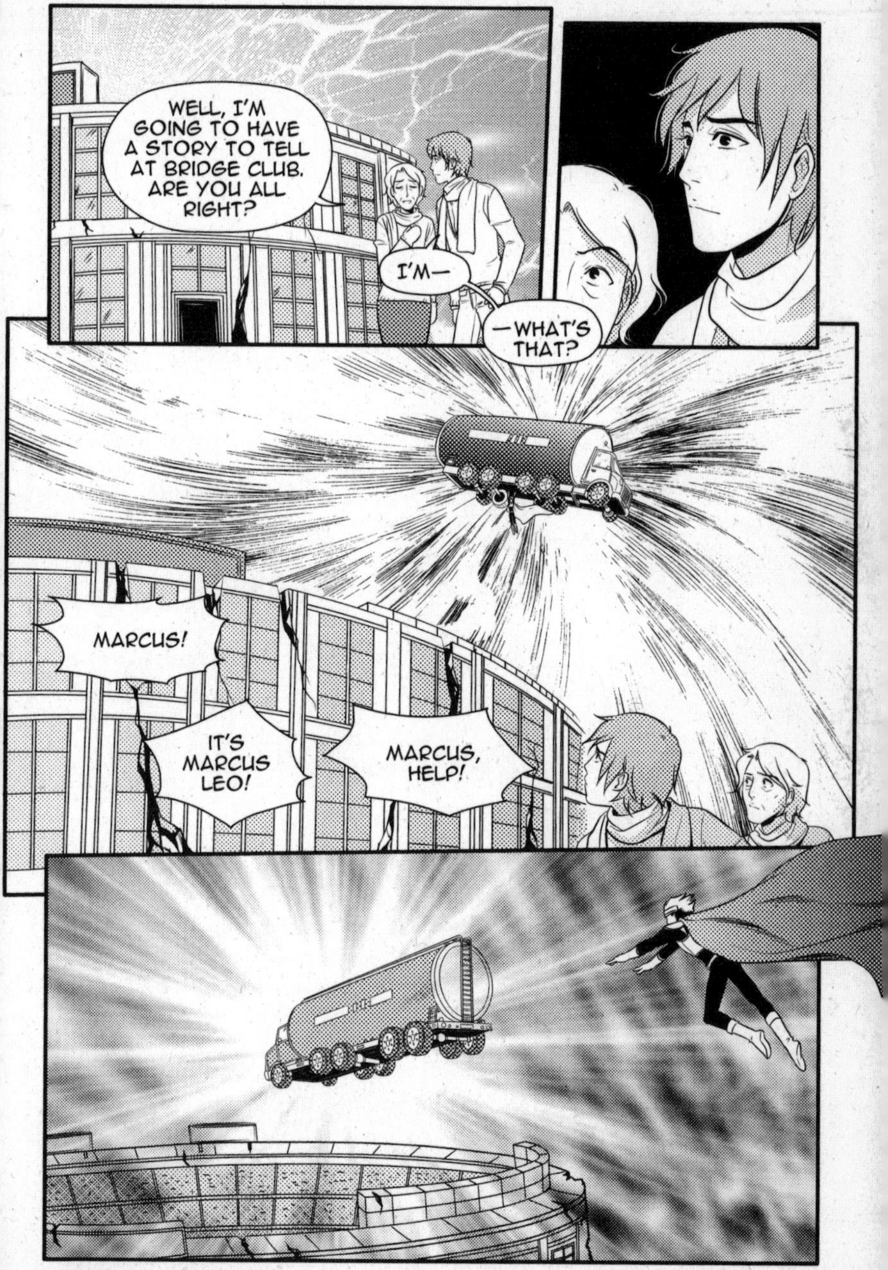
WELL, I'M GOING TO HAVE A STORY TO TELL AT BRIDGE CLUB. ARE YOU ALL RIGHT?
I'M—
—WHAT'S THAT?
MARCUS!
IT'S MARCUS LEO!
MARCUS, HELP!

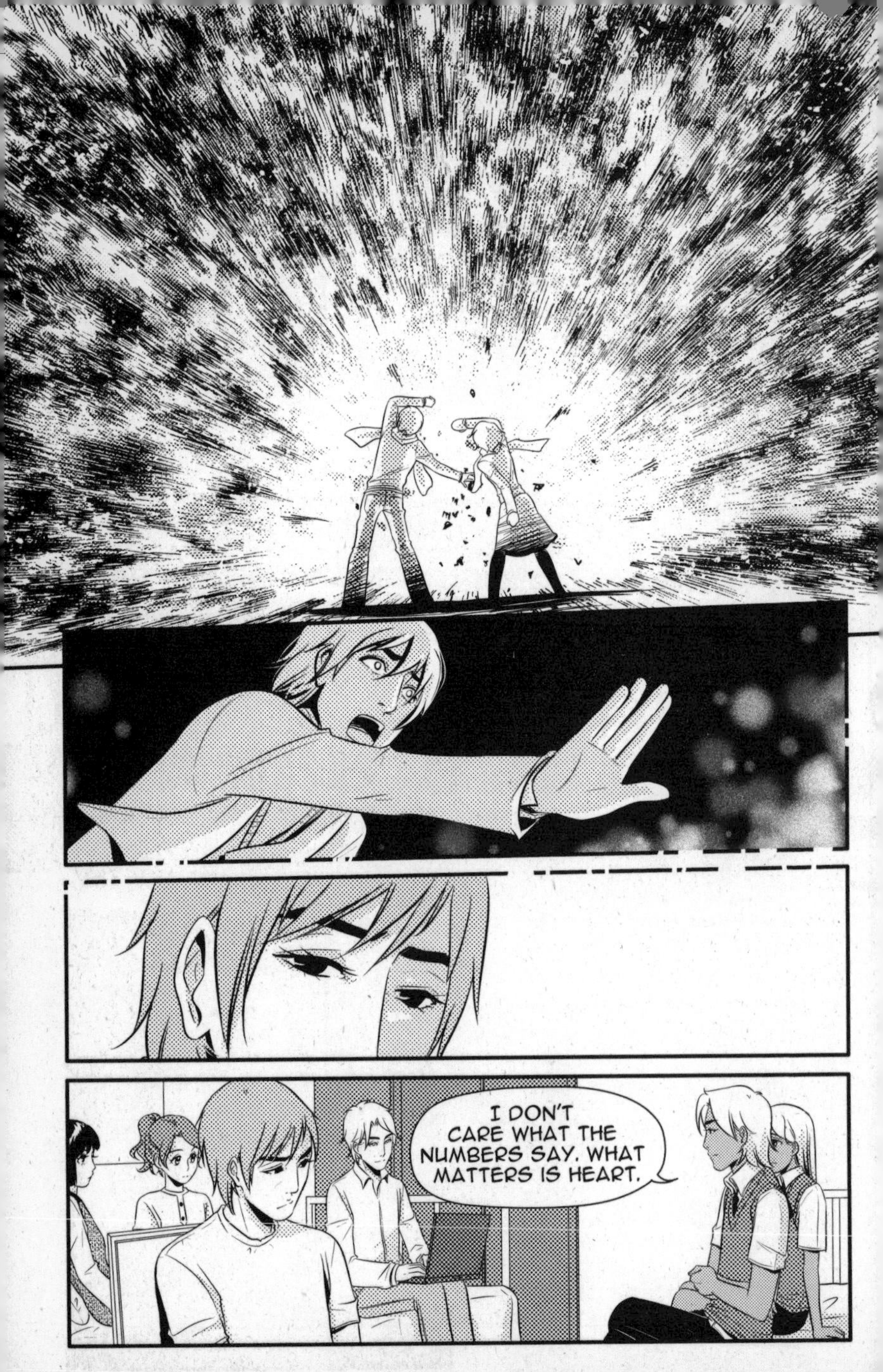
I DON'T CARE WHAT THE NUMBERS SAY. WHAT MATTERS IS HEART.

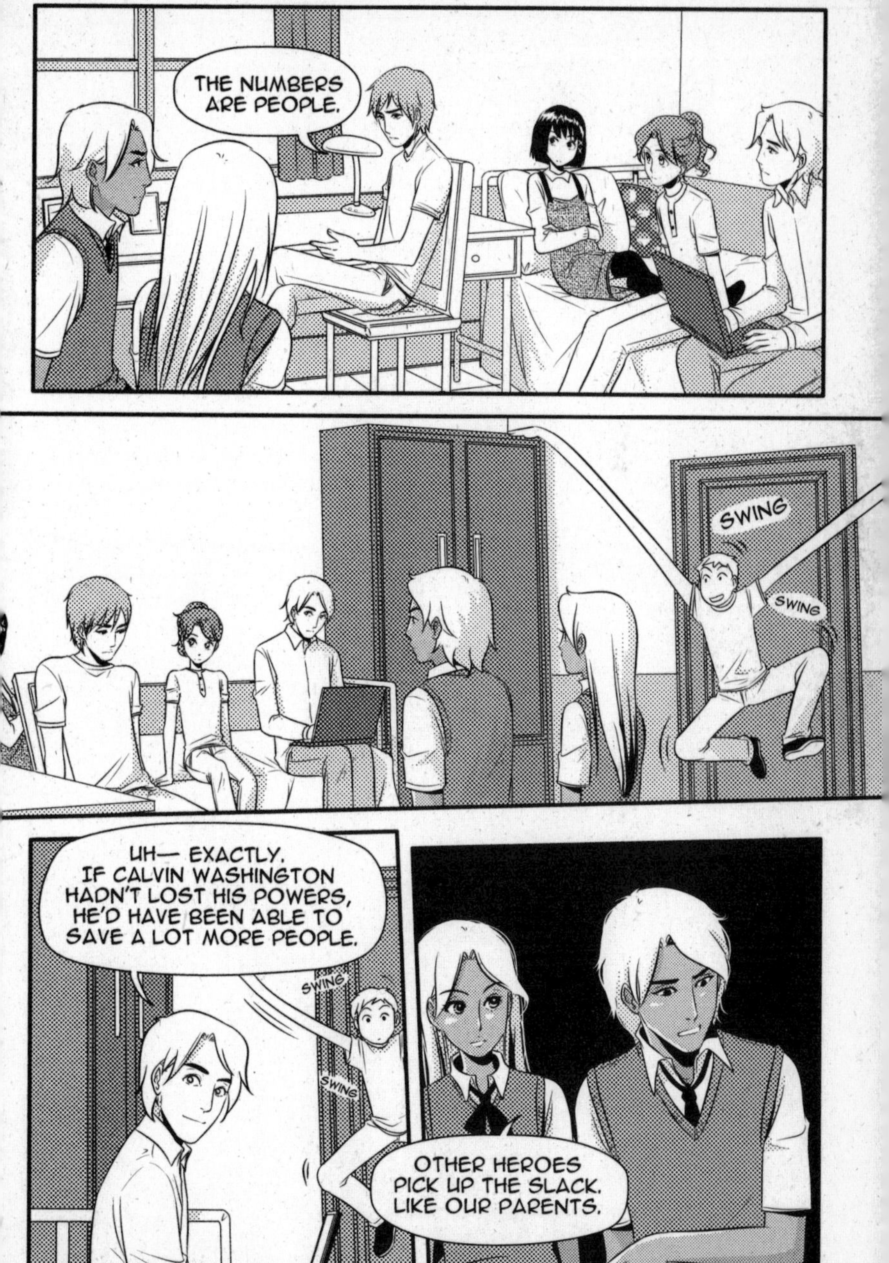
THE NUMBERS ARE PEOPLE.
SWING
SWING
UH— EXACTLY. IF CALVIN WASHINGTON HADN'T LOST HIS POWERS, HE'D HAVE BEEN ABLE TO SAVE A LOT MORE PEOPLE.
SWING
SWING
OTHER HEROES PICK UP THE SLACK. LIKE OUR PARENTS.

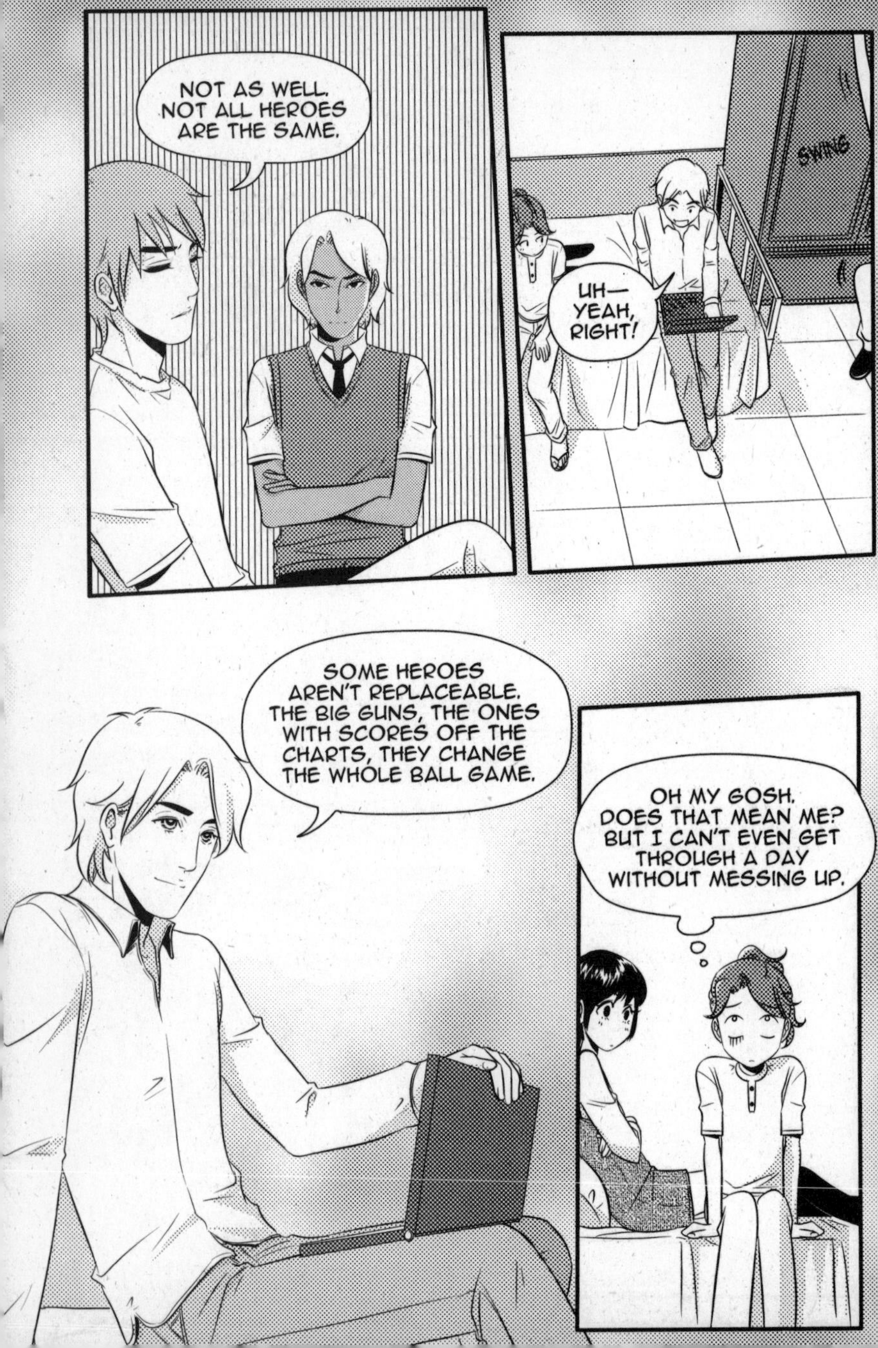
NOT AS WELL. NOT ALL HEROES ARE THE SAME.
SWING
UH— YEAH, RIGHT!
SOME HEROES AREN'T REPLACEABLE. THE BIG GUNS, THE ONES WITH SCORES OFF THE CHARTS, THEY CHANGE THE WHOLE BALL GAME.
OH MY GOSH. DOES THAT MEAN ME? BUT I CAN'T EVEN GET THROUGH A DAY WITHOUT MESSING UP.

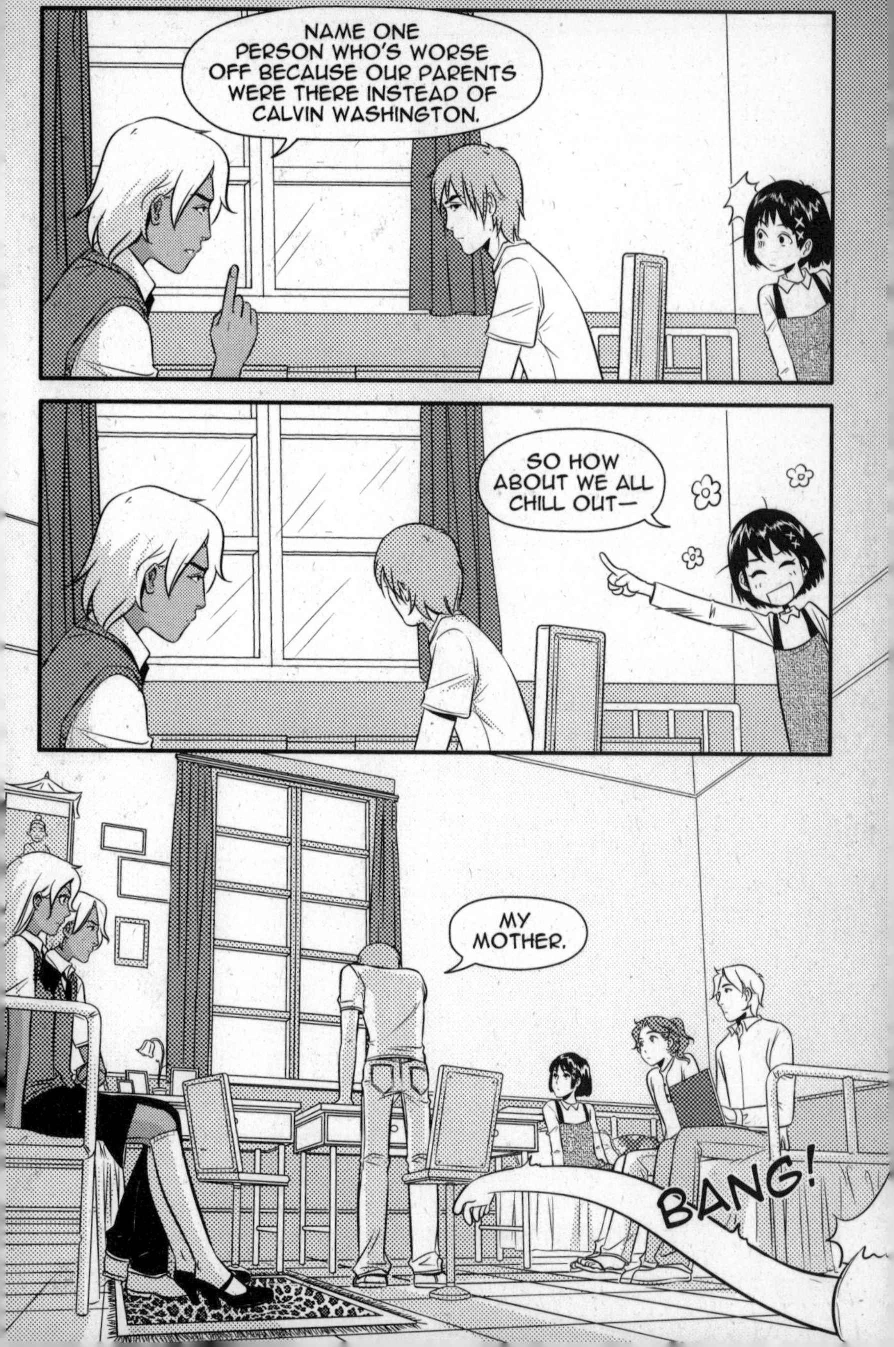
NAME ONE PERSON WHO'S WORSE OFF BECAUSE OUR PARENTS WERE THERE INSTEAD OF CALVIN WASHINGTON.
SO HOW ABOUT WE ALL CHILL OUT—
MY MOTHER.
BANG!

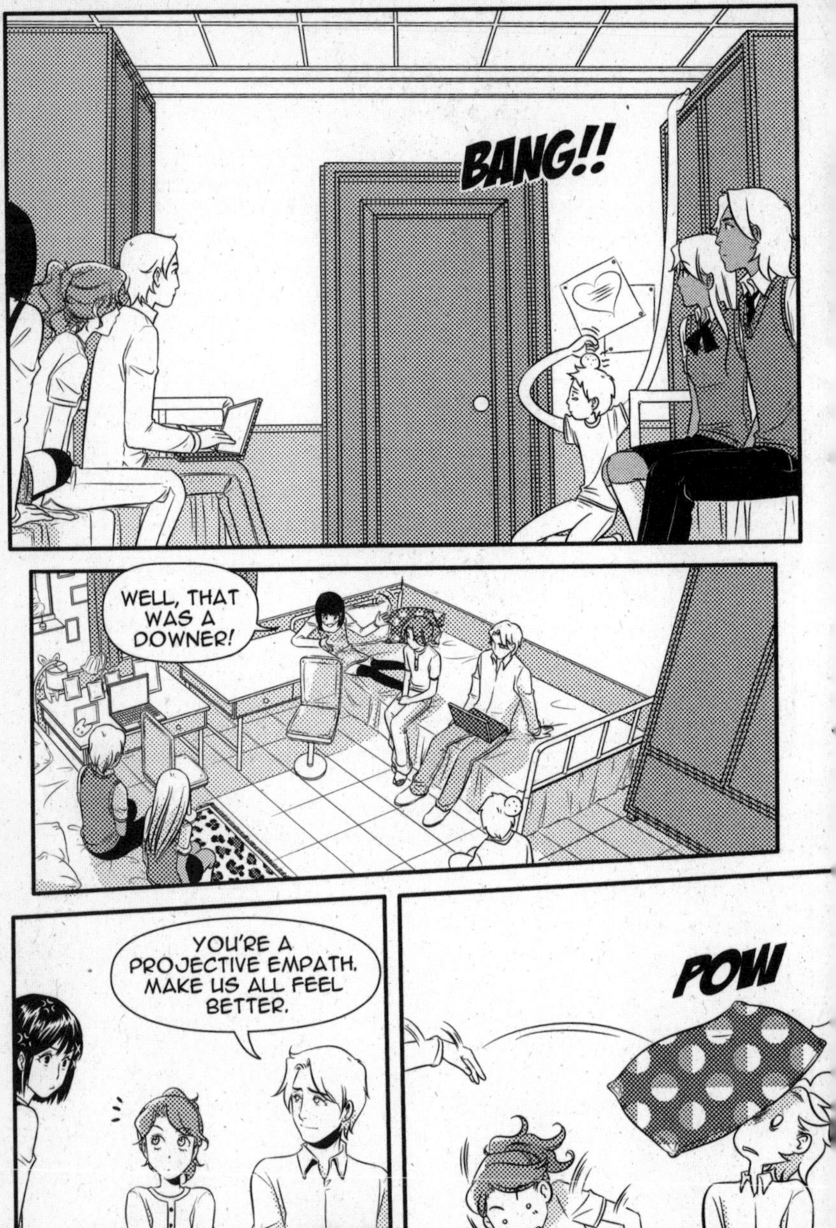
BANG!!
WELL, THAT WAS A DOWNER!
YOU'RE A PROJECTIVE EMPATH. MAKE US ALL FEEL BETTER.
POW

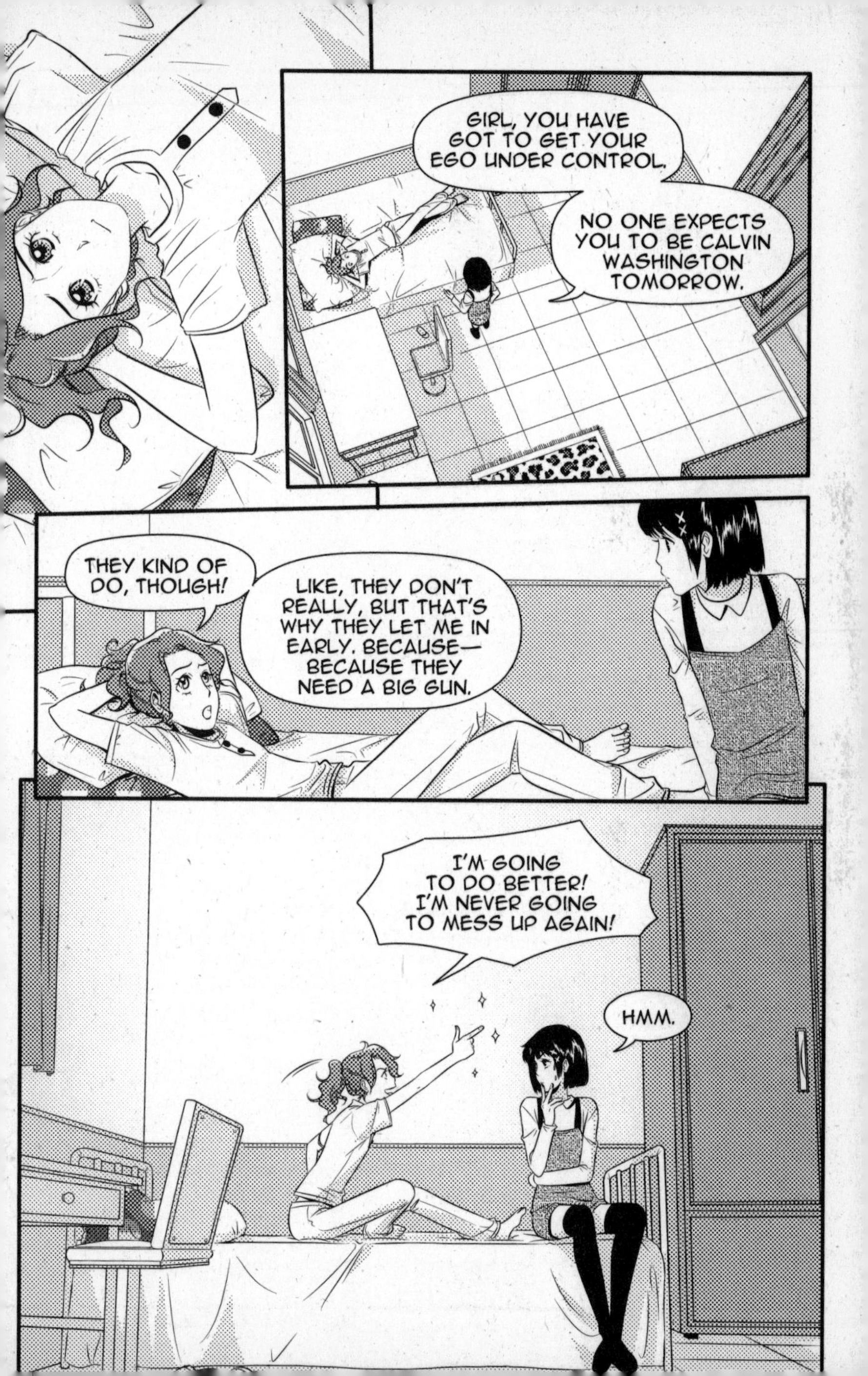
GIRL, YOU HAVE GOT TO GET YOUR EGO UNDER CONTROL.
NO ONE EXPECTS YOU TO BE CALVIN WASHINGTON TOMORROW.
THEY KIND OF DO, THOUGH!
LIKE, THEY DON'T REALLY, BUT THAT'S WHY THEY LET ME IN EARLY. BECAUSE— BECAUSE THEY NEED A BIG GUN.
I'M GOING TO DO BETTER! I'M NEVER GOING TO MESS UP AGAIN!
HMM.

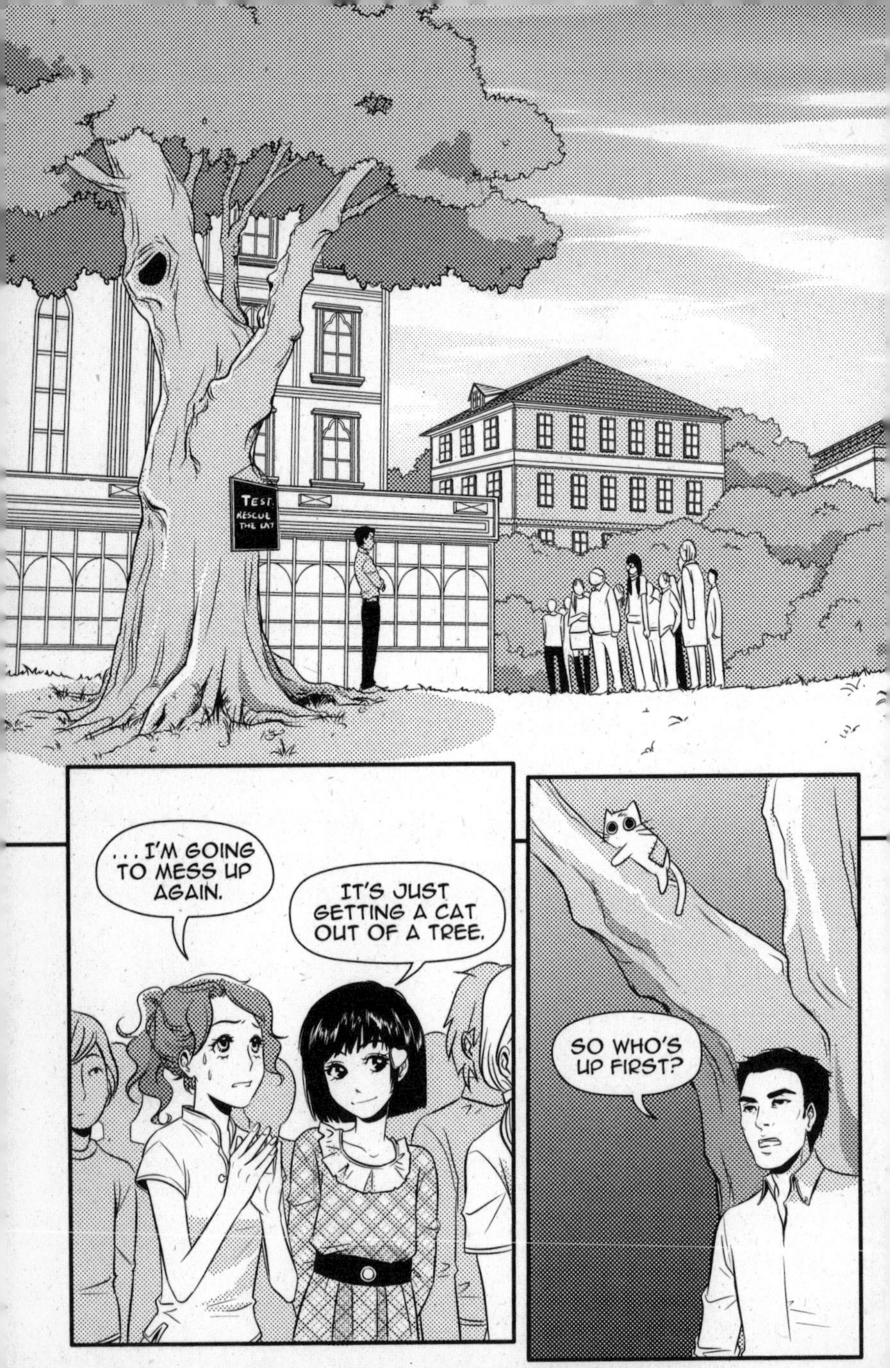
TEST.
RESCUE THE CAT
. . . I'M GOING TO MESS UP AGAIN.
IT'S JUST GETTING A CAT OUT OF A TREE.
SO WHO'S UP FIRST?

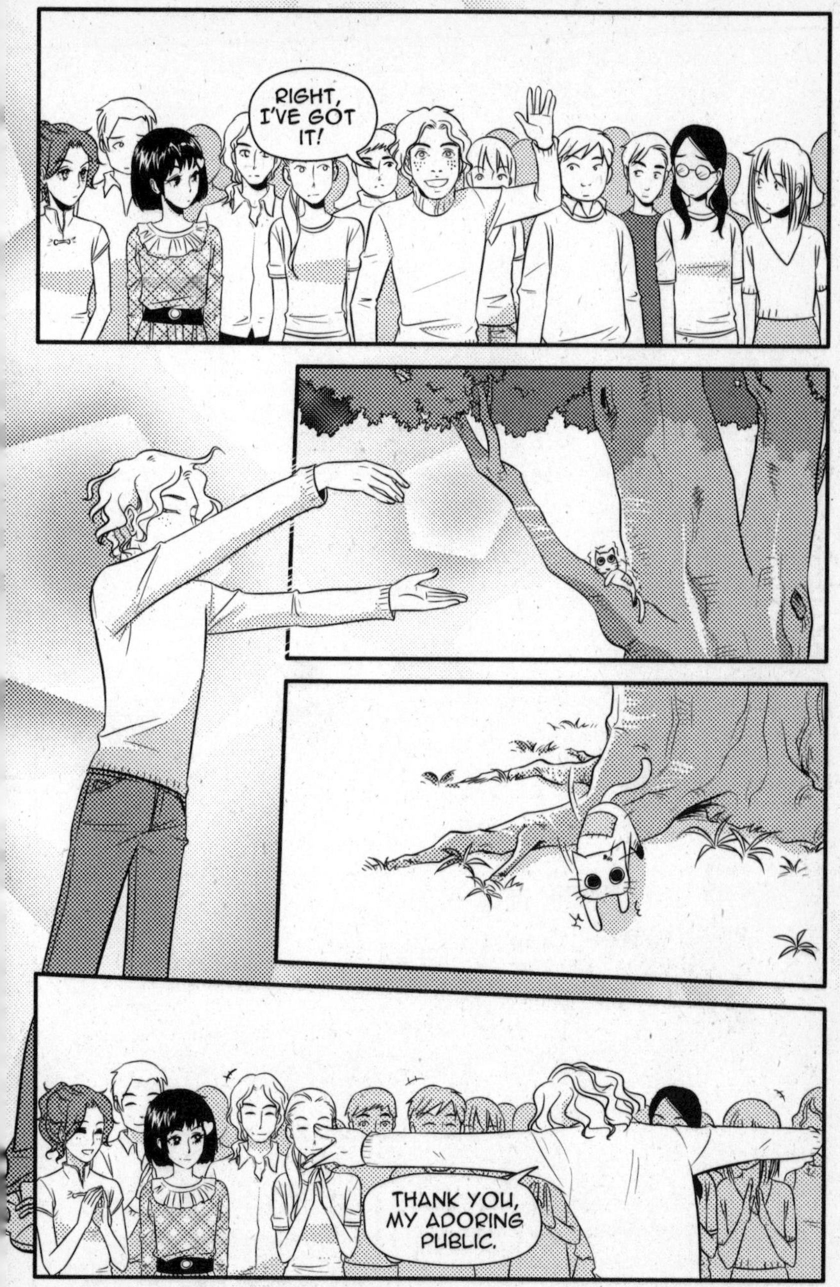
RIGHT, I'VE GOT IT!
THANK YOU, MY ADORING PUBLIC.

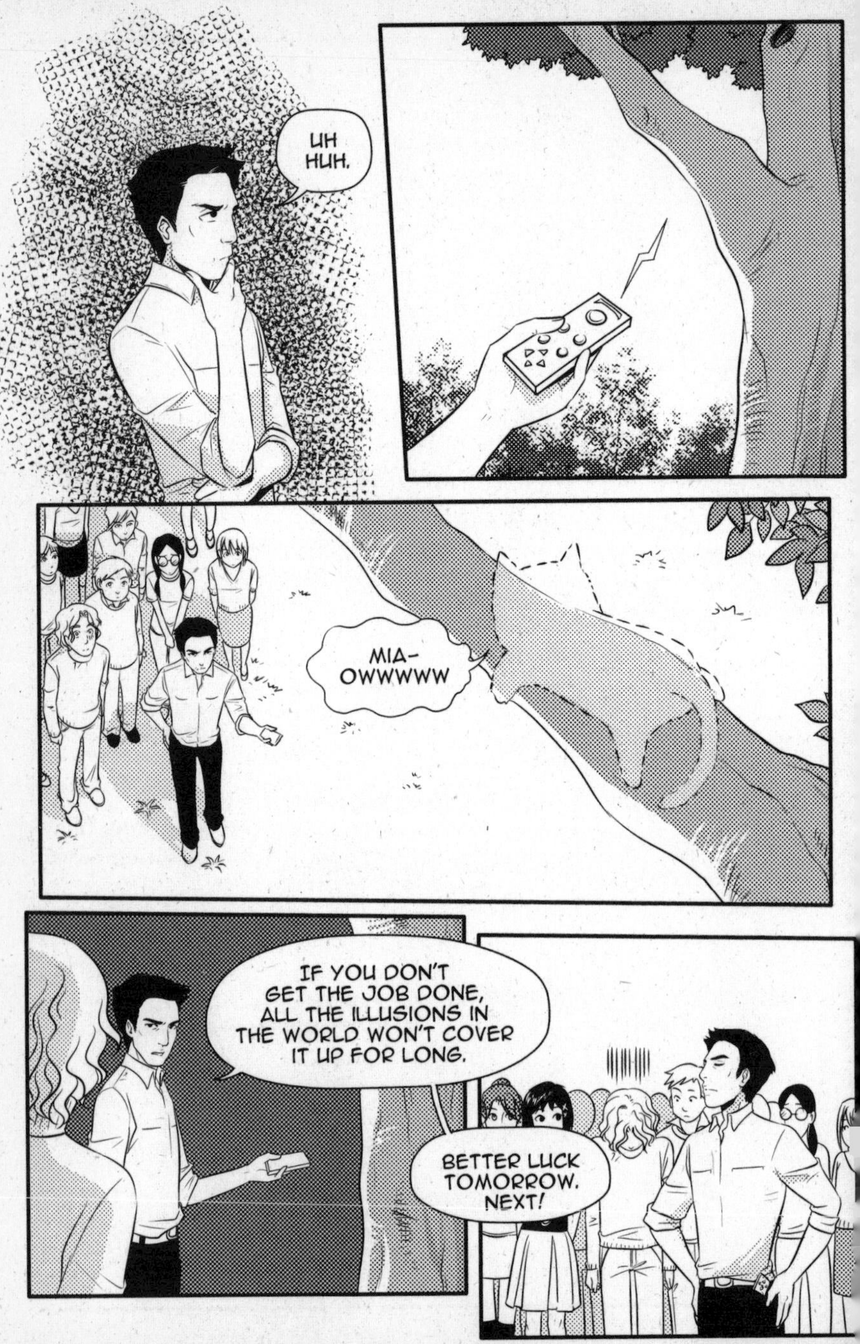
UH HUH.
MIA-OWWWWW
IF YOU DON'T GET THE JOB DONE, ALL THE ILLUSIONS IN THE WORLD WON'T COVER IT UP FOR LONG.
BETTER LUCK TOMORROW. NEXT!

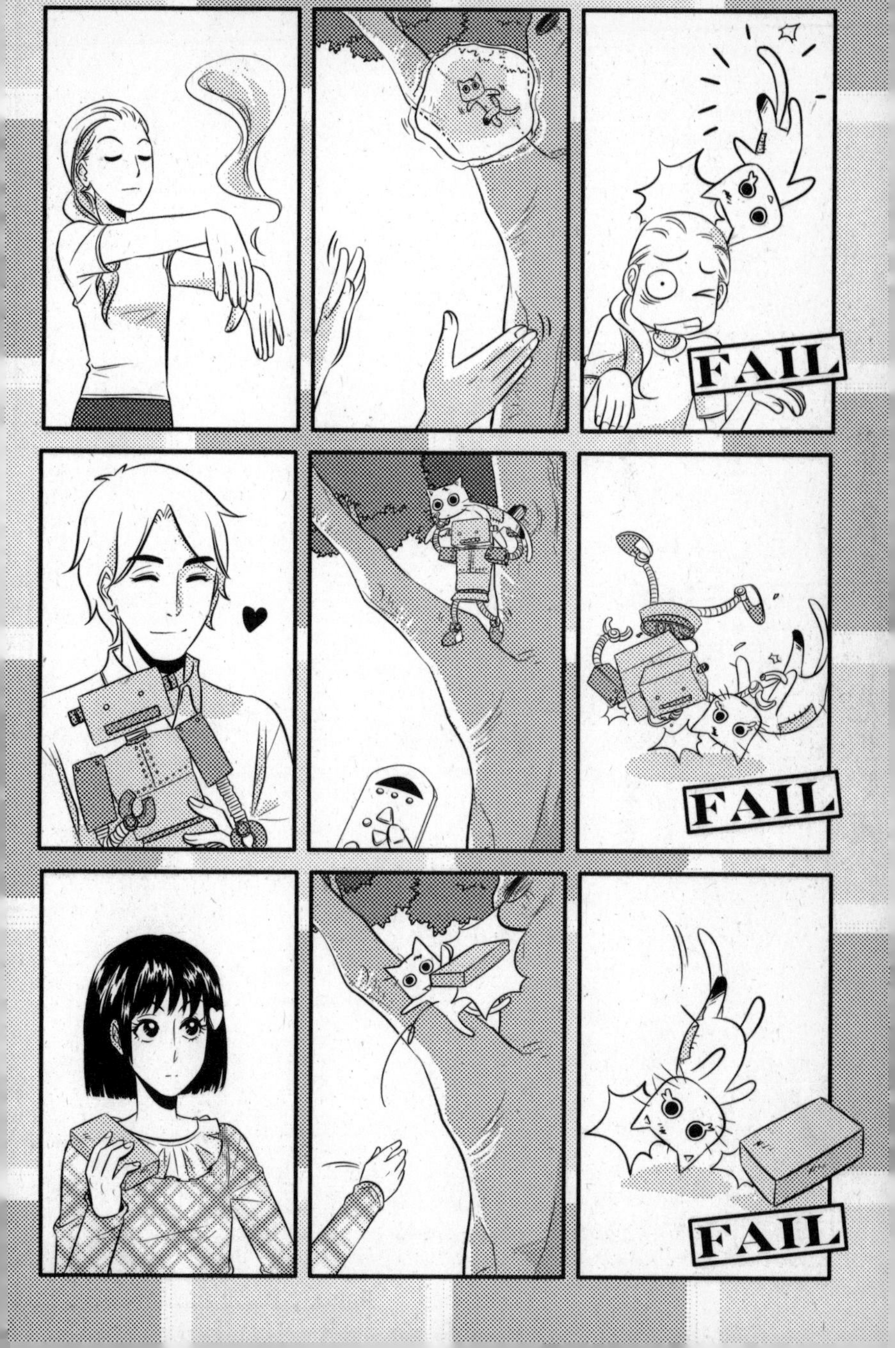
FAIL
FAIL
FAIL

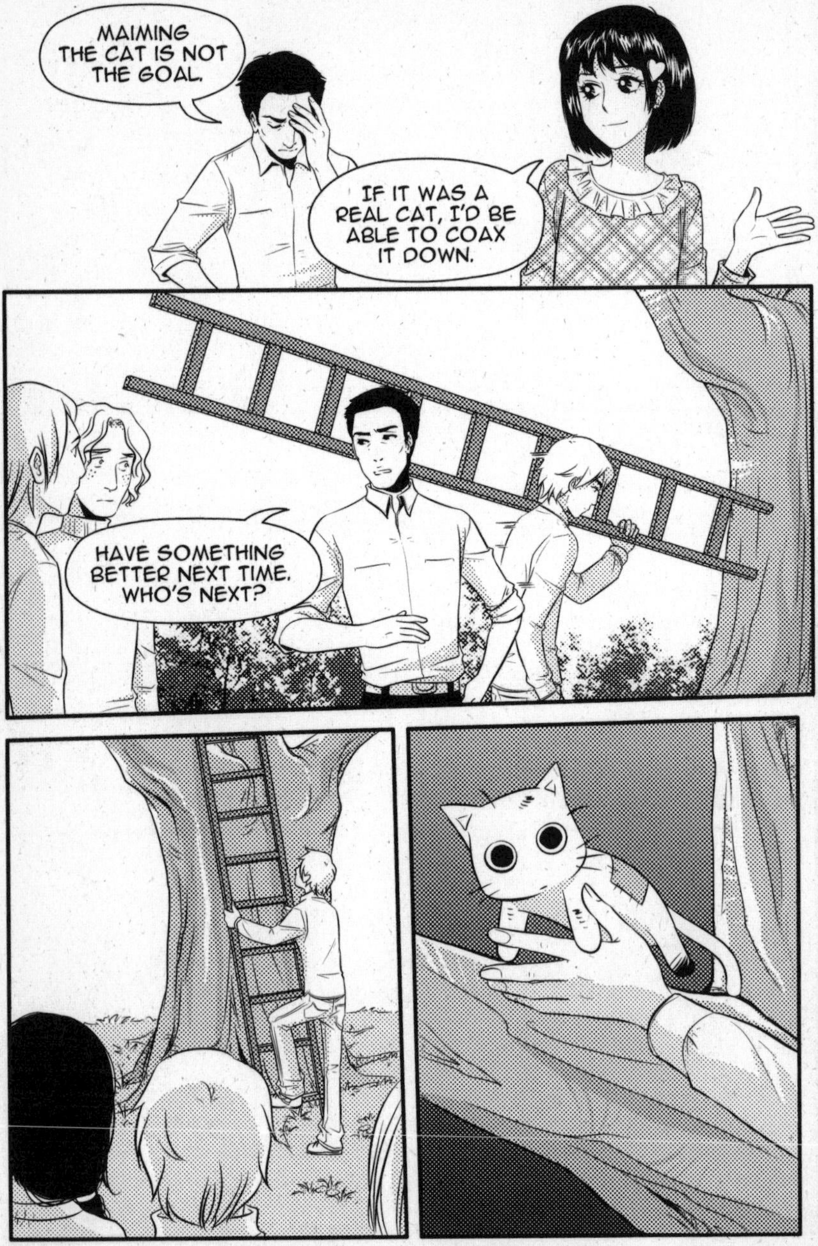
MAIMING THE CAT IS NOT THE GOAL.
IF IT WAS A REAL CAT, I'D BE ABLE TO COAX IT DOWN.
HAVE SOMETHING BETTER NEXT TIME. WHO'S NEXT?

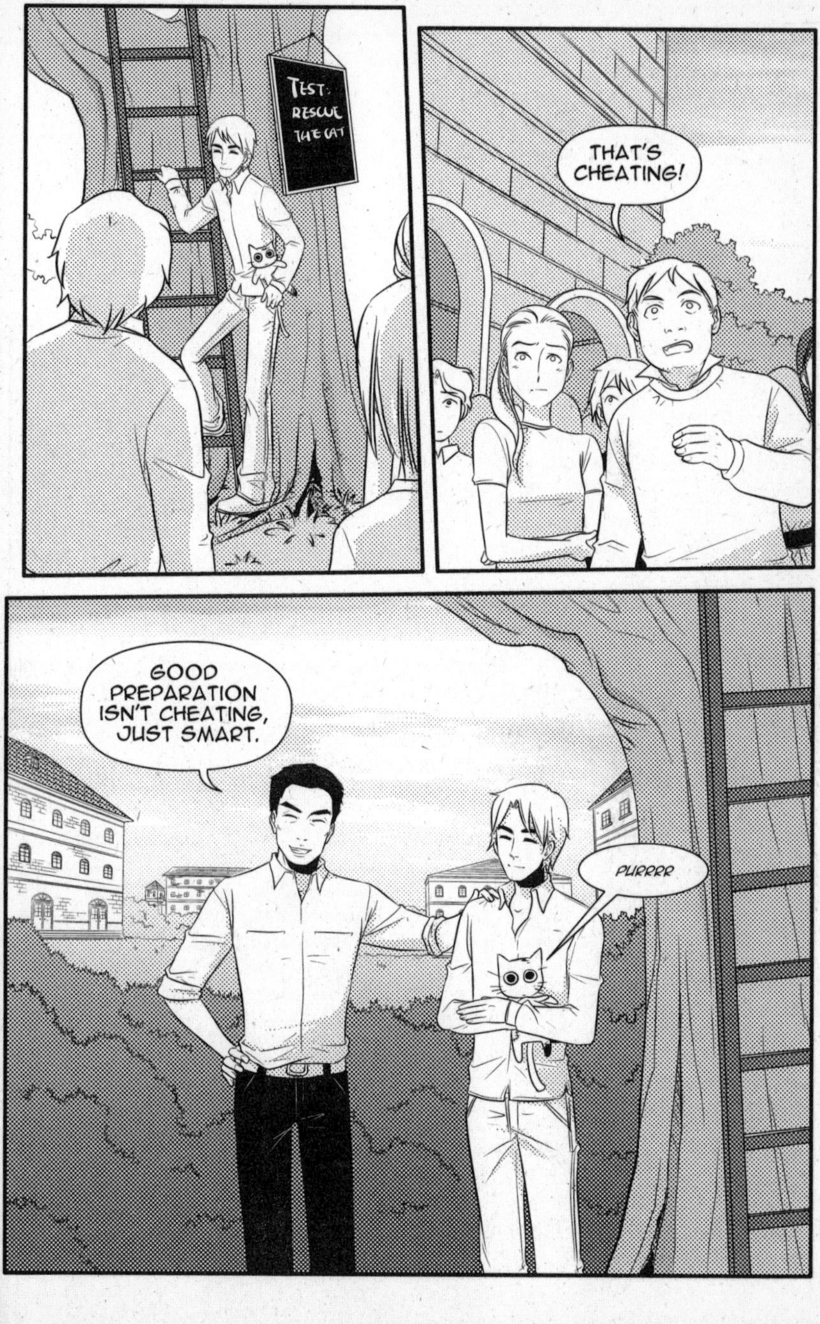
TEST: RESCUE THE CAT
THAT'S CHEATING!
GOOD PREPARATION ISN'T CHEATING, JUST SMART.
PURRRR

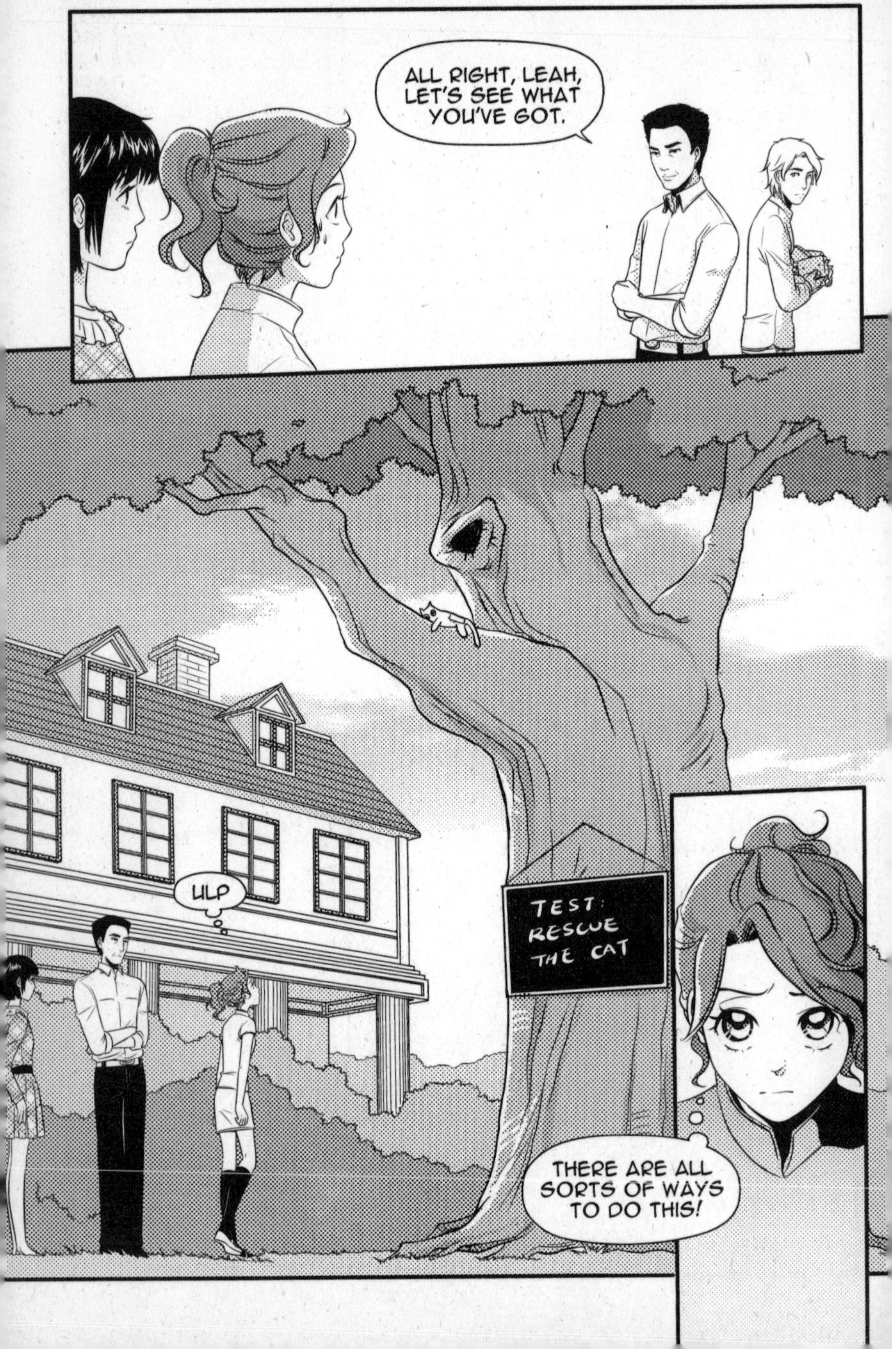
ALL RIGHT, LEAH, LET'S SEE WHAT YOU'VE GOT.
ULP
TEST: RESCUE THE CAT
THERE ARE ALL SORTS OF WAYS TO DO THIS!

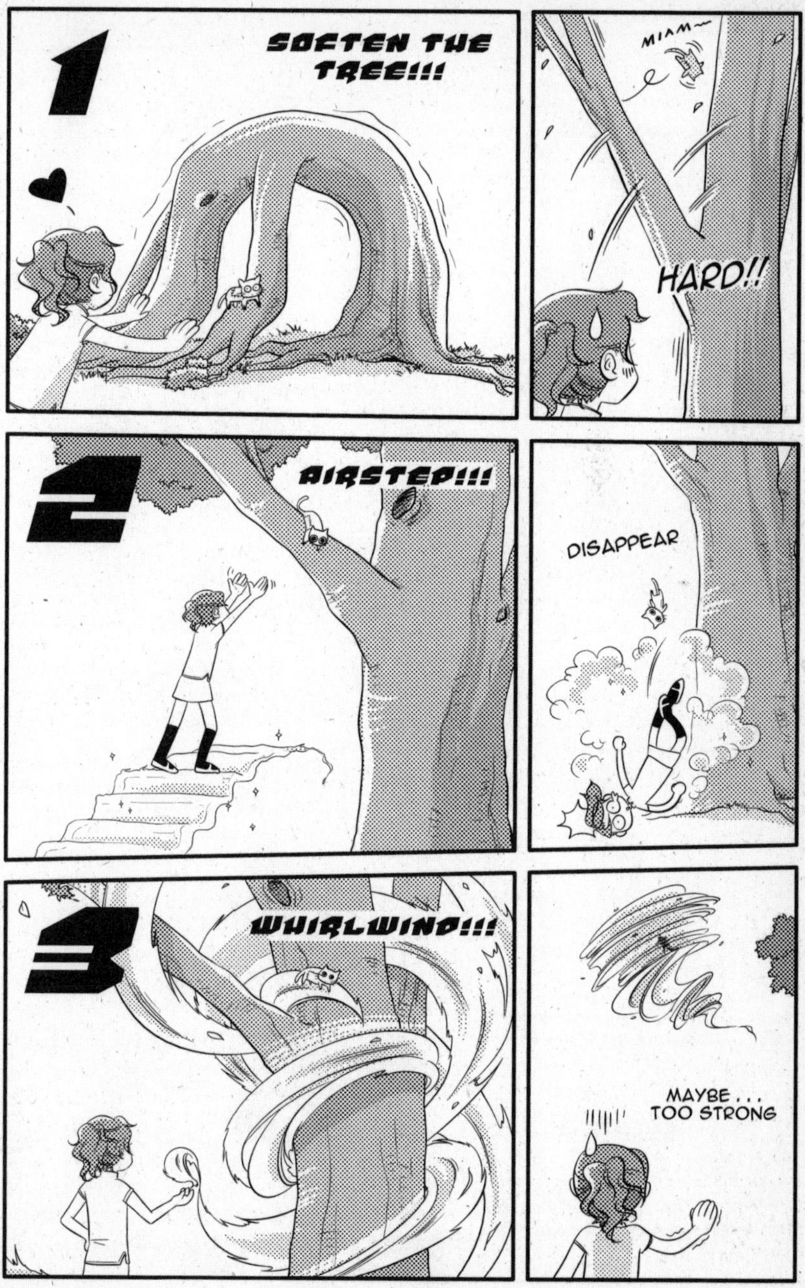
1
SOFTEN THE TREE!!!
MIAM~~
HARD!!
2
AIRSTEP!!!
DISAPPEAR
3
WHIRLWIND!!!
MAYBE . . .
TOO STRONG

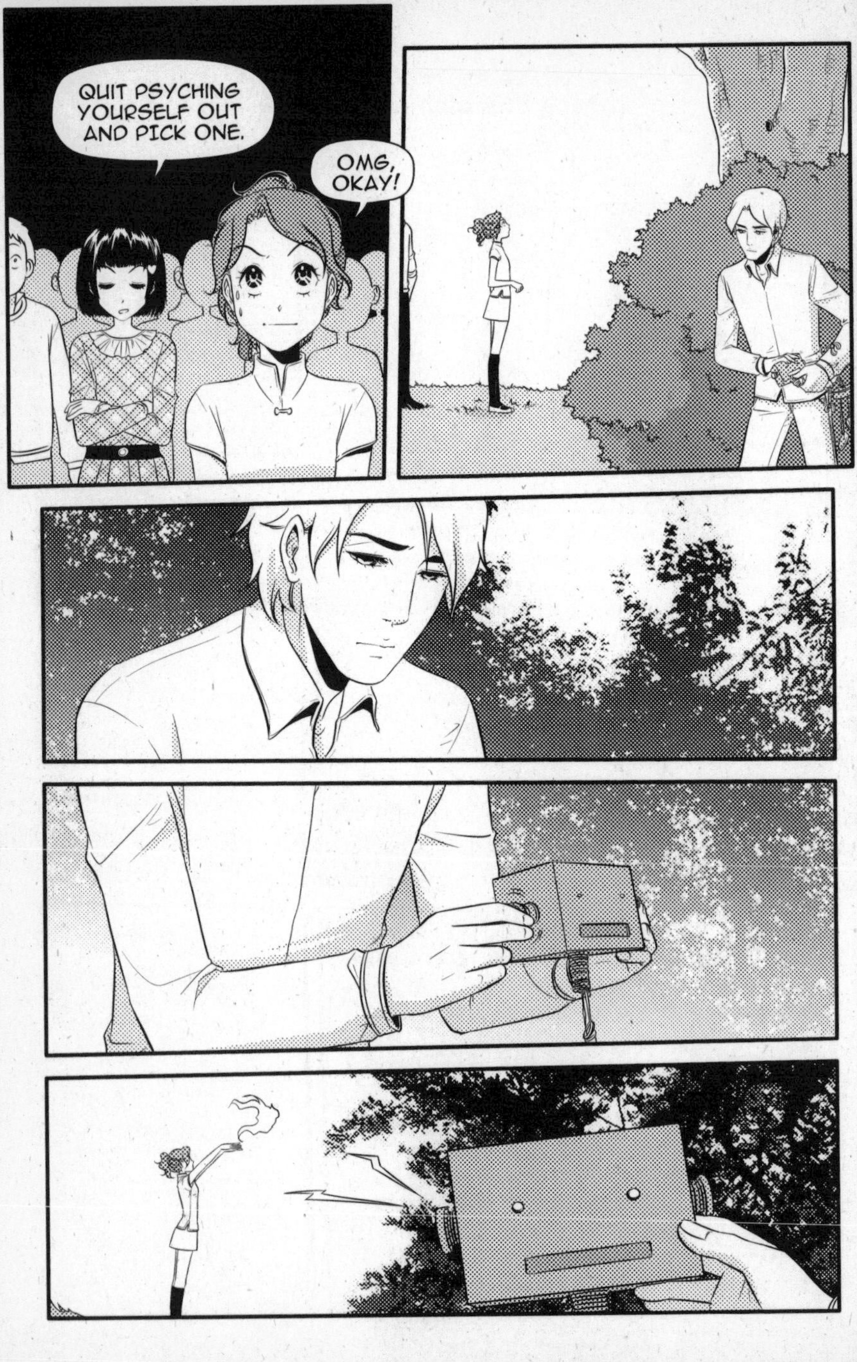
QUIT PSYCHING YOURSELF OUT AND PICK ONE.
OMG, OKAY!

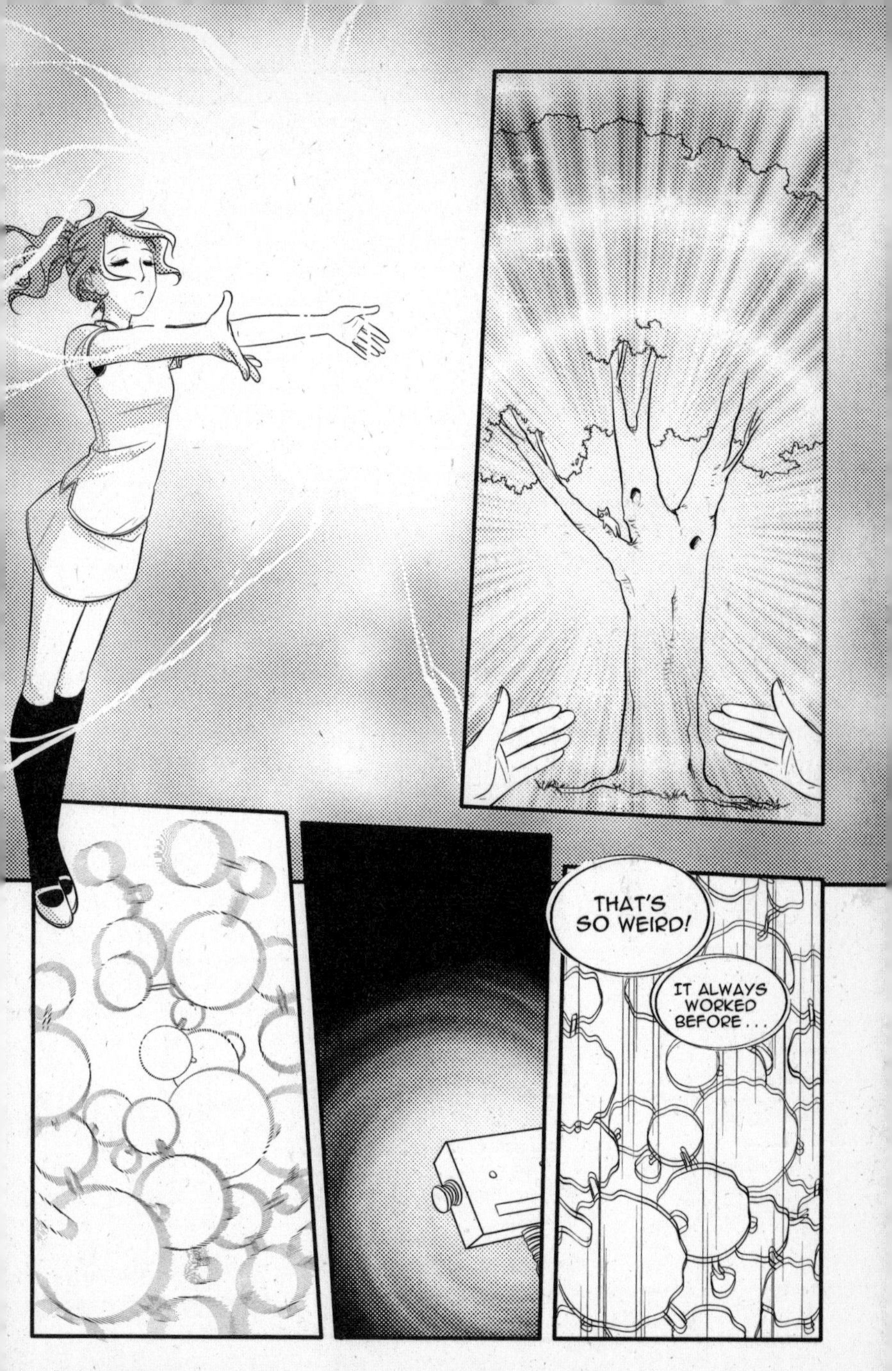
THAT'S SO WEIRD!
IT ALWAYS WORKED BEFORE...

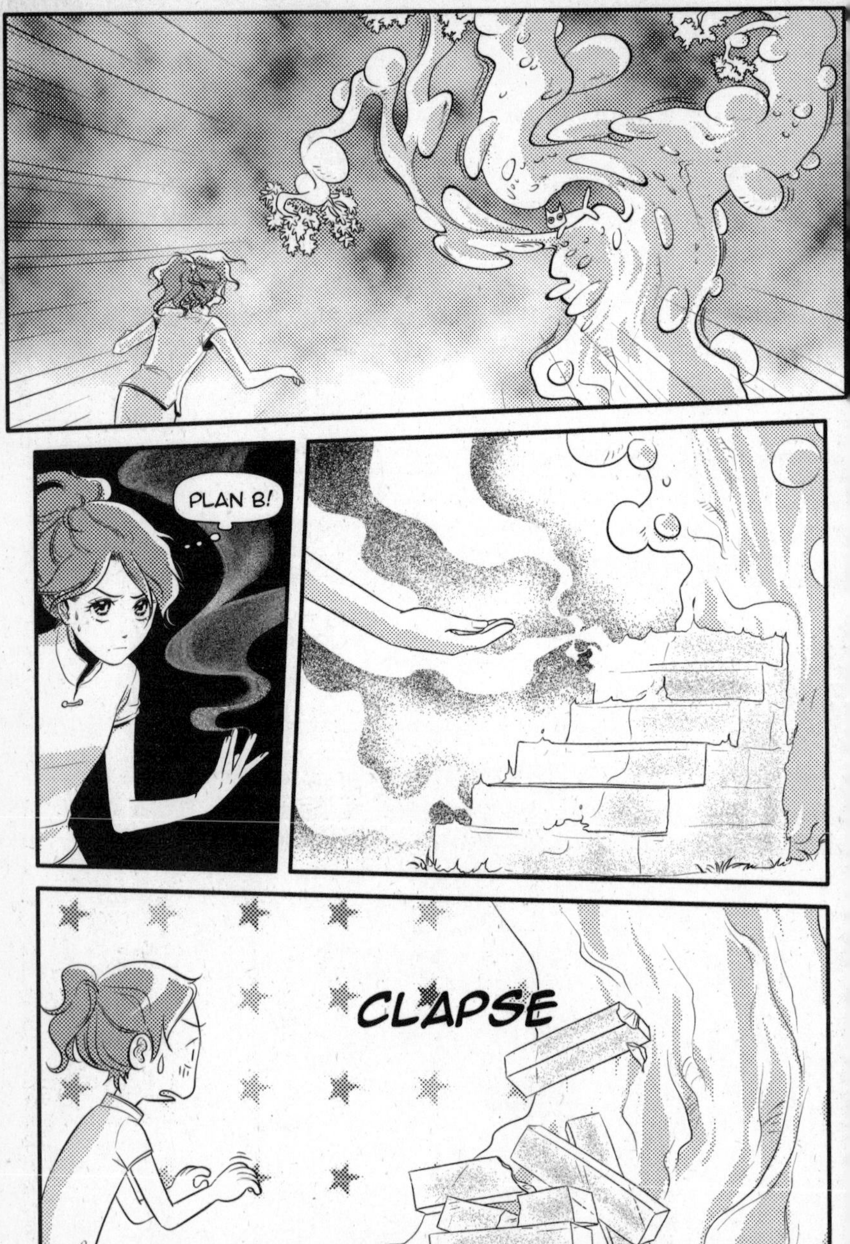
PLAN B!
...
CLAPSE

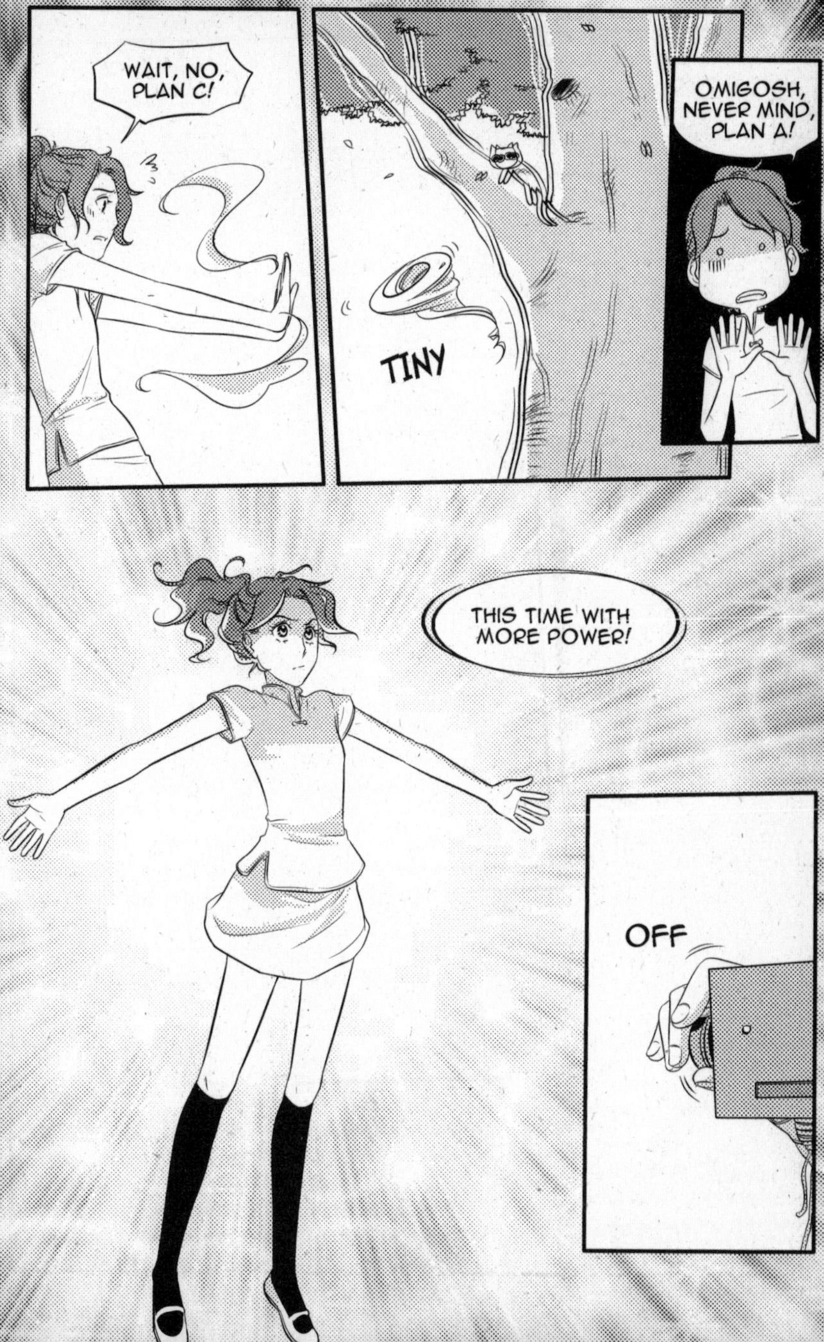
WAIT, NO, PLAN C!
TINY
OMIGOSH, NEVER MIND, PLAN A!
THIS TIME WITH MORE POWER!
OFF

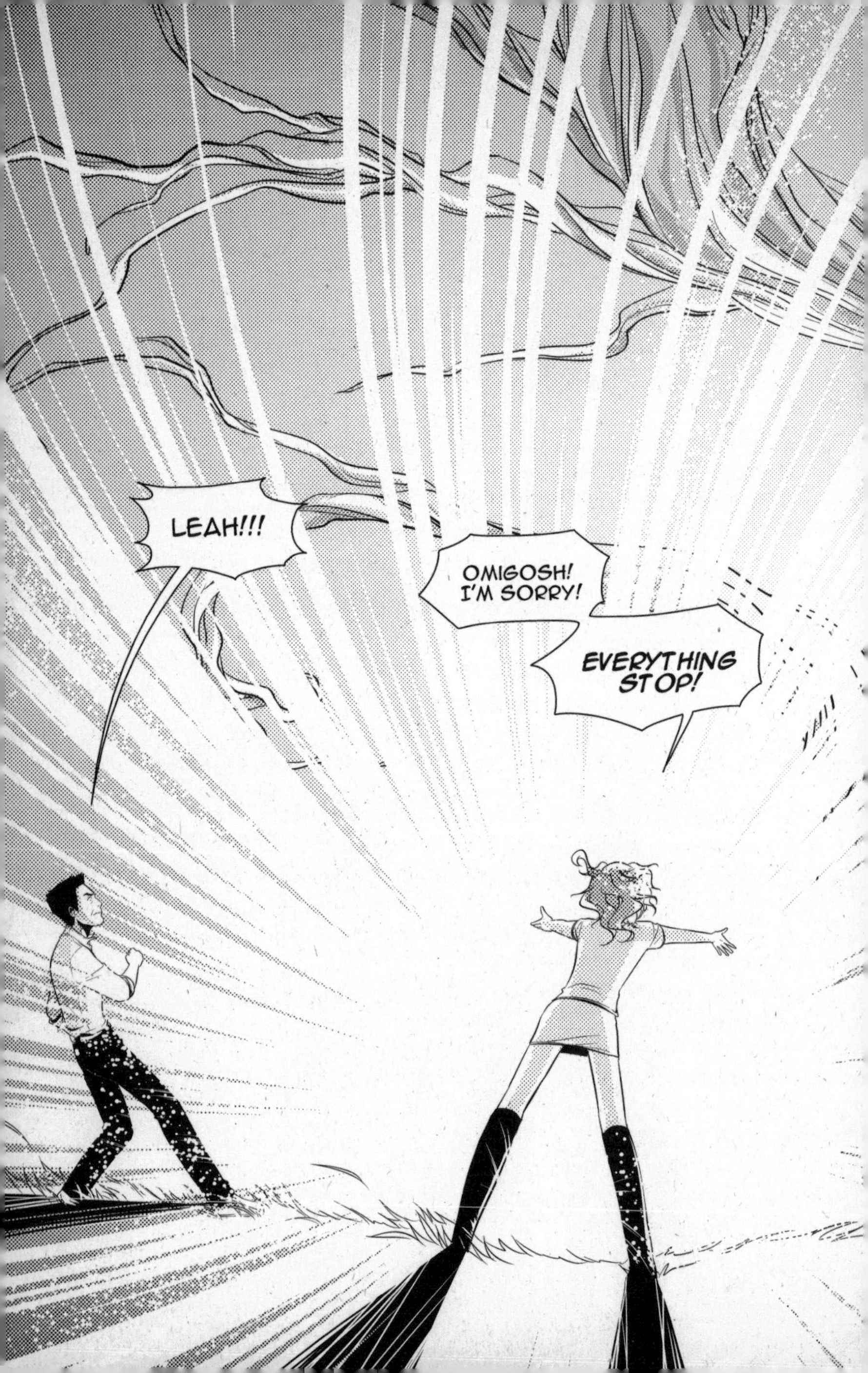
LEAH!!!
OMIGOSH! I'M SORRY!
EVERYTHING STOP!

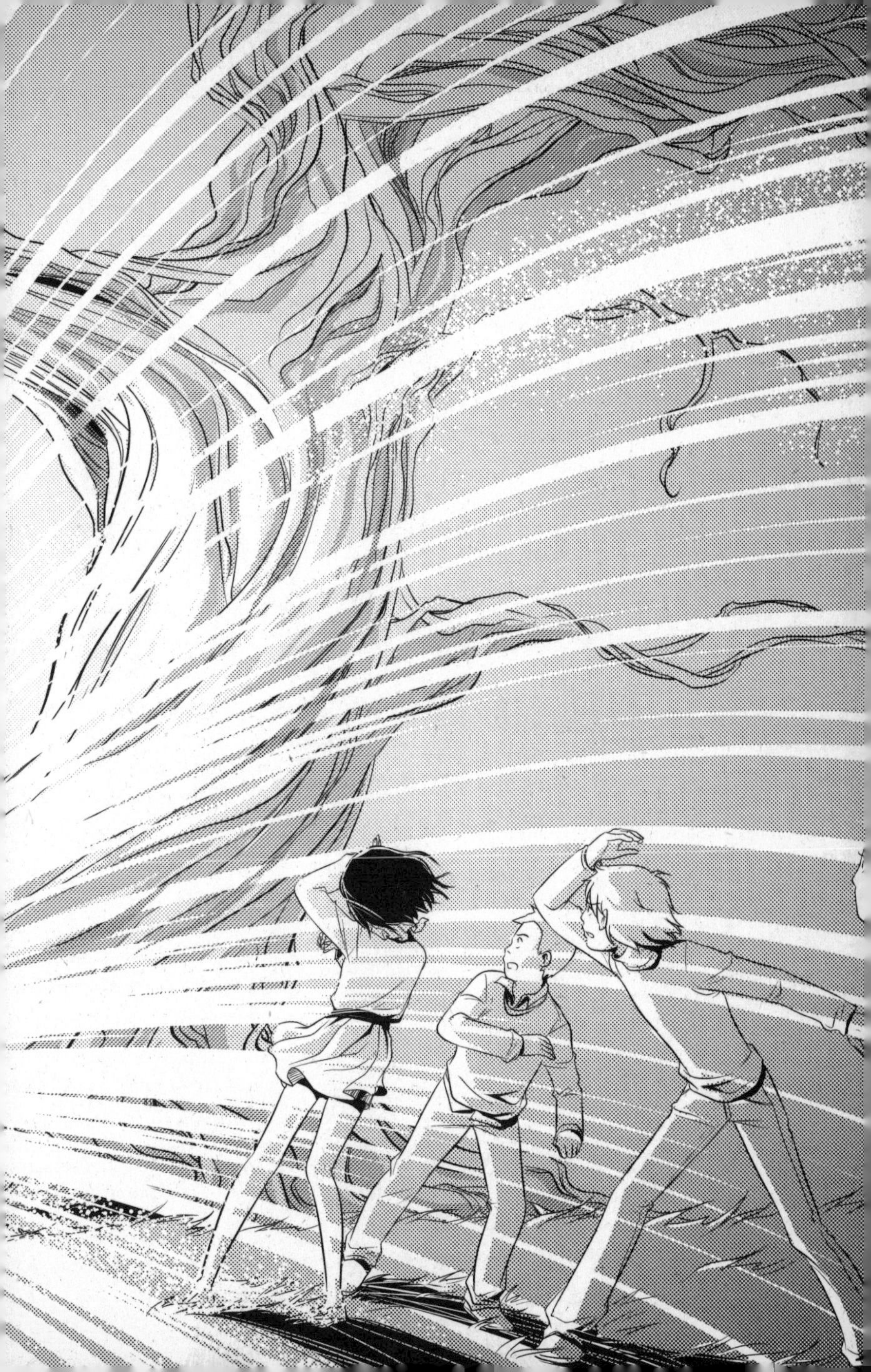

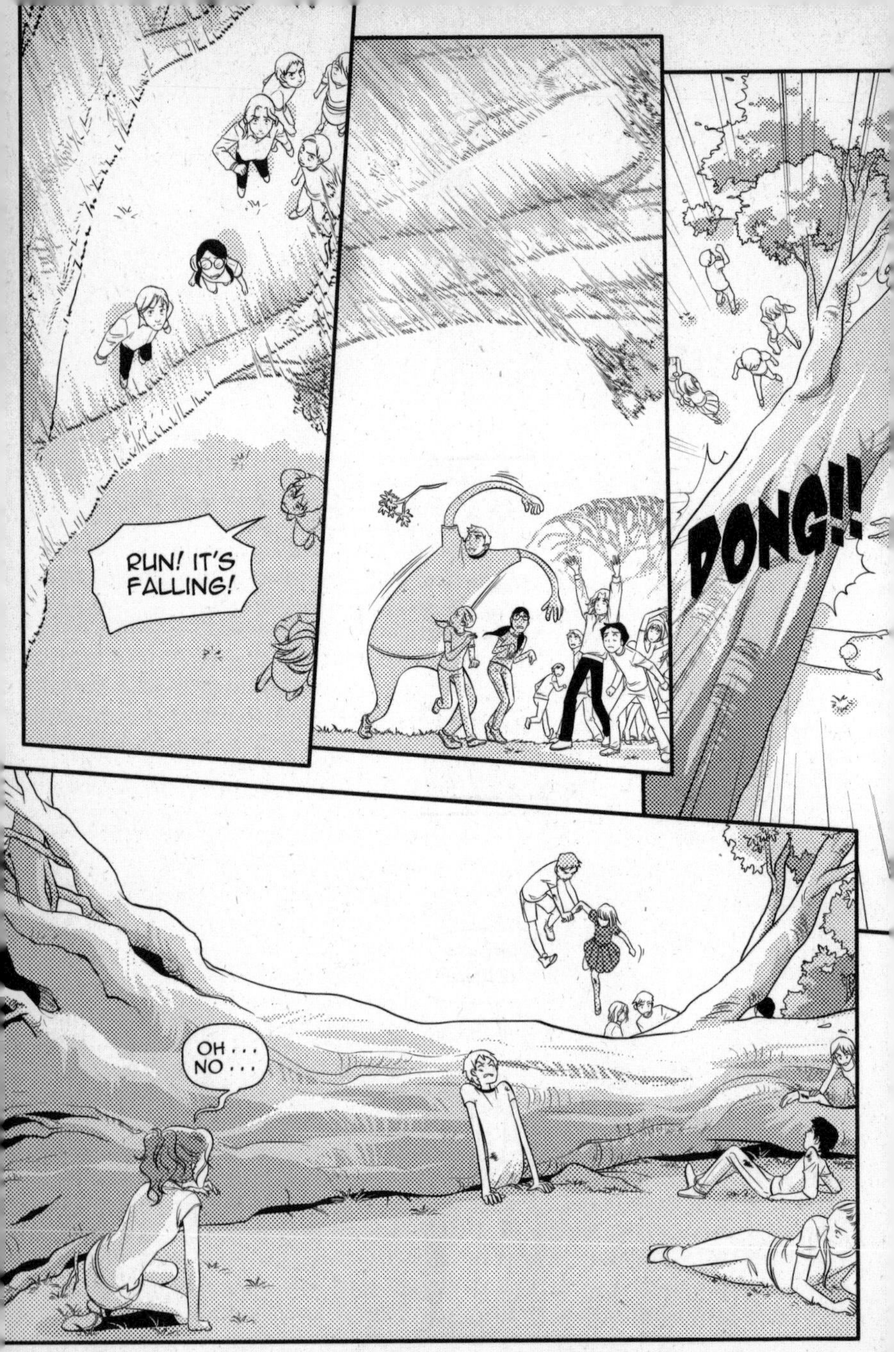
RUN! IT'S FALLING!
DONG!!
OH . . . NO . . .

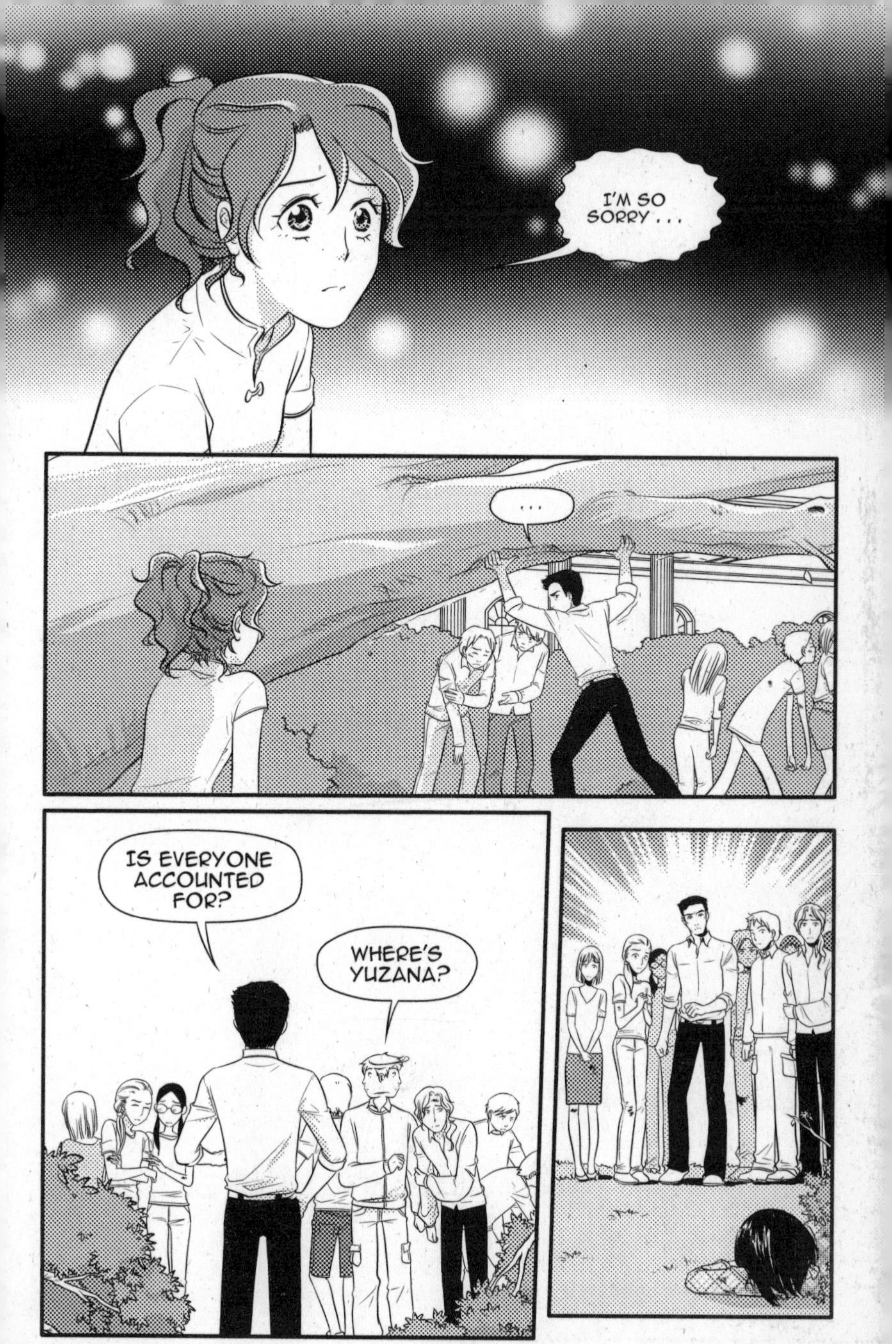
I'M SO SORRY . . .
. . .
IS EVERYONE ACCOUNTED FOR?
WHERE'S YUZANA?

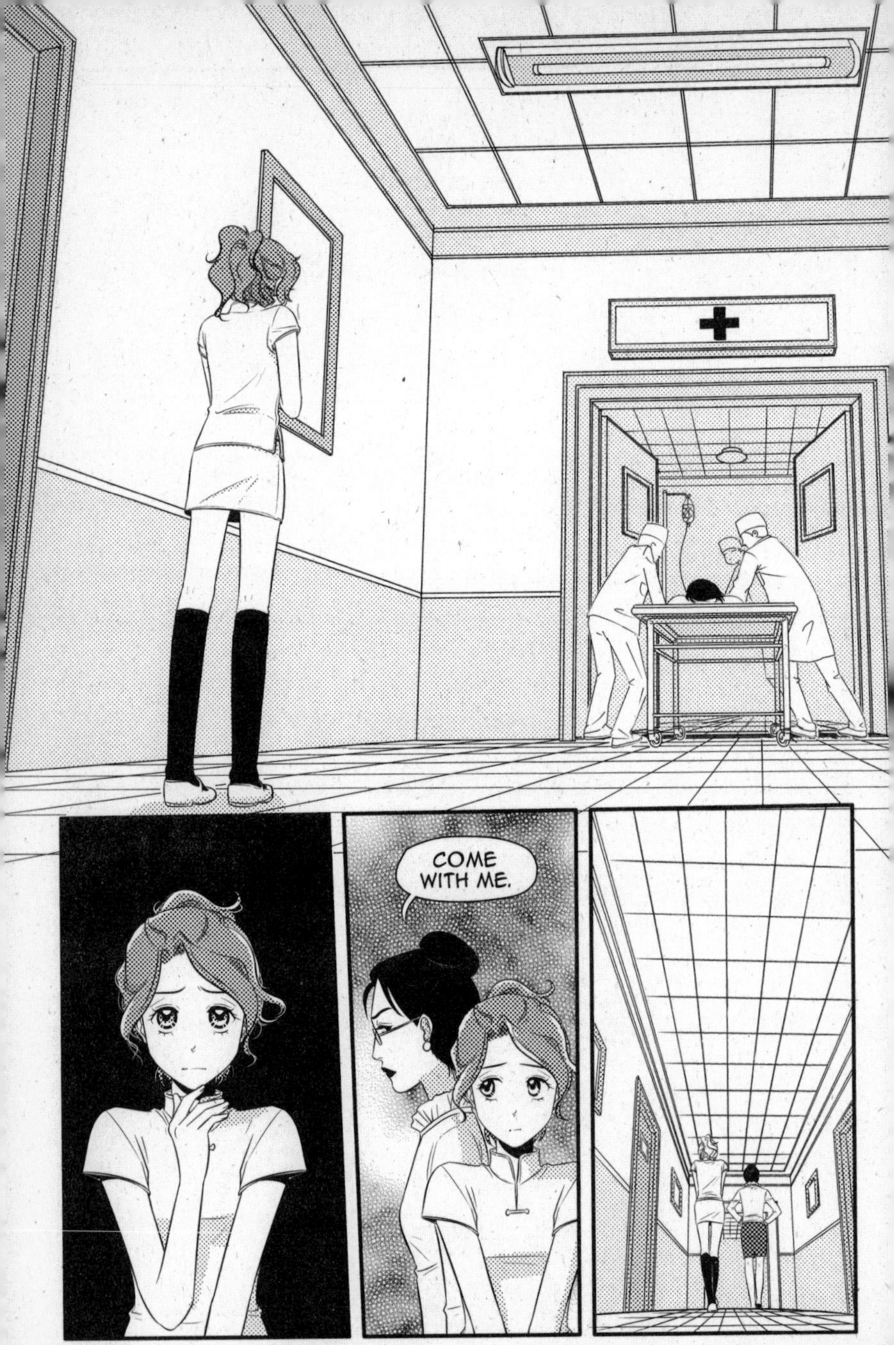
COME WITH ME.

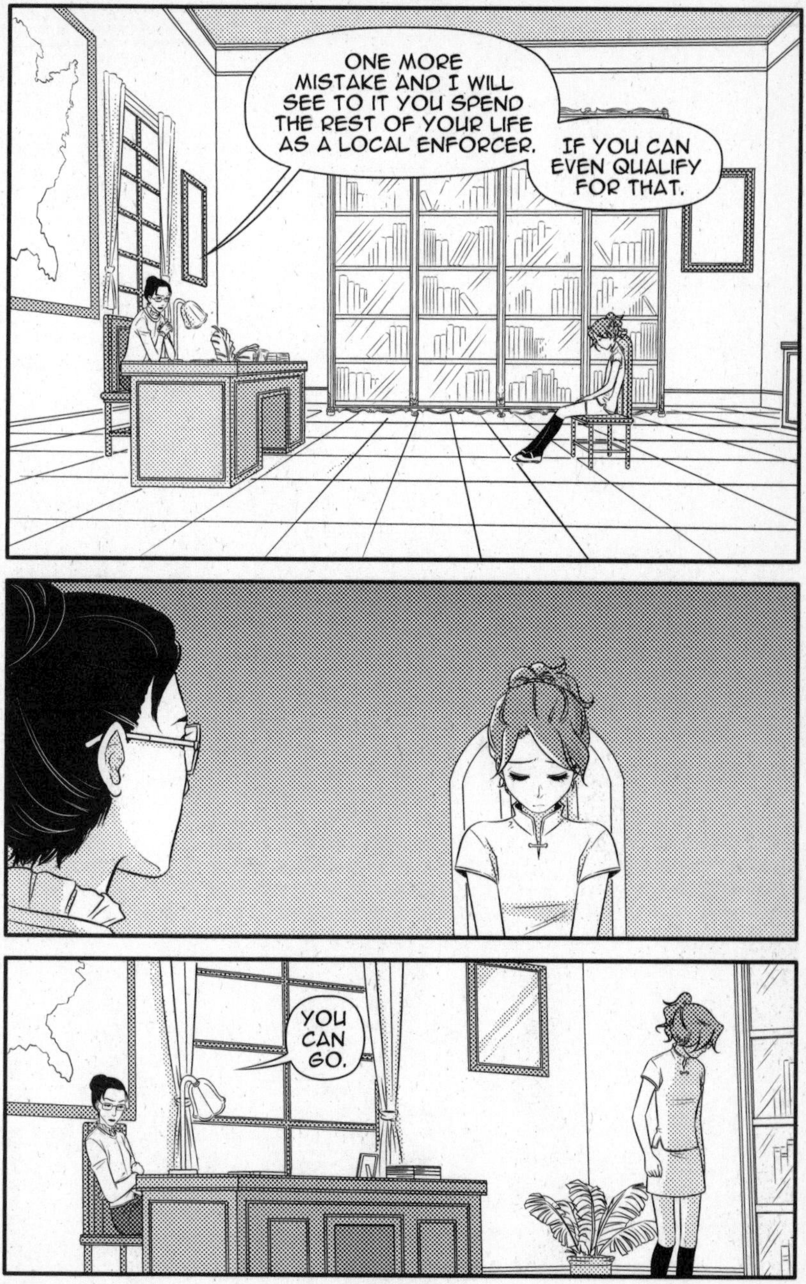
ONE MORE MISTAKE AND I WILL SEE TO IT YOU SPEND THE REST OF YOUR LIFE AS A LOCAL ENFORCER.
IF YOU CAN EVEN QUALIFY FOR THAT.
YOU CAN GO.

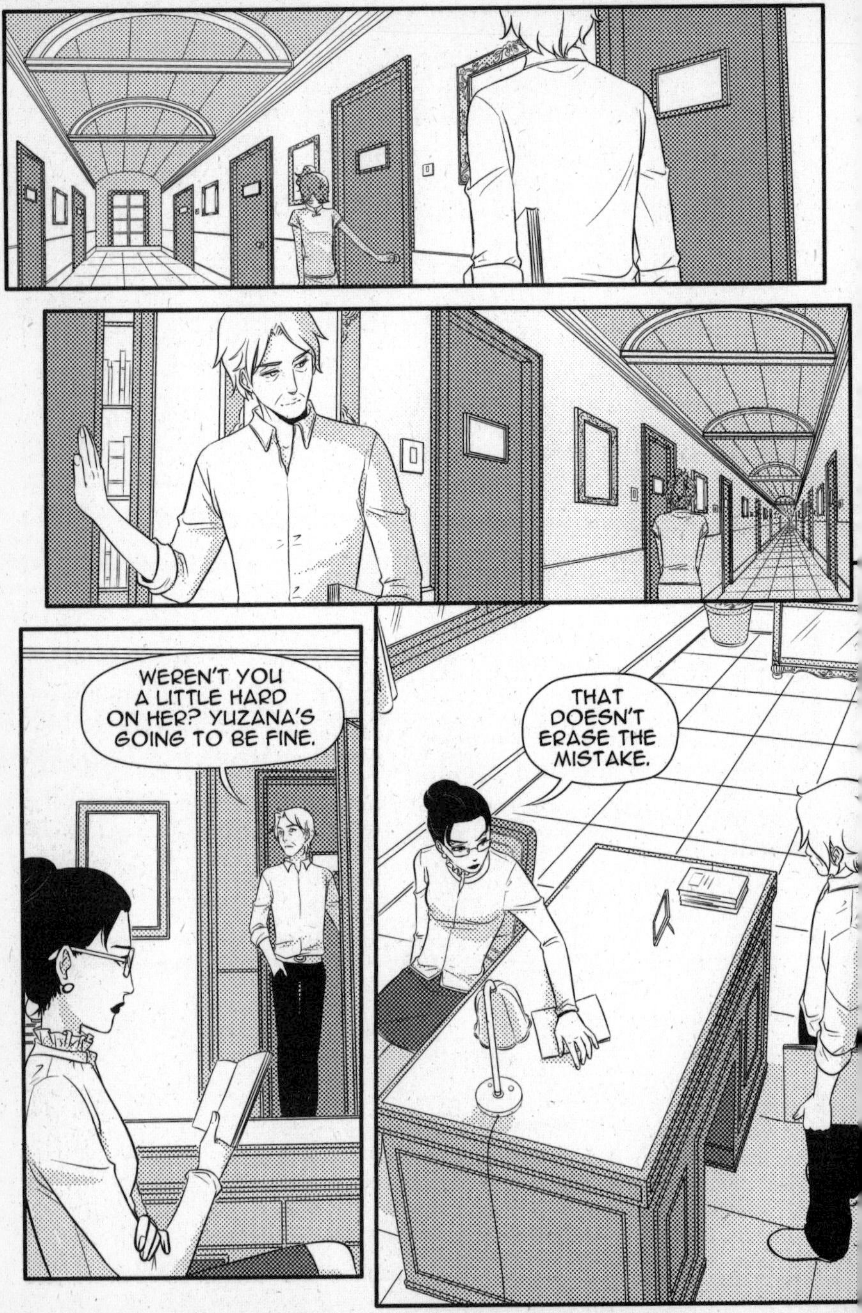
WEREN'T YOU A LITTLE HARD ON HER? YUZANA'S GOING TO BE FINE.
THAT DOESN'T ERASE THE MISTAKE.

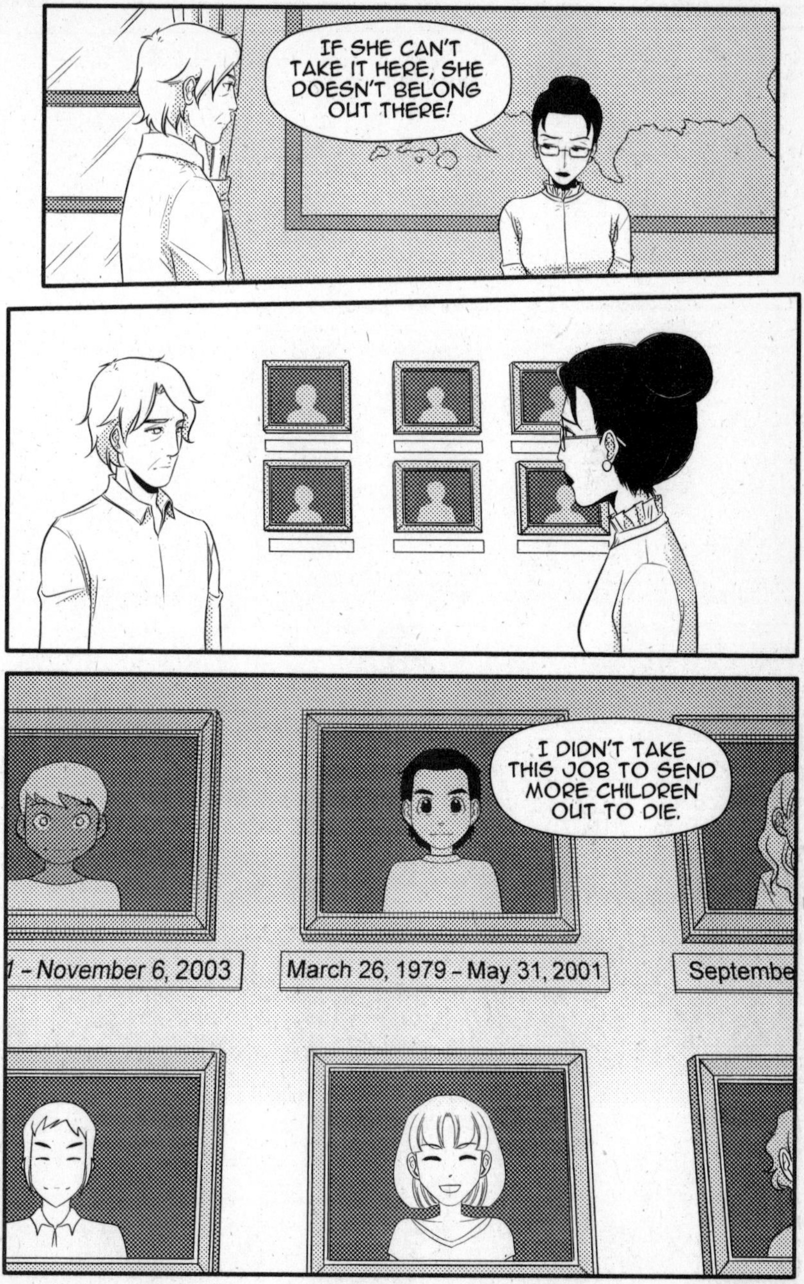
IF SHE CAN'T TAKE IT HERE, SHE DOESN'T BELONG OUT THERE!
I DIDN'T TAKE THIS JOB TO SEND MORE CHILDREN OUT TO DIE.
- November 6, 2003
March 26, 1979 - May 31, 2001
Septembe

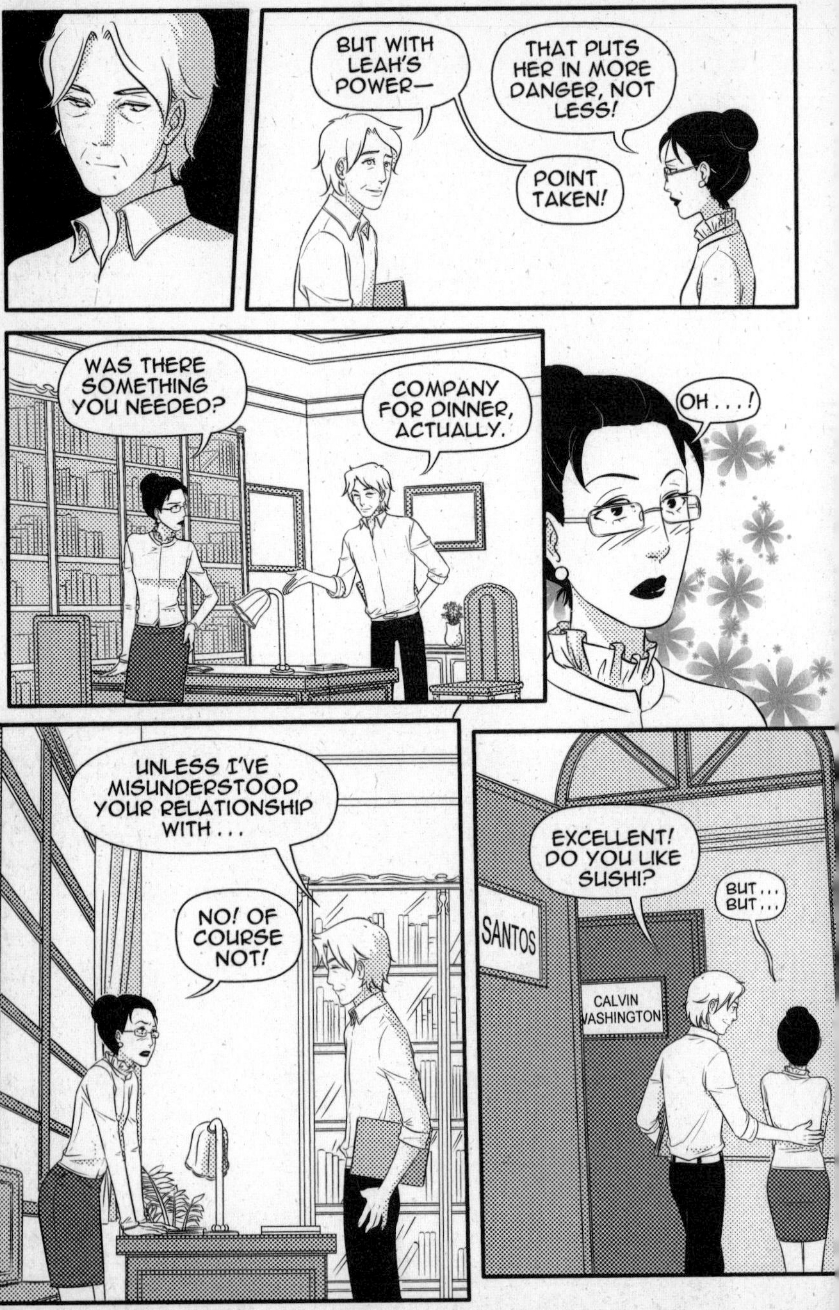
BUT WITH LEAH'S POWER—
THAT PUTS HER IN MORE DANGER, NOT LESS!
POINT TAKEN!
WAS THERE SOMETHING YOU NEEDED?
COMPANY FOR DINNER, ACTUALLY.
OH . . . !
UNLESS I'VE MISUNDERSTOOD YOUR RELATIONSHIP WITH . . .
NO! OF COURSE NOT!
EXCELLENT! DO YOU LIKE SUSHI?
SANTOS
CALVIN WASHINGTON
BUT . . . BUT . . .

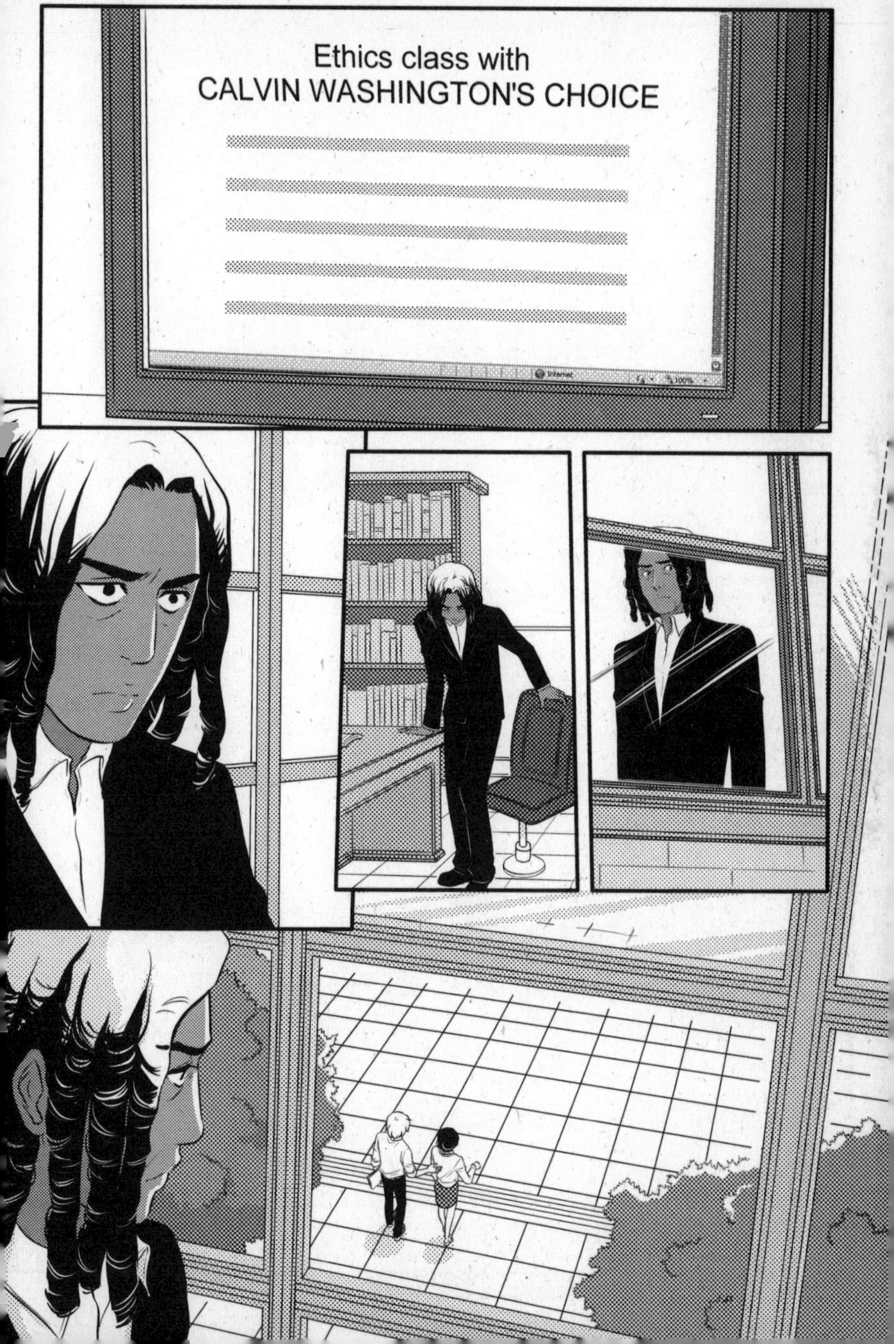
Ethics class with
CALVIN WASHINGTON'S CHOICE
Internet
100%

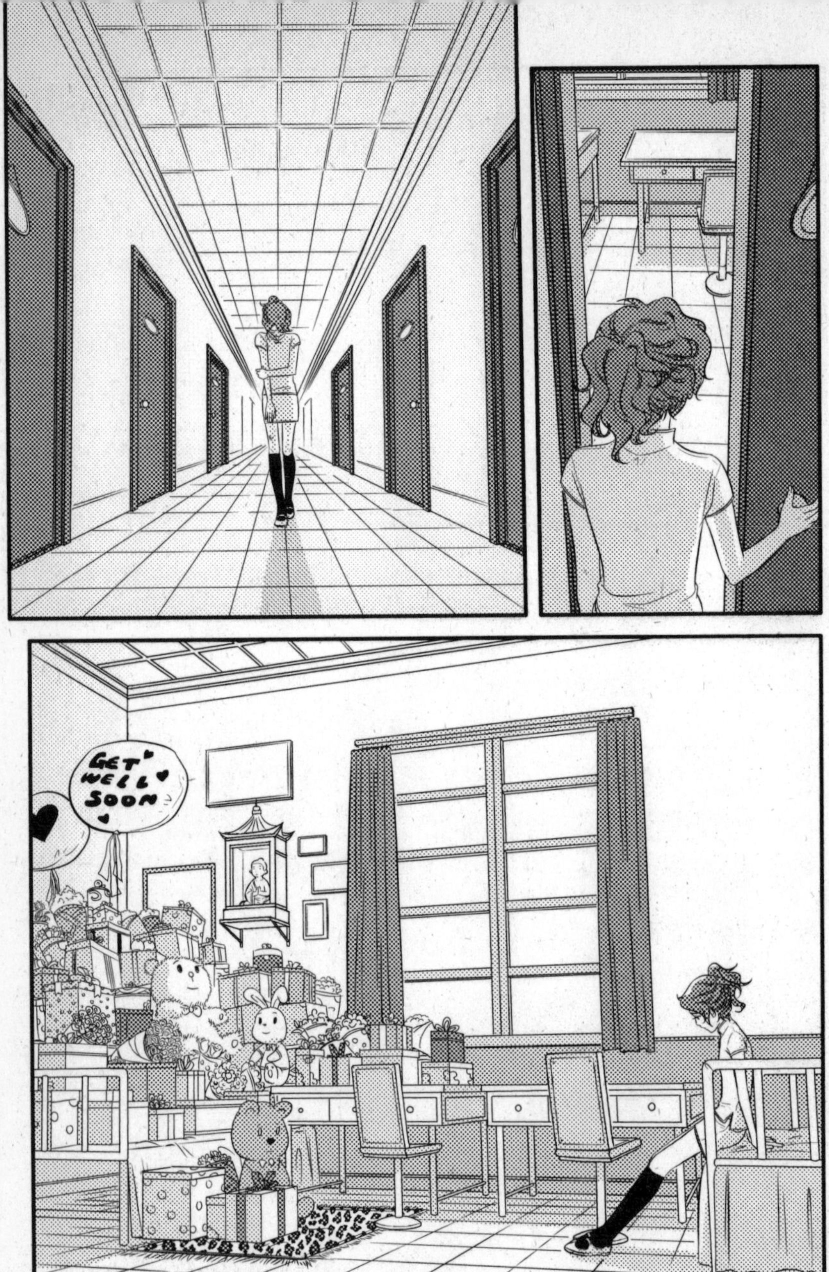
GET WELL SOON

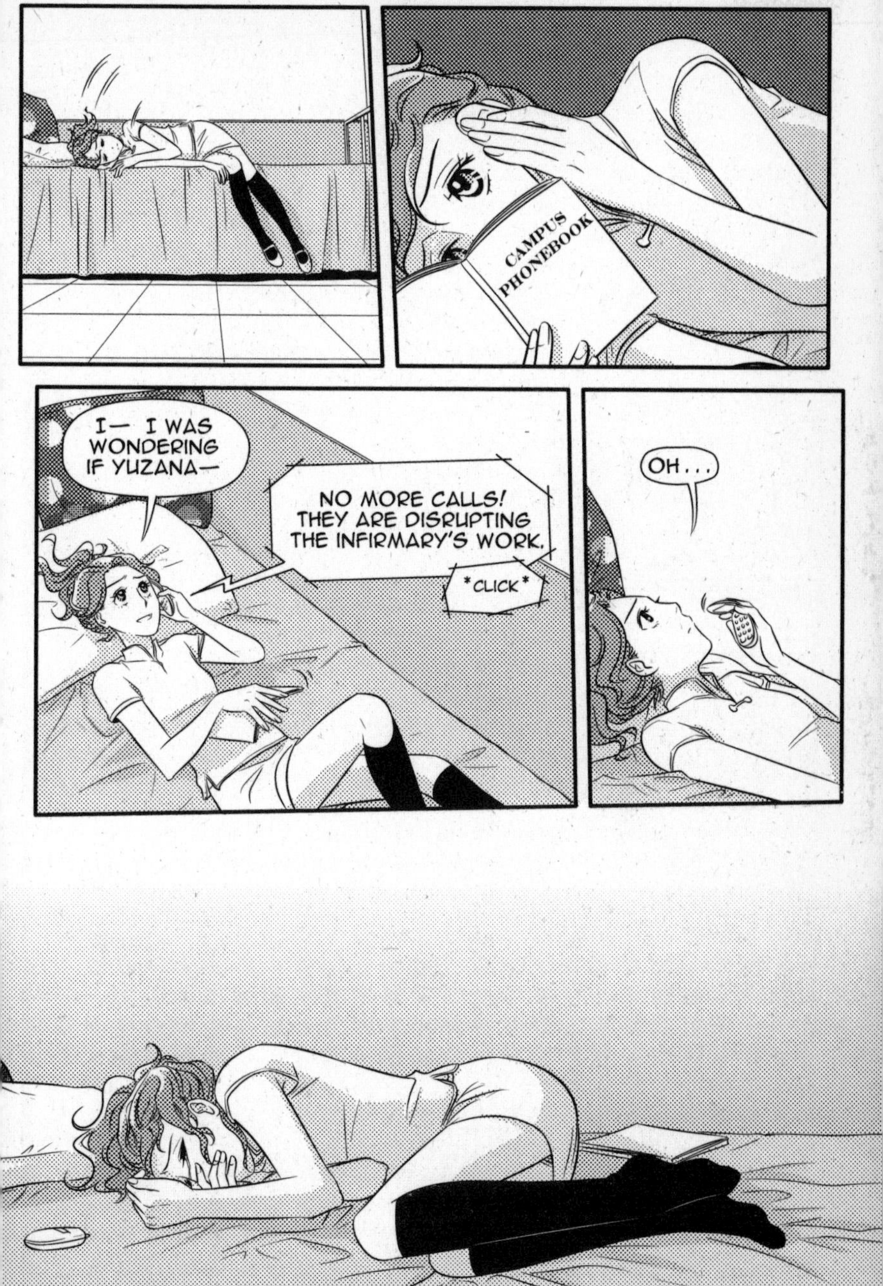
CAMPUS PHONEBOOK
I— I WAS WONDERING IF YUZANA—
NO MORE CALLS! THEY ARE DISRUPTING THE INFIRMARY'S WORK.
CLICK
OH . . .

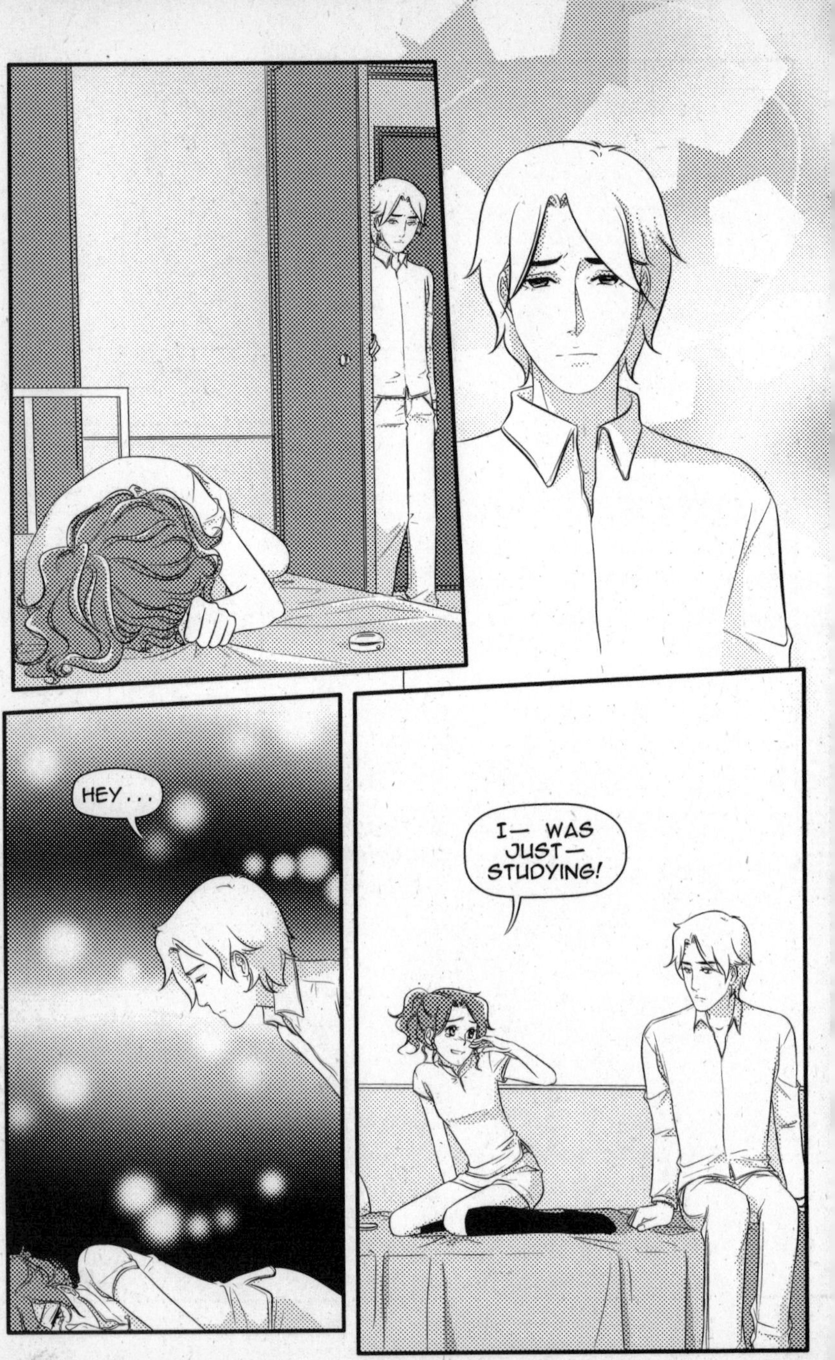
HEY . . .
I— WAS JUST— STUDYING!

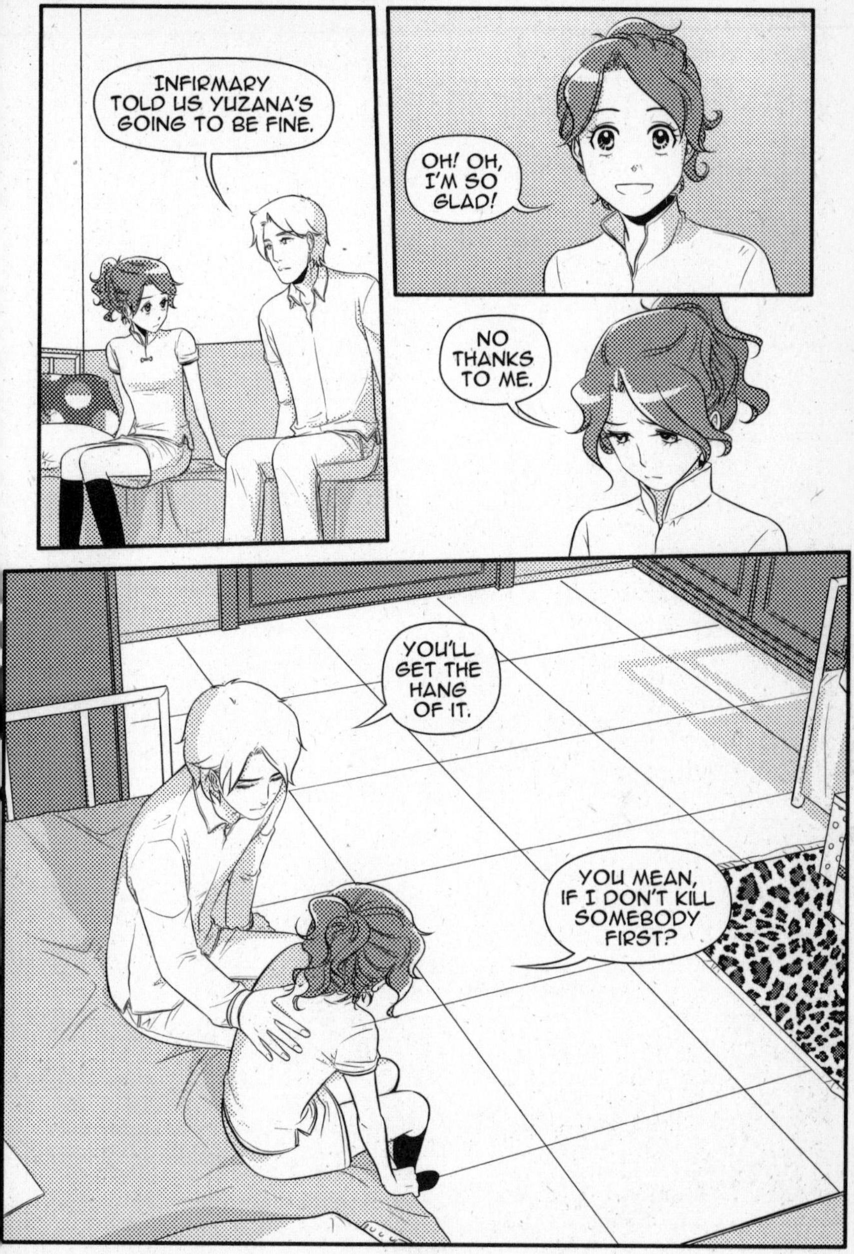
INFIRMARY TOLD US YUZANA'S GOING TO BE FINE.
OH! OH, I'M SO GLAD!
NO THANKS TO ME.
YOU'LL GET THE HANG OF IT.
YOU MEAN, IF I DON'T KILL SOMEBODY FIRST?

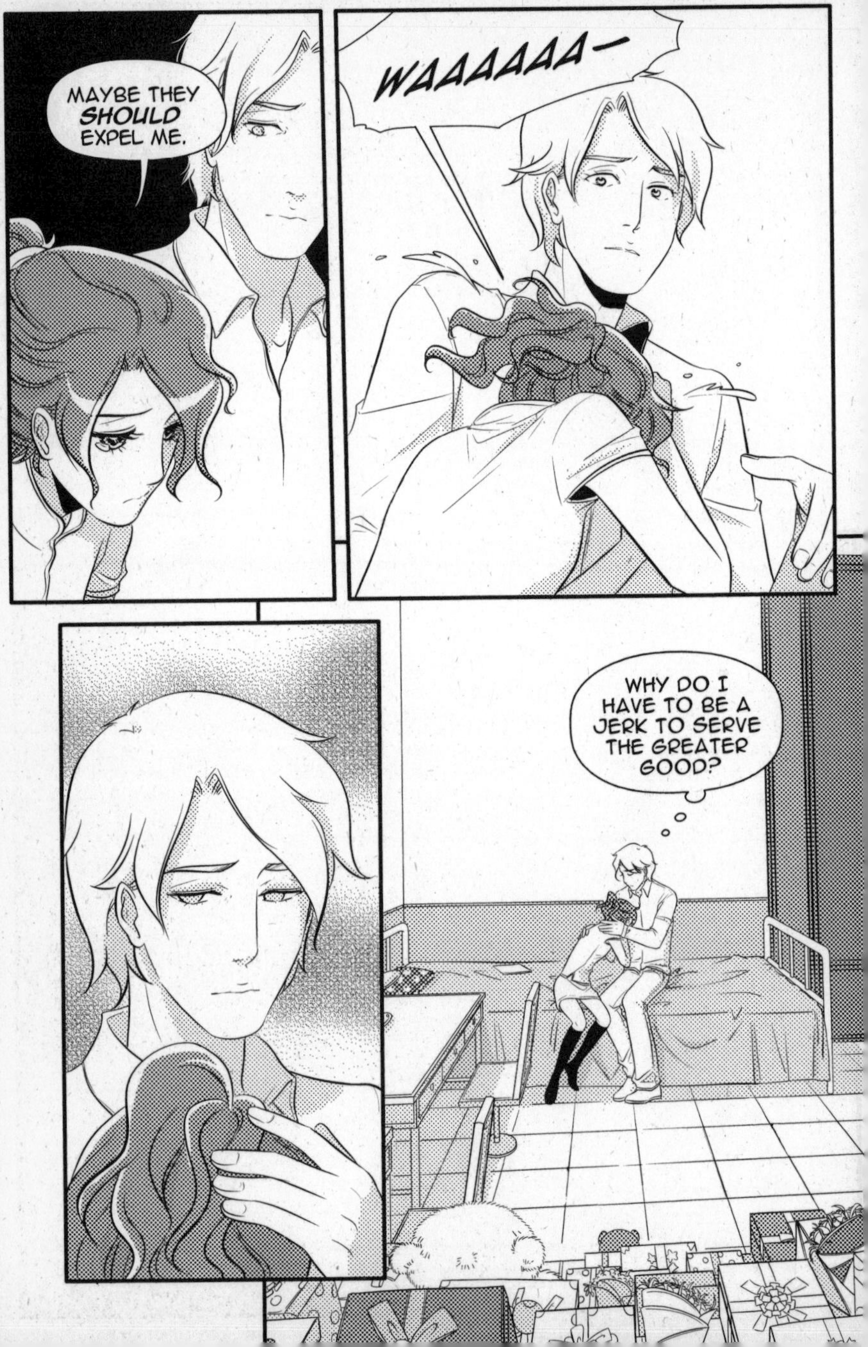
MAYBE THEY SHOULD EXPEL ME.
WAAAAAA—
WHY DO I HAVE TO BE A JERK TO SERVE THE GREATER GOOD?

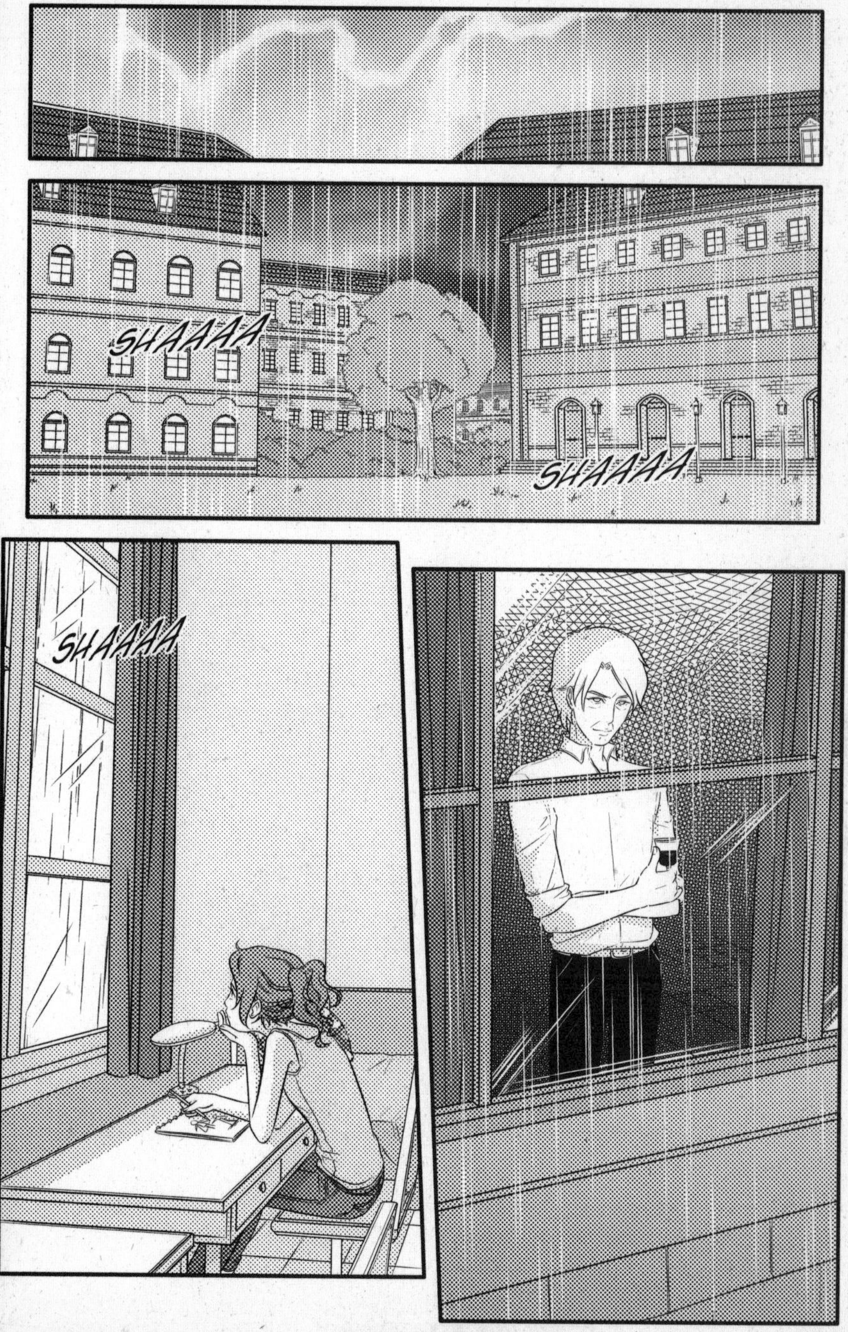
SHAAAAA
SHAAAAA
SHAAAAA

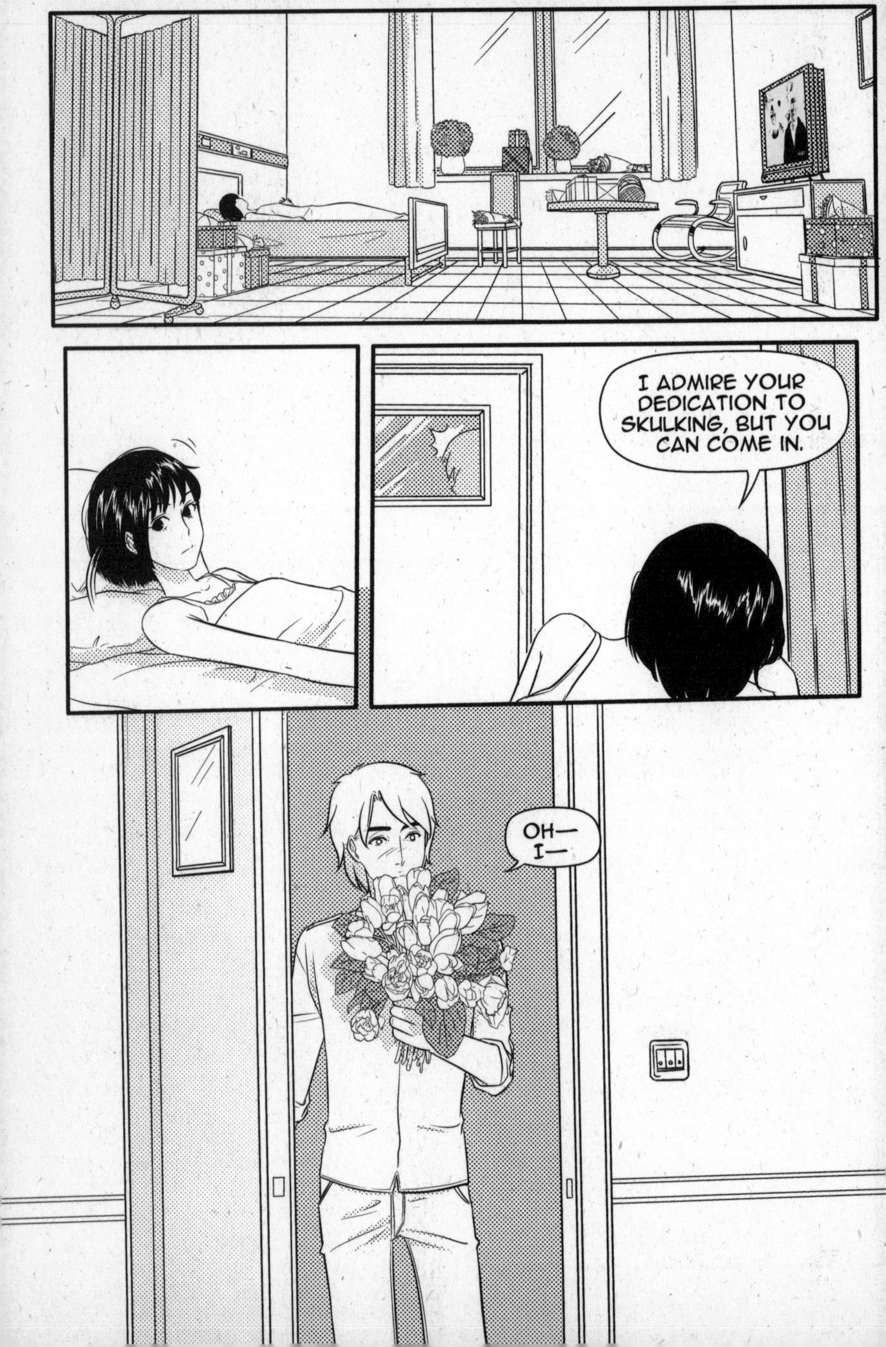
I ADMIRE YOUR DEDICATION TO SKULKING, BUT YOU CAN COME IN.
OH— I—

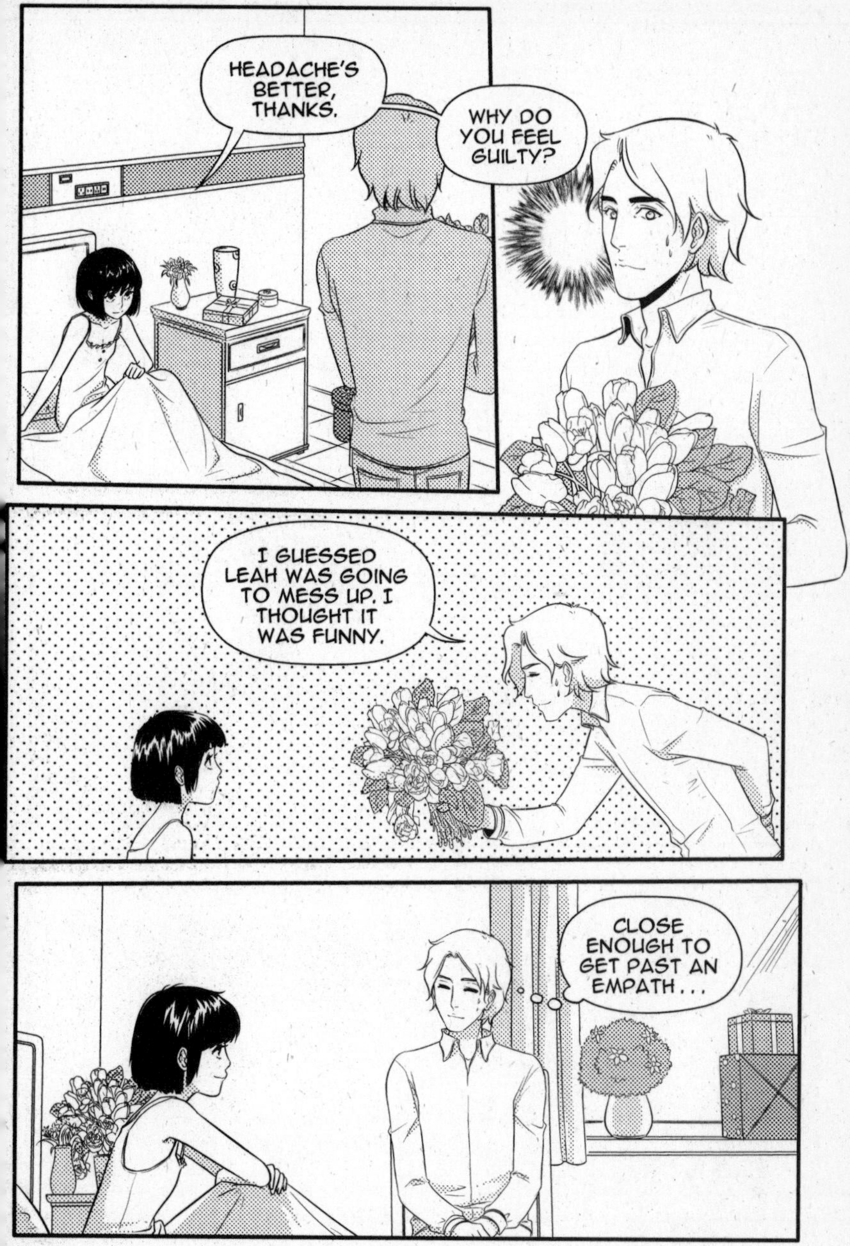
HEADACHE'S BETTER, THANKS.
WHY DO YOU FEEL GUILTY?
I GUESSED LEAH WAS GOING TO MESS UP. I THOUGHT IT WAS FUNNY.
CLOSE ENOUGH TO GET PAST AN EMPATH...

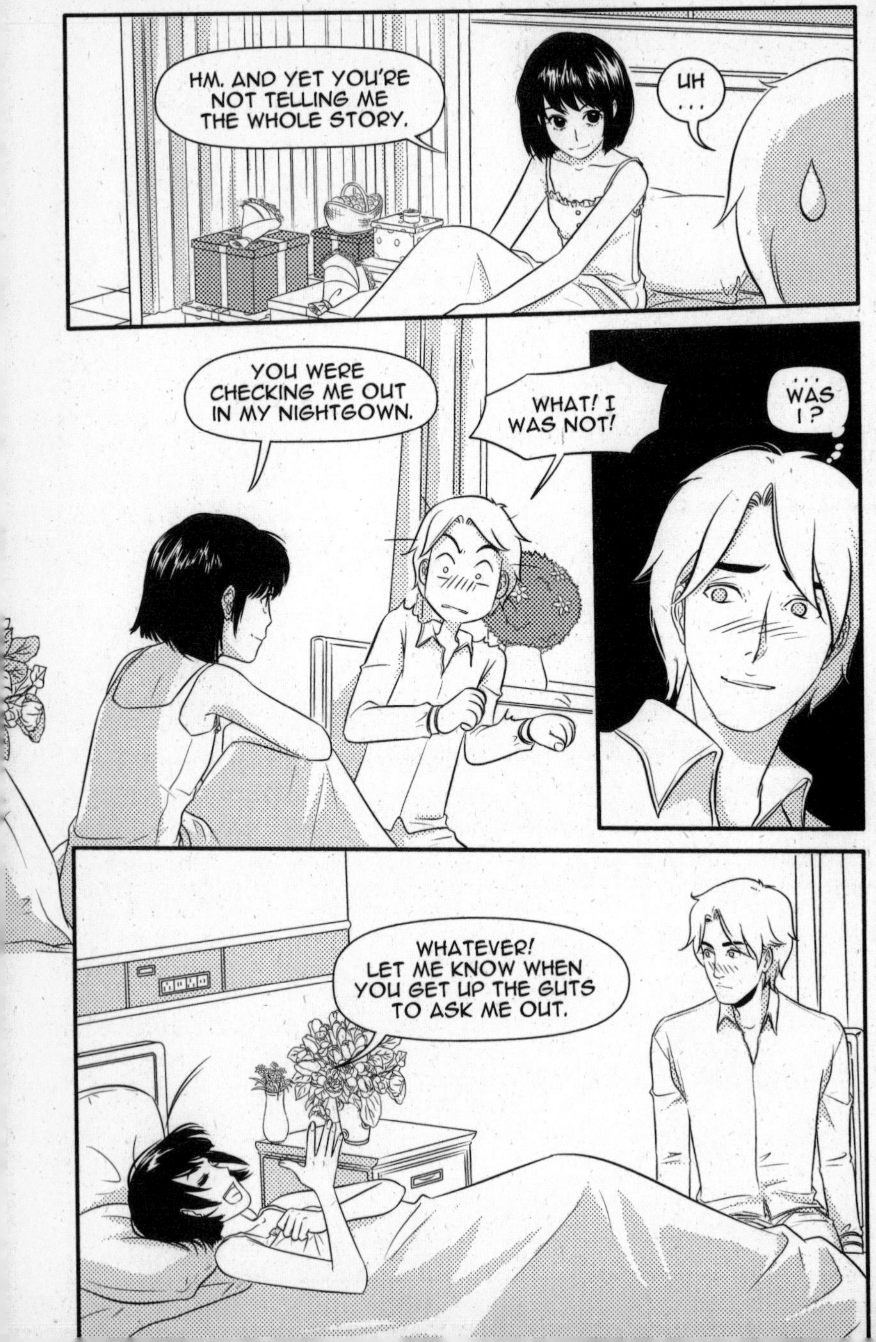
HM. AND YET YOU'RE NOT TELLING ME THE WHOLE STORY.
UH . . .
YOU WERE CHECKING ME OUT IN MY NIGHTGOWN.
WHAT! I WAS NOT!
. . . WAS I?
WHATEVER! LET ME KNOW WHEN YOU GET UP THE GUTS TO ASK ME OUT.

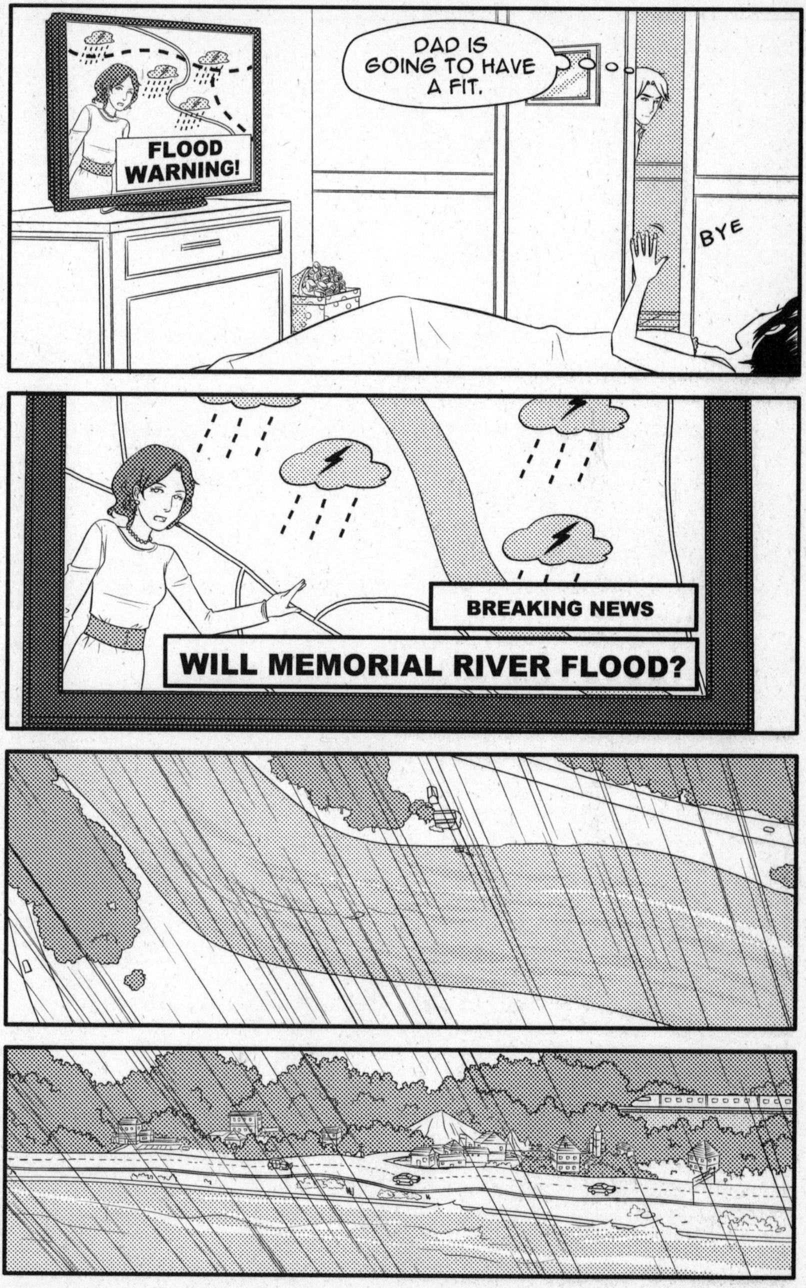
FLOOD WARNING!
DAD IS GOING TO HAVE A FIT.
BYE
BREAKING NEWS
WILL MEMORIAL RIVER FLOOD?

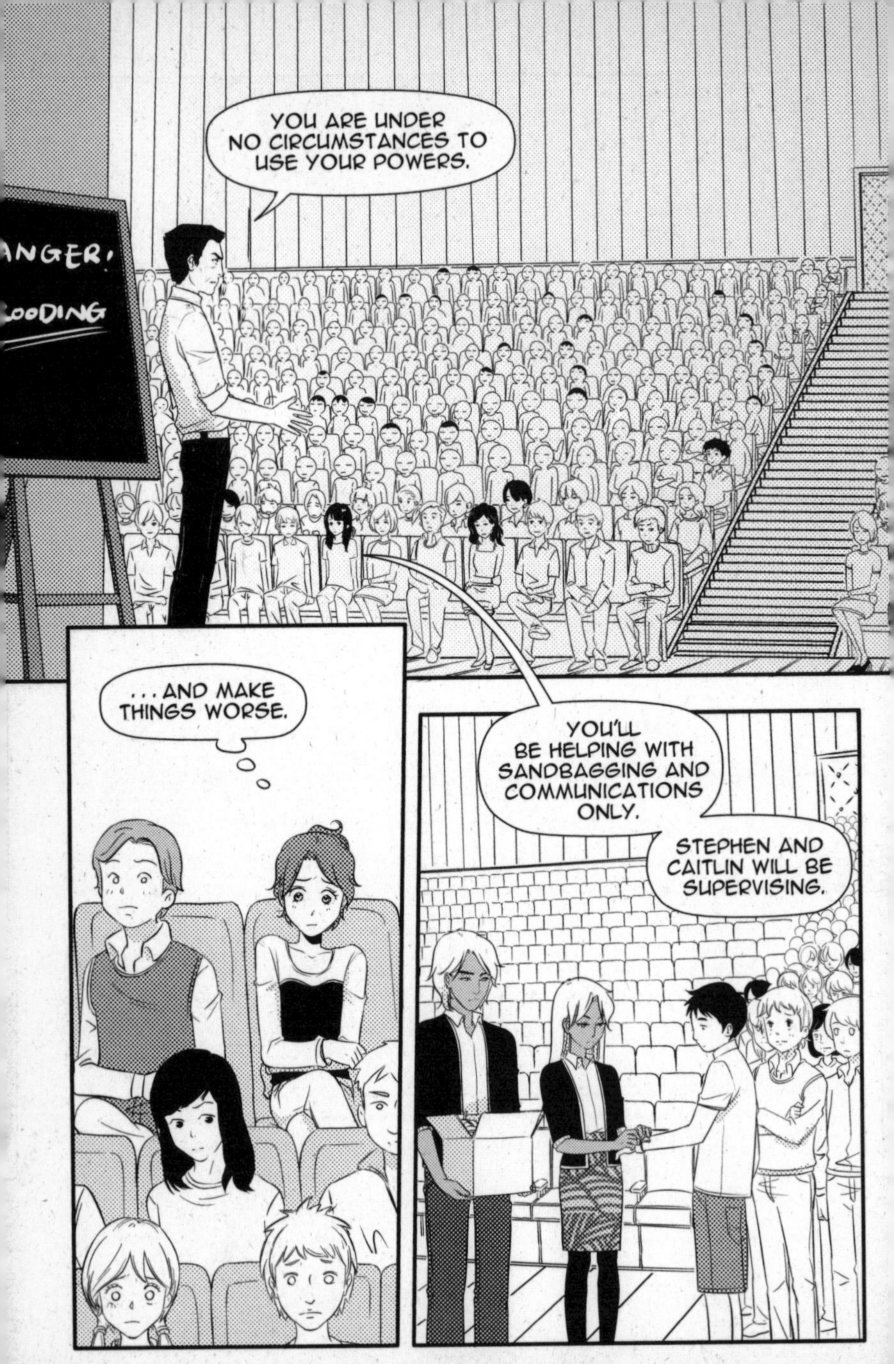
YOU ARE UNDER NO CIRCUMSTANCES TO USE YOUR POWERS.
...AND MAKE THINGS WORSE.
YOU'LL BE HELPING WITH SANDBAGGING AND COMMUNICATIONS ONLY.
STEPHEN AND CAITLIN WILL BE SUPERVISING.

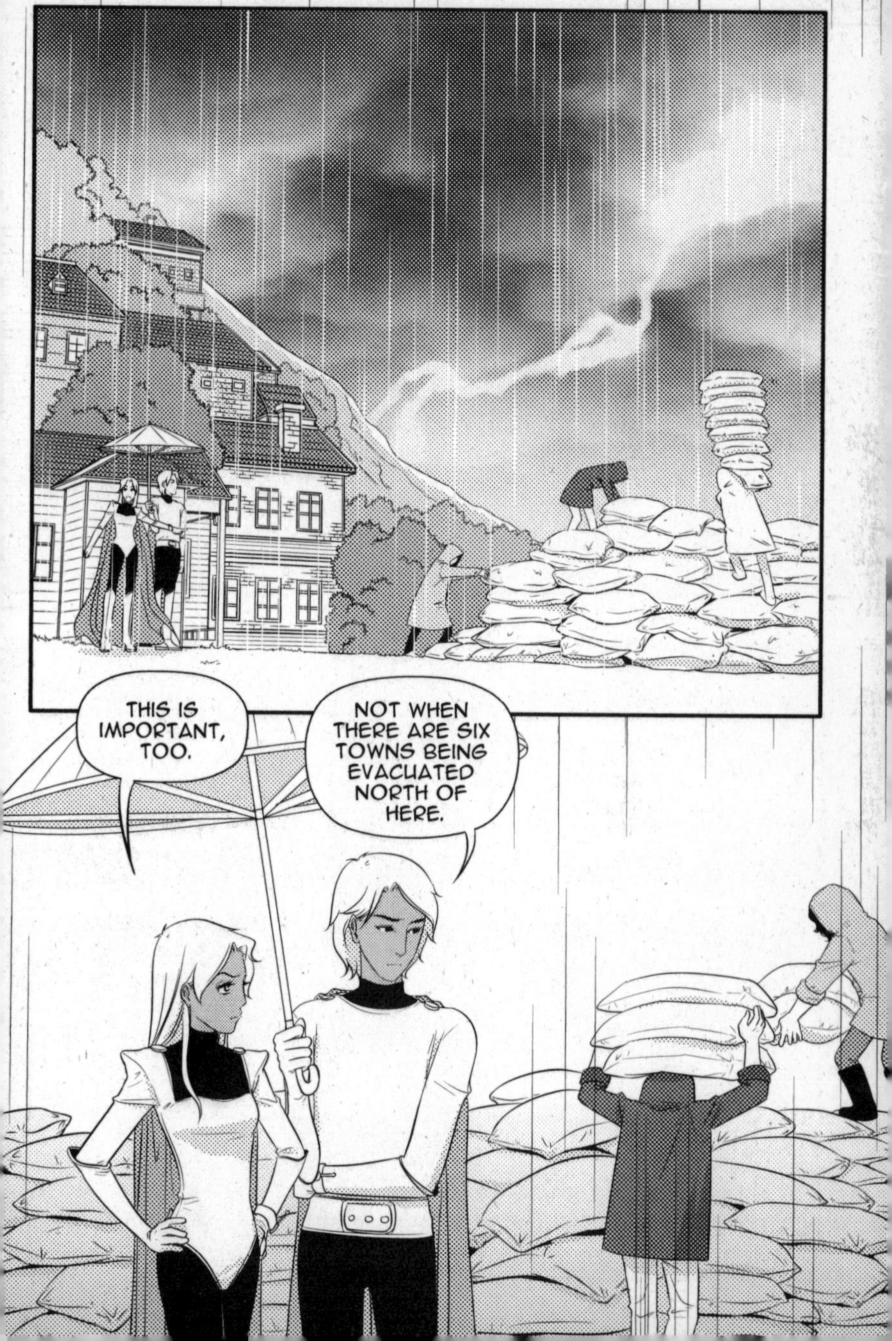
THIS IS IMPORTANT, TOO.
NOT WHEN THERE ARE SIX TOWNS BEING EVACUATED NORTH OF HERE.

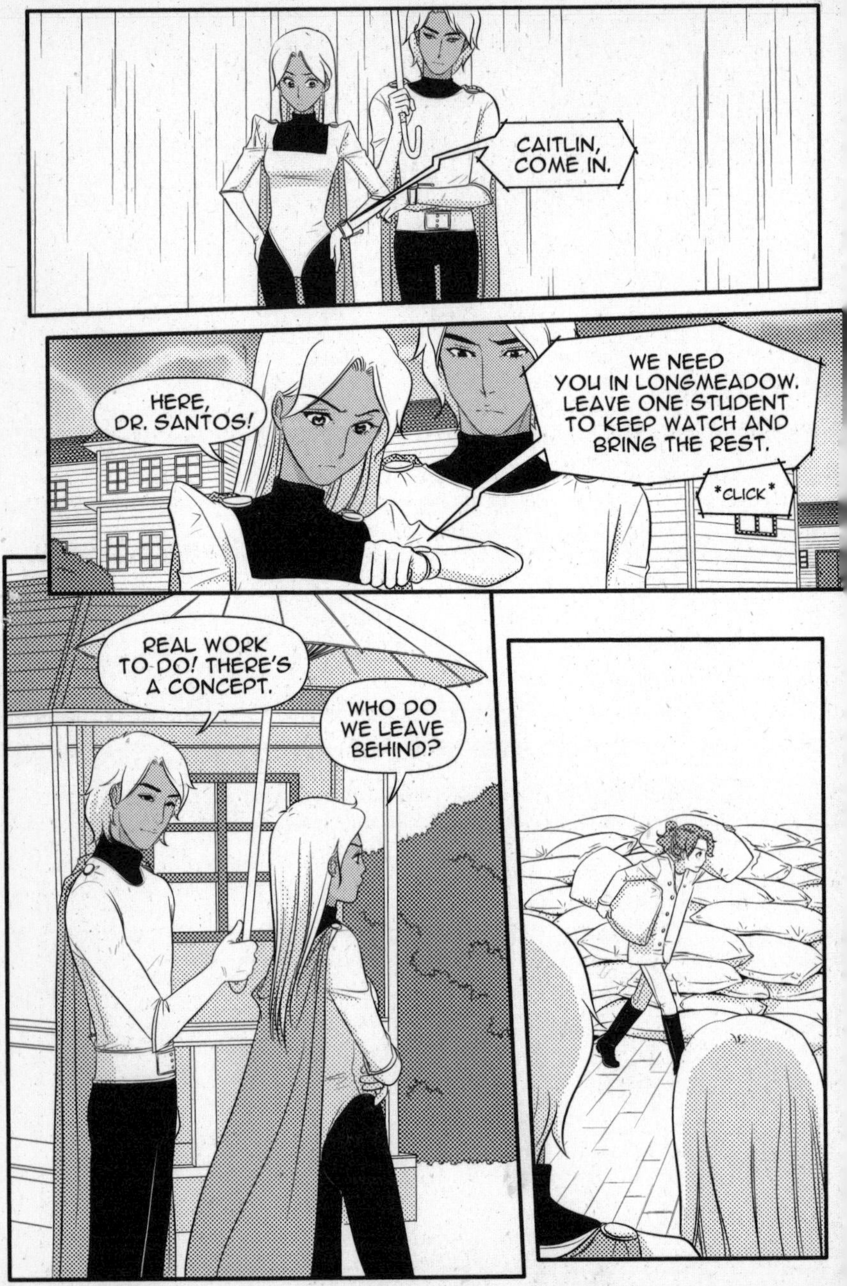
CAITLIN, COME IN.
HERE, DR. SANTOS!
WE NEED YOU IN LONGMEADOW. LEAVE ONE STUDENT TO KEEP WATCH AND BRING THE REST.
CLICK
REAL WORK TO DO! THERE'S A CONCEPT.
WHO DO WE LEAVE BEHIND?

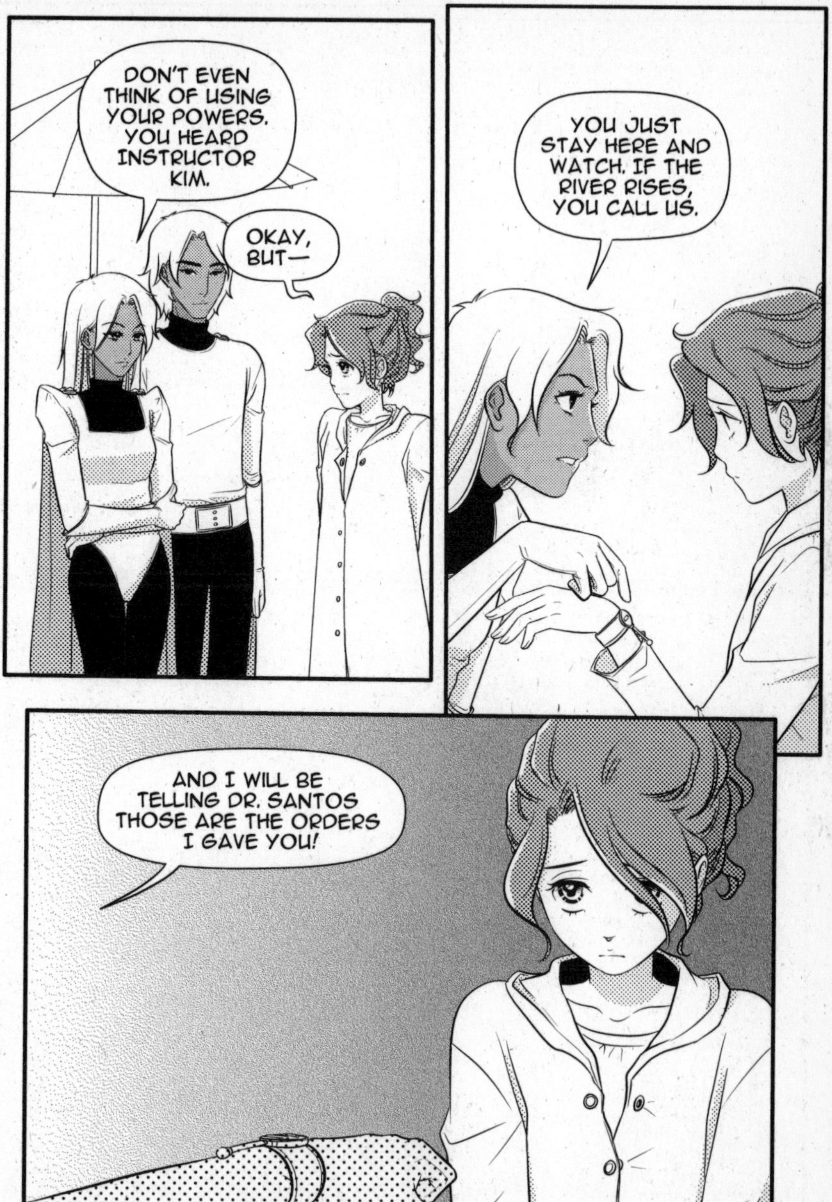
DON'T EVEN THINK OF USING YOUR POWERS. YOU HEARD INSTRUCTOR KIM.
OKAY, BUT—
YOU JUST STAY HERE AND WATCH. IF THE RIVER RISES, YOU CALL US.
AND I WILL BE TELLING DR. SANTOS THOSE ARE THE ORDERS I GAVE YOU!

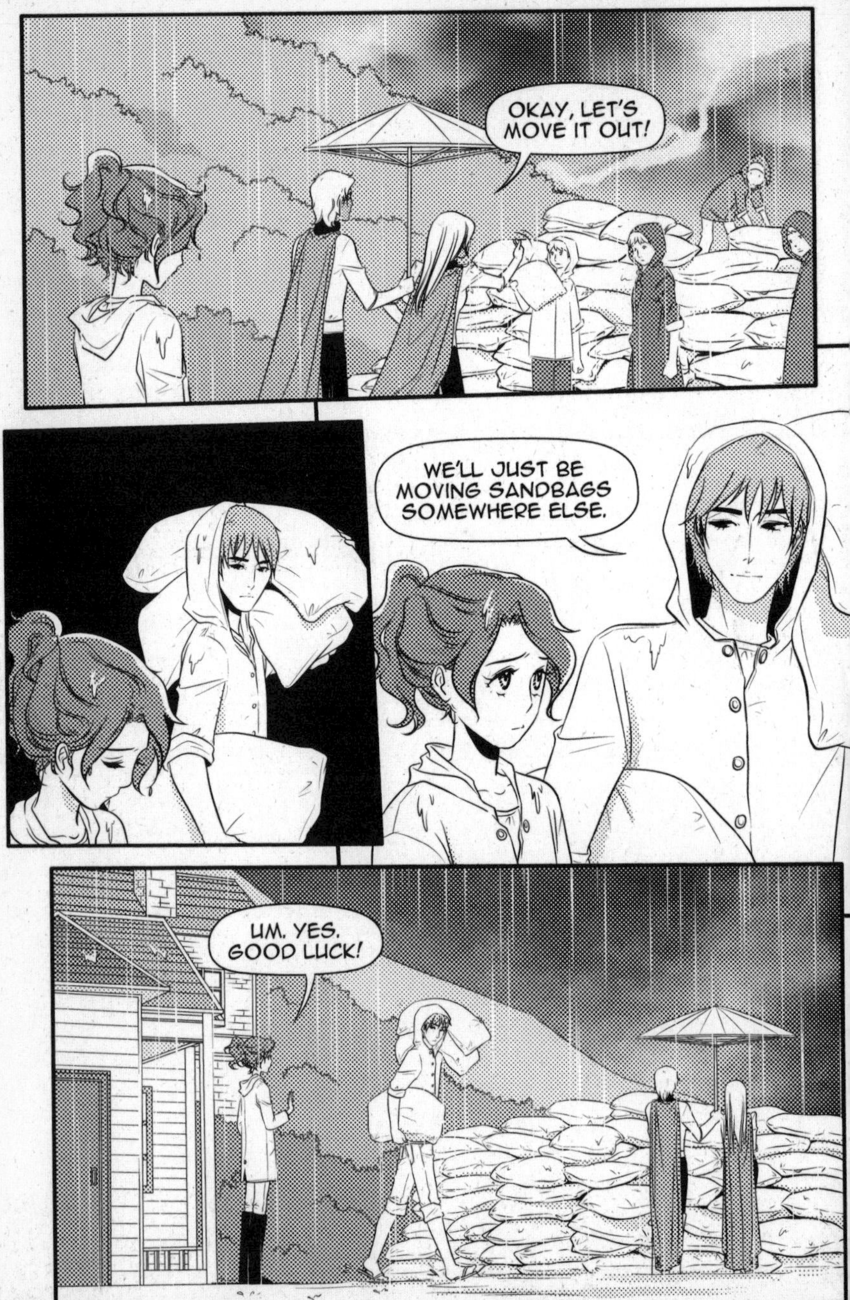
OKAY, LET'S MOVE IT OUT!
WE'LL JUST BE MOVING SANDBAGS SOMEWHERE ELSE.
UM. YES. GOOD LUCK!

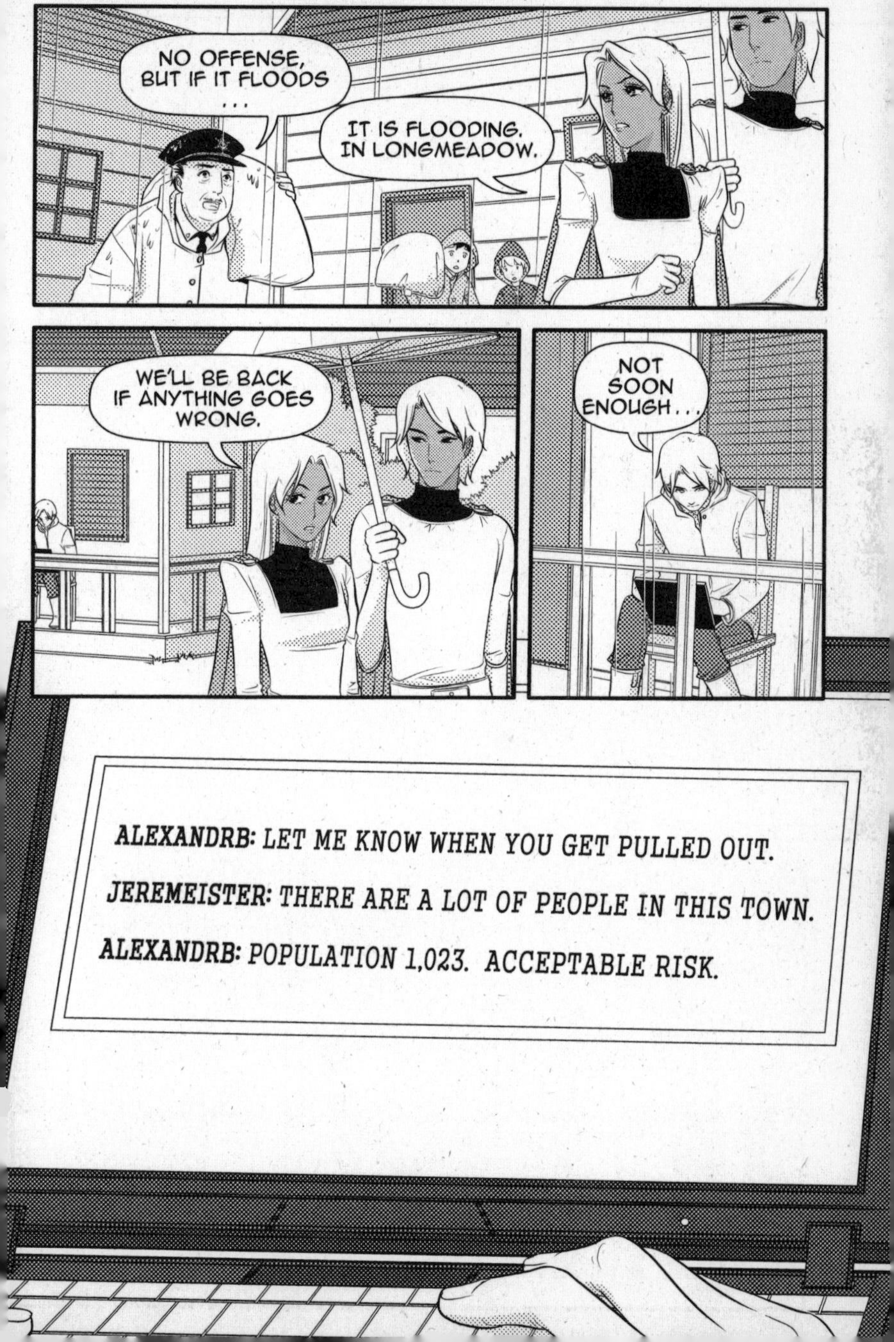
NO OFFENSE, BUT IF IT FLOODS . . .
IT IS FLOODING. IN LONGMEADOW.
WE'LL BE BACK IF ANYTHING GOES WRONG.
NOT SOON ENOUGH. . .
ALEXANDRB: LET ME KNOW WHEN YOU GET PULLED OUT.
JEREMEISTER: THERE ARE A LOT OF PEOPLE IN THIS TOWN.
ALEXANDRB: POPULATION 1,023. ACCEPTABLE RISK.

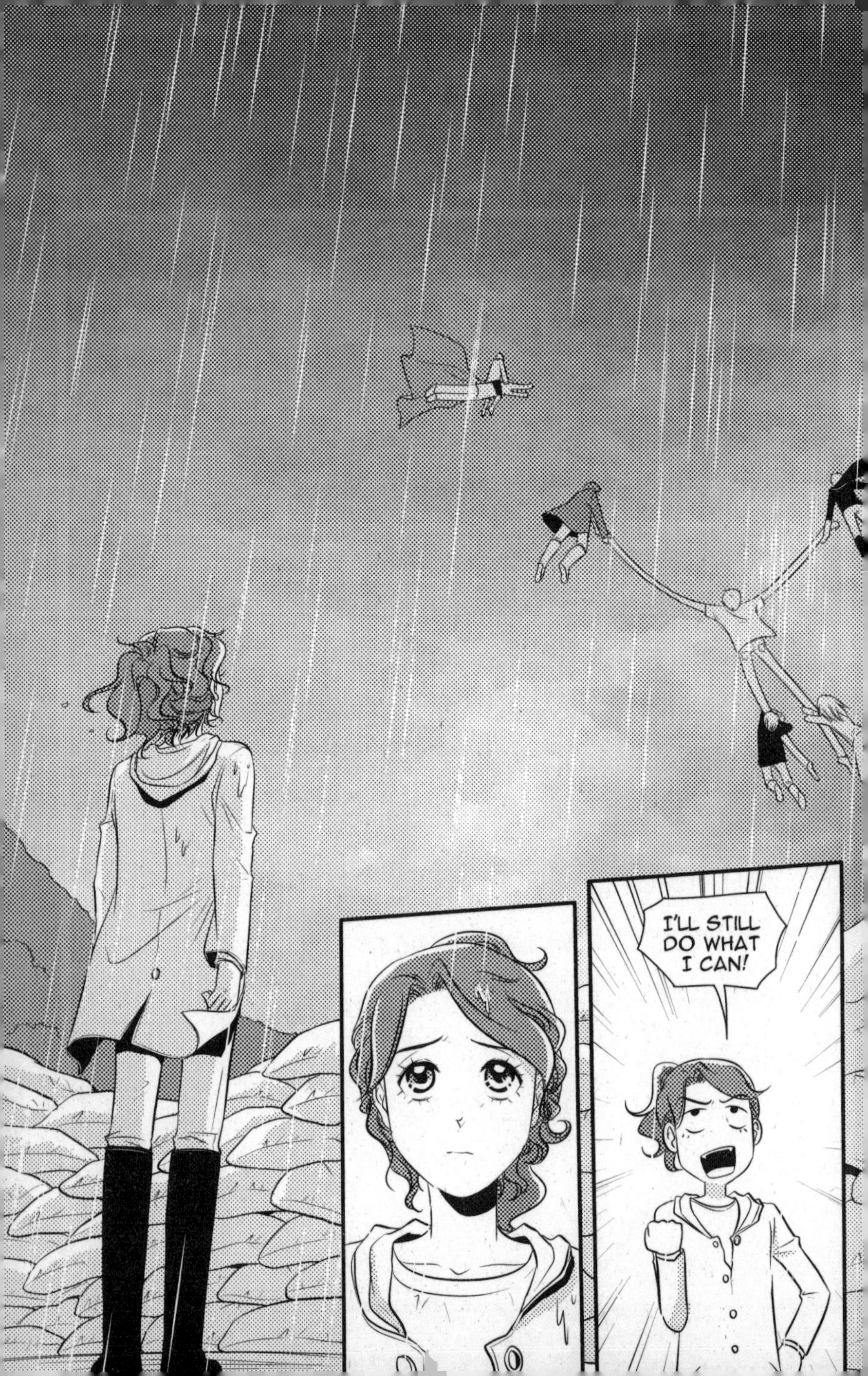
I'LL STILL DO WHAT I CAN!

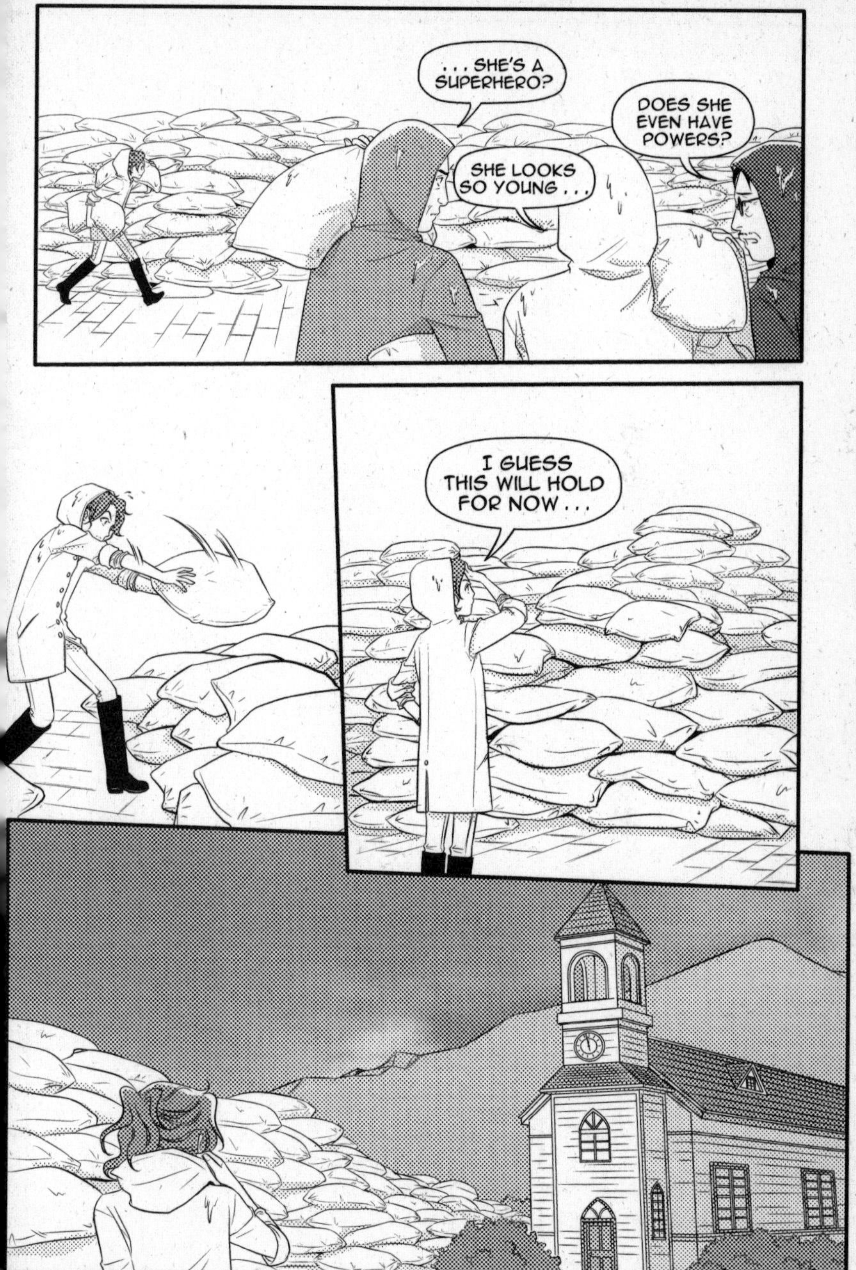
. . . SHE'S A SUPERHERO?
SHE LOOKS SO YOUNG . . .
DOES SHE EVEN HAVE POWERS?
I GUESS THIS WILL HOLD FOR NOW . . .

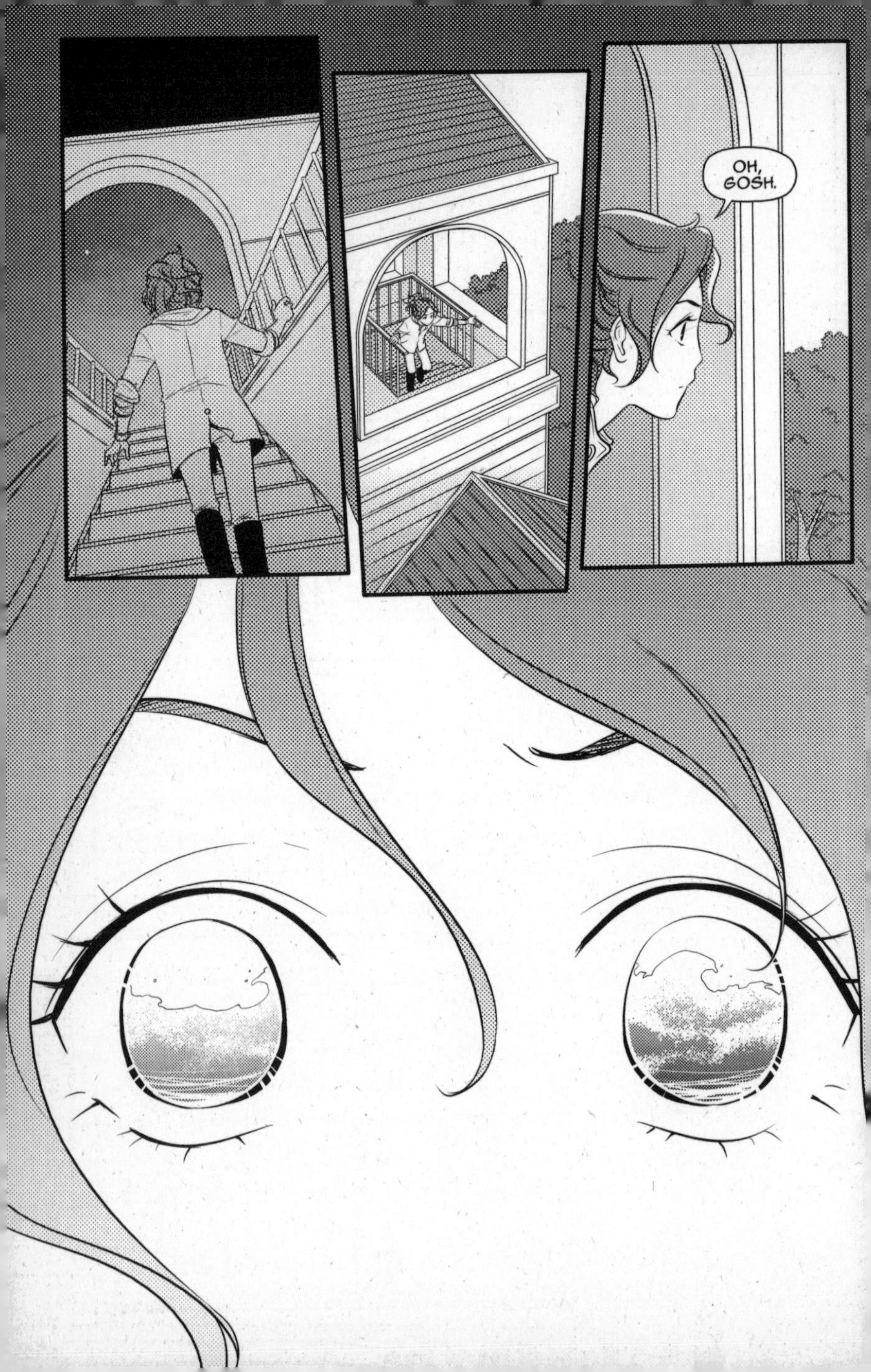
OH, GOSH.

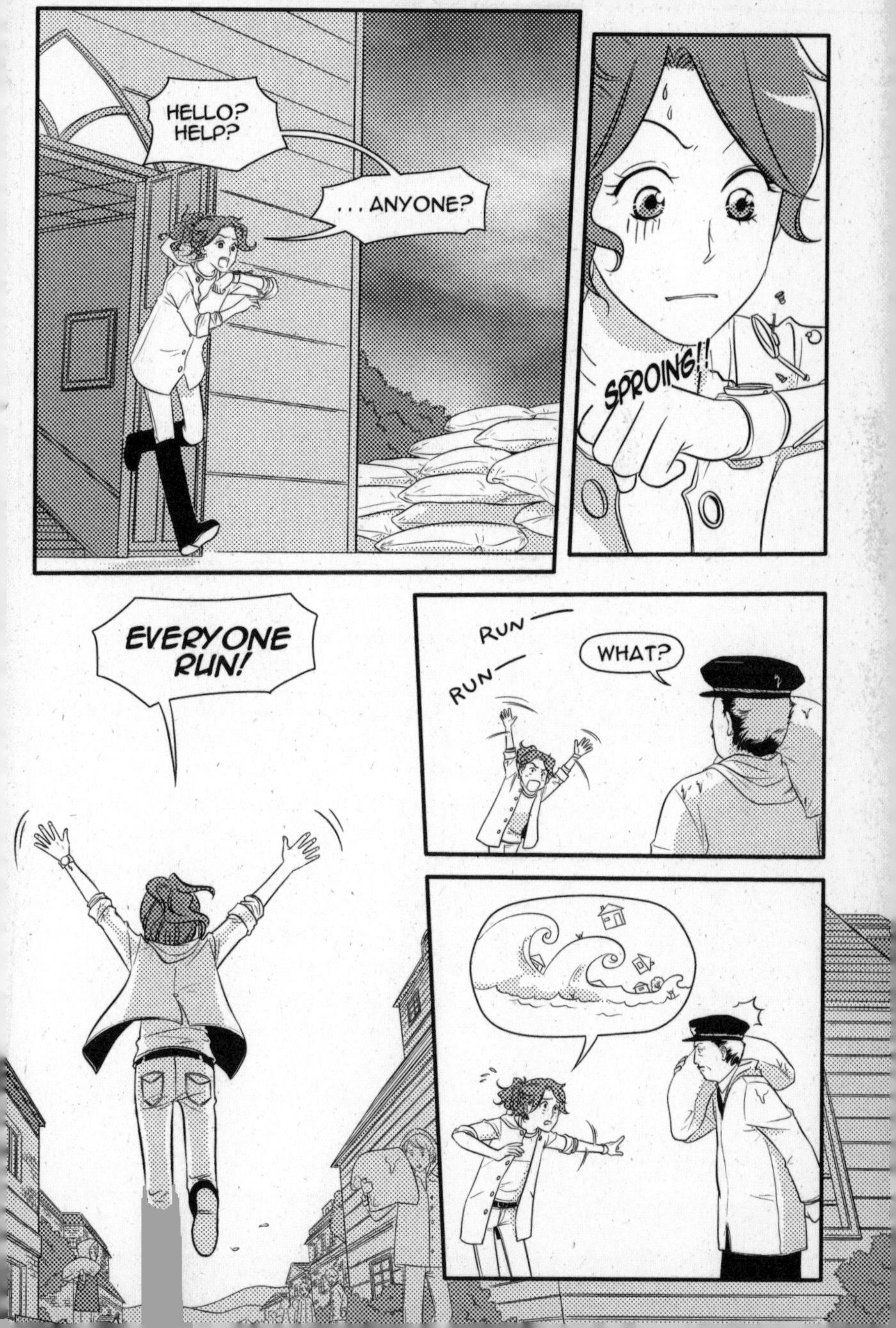
HELLO?
HELP?
...ANYONE?
SPROING!!
EVERYONE RUN!
RUN—
RUN—
WHAT?

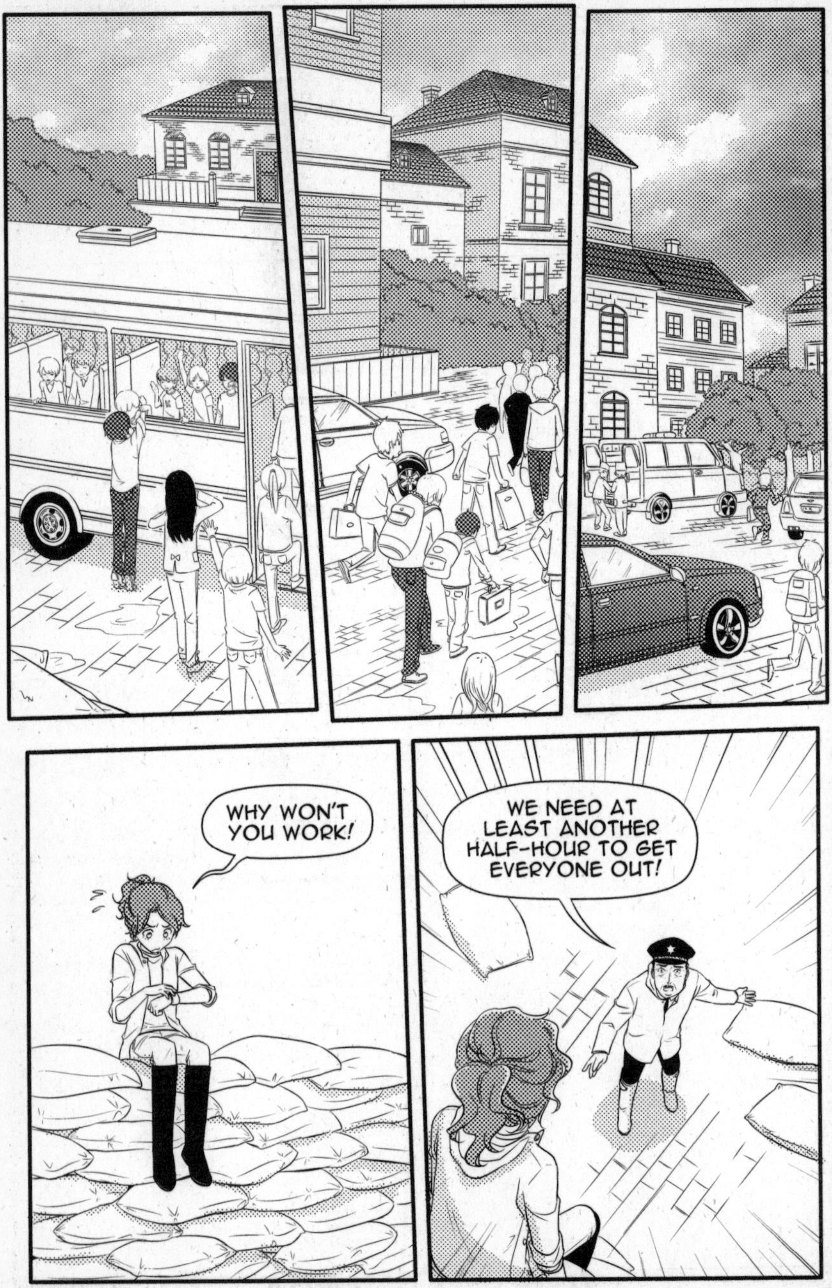
WHY WON'T YOU WORK!
WE NEED AT LEAST ANOTHER HALF-HOUR TO GET EVERYONE OUT!

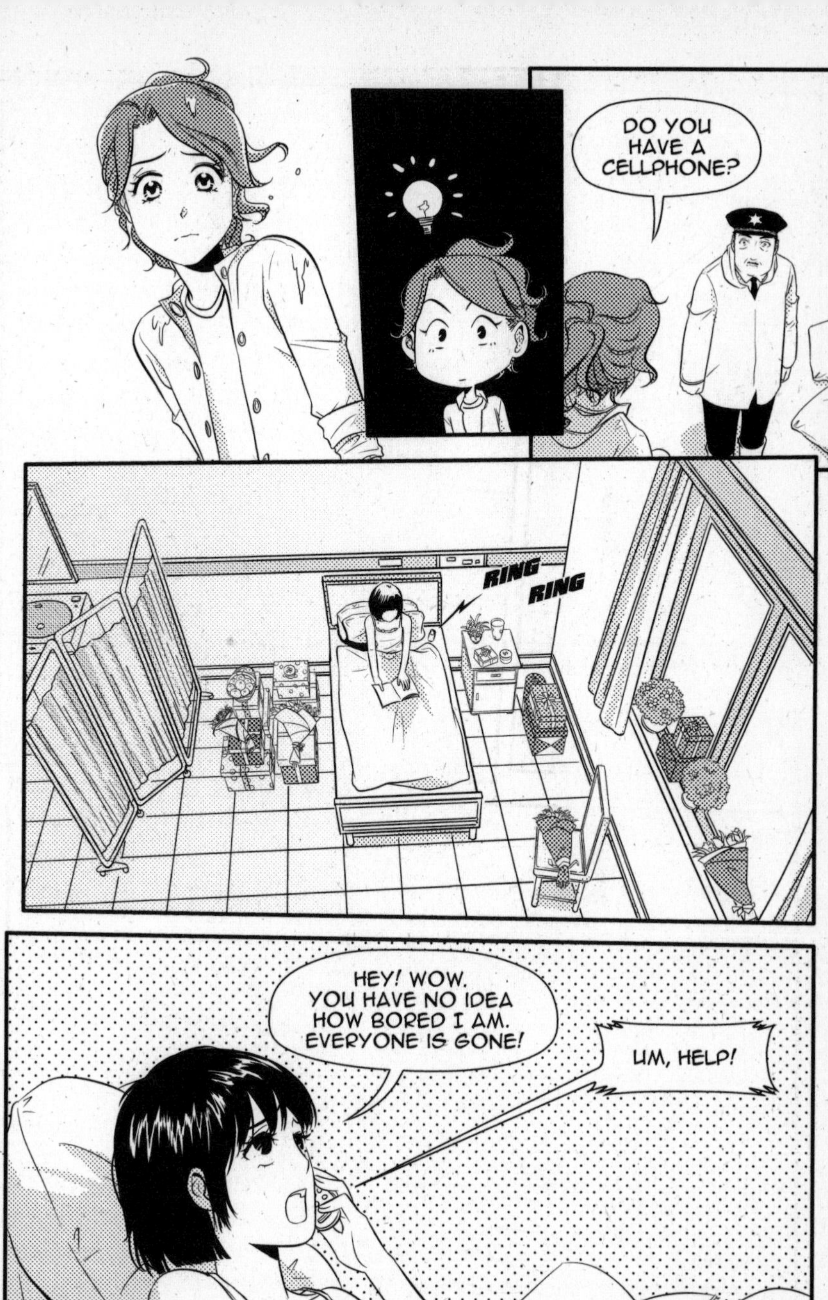
DO YOU HAVE A CELLPHONE?
RING RING
HEY! WOW. YOU HAVE NO IDEA HOW BORED I AM. EVERYONE IS GONE!
UM, HELP!

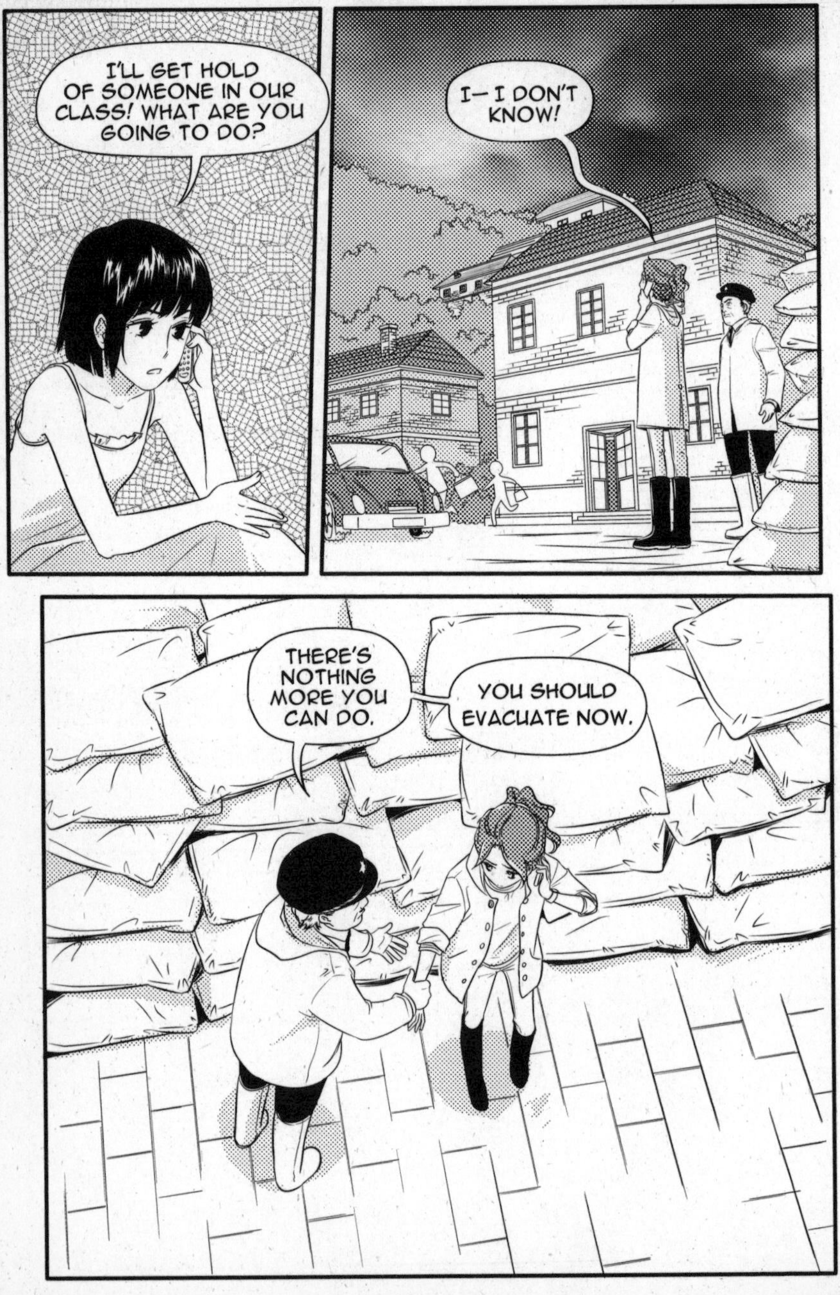
I'LL GET HOLD OF SOMEONE IN OUR CLASS! WHAT ARE YOU GOING TO DO?
I— I DON'T KNOW!
THERE'S NOTHING MORE YOU CAN DO.
YOU SHOULD EVACUATE NOW.

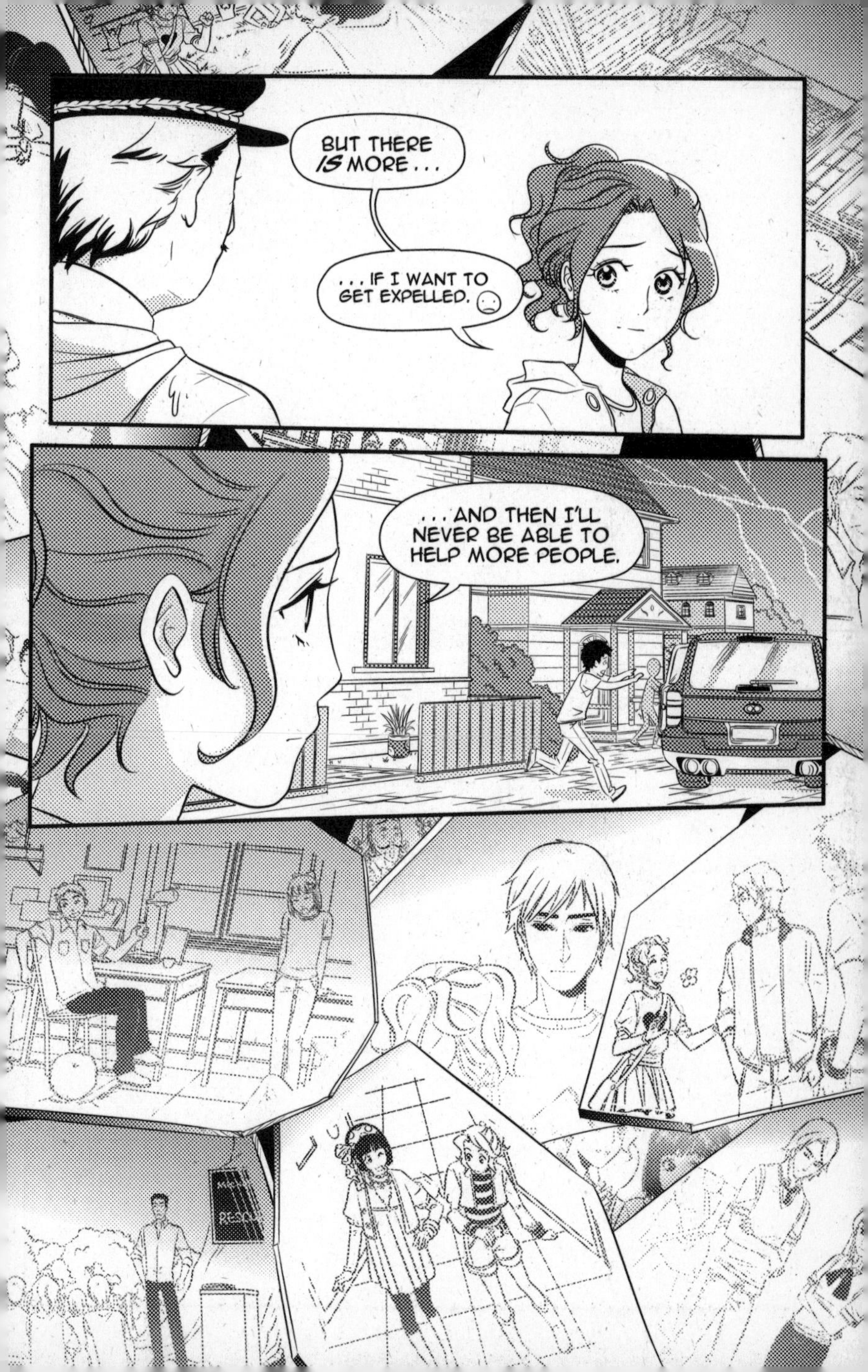
BUT THERE *IS* MORE . . .
. . . IF I WANT TO GET EXPELLED.
. . . AND THEN I'LL NEVER BE ABLE TO HELP MORE PEOPLE.

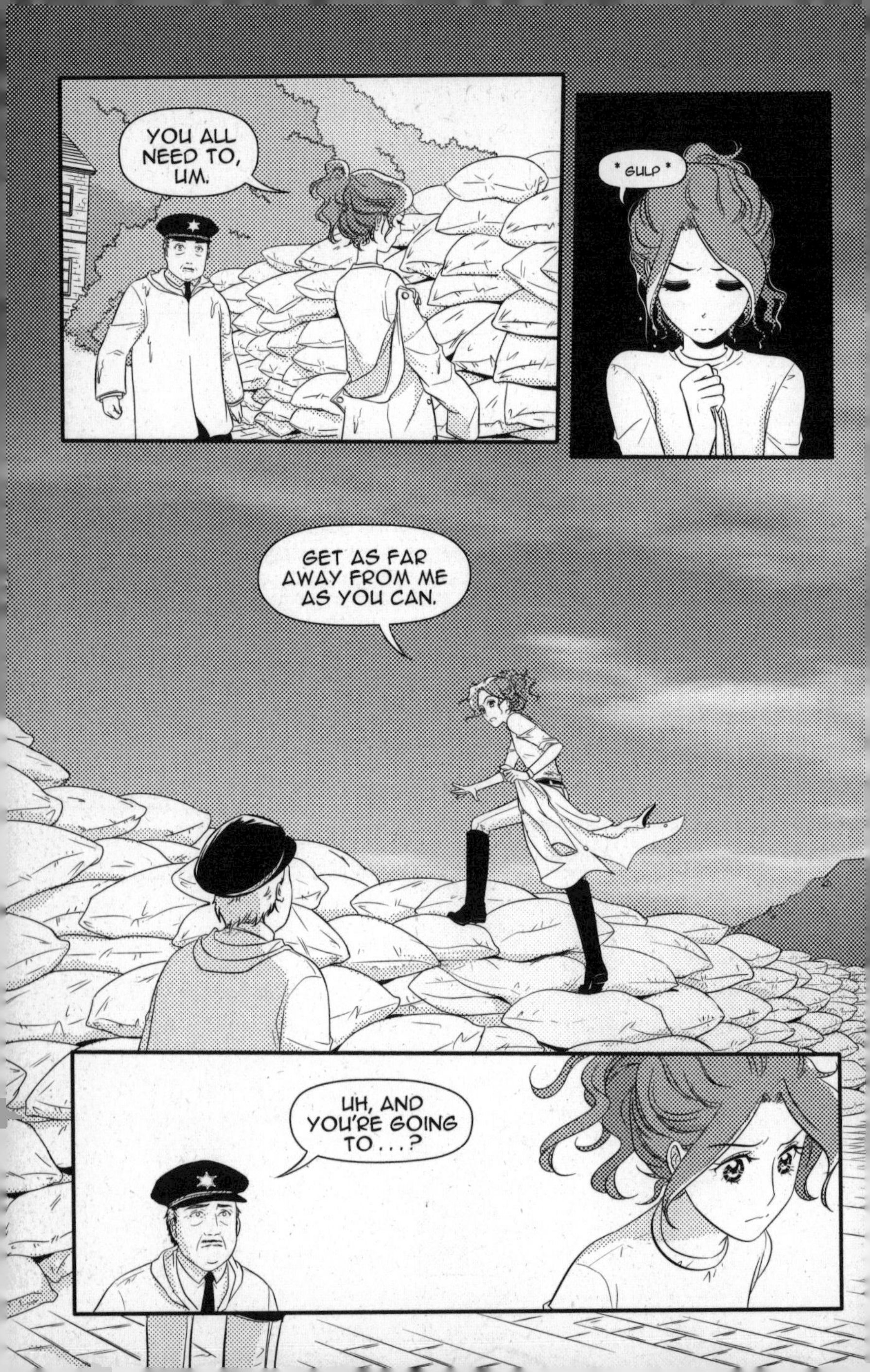
YOU ALL NEED TO, UM.
* GULP *
GET AS FAR AWAY FROM ME AS YOU CAN.
UH, AND YOU'RE GOING TO . . . ?

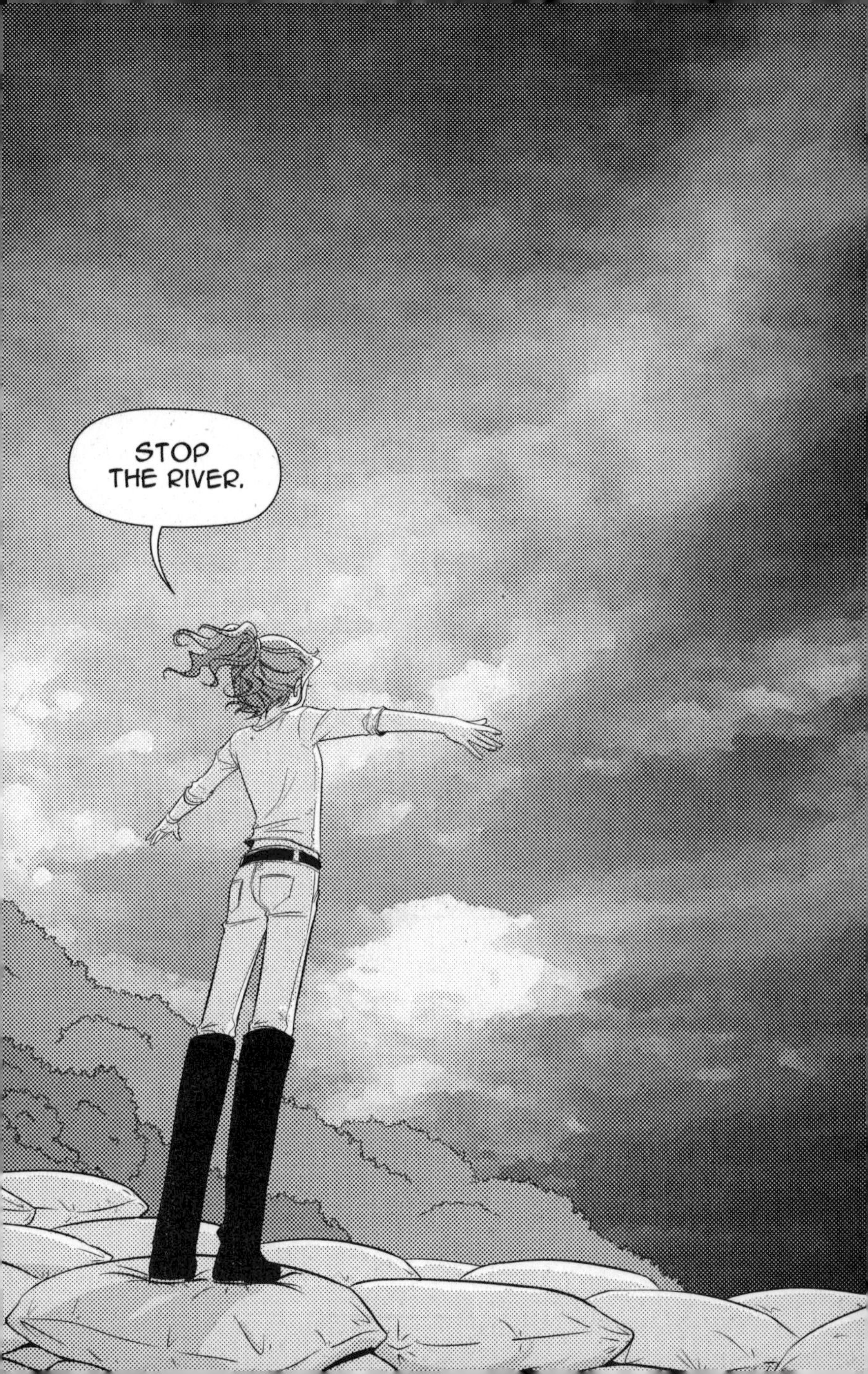
STOP THE RIVER.

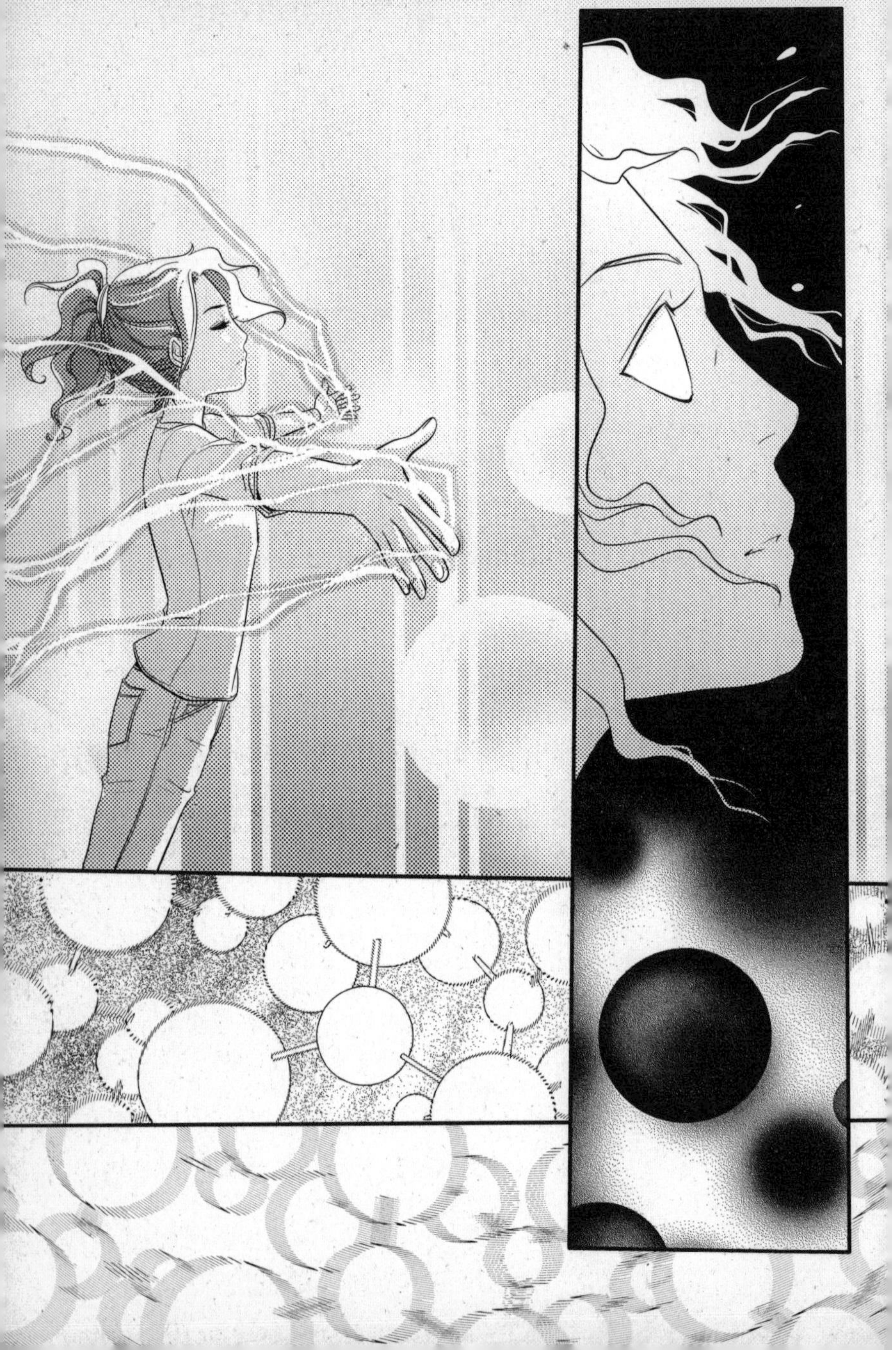

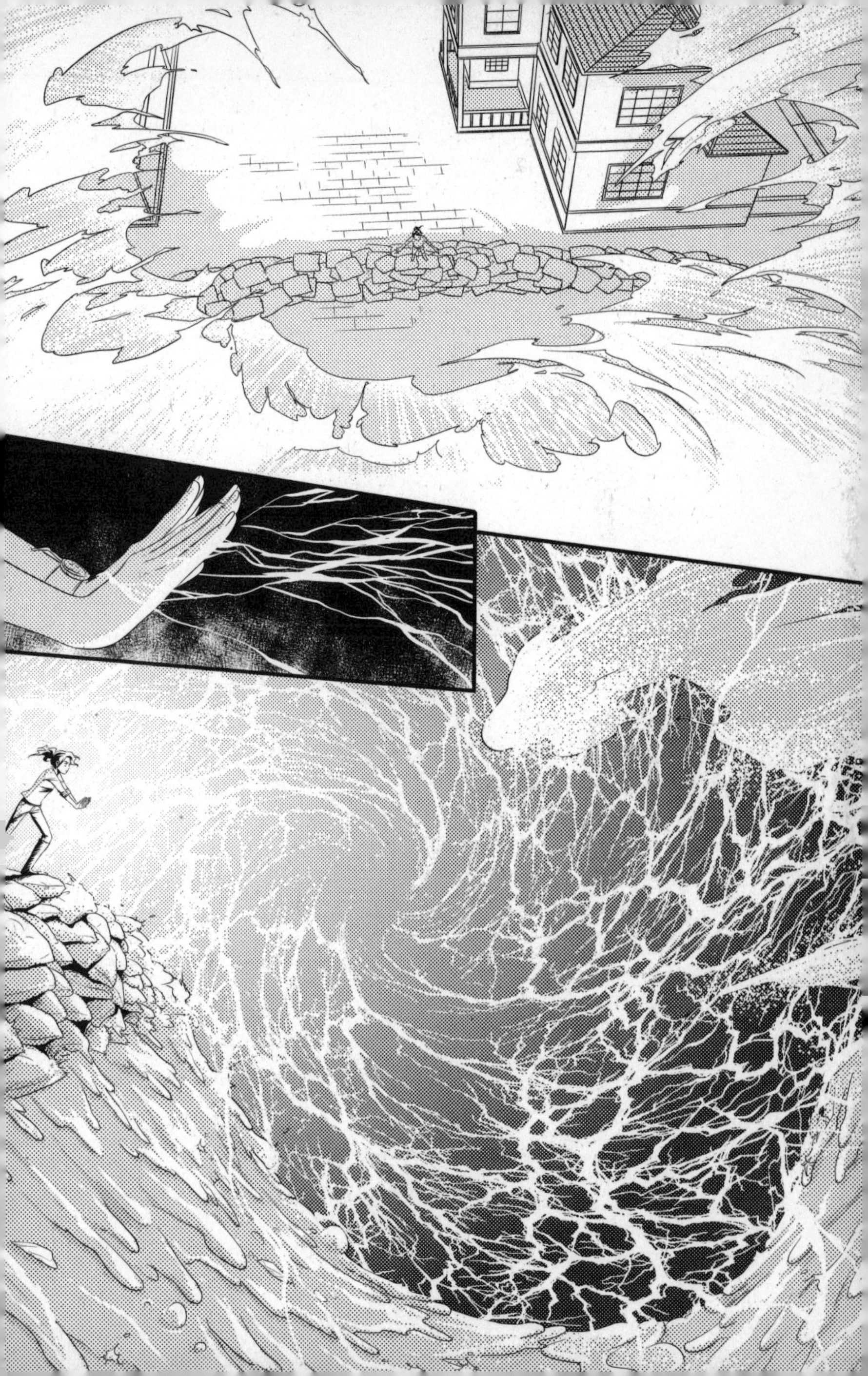

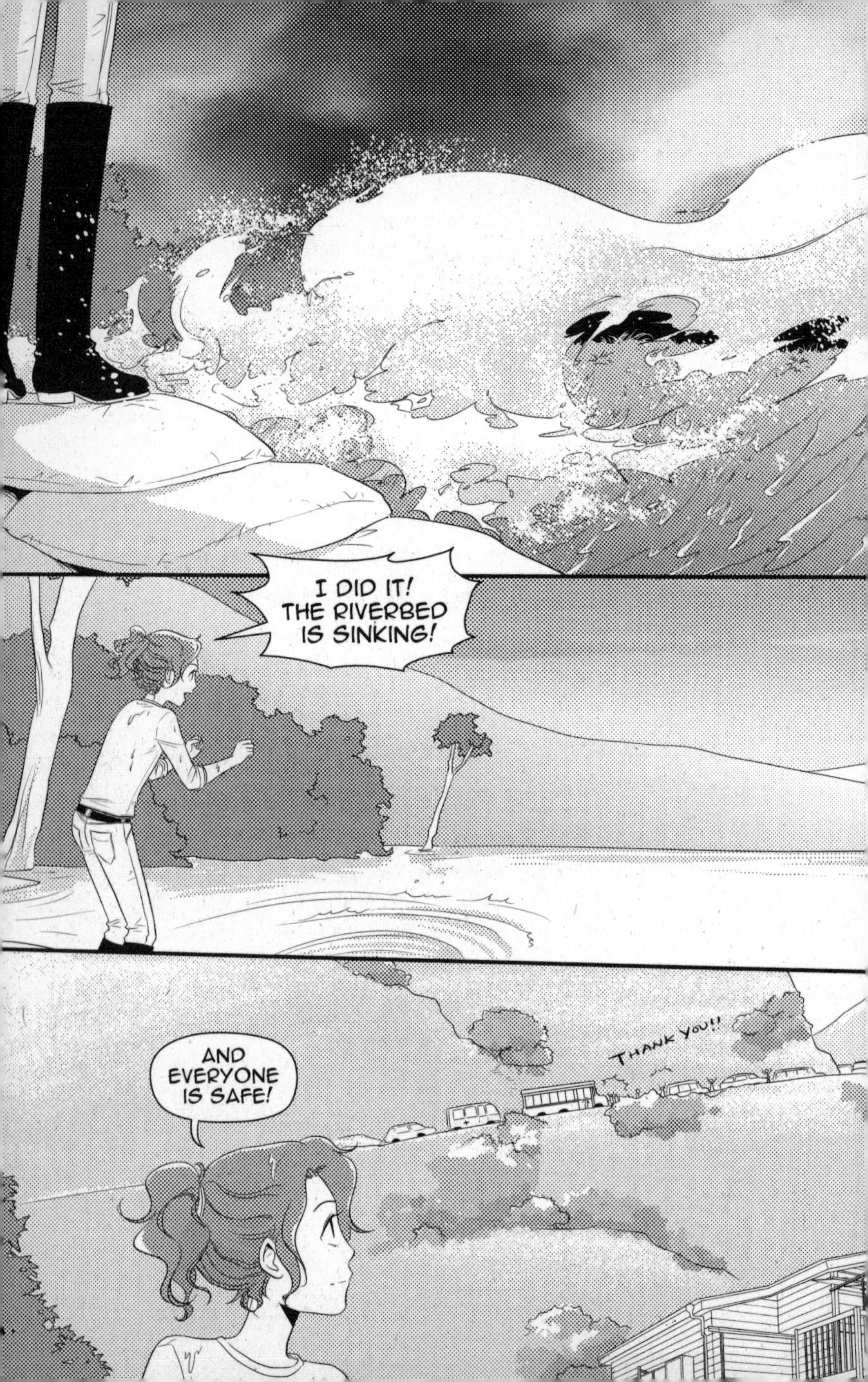
I DID IT! THE RIVERBED IS SINKING!
AND EVERYONE IS SAFE!
THANK YOU!!

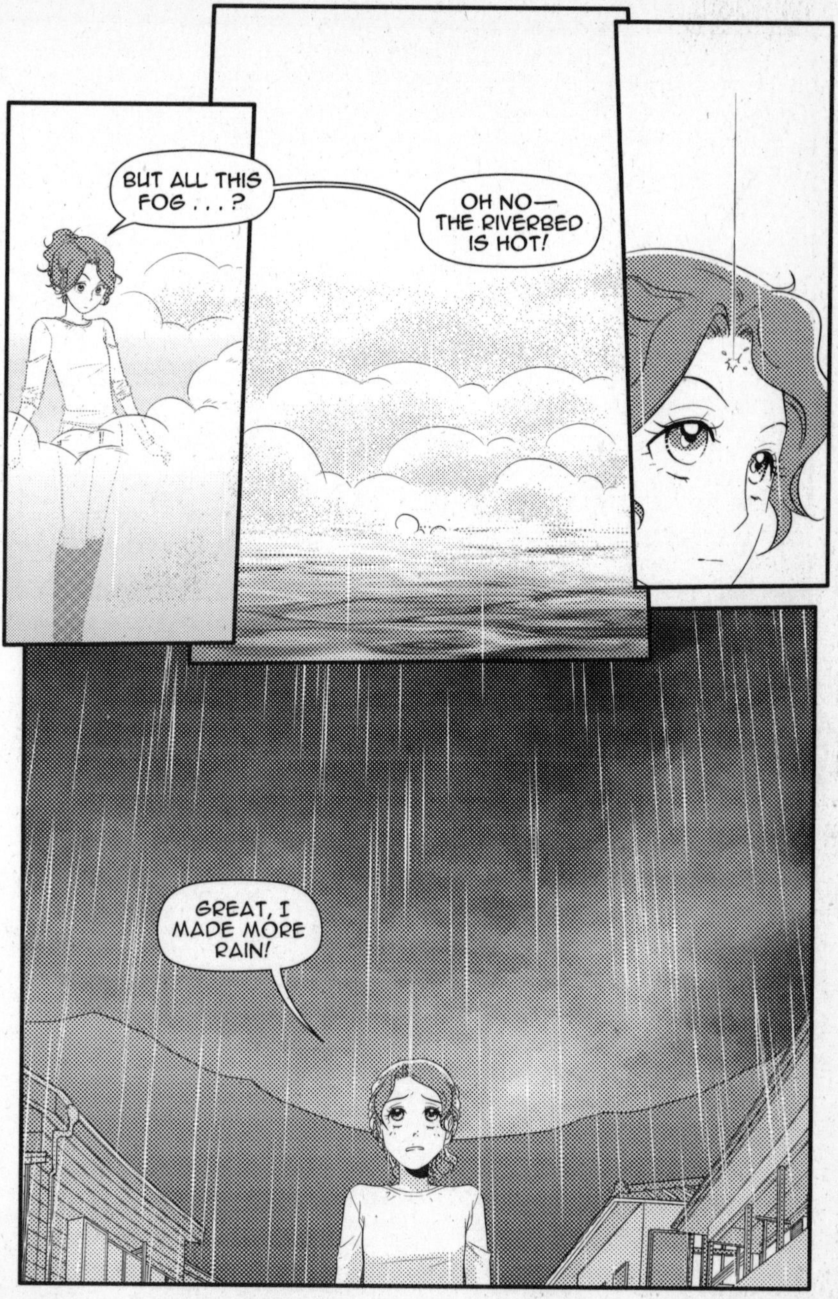
BUT ALL THIS FOG . . . ?
OH NO— THE RIVERBED IS HOT!
GREAT, I MADE MORE RAIN!

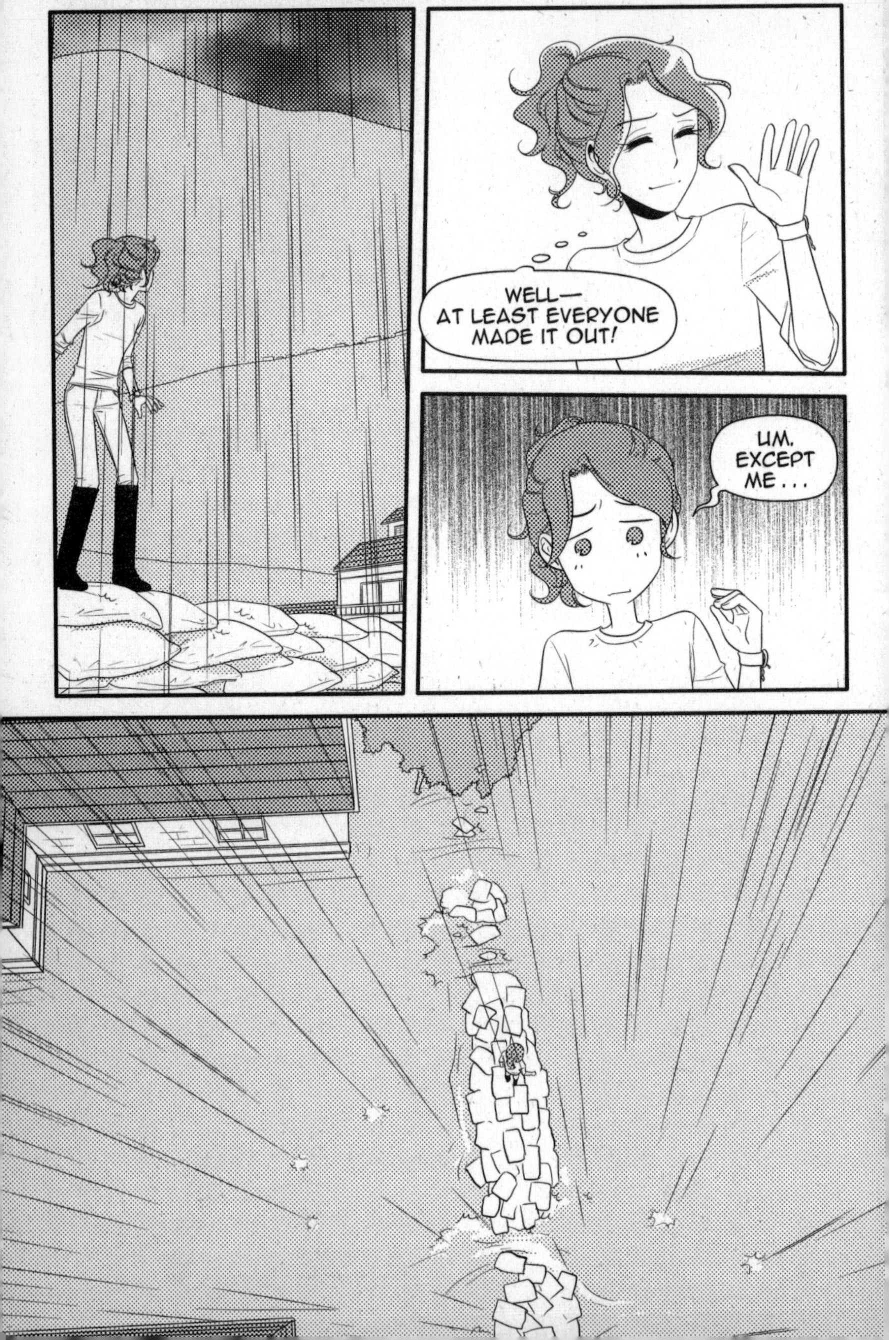
WELL— AT LEAST EVERYONE MADE IT OUT!
UM. EXCEPT ME . . .

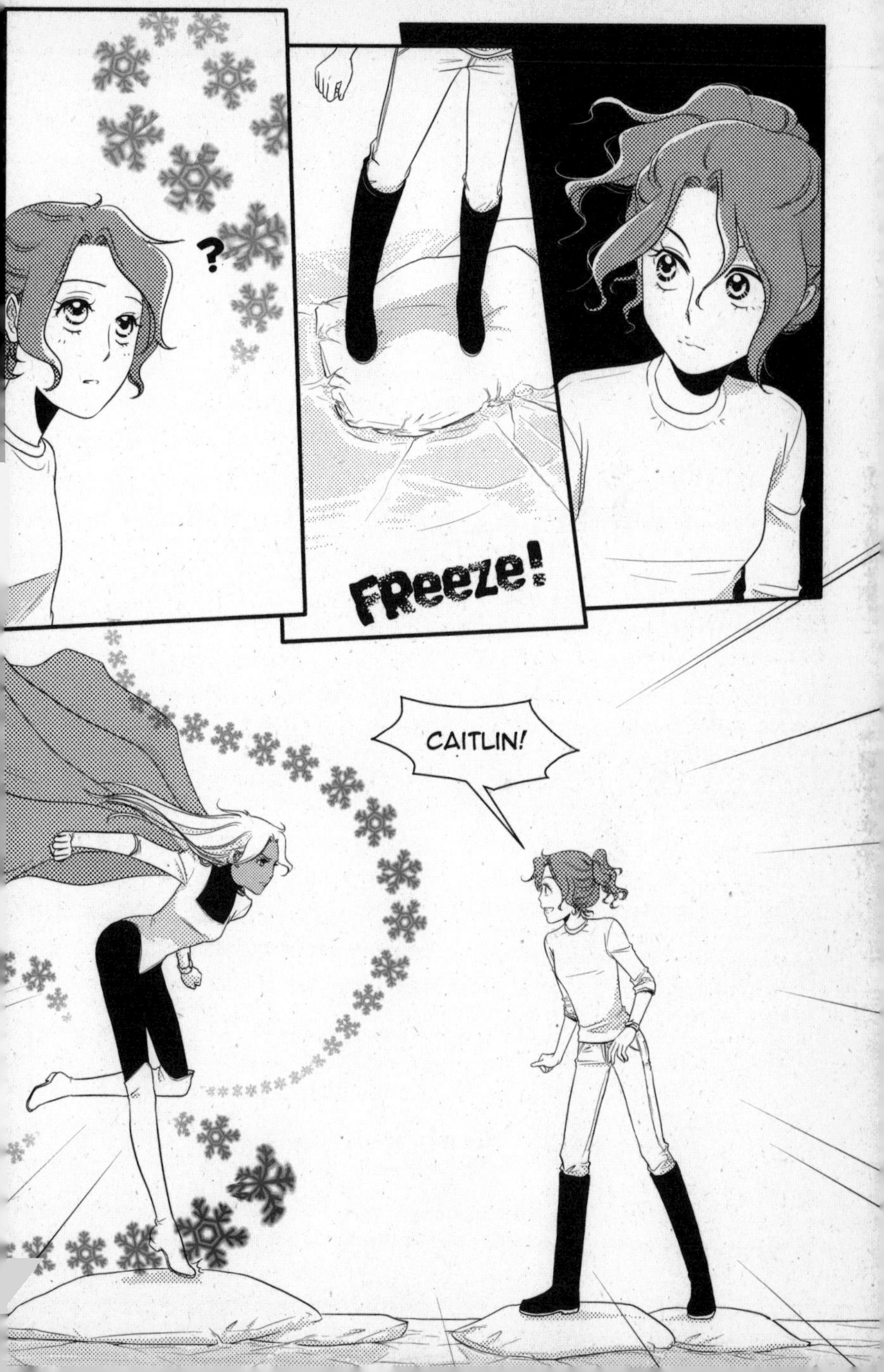
?
FREEZE!
CAITLIN!

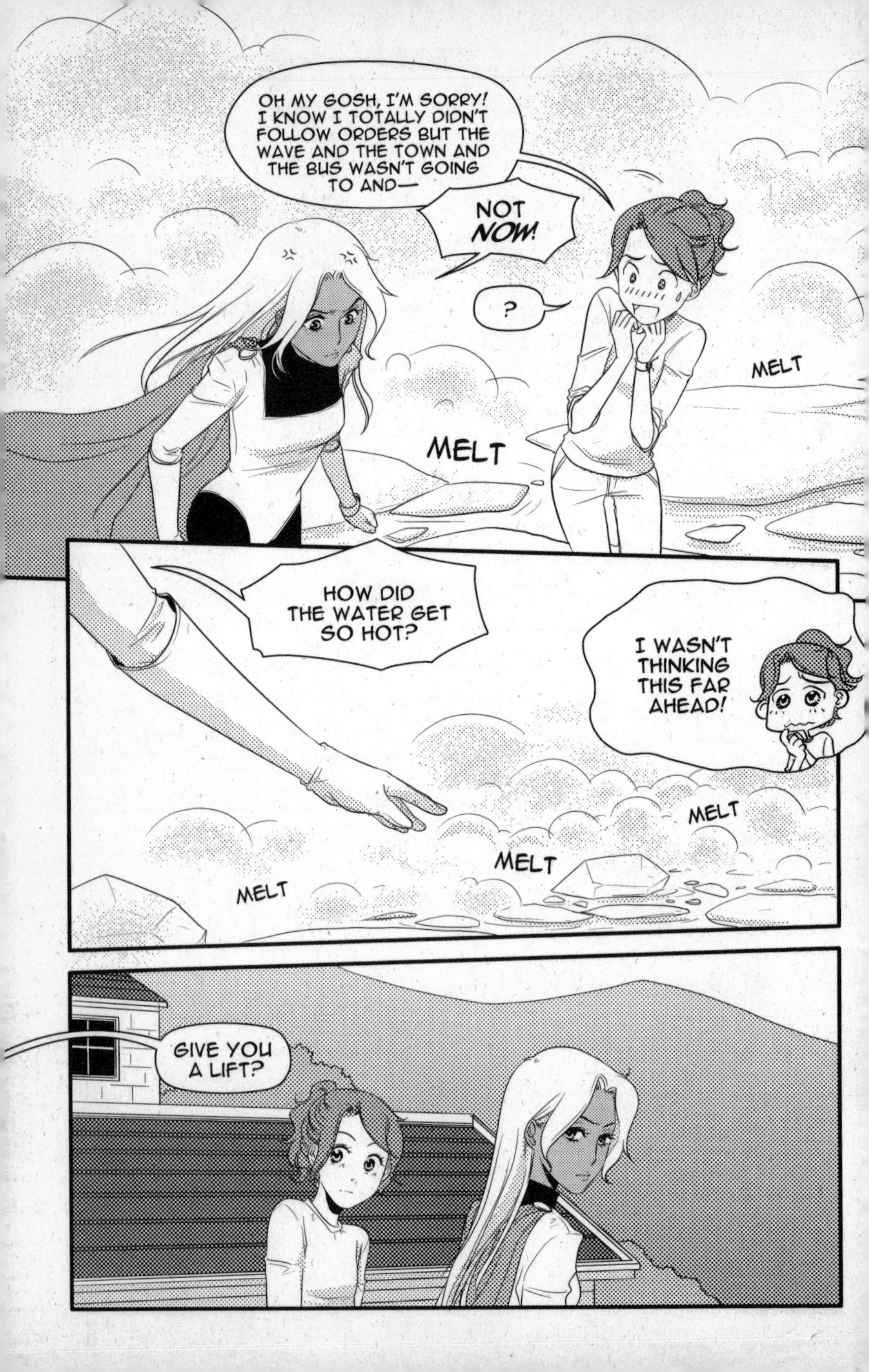
OH MY GOSH, I'M SORRY! I KNOW I TOTALLY DIDN'T FOLLOW ORDERS BUT THE WAVE AND THE TOWN AND THE BUS WASN'T GOING TO AND—
NOT NOW!
?
MELT
MELT
HOW DID THE WATER GET SO HOT?
I WASN'T THINKING THIS FAR AHEAD!
MELT
MELT
MELT
GIVE YOU A LIFT?

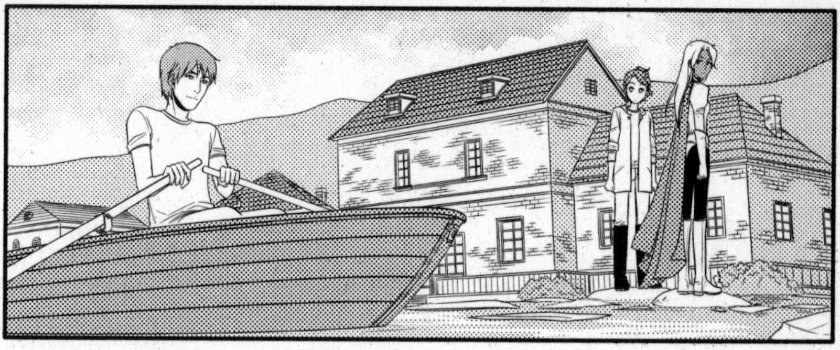
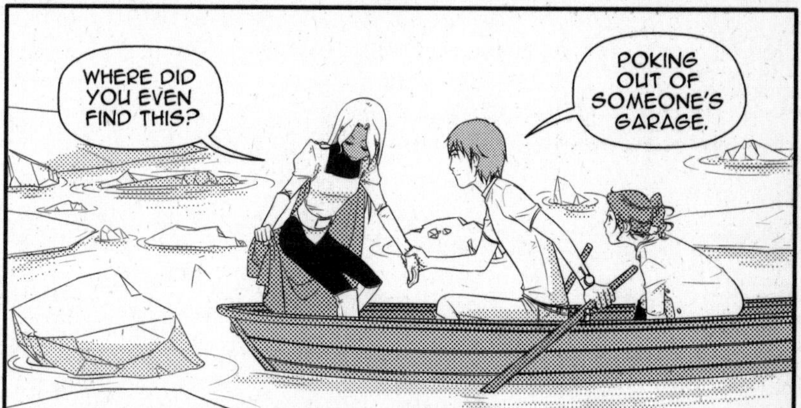
WHERE DID YOU EVEN FIND THIS?
POKING OUT OF SOMEONE'S GARAGE.
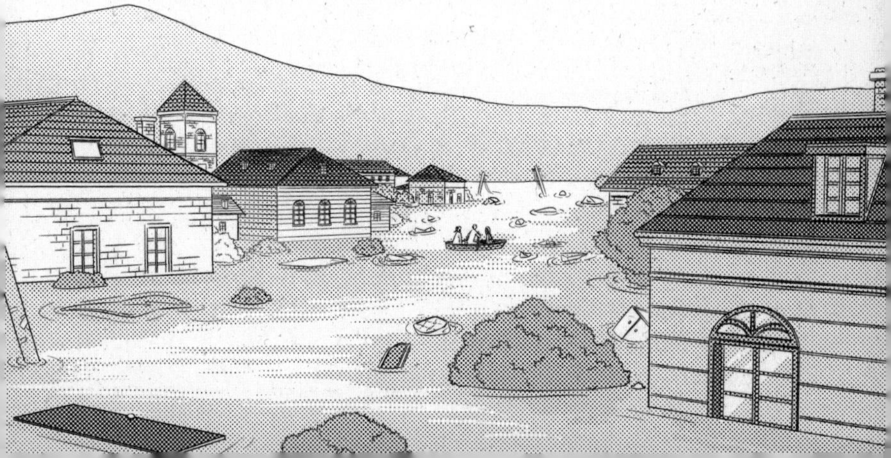

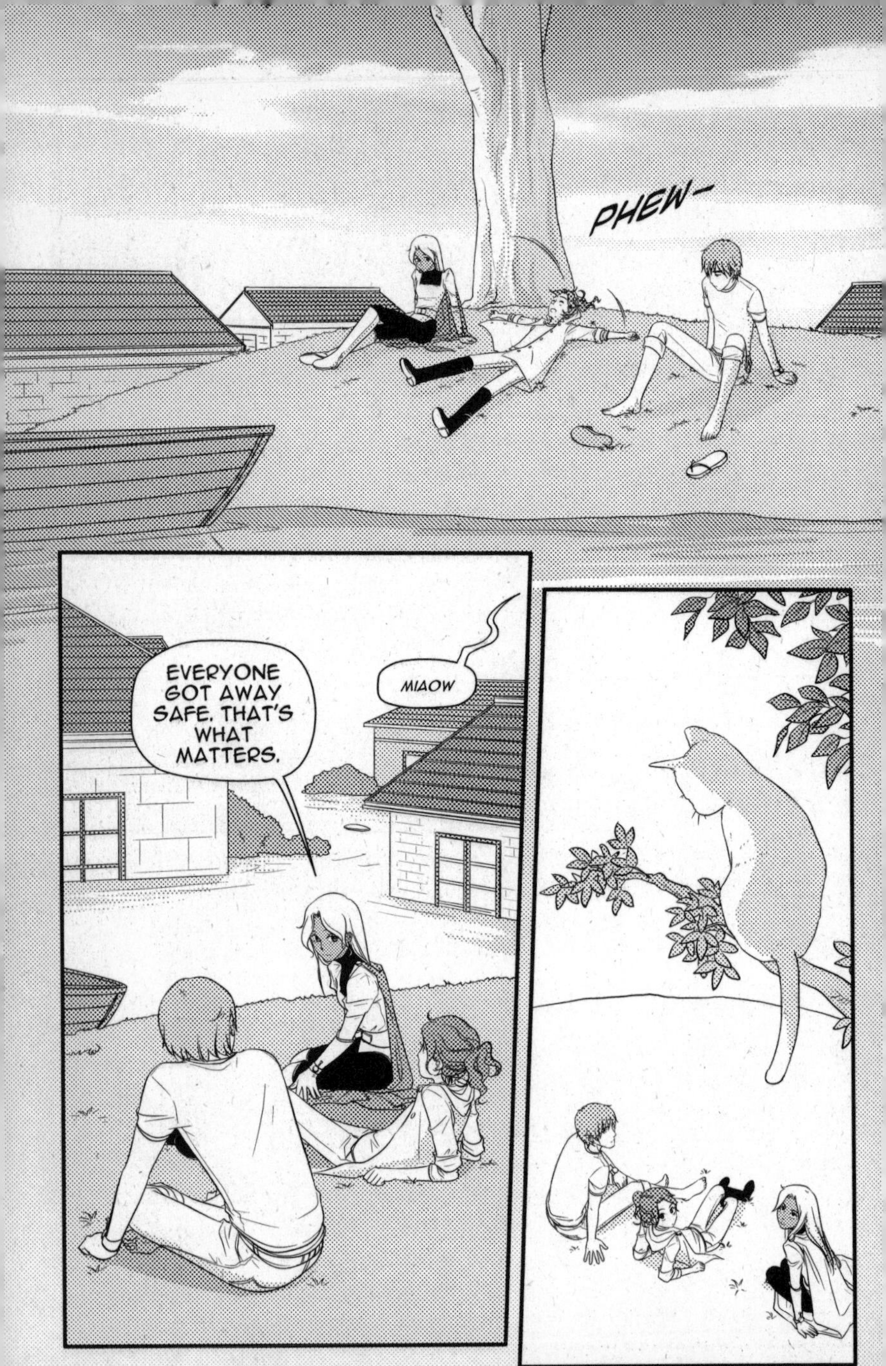
PHEW–
EVERYONE GOT AWAY SAFE. THAT'S WHAT MATTERS.
MIAOW

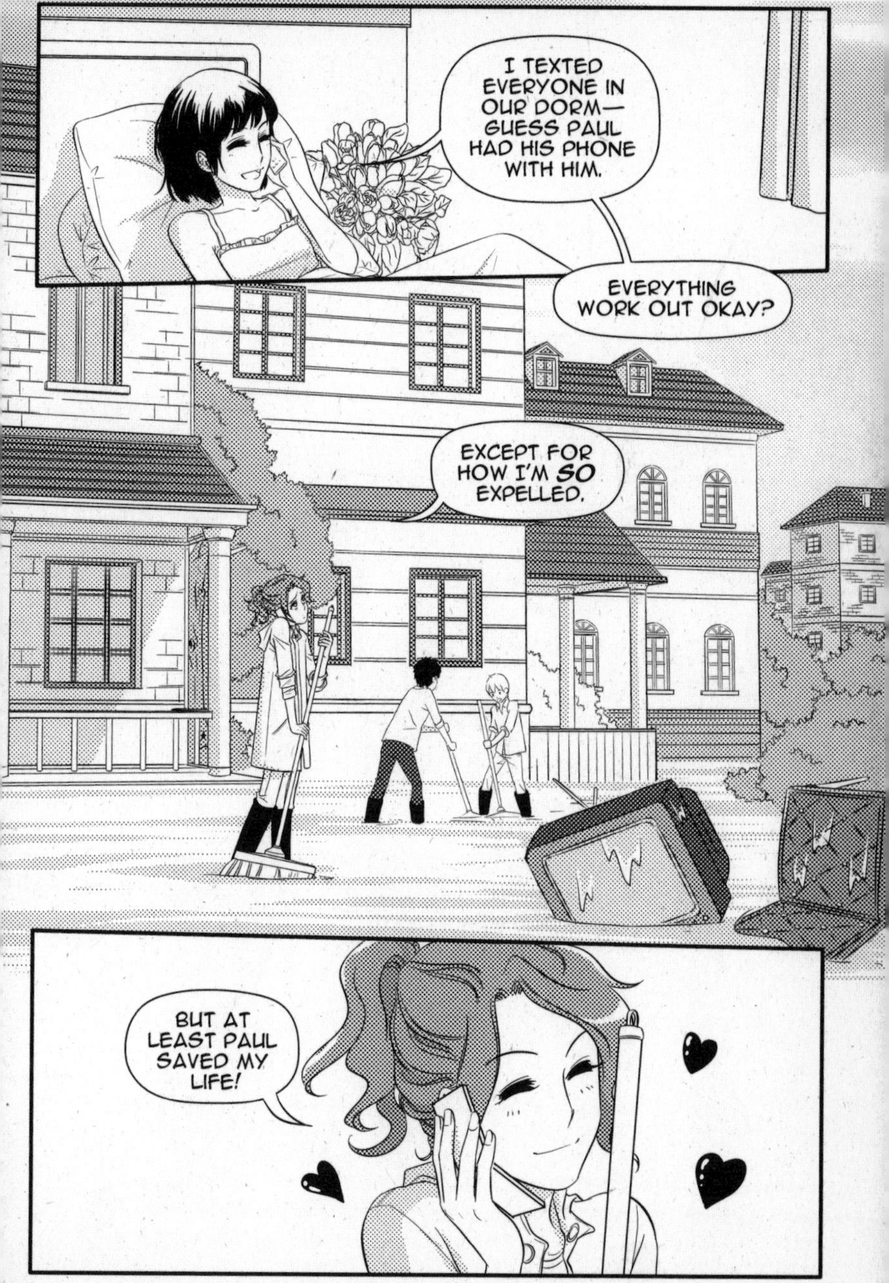
I TEXTED EVERYONE IN OUR DORM— GUESS PAUL HAD HIS PHONE WITH HIM.
EVERYTHING WORK OUT OKAY?
EXCEPT FOR HOW I'M *SO* EXPELLED.
BUT AT LEAST PAUL SAVED MY LIFE!

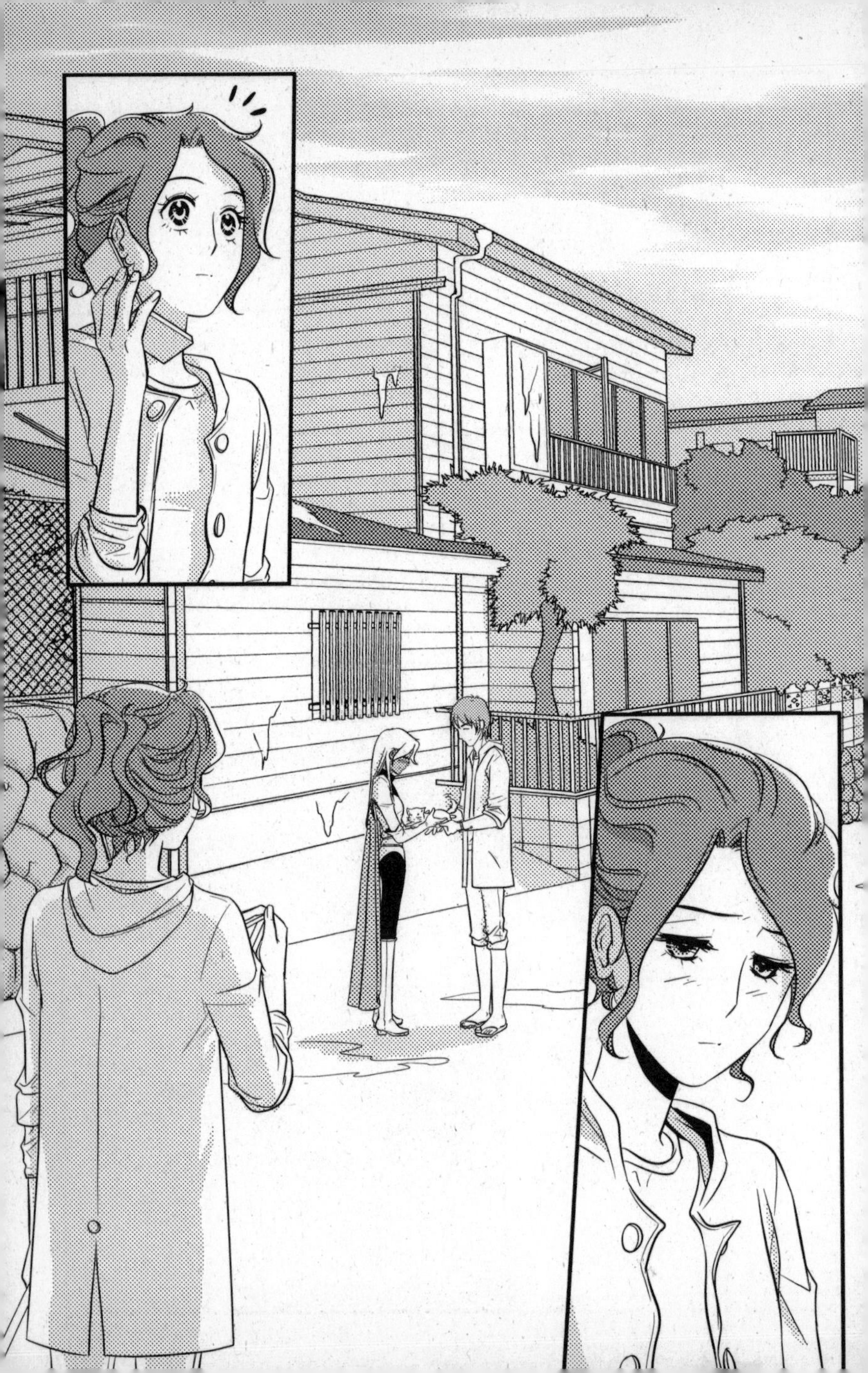

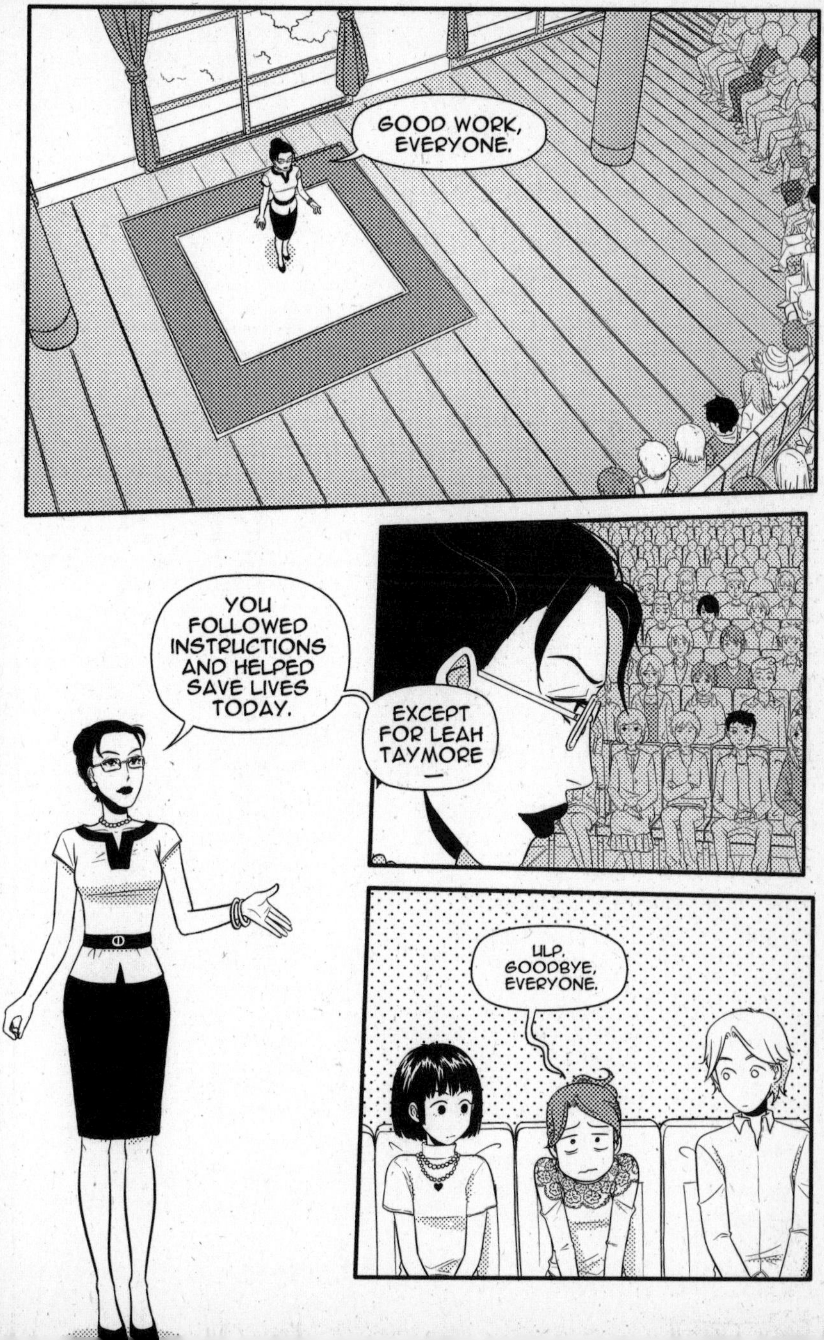
GOOD WORK, EVERYONE.
YOU FOLLOWED INSTRUCTIONS AND HELPED SAVE LIVES TODAY.
EXCEPT FOR LEAH TAYMORE —
ULP. GOODBYE, EVERYONE.

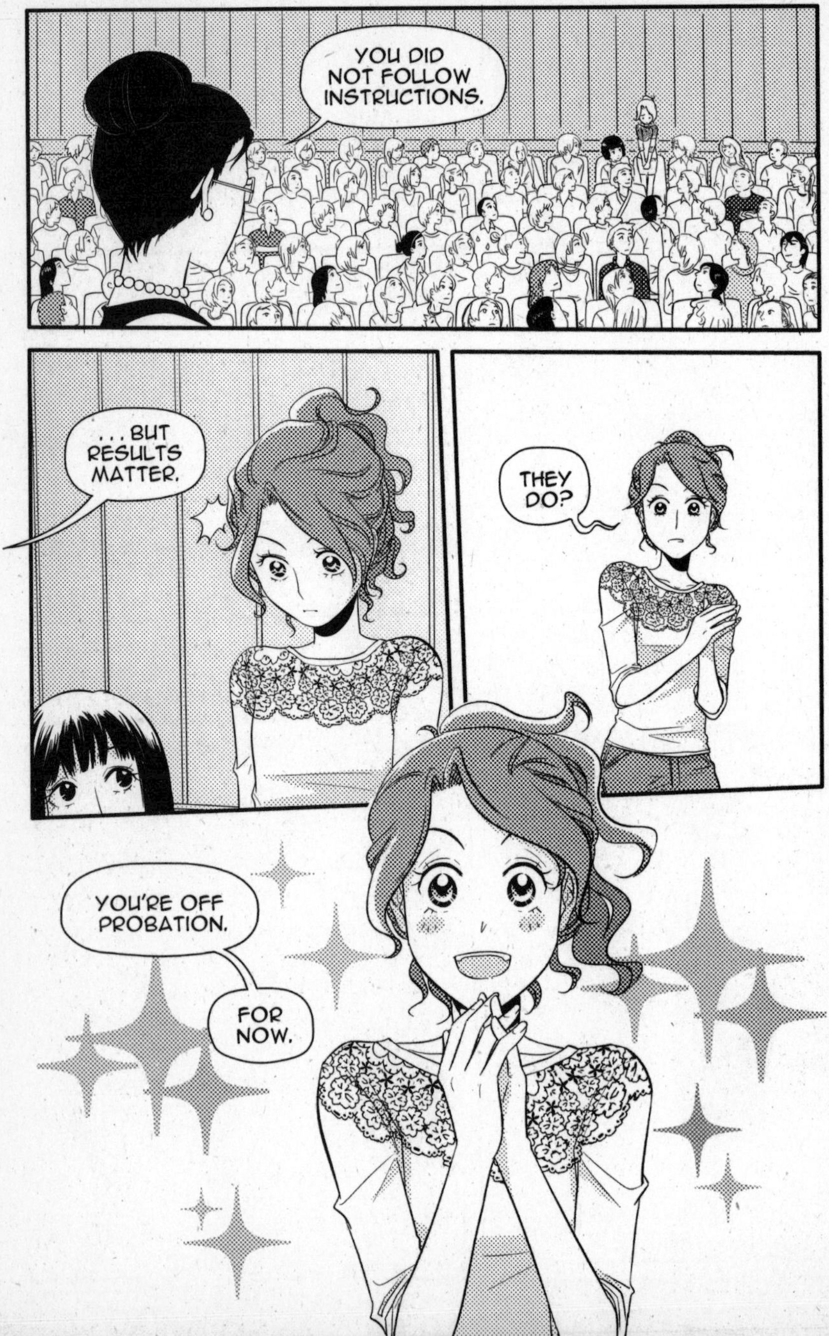
YOU DID NOT FOLLOW INSTRUCTIONS.
. . . BUT RESULTS MATTER.
THEY DO?
YOU'RE OFF PROBATION.
FOR NOW.

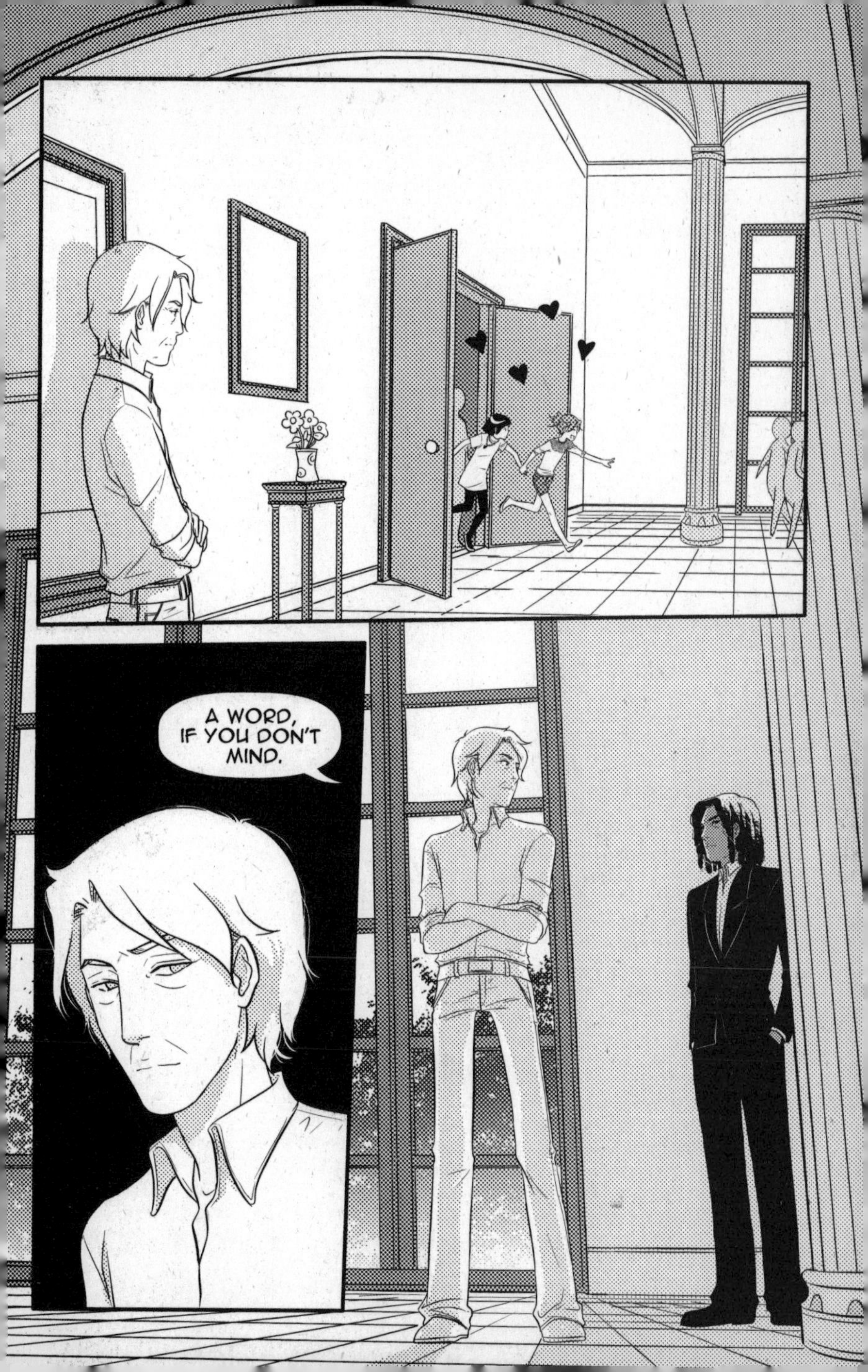
A WORD, IF YOU DON'T MIND.

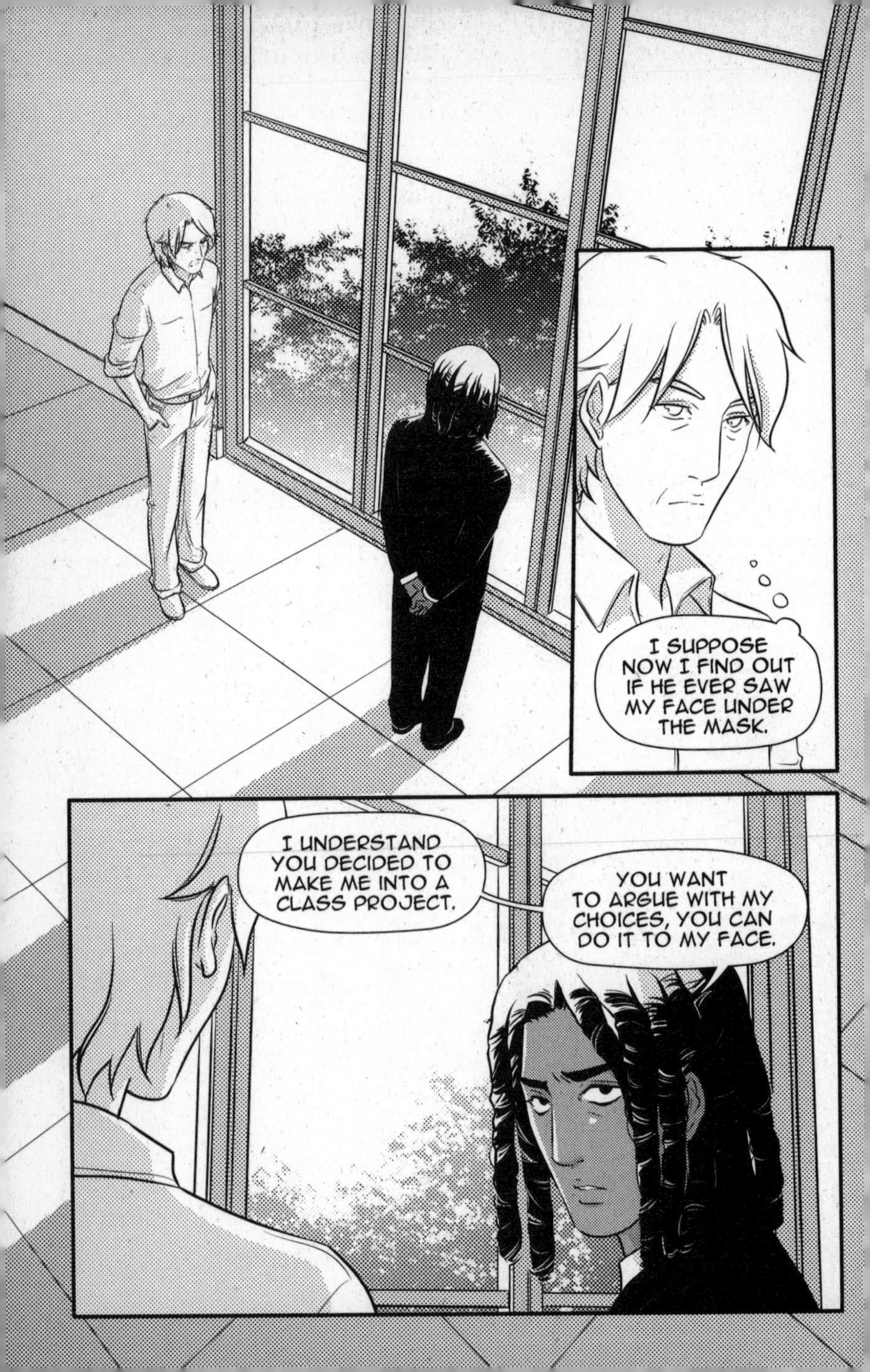
I SUPPOSE NOW I FIND OUT IF HE EVER SAW MY FACE UNDER THE MASK.
I UNDERSTAND YOU DECIDED TO MAKE ME INTO A CLASS PROJECT.
YOU WANT TO ARGUE WITH MY CHOICES, YOU CAN DO IT TO MY FACE.

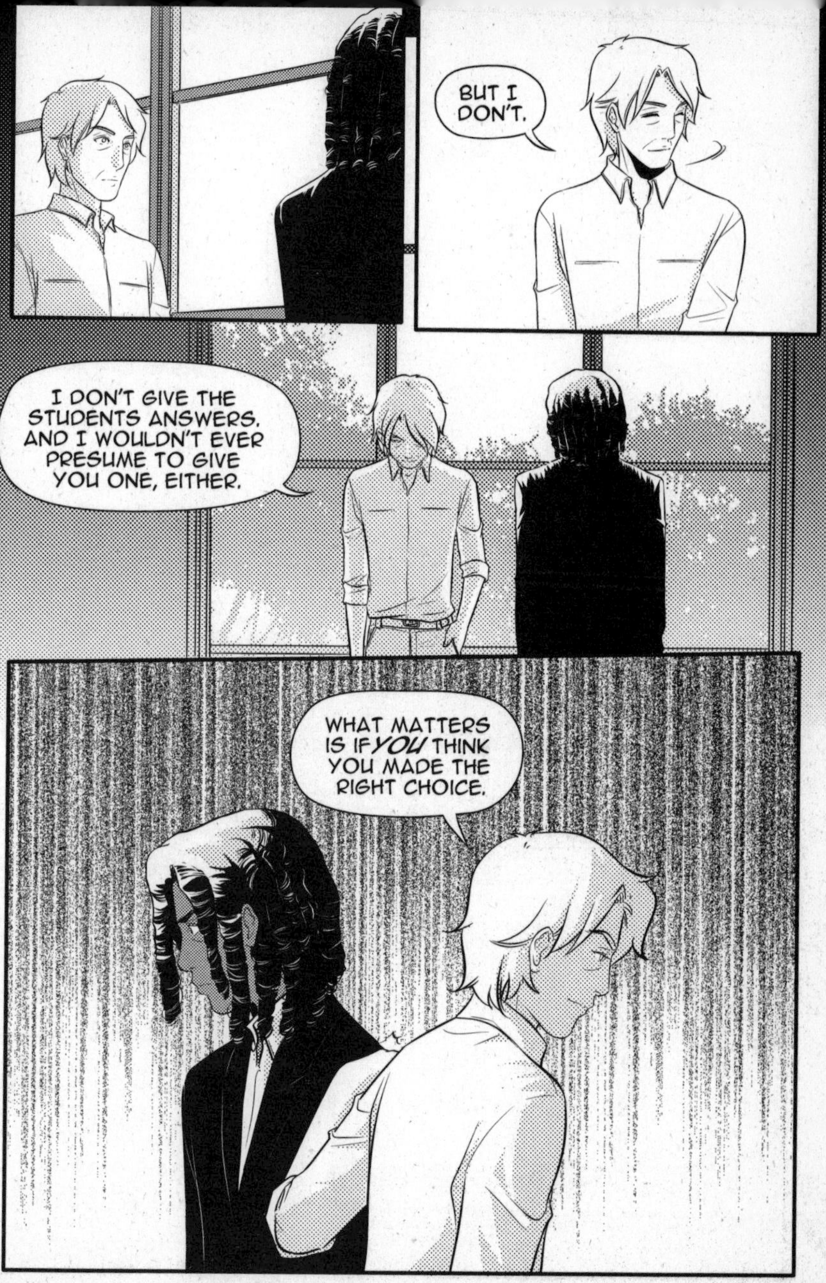
BUT I DON'T.
I DON'T GIVE THE STUDENTS ANSWERS. AND I WOULDN'T EVER PRESUME TO GIVE YOU ONE, EITHER.
WHAT MATTERS IS IF *YOU* THINK YOU MADE THE RIGHT CHOICE.

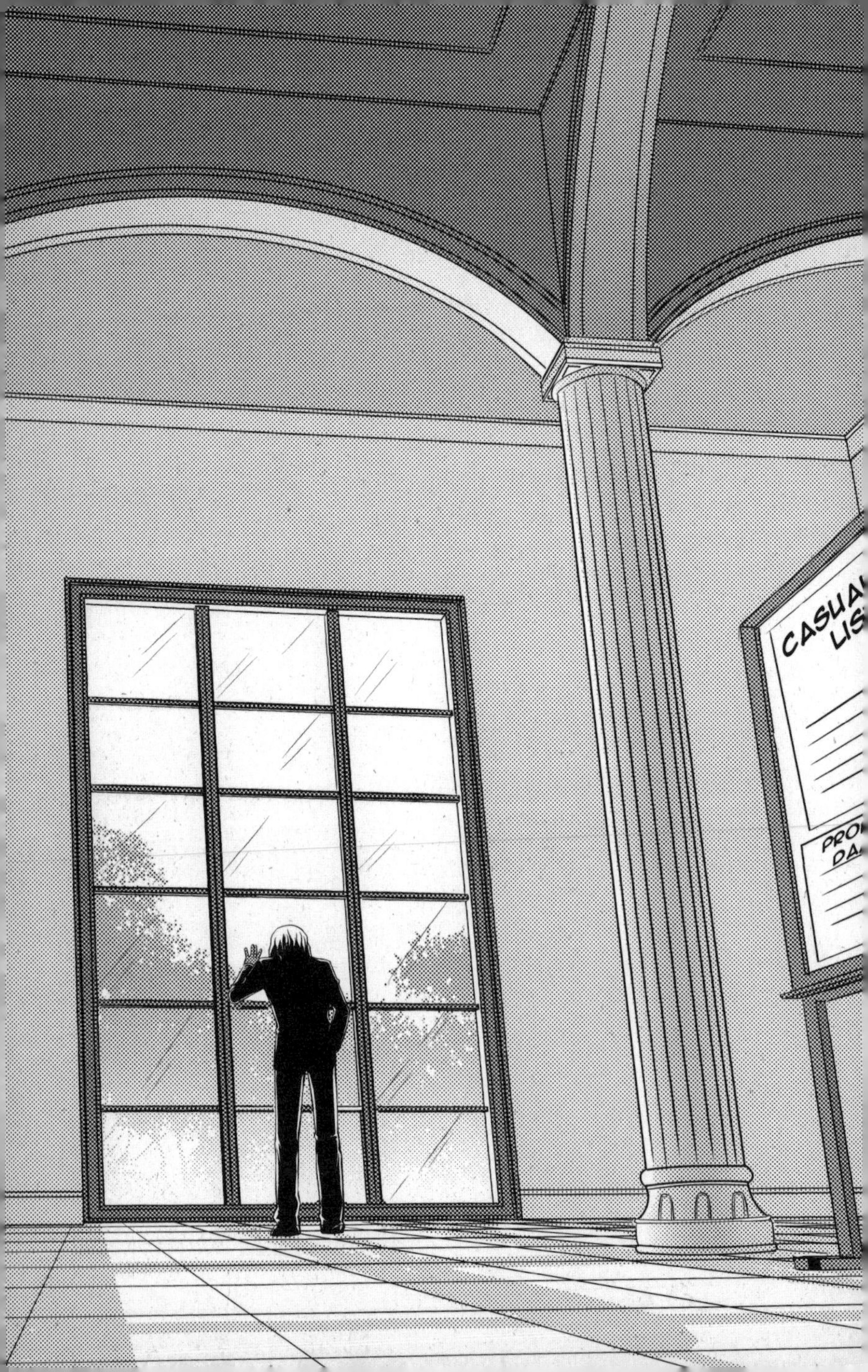
CASUA
LIS
PRO
DA

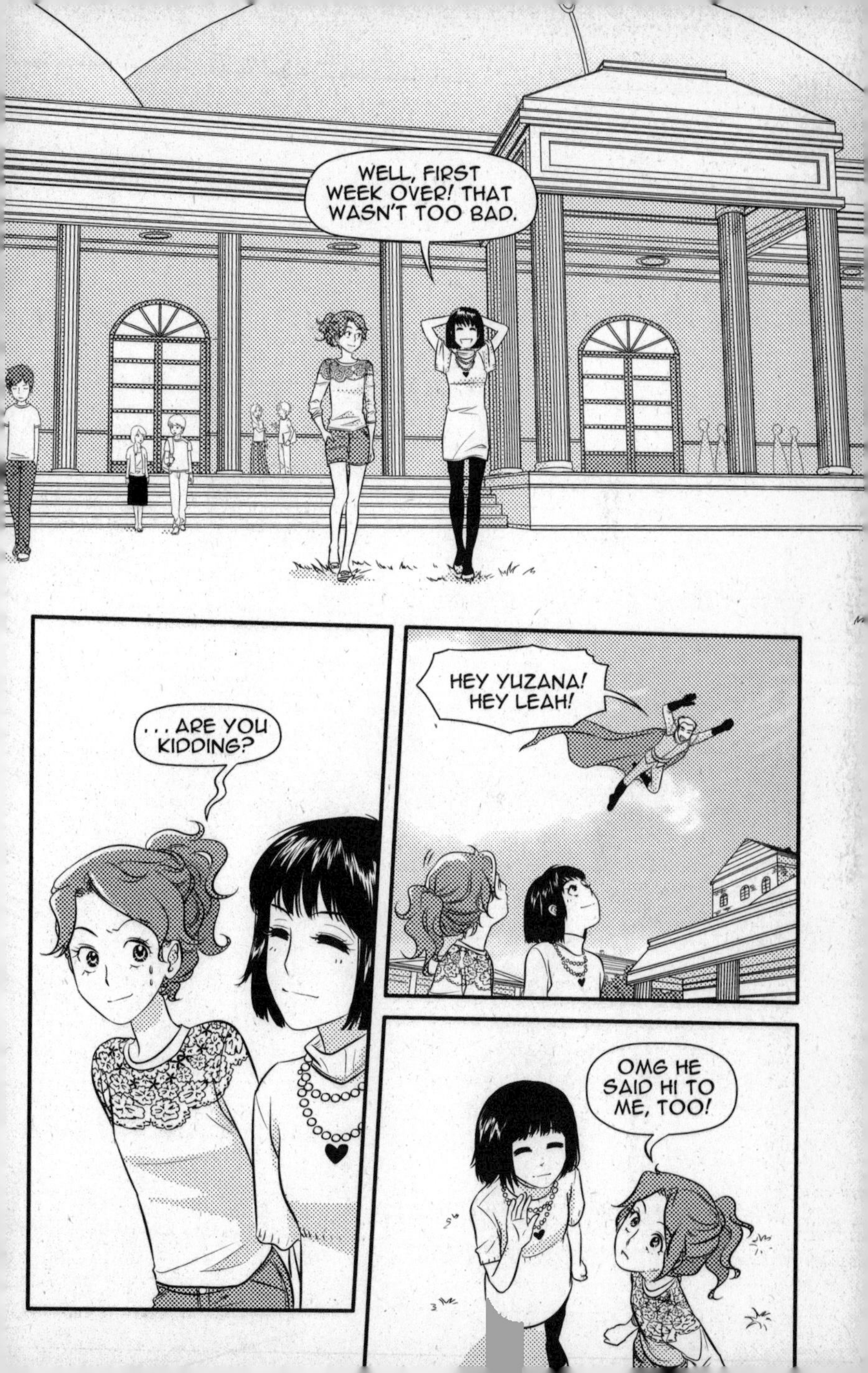
WELL, FIRST WEEK OVER! THAT WASN'T TOO BAD.
. . . ARE YOU KIDDING?
HEY YUZANA! HEY LEAH!
OMG HE SAID HI TO ME, TOO!

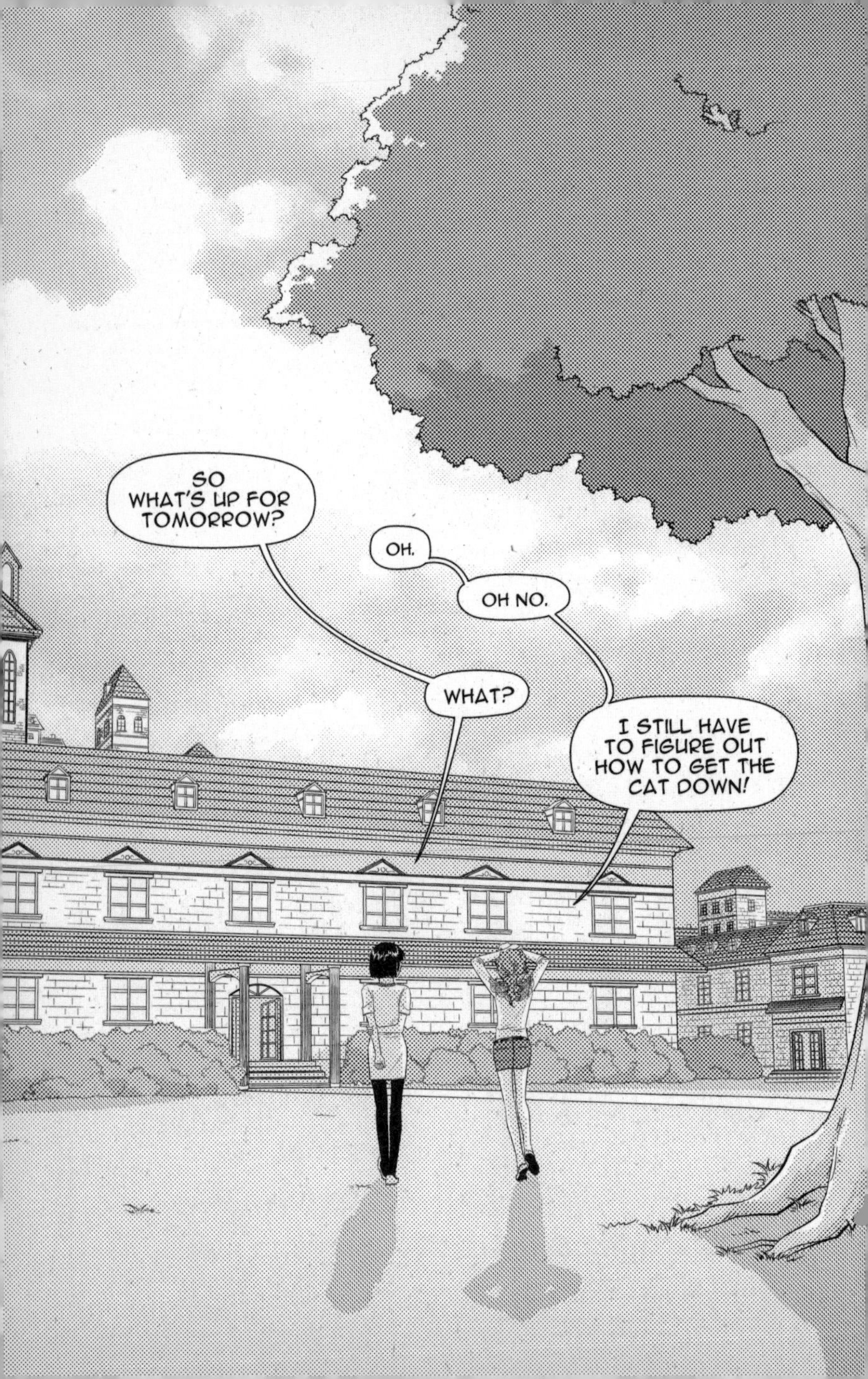
SO WHAT'S UP FOR TOMORROW?
OH.
OH NO.
WHAT?
I STILL HAVE TO FIGURE OUT HOW TO GET THE CAT DOWN!

LIBERTY VOCATIONAL ACADEMY
Semester Grade Report
Leah Taymore

RESCUE

Instructor: Michael Kim

Grade: 87

Shows significant improvement, but more work needed on fundamentals of control. Needs to concentrate on defining a course of action before applying power.

COSTUME DESIGN

Instructor: Dane Dragovich

Grade: 76

Designs lack consistency and originality! Student must work to capture the ESSENCE of her powers with BOLDNESS and ENERGY. Beware an excessive tendency toward indulgence in current fashion—that way lies inevitable obsolescence! Student has however made progress on the basics of color theory and approaches her work with enthusiasm.

PHYSICAL EDUCATION

Instructor: Risha Wuornos

Grade: PASS

Student needs some work on balance, but is in good overall physical condition. Note: Impossible to judge student strength, since student seems to unconsciously adjust weight of items to her carrying capacity and has so far been unable to prevent herself from doing so.

INTRO TO CONSTRUCTION MATERIALS AND PROCESSES

Instructor: Carla Guarnacci

Grade: 93

Student has intuitive grasp of materials composition.

ETHICS

Instructor: Alexander Locke

Grade: 91

Student demonstrates thoughtful contemplation of ethical issues and shows signs of working past knee-jerk first reactions to more subtle analysis. High hopes for her further progress!

ARTIST'S SKETCHBOOK

Yishan Li and Naomi Novik worked closely together to create the visual look of Leah, Paul, Alexander Bane, and the other main characters of *Will Supervillains Be on the Final?*

Here are some of Naomi's original character descriptions and the designs that Yishan submitted for approval.

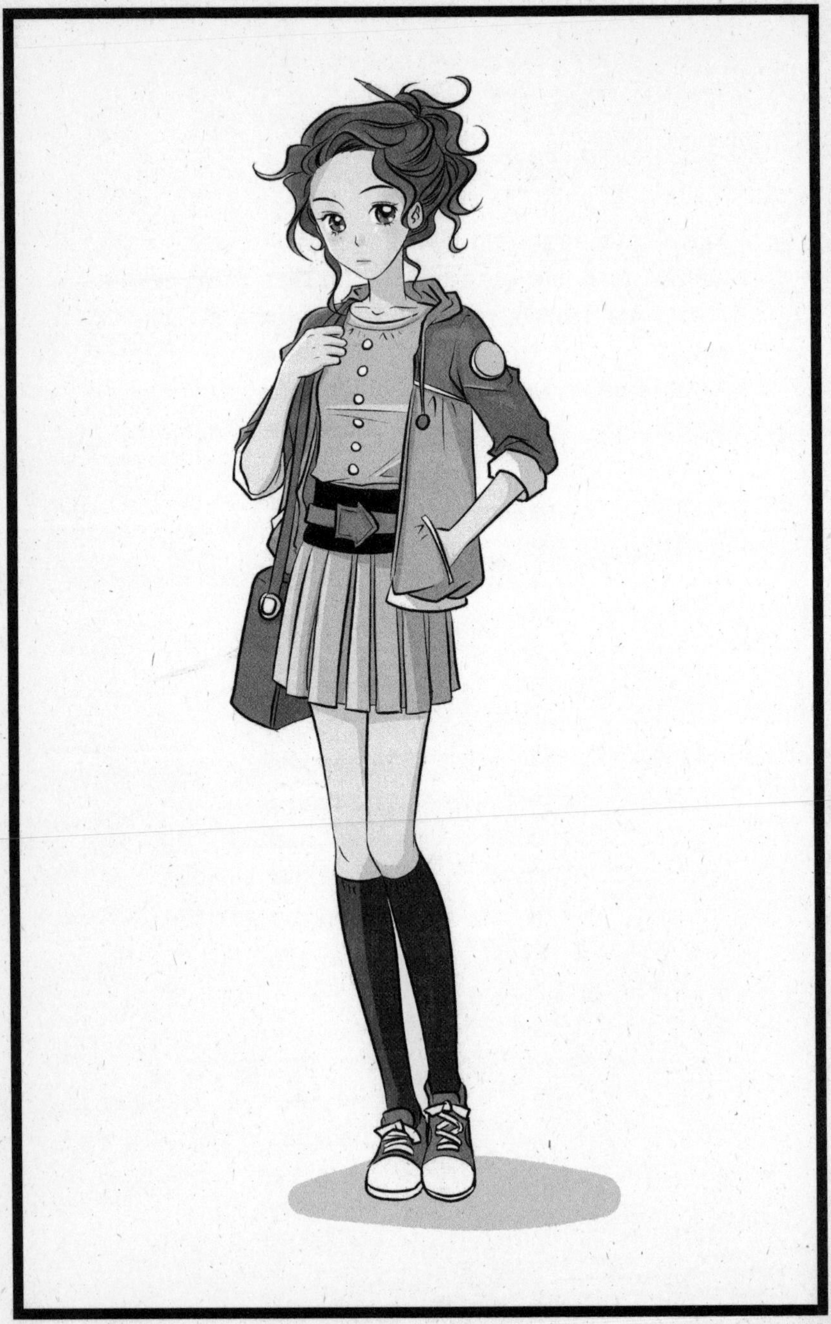

LEAH TAYMORE—protagonist

Leah has the height and the muscle density to be a Wonder Woman type, tall and muscular, but she's prone to day-dreaming and totally unsuited to sports, the kind of person who only notices the ball coming at them when it hits them in the face. Plus she's painfully bored by exercise and by eating, which she's been harassed to do all her life, since her high-powered metabolism keeps her too thin.

She's now sixteen, fresh from a growth spurt and still awkward with her new height, prone to stumbling and knocking into things. She's of Czech Jewish descent. Her face is a little pinched, with wide brown eyes and high cheekbones, and she's got brown hair. She occasionally tries to do something more exciting with it, but it grows fast, so her attempt at getting highlights before coming to school for the first time left her with four-inch-long roots before she even got there. She finally gave up in despair the night before leaving and chopped it all off herself near the ends, so for the moment she's got ragged tips that are lighter than the rest of her hair, and it's a bit of a messy short crop that she tries to keep pulled back in a ponytail, though wisps escape around her face and down her neck.

Yishan wrote, when she delivered her sketch:
I didn't make Leah muscular or particularly tall. Reason for this is, the only muscular female characters in shojo manga are villains (most of the time there isn't any muscular female in shojo at all!). So instead, I made her a bit cuter.

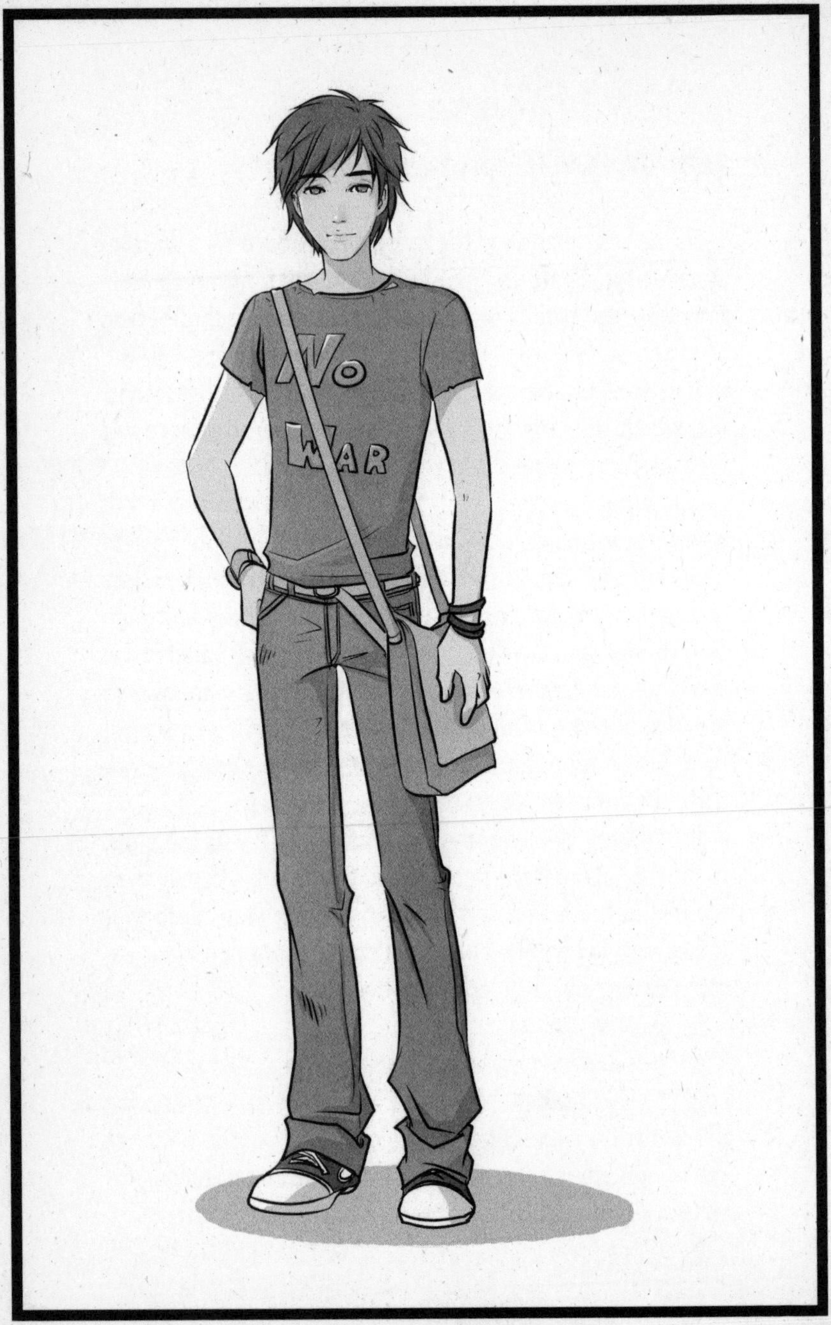
No
War

PAUL LYMAN—Leah's romantic interest

Paul is nineteen and has a scruffy hipster look by accident, largely because money is tight for him and his family and it shows a little bit: forgets to shave or cut his hair sometimes, worn jeans because he's actually worn them too much rather than because he bought them that way, tight faded T-shirts with lefty political statements because T-shirts are cheap and he wears them until they fall apart (unraveled seams and a few holes don't count).

He carries himself older than he looks, and he's still lanky but starting to fill out some, with broad shoulders and strong arms. Floppy dark hair and green eyes, often downturned and serious, although when he laughs, he laughs all the way, head flung back, really into it. Ethnicity-wise, he's of French-Arabic descent.

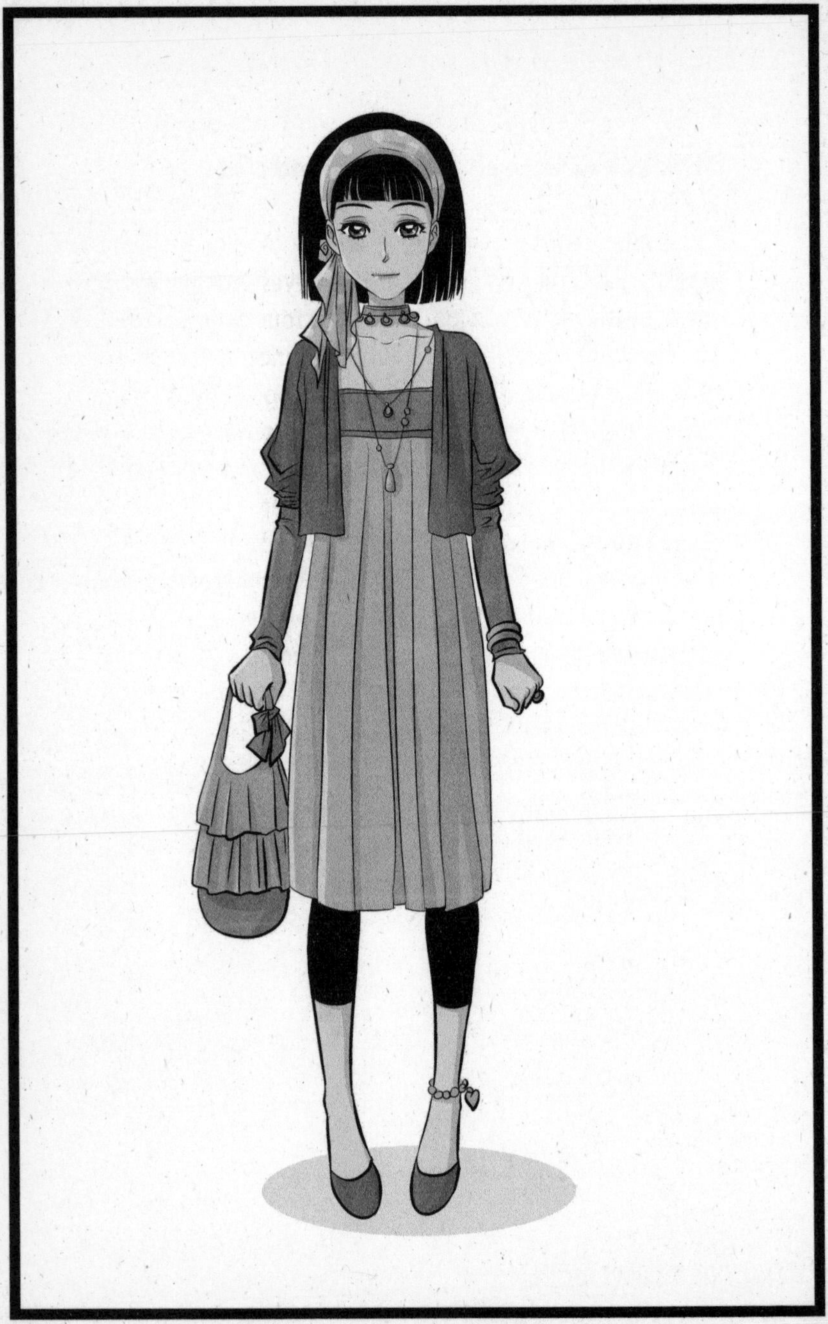

YUZANA MYAT—Leah's best friend and roommate

Yuzana is seventeen, with dark brown eyes and black hair; she's Burmese. She's a bit plump with a round face, and she smiles a lot, warmly. She has a very distinctive style that's cute, bohemian, and sunny rather than polished—chances are when you see her you'd say "That's neat, I've never seen that before" about *something* she's wearing, without ever feeling intimidated by how well put together she is—and that's deliberate on her part; she's put together a style that makes people comfortable and react positively. She has dark hair in a swingy bob of a haircut with the ends even, often with funky barettes of some kind, maybe a headband, often some odd earrings.

ORIGINAL SKETCH

ALEXANDER BANE—supervillain, aka Alexander Locke, Ethics teacher

My mental casting here is Jason Bateman from *Hancock*. Bane is very safe- and pleasant-looking: a cheerful, open face with a square jaw, nice smile, and clear blue eyes. He's a typical mongrel Midwesterner, a mix of Scandinavian/British ethnicities. By choice (and at the school), he wears thin wire-rimmed glasses and slightly rumpled suits (that only an expert eye would realize are actually Savile Row work, custom-tailored for comfort), usually with the jacket off, the sleeves of his white dress shirt rolled up, tie a little loose, sneaking in casual jeans and a Henley instead whenever he thinks he can get away with it.

When meeting with other supervillains, though, he swaps in the kind of suit that *looks* expensive, dark with a French-cuffed shirt with small subtle cufflinks, jacket always on, tie choker-tight, very sharp and hard-looking. When fighting superheroes, he wears a helmet and a carefully designed partially mechanized suit that conceals most of his face and makes his body look bigger than it actually is. In person he's six feet tall, not hugely muscled; in the suit he's six-three and looks Superman-like in build.

Naomi's response to Yishan's original sketch for Alexander Bane:
The sketch of Bane actually more resembles my mental idea of Calvin Washington (Leah's student advisor, the ex-superhero whose powers got burned out and who is deeply bitter). Can we maybe use this sketch as the basis for Calvin,

REVISED SKETCH

and make Alexander a little cuter perhaps? I'm actually thinking I want to have an eventual romance going between him and Alaide, and just generally want him to be an attractive sort of person (the kind of teacher girls would have a crush on).

The revised version was approved.

Caitlin and Stephen Victoire

Basically Caitlin and Stephen are what you'd expect to get if Superman had twins with Storm of the X-Men. Their parents had a brief reckless fling while unhappy and on the outs with their respective non-superhero partners and ended up marrying for the sake of the kids. Both Stephen and Caitlin have been aware of that sacrifice as far back as they can remember and feel they have to be perfect to make up for it.

Dr. Alaide Silva Santos

In her forties, Alaide is a remarkably beautiful (not pretty) woman. She's Latina, with a strong flavor of Native American in her face: an oval-shaped face with a broad forehead (no widow's peak at all), a strong nose, pencil-thin elegant brows, with dark brown eyes and very long black hair that she usually wears pinned up into a knot, with not a tendril daring to escape.

ABOUT THE CREATORS

NAOMI NOVIK is the acclaimed author of *His Majesty's Dragon, Throne of Jade, Black Powder War, Empire of Ivory, Victory of Eagles,* and *Tongues of Serpents,* the first six volumes of the Temeraire series, recently optioned by Peter Jackson, the Academy Award–winning director of the *Lord of the Rings* trilogy. In 2007 Novik received the John W. Campbell Award for Best New Writer at the World Science Fiction Convention. A history buff with a particular interest in the Napoleonic era, Novik studied English literature at Brown University, then did graduate work in computer science at Columbia University before leaving to participate in the design and development of the computer game Neverwinter Nights: Shadows of Undrentide. Novik lives in New York City with her family and six computers.

YISHAN LI is a British/Chinese manga artist currently living in Shanghai. She has been drawing for more than ten years, and her work has been published in the United States, France, Great Britain, China, and elsewhere. Among her projects are *Cutie B, 500 Manga Creatures, Shojo Art Studio, Shounen Art Studio,* and *The Clique.*

AN INTRODUCTION TO EMILY ROLAND

We hope you've enjoyed *Will Supervillains Be on the Final?* Naomi Novik is also the author of a series of novels starring the dragon Temeraire and his captain, William Laurence, and set during the Napoleonic Wars. Dragons play an extremely important part in Naomi's stories; they protect England's ships, deliver messages, spy on the enemy and—when necessary—engage in aerial combat.

A popular character in the Temeraire series is Emily Roland, who dreams one day of captaining a dragon of her own. Here is an excerpt from the first book in the series, *His Majesty's Dragon,* in which Emily first appears—although on first glance, Laurence doesn't recognize the "sandy-haired boy" as being female. He doesn't expect to see a girl training alongside young men, and yet it doesn't take long before Emily will become an important member of Temeraire's crew.

The other novels in the Temeraire series include: *Throne of Jade, Black Powder War, Empire of Ivory, Victory of Eagles,* and *Tongues of Serpents.* Naomi is working on the next in the series.

CHAPTER 5

The sky over Loch Laggan was full of low-hanging clouds, pearl grey, mirrored in the black water of the lake. Spring had not yet arrived; a crust of ice and snow lay over the shore, ripples of yellow sand from an autumn tide still preserved beneath. The crisp cold smell of pine and fresh-cut wood rose from the forest. A gravel road wound up from the northern shores of the lake to the complex of the covert, and Temeraire turned to follow it up the low mountain.

A quadrangle of several large wooden sheds stood together on a level clearing near the top, open in the front and rather like half a stable in appearance; men were working outside on metal and leather: obviously the ground crews, responsible for the maintenance of the aviators' equipment. None of them so much as glanced up at the dragon's shadow crossing over their workplace, as Temeraire flew on to the headquarters.

The main building was a very medieval sort of fortification: four bare towers joined by thick stone walls, framing an enormous courtyard in the front and a squat, imposing hall that sank directly into the mountaintop and seemed to have grown out of it. The courtyard was almost entirely overrun. A young Regal Copper, twice Temeraire's size, sprawled drowsing over the flagstones with a pair of brown-and-purple Winchesters even smaller than Volatilus sleeping right on his back. Three mid-sized Yellow Reapers were in a mingled heap on the opposite side of the courtyard, their white-striped sides rising and falling in rhythm.

As Laurence climbed down, he discovered the reason for the dragons' choice of resting place: the flagstones were warm, as if heated from below, and Temeraire murmured happily and stretched himself on the stones beside the Yellow Reapers as soon as Laurence had unloaded him.

A couple of servants had come out to meet him, and they took the baggage off his hands. He was directed to the back of the building, through narrow dark corridors, musty smelling, until he came out into another open courtyard that emerged from the mountainside and ended with no railing, dropping off sheer into another ice-strewn valley. Five dragons were in the air, wheeling in graceful formation like a flock of birds; the point-leader was a Longwing, instantly recognizable by the black-and-white ripples bordering its orange-tipped wings, which faded to a dusky blue along their extraordinary length. A couple of Yellow Reapers held the flanking positions, and the ends were anchored by a pale greenish Grey Copper to the left, and a silver-grey dragon spotted with blue and black patches to the right; Laurence could not immediately identify its breed.

Though their wings beat in wholly different time, their relative positions hardly changed, until the Longwing's signal-midwingman waved a flag; then they switched off smoothly as dancers, reversing so the Longwing was flying last. At some other signal Laurence did not see, they all backwinged at once, performing a perfect loop and coming back into the original formation. He saw at once that the maneuver gave the Longwing the greatest sweep over the ground during the pass while retaining the protection of the rest of the wing around it; naturally it was the greatest offensive threat among the group.

"Nitidus, you are still dropping low in the pass; try changing to a six-beat pattern on the loop." It was the deep resounding voice of a dragon, coming from above; Laurence turned and saw a golden-hued dragon with the Reaper markings in pale green and the edges of his wings deep orange, perched on an outcropping to the right of the courtyard: he bore no rider and no harness, save, if it could be called so, a broad golden neck-ring studded with rounds of pale green jade stone.

Laurence stared. Out in the valley, the wing repeated its looping pass. "Better," the dragon called approvingly. Then he turned his head and looked down. "Captain Laurence?" he said. "Admiral Powys said you would be arriving; you come in good time. I am Celeritas, training master here." He spread his wings for lift and leapt easily down into the courtyard.

Laurence bowed mechanically. Celeritas was a mid-weight dragon, perhaps a quarter of the size of a Regal Copper; smaller even than Temeraire's present juvenile size. "Hm," he said, lowering his head to inspect Laurence closely; the deep green irises of his eyes seemed to turn and contract around the narrowed pupil. "Hm, well, you are a good deal older than most handlers; but that is often all to the good when we must hurry along a young dragon, as in Temeraire's case I think we must."

He lifted his head and called out into the valley again, "Lily, remember to keep your neck straight on the loop." He turned back to Laurence. "Now then. He has no special offensive capabilities showing, as I understand it?"

"No, sir." The answer and the address were automatic; tone and attitude alike both declared the dragon's rank, and habit carried Laurence along through his surprise. "And Sir Edward Howe, who identified his species, was of the opinion that it was unlikely he should develop such, though not out of the question—"

"Yes, yes," Celeritas interrupted. "I have read Sir Edward's work; he is an expert on the Oriental breeds, and I would trust his judgment in the matter over my own. It is a pity, for we could well do with one of those Japanese poison-spitters, or waterspout-makers: now that would be useful against a French Flamme-de-Gloire. But heavy-combat weight, I understand?"

"He is at present some nine tons in weight, and it is nearly six weeks since he was hatched," Laurence said.

"Good, that is very good, he ought to double that," Celeritas said, and he rubbed the side of a claw over his forehead thoughtfully. "So. All is as I had heard. Good. We will be pairing Temeraire with Maximus, the Regal Copper currently here in training. The two of them together will serve as a loose backing arc for

Lily's formation—that is the Longwing there." He gestured with his head out at the formation wheeling in the valley, and Laurence, still bewildered, turned to watch it for a moment.

The dragon continued, "Of course, I must see Temeraire fly before I can determine the specific course of your training, but I need to finish this session, and after a long journey he will not show to advantage in any case. Ask Lieutenant Granby to show you about and tell you where to find the feeding grounds; you will find him in the officers' club. Come back with Temeraire tomorrow, an hour past first light."

This was a command; an acknowledgment was required. "Very good, sir," Laurence said, concealing his stiffness in formality. Fortunately, Celeritas did not seem to notice; he was already leaping back up to his higher vantage point.

Laurence was very glad that he did not know where the officers' club was; he felt he could have used a quiet week to adjust his thinking, rather than the fifteen minutes it took him to find a servant who could point him in the right direction. Everything which he had ever heard about dragons was turned upon its head: that dragons were useless without their handlers; that unharnessed dragons were only good for breeding. He no longer wondered at all the anxiety on the part of the aviators; what would the world think, to know they were trained—given orders—by one of the beasts they supposedly controlled?

Of course, considered rationally, he had long possessed proofs of dragon intelligence and independence, in Temeraire's person; but these had developed gradually over time, and he had unconsciously come to think of Temeraire as a fully realized individual without extending the implication to the rest of dragonkind. The first surprise past, he could without too much difficulty accept the idea of a dragon as instructor, but it would certainly create a scandal of extraordinary proportions among those who had no similar personal experience.

It had not been so long, only shortly before the Revolution in France had cast Europe into war again, since the proposal had been

HALF HOLLOW HILLS
COMMUNITY LIBRARY

Welcome to your beautiful new library at 55
Vanderbilt Parkway! We look forward to seeing you!

Melville Branch
510 Sweet Hollow Rd
Melville, NY 11747
(631) 421-4535

Dix Hills Branch
55 Vanderbilt Parkway
Dix Hills, NY 11746
(631) 421-4530

05/23/2023

Items checked out to:
   p45130000

Title: **Americus / MK Reed ; [illustrations by]**
Barcode: 3 1974 01053 8410
Call #: YA GN REED
Due: **06-13-23**

Title: **Will super villains be on the final? / by**
Barcode: 3 1974 01087 6950
Call #: YA GN LIBERTY
Due: **06-13-23**

Total items checked out: 2

You just saved an estimated $30 by
using the Library today.

Thank you for visiting!

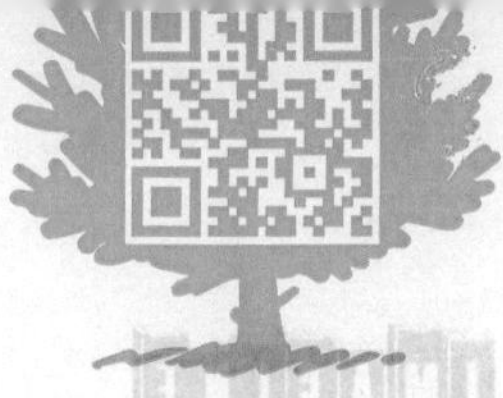

EcoChit veritree

BPA/BPS Free

Recyclable

Sustainably Sourced

This receipt helps plant a forest.

(scan to learn more)

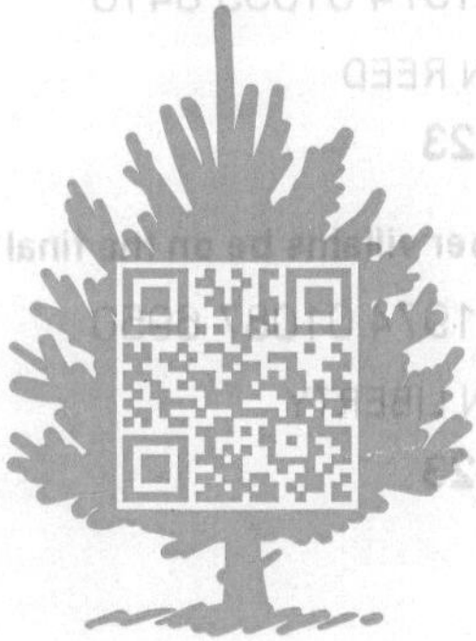

EcoChit veritree

BPA/BPS Free

Recyclable

Sustainably Sourced

made by Government that unharnessed dragons ought to be killed, rather than supported at the public expense and kept for breeding; the rationale offered had been a lack of need at that present time, and that their recalcitrance likely only hurt the fighting bloodlines. Parliament had calculated a savings of more than ten million pounds per annum; the idea had been seriously considered, then dropped abruptly without public explanation. It was whispered, however, that every admiral of the Corps stationed in range of London had jointly descended upon the Prime Minister and informed him that if the law were passed, the entire Corps would mutiny.

He had previously heard the story with disbelief; not for the proposal, but for the idea that senior officers—any officers— would behave in such a way. The proposal had always seemed to him wrong-minded, but only as the sort of foolish short-sightedness so common among bureaucrats, who thought it better to save ten shillings on sailcloth and risk an entire ship worth six thousand pounds. Now he considered his own indifference with a sense of mortification. Of course they would have mutinied.

Still preoccupied with his thoughts, he walked through the archway to the officers' club without attention, and only caught the ball that hurtled at his head by reflex. A mingled cheer and cry of protest both went up at once.

"That was a clear goal, he's not on your team!" a young man, barely out of boyhood, with bright yellow hair, was complaining.

"Nonsense, Martin. Certainly he is; aren't you?" Another of the participants, grinning broadly, came up to Laurence to take the ball; he was a tall, lanky fellow, with dark hair and sunburnt cheekbones.

"Apparently so," Laurence said, amused, handing over the ball. He was a little astonished to find a collection of officers playing children's games indoors, and in such disarray. In his possession of coat and neckcloth, he was more formally dressed than all of them; a couple had even taken off their shirts entirely. The furniture had been pushed pell-mell into the edges of the room, and the carpet rolled up and thrust into a corner.

"Lieutenant John Granby, unassigned," the dark-haired man said. "Have you just arrived?"

"Yes; Captain Will Laurence, on Temeraire," Laurence said, and was startled and not a little dismayed to see the smile fall off Granby's face, the open friendliness vanishing at once.

"The Imperial!" The cry was almost general, and half the boys and men in the room disappeared past them, pelting towards the courtyard. Laurence, taken aback, blinked after them.

"Don't worry!" The yellow-haired young man, coming up to introduce himself, answered his look of alarm. "We all know better than to pester a dragon; they're only going to have a look. Though you might have some trouble with the cadets; we have around two dozen of 'em here, and they make it their mission to plague the life out of everyone. Midwingman Ezekiah Martin, and you can forget my first name now that you have it, if you please."

Informality was so obviously the usual mode among them that Laurence could hardly take offense, though it was not in the least what he was used to. "Thank you for the warning; I will see Temeraire does not let them bother him," he said. He was relieved to see no sign of Granby's attitude of dislike in Martin's greeting, and wished he might ask the friendlier of the two for guidance. However, he did not mean to disobey orders, even if given by a dragon, so he turned to Granby and said formally, "Celeritas tells me to ask you to show me about; will you be so good?"

"Certainly," Granby said, trying for equal formality; but it sat less naturally on him, and he sounded artificial and wooden. "Come this way, if you please."

Laurence was pleased when Martin fell in with them as Granby led the way upstairs; the midwingman's light conversation, which did not falter for an instant, made the atmosphere a great deal less uncomfortable. "So you are the naval fellow who snatched an Imperial out of the jaws of France. Lord, it is a famous story; the Frogs must be gnashing their teeth and tearing their hair over it," Martin said exultantly. "I hear you took the egg off a hundred-gun ship; was the battle very long?"

"I am afraid rumor has magnified my accomplishments," Laurence said. "The *Amitié* was not a first-rate at all, but a thirty-six, a frigate; and her men were nearly falling down for thirst. Her captain offered a very valiant defense, but it was not a very great contest; ill fortune and the weather did our work for us. I can claim only to have been lucky."

"Oh! Well, luck is nothing to sneeze at, either; we would not get very far if luck were against us," Martin said. "Hullo, have they put you at the corner? You will have the wind howling at all hours."

Laurence came into the circular tower room and looked around his new accommodation with pleasure; to a man used to the confines of a ship's cabin, it seemed spacious, and the large, curved windows a great luxury. They looked out over the lake, where a thin grey drizzle had started; when he opened them, a cool wet smell came blowing in, not unlike the sea, except for the lack of salt.

It was some time later that Laurence walked into the courtyard and found Temeraire awake and waiting for him. "I am sorry to have abandoned you so long," Laurence said, leaning against his side and petting him. "Have you been very bored?"

"No, not at all," Temeraire said. "There were a great many people who came by and spoke to me; some of them measured me for a new harness. Also, I have been talking to Maximus here, and he tells me we are to train together."

Laurence nodded a greeting to the Regal Copper, who had acknowledged the mention of his name by opening a sleepy eye; Maximus lifted his massive head enough to return the gesture, and then sank back down. "Are you hungry?" Laurence asked, turning back to Temeraire. "We must be up early to fly for Celeritas—that is the training master here," he added, "so you will likely not have time in the morning."

"Yes, I would like to eat," Temeraire said; he seemed wholly unsurprised to have a dragon as training master, and in the face of his pragmatic response, Laurence felt a little silly for his own first shock; of course Temeraire would see nothing strange in it.

Laurence did not bother strapping himself back on completely for the short hop to the ledge, and there he dismounted to let Temeraire hunt without a passenger. The uncomplicated pleasure of watching the dragon soar and dive so gracefully did a great deal to ease Laurence's mind. No matter how the aviators should respond to him, his position was secure in a way that no sea captain could hope for; he had experience in managing unwilling men, if it came to that in his crew, and at least Martin's example showed that not all the officers would be prejudiced against him from the beginning.

There was some other comfort also: as Temeraire swooped and snatched a lumbering shaggy-haired cow neatly off the ground and settled down to eat it, Laurence heard enthusiastic murmuring and looked up to see a row of small heads poking out of the windows above. "That is the Imperial, sir, is he not?" one of the boys, sandy-haired and round-faced, called out to him.

"Yes, that is Temeraire," Laurence answered. He had always made an effort towards the education of his young gentlemen, and his ship had been considered a prime place for a squeaker; he had many family and service friends to do favors for, so he had fairly extensive experience of boys, most of it favorable. Unlike many grown men, he was not at all uncomfortable in their company, even if these were younger than most of his midshipmen ever had been.

"Look, look, how smashing," another one, smaller and darker, cried and pointed; Temeraire was skimming low to the ground and collecting up all three sheep that had been released for him, before stopping to eat again.

"I dare say you all have more experience of dragonflight than I; does he show to advantage?" he asked them.

"Oh, yes" was the general and enthusiastic response. "Corners on a wink and a nod," the sandy-haired boy said, adopting a professional tone, "and splendid extension; not a wasted wingbeat. Oh, ripping," he added, dissolving back into a small boy, as Temeraire backwinged to take the last cow.

"Sir, you haven't picked your runners yet, have you?" another dark-haired one asked hopefully, which at once set up a clamor among all the others; all of them announcing their worthiness for what Laurence gathered was some position to which particularly favored cadets were assigned, in a dragon-crew.

"No; and I imagine when I do it will be on the advice of your instructors," he said, with mock severity. "So I dare say you ought to mind them properly the next few weeks. There, have you had enough?" he asked, as Temeraire rejoined him on the ledge, landing directly on the edge with perfect balance.

"Oh yes, they were very tasty; but now I am all over blood, may we go and wash up?" Temeraire said.

Laurence realized belatedly this had been omitted from his tour; he glanced up at the children. "Gentlemen, I must ask you for direction; shall I take him to the lake for bathing?"

They all stared down at him with round surprised eyes. "I have never heard of bathing a dragon," one of them said.

The sandy-haired one added, "I mean, can you imagine trying to wash a Regal? It would take ages. Usually they lick their chops and talons clean, like a cat."

"That does not sound very pleasant; I like being washed, even if it is a great deal of work," Temeraire said, looking at Laurence anxiously.

Laurence suppressed an exclamation and said equably, "Certainly it is a great deal of work, but so are many other things that ought to be done; we shall go to the lake at once. Only wait here a moment, Temeraire; I will go and fetch some linens."

"Oh, I will bring you some!" The sandy-haired boy vanished from the windows; the rest immediately followed, and scarcely five minutes later the whole half a dozen of them had come spilling out onto the ledge with a pile of imperfectly folded linens whose provenance Laurence suspected.

He took them anyway, thanking the boys gravely, and climbed back aboard, making a mental note of the sandy-haired fellow; it was the sort of initiative he liked to see and considered the making of an officer.

"We could bring our carabiner belts tomorrow, and then we could ride along and help," the boy added now, with a too-guileless expression.

Laurence eyed him and wondered if this was forwardness to discourage, but he was secretly cheered by the enthusiasm, so he contented himself with saying firmly, "We shall see."